SELF-STUDY PROBLEMS/SOLUTIONS BOOK

VOLUME I: CHAPTERS 1–14

INTERMEDIATE ACCOUNTING

NINTH EDITION

MARILYN F. HUNT, M.A., C.P.A.
University of Central Florida
Orlando, Florida

DONALD E. KIESO, Ph.D., C.P.A.
KPMG Peat Marwick Emeritus Professor of Accountancy
Northern Illinois University
DeKalb, Illinois

JERRY J. WEYGANDT, Ph.D., C.P.A.
Arthur Andersen Alumni Professor of Accounting
University of Wisconsin
Madison, Wisconsin

JOHN WILEY & SONS, INC.
NEW YORK • CHICHESTER • WEINHEIM
BRISBANE • SINGAPORE • TORONTO

ISBN 0-471-15900-X

Printed in the United States of America

10 9 8 7 6 5 4 3 2

Printed and bound by Bradford & Bigelow, Inc.

CONTENTS

PREFACE: To the Student

The purpose of this self-study tutorial is to help you to improve your success rate in solving accounting homework assignments and in answering accounting exam questions. For each chapter we provide you with:

OVERVIEW To briefly introduce the chapter topics and their importance.

STUDY OBJECTIVES To provide you with a learning framework. Explanations of these objectives also provide you with a summary of the major points covered in the chapter.

TIPS To alert you to common pitfalls and misconceptions and to remind you of important terminology, concepts, and relationships that are relevant to answering specific questions or solving certain problems. To help you to understand the intricacies of a problematic situation and to tell you what to do in similar circumstances.

EXERCISES To provide you with a selection of problems which are representative of homework assignments which an intermediate accounting student may encounter.

MULTIPLE CHOICE To provide you with a selection of multiple-choice questions which are representative of common exam questions covering topics in the chapter.

PURPOSES To identify the essence of each question or exercise and to link them to learning objectives.

SOLUTIONS To show you the appropriate solution for each exercise and multiple-choice question presented.

EXPLANATIONS To give you the details of how selected solutions were derived and to explain why things are done as shown.

APPROACHES To coach you on the particular model, computational format, or other strategy to be used to solve particular problems. To teach you how to analyze and solve multiple-choice questions.

This book will be a welcome teaching/learning aid because it provides you with the opportunity to solve accounting problems in addition to the ones assigned by your instructor without having to rely on your teacher for solutions. Many of the exercises and questions contained herein are very similar to items in your intermediate accounting textbook; the difference is, the ones in this book are accompanied with detailed clearly-laid out solutions.

The use of the multiple choice questions in this volume and the related suggestions on how to approach them can easily increase your ability (and confidence in your ability) to deal with exam questions of this variety.

We are grateful to Jennifer Laudermilch of Coopers & Lybrand, Atlanta, Georgia, for her constructive suggestions and editorial comments. Also thanks to Chelsea Hunt, James S. Hunt, Annabelle Specie, and M.F. Specie for their assistance and support. Our appreciation to Mary Ann Benson who skillfully prepared the manuscript and performed the composition of this book.

Marilyn F. Hunt
Donald E. Kieso
Jerry J. Weygandt

HOW TO STUDY ACCOUNTING

The successful study of accounting requires a different approach than most other subjects. In addition to reading a chapter, applying the material through the completion of exercises or problems is necessary to develop a true and lasting understanding of the concepts introduced in the text chapter. The study of accounting principles is a combination of theory and practice; theory describes what to do and why, and practice is the application of guidelines to actual situations. We use illustrations (practice) to demonstrate how theory works and we use theory to explain why something is done in practice. Therefore, it is impossible to separate the two in the study of accounting.

Learning accounting is a cumulative process. It is difficult to master Chapter 4 until you are thoroughly familiar with Chapters 1-3, and so on. Therefore, it is imperative that you keep up with class assignments. And because accounting is a technical subject, you must pay particular attention to terminology.

Accounting is the language of business. It is an exciting subject that provides a challenge for most business majors. Your ultimate success in life may well depend on your ability to grasp financial data. The effort you expend now will provide rewards for years to come.

We encourage you to follow the four steps for study outlined below to give yourself the best possible chance for a successful learning experience and to make the most efficient use of your time. These steps provide a system of study for each new chapter in your text.

Step 1

- Scan the study objectives in the text.
- Scan the chapter (or chapter section) rather quickly.
- Glance over the questions at the end of the chapter.

This first step will give you an overview of the material to be mastered.

Step 2

- Read the assigned pages slowly.
- Use the marginal notes to review and to locate topics within each chapter.
- Study carefully and mark for later attention any portions not clearly understood.
- Pay particular attention to examples and illustrations.
- Try to formulate tentative answers to end-of-chapter questions.

During this phase, you will be filling in the "outline" you formed in Step 1. Most of the details will fall into place during this part of your study. The remaining steps are necessary, however, for a keen understanding of the subject.

Step 3

- Carefully read the **Overview, Learning Objectives,** and **Tips** sections of this *Self-Study* volume.
- Do the **Exercises** and **Cases** in the *Self-Study* that pertain to the same learning objectives as your homework assignments. Review the relevant **Illustrations** in this book.
- Do the **Multiple-Choice Type Questions** in the *Self-Study* that pertain to the same study objectives as your homework assignments.
- Refer back to the sections of the chapter in the text that you marked as unclear if any. It is likely that any confusion or questions on your part will have been cleared up through your work in the *Self-Study* book. If a section remains unclear, carefully reread it and rework relevant pages of the *Self-Study.*
- Repeat this process for each assigned topic area.

Step 4 • Write out formal answers to homework assignments in the text.

This step is crucial because you find out whether you can independently **apply** the material you have been studying to fresh situations. You may find it necessary to go back to the text and/or *Self-Study* to restudy certain sections. This is common and merely shows that the study assignments are working for you.

Additional comments pertaining to Step 3 and your usage of this *Self-Study* volume are as follows:

- The **Learning Objectives** and **Tips** sections, along with **Illustrations** will aid your understanding and retention of the material. **Exercises** provide examples of application of the text material. These should be very valuable in giving you guidance in completing homework assignments which are often similar in nature and content.

- The **Approach** stated for an exercise or question is likely the most valuable feature of this *Self-Study* volume because it tells you how to **think** through the situation at hand. This thought process can then be used for similar situations. It is impossible to illustrate every situation you may encounter. You can, however, handle new situations by simply applying what you know and making modifications where appropriate. Many students make the mistake of attempting to memorize their way through an accounting book. That too is an impossible feat. **Do not rely on memorization.** If this material is going to be useful to you, you must **think** about what you are reading and always be thinking of **why** things are as they are. If you know the reasoning for a particular accounting treatment, it will be much easier to remember that treatment and reconstruct it even weeks after your initial study of it.

- **Explanations** are provided for exercise and questions. These are very detailed so that you will thoroughly understand what is being done and why. These details will serve you well when you complete your homework assignments.

- Always make an honest effort to solve the exercises and answer the questions contained in this *Self-Study* volume **before** you look at the solutions. Answering the questions on your own will maximize the benefits you can expect to reap from this book.

- The **Multiple-Choice Type Questions** are self-tests to give you immediate feedback on how well you understand the material. Study the **Approaches** suggested for answering these questions in the *Self-Study.* Practice them when answering the multiple choice questions in the text. Apply them when taking examinations. By doing so, you will learn to calmly, methodically, and successfully process examination questions. This will definitely improve your exam scores.

- When you work an **Exercise** or **Case** in the *Self-Study* or in the text, always read the instructions **before** you read all of the given data. This allows you to determine what you are to accomplish. Therefore, as you now read through the data, you can begin to process it because you can determine its significance and relevance. If you read the data before the instructions, you are likely to waste your time because you will have to reread the facts once you find out what you are to do with them. Also, more importantly, you are likely to begin to anticipate what the problem is about, which will often cause you to do things other than what is requested in the question.

Good luck and best wishes for a positive learning experience!

CHAPTER 1

FINANCIAL ACCOUNTING AND ACCOUNTING STANDARDS

OVERVIEW

Accounting is the language of business. As such, accountants collect and communicate economic information about business enterprises or other entities to a wide variety of persons. To be useful, financial statements must be clearly understandable and comparable so that users may compare the performance of one business with the performance of the same business for a prior period or with the performance of another similar business. Therefore, all general purpose financial statements should be prepared in accordance with the same uniform guidelines. In this chapter, we will examine the history and sources of current financial accounting standards (generally accepted accounting principles).

SUMMARY OF LEARNING OBJECTIVES

1. **Describe the essential characteristics of accounting.** The essential characteristics of accounting are: (1) identification, measurement, and communication of financial information about (2) economic entities to (3) interested persons.

2. **Identify the major financial statements and other means of financial reporting.** The financial statements most frequently provided are (1) the balance sheet, (2) the income statement, (3) the statement of cash flows, and (4) the statement of owners' or stockholders' equity. Financial reporting other than financial statements may take various forms. Examples include the president's letter or supplementary schedules in the corporate annual report, prospectuses, reports filed with government agencies, news releases, management's forecasts, and descriptions of an enterprise's social or environmental impact.

3. **Explain how accounting assists in the efficient use of scarce resources.** Accounting provides reliable, relevant, and timely information to managers, investors, and creditors so that resources are allocated to the most efficient enterprises. Accounting also provides measurements of efficiency (profitability) and financial soundness.

4. **Identify some of the challenges facing accounting.** Financial reports fail to provide (1) some key performance measures widely used by management, (2) forward-looking information needed by investors and creditors, (3) sufficient information about a company's soft assets (intangibles) and (4) real-time financial information.

5. **Identify the objectives of financial reporting.** The objectives of financial reporting are to provide (1) information that is useful in investment and credit decisions, (2) information that is useful in assessing cash flow prospects, and (3) information about enterprise resources, claims to those resources, and changes in the resources and claims to resources.

6. **Explain the need for accounting standards.** In preparing financial statements, accountants are confronted with the potential dangers of bias, misinterpretation, inexactness, and ambiguity. In order to minimize these dangers, the accounting profession has attempted to develop a set of standards that is generally accepted and universally practiced. Without this set of standards, each accountant or enterprise would have to develop its own standards, and readers of financial statements would have to familiarize themselves with every company's peculiar accounting and reporting practices. As a result, it would be almost impossible to prepare statements that could be compared.

7. **Identify the major policy-setting bodies and their role in the standard-setting process.** The **Securities and Exchange Commission (SEC)** is an agency of the federal government that has the broad powers to prescribe, in whatever detail it desires, the accounting standards to be employed by companies that fall within its jurisdiction. The **American Institute of Certified Public Accountants (AICPA)** issued standards through its Committee on Accounting Procedure (CAP) and Accounting Principles Board (APB). The **Financial Accounting Standards Board (FASB)** establishes and improves standards of financial accounting and reporting for the guidance and education of the public, which includes issuers, auditors, and users of financial information. The **Governmental Accounting Standards Board (GASB)** establishes and improves standards of financial accounting for state and local governments.

8. **Explain the meaning of "generally accepted accounting principles."** Generally accepted accounting principles are those principles that have substantial authoritative support, such as FASB Standards and Interpretations, APB Opinions and Interpretations, AICPA Accounting Research Bulletins, and other authoritative pronouncements.

9. **Describe the impact of user groups on the standard-setting process.** User groups may want particular economic events accounted for or reported in a particular way, and they fight hard to get what they want. Therefore, the FASB has become the target of many pressures and efforts to influence changes in the existing standards and the development of new ones. Because of the accelerated rate of change and the increased complexity of our economy, these pressures have been multiplying. As a result, accounting standards are as much a product of political action as they are of careful logic or empirical findings.

10. **Understand issues related to ethics and financial accounting.** Financial accountants in the performance of their professional duties are called on for moral discernment and ethical decision making. Decisions are more difficult because a public consensus has not emerged to formulate a comprehensive ethical system that provides guidelines in making ethical judgments.

TIPS ON CHAPTER TOPICS

TIP: The accounting profession has adopted a common set of standards and procedures called **generally accepted accounting principles** (often referred to as **GAAP**). The term "generally accepted" can mean either that an authoritative accounting rule-making body has established a principle of reporting in a given area or that over time a given practice has been accepted as appropriate because of its universal application.

TIP: Because most business owners (stockholders of corporations) are not involved with the operation of the business, the **stewardship function**—measuring and reporting data to absentee owners—has emerged as a critical role for accounting. This situation greatly increases the need for accounting standards.

TIP: The financial statements most frequently provided by an entity (often called the **basic financial statements** or **general purpose financial statements**) are: (1) the income statement, (2) the statement of owners' equity (or statement of stockholders' equity), (3) the balance sheet, and (4) the statement of cash flows. In addition, note disclosures are an integral part of the financial statements.

TIP: The primary focus of this textbook concerns the development of two types of financial information which are governed by generally accepted accounting principles: (1) the basic financial statements and (2) the related note disclosures.

TIP: The terms **principles** and **standards** are used interchangeably in practice and throughout this book.

TIP: The **accrual basis of accounting** is used in preparing the basic financial statements. The accrual basis provides for (1) reporting revenues in the period they are earned (which may not be the same period in which the related cash is received), and (2) reporting expenses in the period they are incurred (which may not be the same period in which the related cash is paid).

CASE 1-1

Purpose: (L.O.7) This case will identify the organizations responsible for various accounting documents.

Instructions

Presented below are a number of accounting organizations and the type of documents they have issued. Match the appropriate document to the organization involved. Note that more than one document may be issued by the same organization. If no document is provided for an organization, write in "None."

Organization		Document
1. ______	Internal Revenue Service	(a) Practice Bulletins
		(b) Accounting Research Bulletins
2. ______	AICPA Committee on Accounting Procedure	(c) Opinions
		(d) Invitations to Comment
		(e) Financial Reporting Releases
3. ______	Financial Accounting Standards Board	(f) Statements of Financial Accounting Standards
		(g) Technical Bulletins
4. ______	Securities and Exchange Commission	(h) Statements of Position
		(i) Regulations S-X
		(j) Industry Accounting and Auditing Guides
5. ______	Accounting Standards Executive Committee of the AICPA	(k) Statements of Financial Accounting Concepts
6. ______	Accounting Principles Board	

Solution to Case 1-1

1.	None	3.	d, f, g, k	5.	a, h, j
2.	b	4.	e, i	6.	c

CASE 1-2

Purpose: (L.O.8) This case will review the meaning of generally accepted accounting principles and their significance.

All publicly-held companies must have their annual financial statements audited by an independent CPA. In accordance with generally accepted auditing standards (which you will study in an auditing class), the auditor expresses an opinion regarding the fairness of the financial statements which are to be in conformity with generally accepted accounting principles.

Instructions

(a) Define generally accepted accounting principles and explain their significance to an auditor of financial statements.

(b) Reconstruct the "House of GAAP" which displays the hierarchy of sources of generally accepted accounting principles.

Solution to Case 1-2

(a) The accounting profession has adopted a common set of standards and procedures called **generally accepted accounting principles** (often referred to as GAAP). The word "principles" refers to methods or procedures or standards. The phrase "generally accepted" means having "substantial authoritative support." A method has substantial authoritative support if it has been approved by a rule-making body or if it has gained acceptance over time because of its universal application.

The AICPA's Code of Professional Conduct requires that members prepare financial statements in accordance with generally accepted accounting principles. Specifically, Rule 203 of this Code prohibits a member from expressing an opinion that financial statements conform with GAAP if those statements contain a material departure from a generally accepted accounting principle, unless the member can demonstrate that because of unusual circumstances the financial statements would otherwise have been misleading. Failure to follow Rule 203 can lead to loss of a CPA's license to practice.

The meaning of generally accepted accounting principles is defined by *Statement on Auditing Standards (SAS) No. 69,* "The Meaning of 'Present Fairly in Conformity With Generally Accepted Accounting Principles' in the Independent Auditor's Report." Under this standard, generally accepted accounting principles covered by Rule 203 are construed to be FASB Standards and Interpretations, APB Opinions, and AICPA (CAP) Accounting Research Bulletins.

Oftentimes, however, a specific accounting transaction that occurs is not covered by any of these documents. In this case, other authoritative literature is used. Major examples are: FASB Technical Bulletins, AICPA Industry Audit and Accounting Guides, and Statements of Position that have been "cleared" by the FASB (these are assumed to be cleared—approved—by the FASB unless the pronouncement states otherwise). These documents are considered to have substantial authoritative support because the recognized professional bodies, after giving interested and affected parties the opportunity to react to exposure drafts and respond at public hearings, have voted their issuance. If these pronouncements are lacking in guidance, then other sources might be considered. The hierarchy of these sources is presented in the House of GAAP [see part (b) of this Solution]. If the accounting treatment of an event is not specified by a category (a) pronouncement, then categories (b) through (d) should be investigated. If there is a conflict between pronouncements in (b) through (d), the higher category [for example (b) is higher than (c)] is to be followed.

In the event that none of these pronouncements addresses the transaction, the accountant should seek support from other accounting literature. Examples of other accounting literature include FASB Concepts Statements; International Accounting Standards Committee Statements; AICPA Issues Papers; and accounting textbooks, handbooks, and articles.

(b)

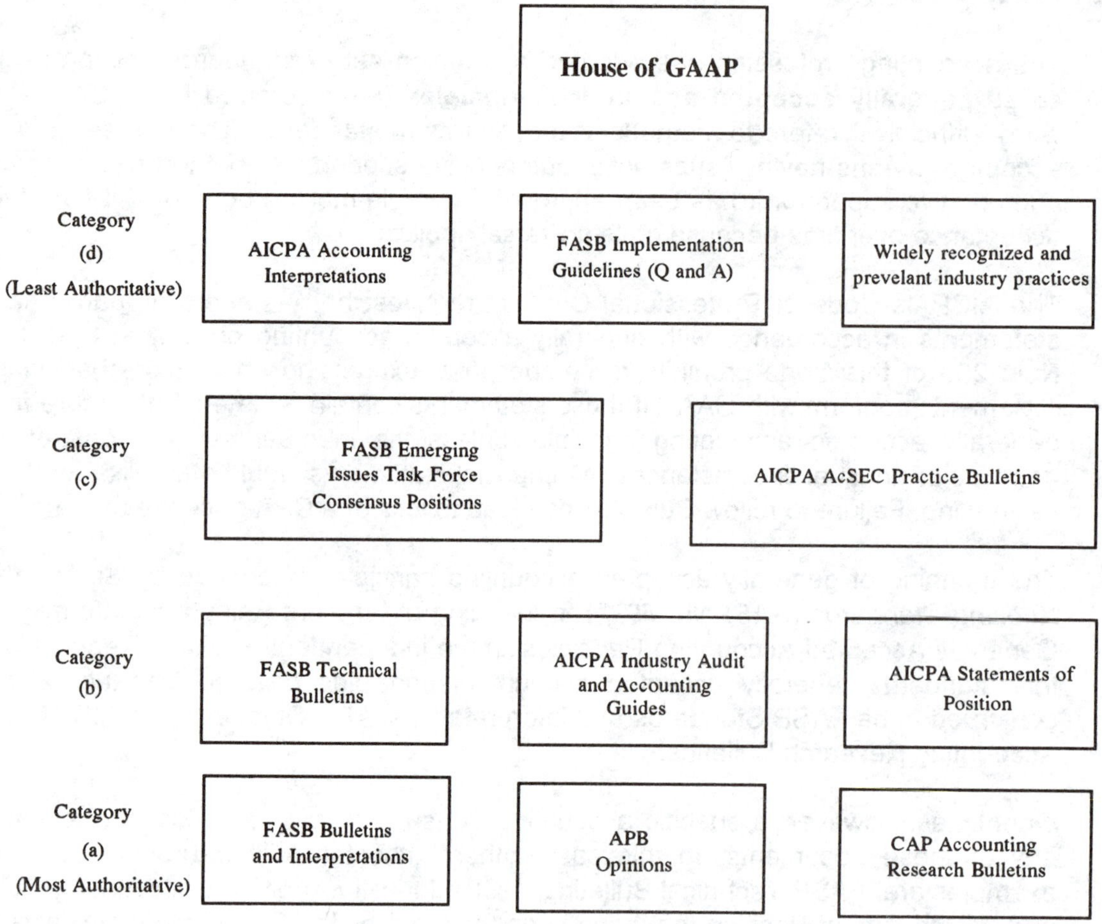

ANALYSIS OF MULTIPLE-CHOICE TYPE QUESTIONS

QUESTION

1. (L.O.1) The process of identifying, measuring, analyzing, and communicating financial information needed by management to plan, evaluate, and control an organization's operations is called:
   a. financial accounting.
   b. managerial accounting.
   c. tax accounting.
   d. auditing.

Approach and Explanation: Define each answer selection. Select the answer item for which your definition matches the stem of the question. **Financial accounting** is the process that culminates in the preparation of financial reports on the enterprise as a whole for use by parties both internal and external to the enterprise. (Users of these financial reports include investors, creditors, managers, unions, and government agencies.) **Managerial accounting** is the process of identifying, measuring, analyzing, and communicating financial information needed by management to plan, evaluate, and control an organization's operations. (These reports are only for the use of parties internal to the enterprise.) **Tax accounting** usually refers to tax planning, advising on tax matters, and/or preparing tax returns. **Auditing** refers to the examination of financial statements by a certified public accountant in order to express an opinion on their fairness. An auditor attests to the fairness of financial statements and their conformity to generally accepted accounting principles. (Solution = b.)

QUESTION

2. (L.O.6) The measuring and reporting of data to absentee owners of a corporation is referred to as management's:
   a. fiduciary responsibility.
   b. stewardship function.
   c. accounting standard-setting function.
   d. audit function.

Explanation: Management's responsibility to manage assets with care and trust is its **fiduciary responsibility**. Management does not set accounting standards. Audits are conducted by independent CPAs, not management. The **stewardship function** involves measuring and reporting data to absentee owners. (Solution = b.)

QUESTION

3. (L.O.7) The most significant current source of generally accepted accounting principles in the nongovernmental sector is the:
   a. NYSE.
   b. SEC.
   c. APB.
   d. FASB.

Explanation: The mission of the Financial Accounting Standards Board (FASB) is to establish and improve standards of financial accounting and reporting. The Governmental Accounting Standards Board (GASB) is responsible for developing standards to regulate state and local government reporting. The Accounting Principles Board (APB) was the predecessor of the FASB. The New York Stock Exchange (NYSE) has nothing to do with the development of generally accepted accounting principles. Generally, the Securities and Exchange Commission (SEC) has relied on the AICPA and the FASB to develop and enforce accounting standards. (Solution = d.)

QUESTION

4. (L.O.7) Members of the Financial Accounting Standards Board are:
   a. employed by the American Institute of Certified Public Accountants (AICPA).
   b. part-time employees.
   c. required to hold a CPA certificate.
   d. independent of any other organization.

Explanation: The members of the FASB are well-paid, full-time members. The FASB is not affiliated with the AICPA; it is not associated with any single professional organization. The FASB is answerable only to the Financial Accounting Foundation. It is not necessary to be a CPA or a member of the AICPA to be a member of the FASB. FASB members must sever all ties with CPA firms, companies, or institutions. (Solution = d.)

QUESTION

5. (L.O.7) Which of the following pronouncements were issued by the Accounting Principles Board?
   a. Accounting Research Bulletins
   b. Opinions
   c. Statements of Position
   d. Statements of Financial Accounting Concepts

Explanation: The Accounting Principles Board issued 31 APB Opinions between the years 1962-1973. Accounting Research Bulletins (51 of them) were issued by the Committee on Accounting Procedure between 1953 and 1959. Statements of Position are issued by the AICPA (but not the APB). The FASB issues Statements on Financial Accounting Concepts (there are 6 of these to date and five of them relate to financial reporting for business enterprises). (Solution = b.)

QUESTION

6. (L.O.7) The body charged with the mission of establishing and improving standards of financial accounting and reporting for business enterprises is the:
   a. Financial Accounting Foundation (FAF).
   b. Financial Accounting Standards Board (FASB).
   c. Financial Accounting Standards Advisory Council (FASAC).
   d. Governmental Accounting Standards Board (GASB).

Explanation: The FASB is responsible for establishing and improving GAAP. The FAF selects the members of the FASB, and the FASAC funds their activities and generally oversees the FASB's activities (from an operational rather than from a technical standpoint). The GASB deals only with standards pertaining to state and local government reporting. (Solution = b.)

QUESTION

7. (L.O.7) The demise of the APB and the creation of the FAF, FASB, and FASAC are largely and most directly attributed to the:
   a. IRS.
   b. Great Depression.
   c. Securities Exchange Act.
   d. recommendations of the Wheat Committee.

Explanation: The Great Depression of the 1930s resulted in the Securities Exchange Act of 1934 which led to the formation of the Securities and Exchange Commission (SEC). These developments prompted the formation of the Committee on Accounting Procedure (CAP) which was replaced by the Accounting Principles Board (APB). When the APB needed an overhaul, it was the recommendations of the Wheat Committee that resulted in the demise of the APB and the creation of the new standard-setting structure composed of three organizations—the Financial Accounting Foundation (FAF), the Financial Accounting Standards Board (FASB), and the Financial Accounting Standards Advisory Council (FASAC). (Solution = d.)

QUESTION

8. (L.O.7) The American Institute of Certified Public Accountants (AICPA) continues to be the leader in:
   a. developing financial accounting standards.
   b. developing auditing standards.
   c. developing and enforcing professional ethics.
   d. providing professional education programs.
   e. all of the above, except a.

Approach and Explanation: Before you read the alternative answers, mentally list the facts you know about the AICPA. Its Accounting Standards Executive Committee is involved in assisting the development of financial accounting and reporting guidelines through (1) Issues Papers, (2) Statements of Position, (3) Practice Bulletins, and (4) Industry Accounting and Auditing Guides. The AICPA develops and grades the CPA Examination. It is still the leader in developing auditing standards through its *Auditing Standards Board*, in regulating auditing practices, in developing and enforcing professional ethics, and in providing continuing professional education (CPE) programs. (Solution = e.)

QUESTION

9. (L.O.7) The following published documents are part of the "due process" system used by the FASB in the evolution of a typical FASB Statement of Financial Accounting Standards:
   1. Exposure Draft
   2. Statement of Financial Accounting Standards
   3. Discussion Memorandum

   The chronological order in which these items are released is as follows:
   a. 1, 2, 3.
   b. 1, 3, 2.
   c. 2, 3, 1.
   d. 3, 1, 2.

Explanation: The following steps are taken in the evolution of a typical FASB Statement of Financial Accounting Standards:

1. A topic or project is identified and placed on the Board's agenda.
2. A task force of experts from various sectors is assembled to define problems, issues, and alternatives related to the topic.
3. Research and analysis are conducted by the FASB technical staff.
4. A **discussion memorandum** is drafted and released.
5. A public hearing is often held, usually 60 days after release of the memorandum.
6. The Board analyzes and evaluates the public response.
7. The Board deliberates on the issues and prepares an **exposure draft** for release.
8. After a 30-day (minimum) exposure period for public comment, the Board evaluates all of the responses received.
9. A committee studies the exposure draft in relation to the public responses, reevaluates its position, and revises the draft if necessary.
10. The full Board gives the revised draft final consideration and votes on issuance of a **Standards Statement**. (Solution = d.)

QUESTION

10. (L.O.7) All of the following organizations are directly involved in the development of financial accounting standards (GAAP) in the United States, except the:
    a. Internal Revenue Service (IRS).
    b. Financial Accounting Standards Board (FASB).
    c. American Institute of Certified Public Accountants (AICPA).
    d. Securities and Exchange Commission (SEC).

Explanation: The Internal Revenue Service (IRS) is responsible for federal income tax rules and administration. Although the IRS and its Internal Revenue Code are influences on accounting practice, they are not directly involved in the development of accounting standards (for financial statements) as are the other organizations listed. (Solution = a.)

QUESTION

11. (L.O.8) In the House of GAAP, is the following on the highest level of authoritative status (meaning among the most authoritative)?

	FASB Technical Bulletin	FASB Statement of Financial Accounting Standards	FASB Interpre-tation	FASB Statement of Financial Accounting Concepts
a.	Yes	Yes	Yes	Yes
b.	Yes	Yes	Yes	No
c.	No	Yes	No	No
d.	No	Yes	Yes	No

Approach and Explanation: Visualize the House of GAAP [see **Solution to Case 1-2, part (b)**]. The accounting guidelines that have the most authoritative status are those in category (a) which are the FASB Statements of Financial Accounting Standards, the FASB Interpretations, the APB Opinions, and the AICPA (CAP) Accounting Research Bulletins. The FASB Technical Bulletins are in category (b), not (a) and the FASB Statements of Financial Accounting Concepts are not even in the House. They would be used to support an accounting treatment only if none of the pronouncements in the House of GAAP contradicted that treatment. (Solution = d.)

CHAPTER 2

CONCEPTUAL FRAMEWORK UNDERLYING FINANCIAL ACCOUNTING

OVERVIEW

Financial statements are needed for decision making. In order to make informed decisions, a financial statement user must understand both the financial information conveyed and how it is derived. To be useful, financial statements must be clearly understandable and comparable so that users may compare the performance of one business with the performance of the same business for a prior period or with the performance of another similar business. Therefore, all general purpose financial statements should be prepared in accordance with the same uniform guidelines. In this chapter, we will examine basic accounting principles.

SUMMARY OF LEARNING OBJECTIVES

1. **Describe the usefulness of a conceptual framework.** A conceptual framework is needed to (1) build on and relate to an established body of concepts and objectives, (2) provide a framework for solving new and emerging practical problems, (3) increase financial statement users' understanding of and confidence in financial reporting, and (4) enhance comparability among companies' financial statements.

2. **Describe the FASB's efforts to construct a conceptual framework.** The FASB has issued five Statements of Financial Accounting Concepts that relate to financial reporting for business enterprises. These concepts statements provide the basis for the conceptual framework and include objectives, qualitative characteristics, and elements. In addition, measurement and recognition concepts are developed.

3. **Understand the objectives of financial reporting.** The objectives of financial reporting are to provide information that is (1) useful to those making investment and credit decisions who have a reasonable understanding of business activities; (2) helpful to present and potential investors, creditors, and other users in assessing future cash flows; and (3) about economic resources and the claims to those resources.

4. **Identify the qualitative characteristics of accounting information.** The over-riding criterion by which accounting choices can be judged is decision usefulness; that is, providing information that is most useful for decision making. Relevance and reliability are the two primary qualities and comparability and consistency are the secondary qualities that make accounting information useful for decision making.

5. **Define the basic elements of financial statements.** The basic elements of financial statements are (1) assets, (2) liabilities, (3) equity, (4) investments by owners, (5) distributions to owners, (6) comprehensive income, (7) revenues, (8) expenses, (9) gains, and (10) losses. These ten elements are defined in **Illustration 2-3**.

6. **Describe the basic assumptions of accounting.** Four basic assumptions underlying the financial accounting structure are (1) **Economic entity:** the assumption that the activity of a business enterprise can be kept separate and distinct from its owners and any other business unit. (2) **Going concern:** the assumption that the business enterprise will have a long life. (3) **Monetary unit:** the assumption that money is the common denominator by which economic activity is conducted, and that the monetary unit provides an appropriate basis for measurement and analysis. (4) **Periodicity:** the assumption that the economic activities of an enterprise can be divided into artificial time periods.

7. **Explain the application of the basic principles of accounting.** (1) **Historical cost principle:** Existing GAAP requires that most assets and liabilities be accounted for and reported on the basis of acquisition price. (2) **Revenue recognition:** Revenue is generally recognized when (a) realized or realizable and (b) earned. (3) **Matching principle:** Expenses are recognized when the work (service) or the product actually makes its contribution to revenue. (4) **Full disclosure principle:** Accountants follow the general practice of providing information that is of sufficient importance to influence the judgment and decisions of an informed user.

8. **Describe the impact that constraints have on reporting accounting information.** The constraints and their impact are: (1) **Cost-benefit relationship:** The costs of providing the information must be weighed against the benefits that can be derived from using the information. (2) **Materiality:** Sound and acceptable standards should be followed if the amount involved is significant when compared with the other revenues and expenses, assets and liabilities, or net income of the entity. (3) **Industry practices:** Follow the general practices in the firm's industry, which sometimes requires departure from basic theory. (4) **Conservatism:** When in doubt, choose the solution that will be least likely to overstate net assets and net income.

TIPS ON CHAPTER TOPICS

TIP: Although it can sometimes be confusing, accountants often use the terms **assumptions**, **concepts**, **principles**, **conventions**, **constraints**, and **standards** interchangeably. Regardless of the particular term used, they are all a part of GAAP (generally accepted accounting principles).

TIP: The revenue recognition principle is applied before the matching principle is applied. The revenue recognition principle gives guidance in determining what revenues to recognize in a given period. The matching principle then gives guidance as to what expenses to recognize during the period. According to the **revenue recognition principle**, revenues are to be recognized in the period earned. Per the **matching principle**, expenses are to be recognized in the same period as the revenues they helped generate.

TIP: The term **recognition** refers to the process of formally recording or incorporating an item in the accounts and financial statements of an entity.

TIP: You should study **Illustration 2-2** on the hierarchy of accounting qualities until you can close your eyes and visualize that diagram. Many exam questions (including CPA Examination questions) over *SFAC No. 2* can be answered by describing what is on that diagram.

TIP: Accounting assumptions underlie the more detailed accounting principles or standards. These assumptions include the economic entity assumption, the going concern assumption, the monetary unit assumption, and the periodicity assumption. They are the foundation for the basic principles which include the historical cost principle, the revenue recognition principle, the matching principle, and the full disclosure principle. For example, the historical cost principle and the matching principle would not be appropriate if it were not for the going concern assumption. If an entity is not expected to continue in business, then plant assets would be reported on the balance sheet at their liquidation or net realizable value (estimated selling price less estimated cost of disposal) rather than at their cost, and depreciation of these assets would not be appropriate.

TIP: There are three common bases of expense recognition: (1) cause and effect, (2) systematic and rational allocation, and (3) immediate recognition. You should be able to explain and give examples for each of these.

ILLUSTRATION 2-1
A CONCEPTUAL FRAMEWORK FOR FINANCIAL REPORTING (L.O.2 THRU 8)

Recognition and Measurement Concepts

ASSUMPTIONS
1. Economic entity
2. Going concern
3. Monetary unit
4. Periodicity

PRINCIPLES
1. Historical cost
2. Revenue recognition
3. Matching
4. Full disclosure

CONSTRAINTS
1. Cost-benefit
2. Materiality
3. Industry practices
4. Conservatism

Third Level: "The how"—implementation

QUALITATIVE CHARACTERISTICS
1. Primary qualities
   - A. Relevance
     - (1) Predictive value
     - (2) Feedback value
     - (3) Timeliness
   - B. Reliability
     - (1) Verifiability
     - (2) Neutrality
     - (3) Representational faithfulness
2. Secondary qualities
   - A. Comparability
   - B. Consistency

ELEMENTS
1. Assets
2. Liabilities
3. Equity
4. Investment by owners
5. Distribution to owners
6. Comprehensive income
7. Revenues
8. Expenses
9. Gains
10. Losses

Second Level: Bridge between first and third levels.

OBJECTIVES

Provide information:
1. Useful in investment and credit decisions
2. Useful in assessing future cash flows
3. About enterprise resources, claims to resources, and changes in them.

First Level: "The Why"—goals and purposes of accounting.

This illustration provides an overview of the FASB's conceptual framework.[1] At the first level, the **objectives** identify the goals and purposes of financial accounting and are the building blocks for the conceptual framework. At the second level are the **qualitative characteristics** that make financial accounting information useful and the **elements** of financial statements (assets, liabilities, and so on). At the final, or third level, are the measurement and recognition concepts that accountants use in establishing and applying financial accounting standards. These concepts include assumptions, principles, and constraints that describe the present reporting environment.

[1] Adapted from William C. Norby, *The Financial Analysts Journal* (March-April, 1982), p. 22.

ILLUSTRATION 2-2
A HIERARCHY OF ACCOUNTING QUALITIES (L.O.4)

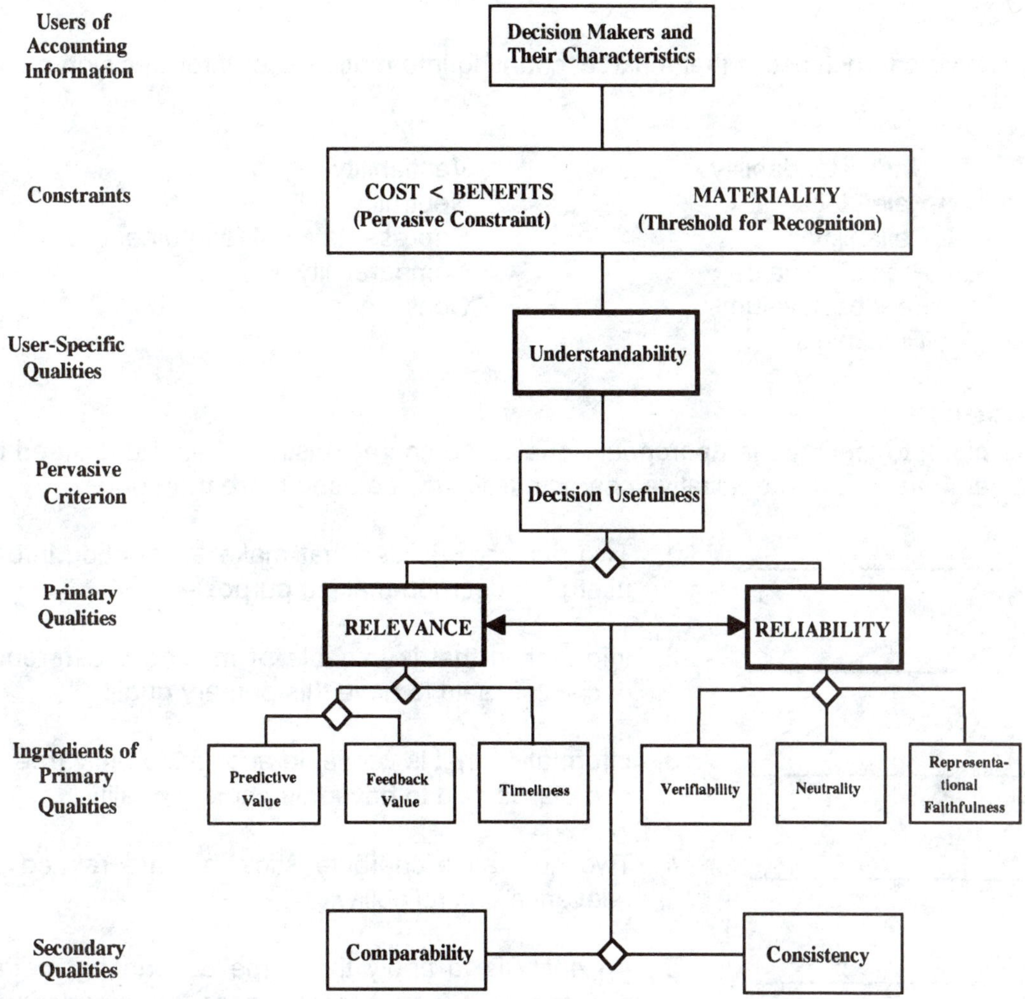

SOURCE: FASB, *Statement of Financial Accounting Concepts No. 2*, "Qualitative Characteristics of Accounting Information."

CASE 2-1

Purpose: (L.O.4) This exercise is designed to review the qualitative characteristics that make accounting information useful for decision making purposes (per *SFAC No. 2*).

The qualitative characteristics that make accounting information useful for decision making are as follows:

Understandability	Verifiability
Relevance	Neutrality
Reliability	Representational faithfulness
Predictive value	Comparability
Feedback value	Consistency
Timeliness	

Instructions

Fill in the blank to identify the appropriate qualitative characteristic(s) being described in each of the statements below. A qualitative characteristic may be used more than once.

______________________ 1. Two primary qualities that make accounting information useful for decision-making purposes.

______________________ 2. Information that is capable of making a difference in a decision is said to have this primary quality.

______________________ 3. Information that is verifiable and reasonably free of error and bias is said to have this primary quality.

______________________ 4. Two qualitative characteristics that are related to both relevance and reliability.

______________________ 5. An entity is to apply the same accounting methods to similar events for successive accounting periods; that is, when an entity selects one method from a list of alternative acceptable methods, that same method is used period after period.

______________________ 6. Information is measured and reported in a similar manner for different enterprises.

______________________ 7. Neutrality is an ingredient of this primary quality of accounting information.

______________________ 8. Requires that information cannot be selected to favor one set of interested parties over another.

________________ 9. Predictive value is an ingredient of this primary quality of information.

________________ 10. When information provides a basis for forecasting annual earnings for future periods, it is said to have this ingredient of a primary quality of accounting information.

________________ 11. Quality of information that confirms or corrects users' prior expectations.

________________ 12. Information must be available to decision makers before it loses its capacity to influence their decisions.

________________ 13. Imperative for providing comparisons of a single firm from period to period.

________________ 14. Qualitative characteristic being employed when companies in the same industry are using the same accounting principles.

________________ 15. A company cannot suppress information just because such disclosure is embarrassing or damaging to the entity.

________________ 16. The amounts and descriptions in financial statements agree with the elements or events that these amounts and descriptions purport to represent.

________________ 17. Independent measurers, using the same measurement methods, obtain similar results.

________________ 18. The numbers and descriptions in financial statements represent what really existed or happened.

________________ 19. Requires information to be free of personal bias.

________________ 20. Requires a high degree of consensus among individuals on a given measurement.

________________ 21. Financial information is a tool and, like most tools, cannot be much direct help to those who are unable or unwilling to use it or who misuse it.

Solution to Case 2-1

1. Relevance and reliability
2. Relevance
3. Reliability
4. Comparability and consistency
5. Consistency
6. Comparability
7. Reliability
8. Neutrality
9. Relevance
10. Predictive value
11. Feedback value
12. Timeliness
13. Consistency
14. Comparability
15. Neutrality
16. Representational faithfulness
17. Verifiability
18. Representational faithfulness
19. Neutrality
20. Verifiability
21. Understandability

Approach: Before beginning to fill in the twenty-one blanks required, visualize the diagram for the hierarchy of accounting qualities (**Illustration 2-2**). Also, take a few minutes to individually consider the eleven characteristics listed and think of the key phrases involved in describing those items. Such as:

- **Understandability:** information provided by financial reporting should be comprehensible to those who have a reasonable understanding of business and economic activities and are willing to study the information with reasonable diligence.
- **Relevance:** capable of making a difference in a decision.
- **Reliability:** users can depend on information to be verifiable, reasonably free of error and bias, and to represent what it purports to represent.
- **Predictive value:** helps users make predictions about the outcome of past, present, and future events.
- **Feedback value:** helps to confirm or correct prior expectations.
- **Timeliness:** information must be available to decision makers before it loses its capacity to influence their decisions.
- **Verifiability:** is demonstrated when a high degree of consensus can be secured among independent measurers using the same measurement methods.
- **Neutrality:** information is not to be selected to favor one set of interested parties over another and is to be free from bias towards a predetermined result.
- **Representational faithfulness:** correspondence or agreement between the accounting numbers and descriptions and the resources or events that these numbers and descriptions purport to represent.
- **Comparability:** information that has been measured and reported in a similar manner for different enterprises is considered comparable.
- **Consistency:** a company is to apply the same methods to similar accountable events from period to period.

ILLUSTRATION 2-3
ELEMENTS OF FINANCIAL STATEMENTS (L.O.5)

Assets: Probable future economic benefits obtained or controlled by a particular entity as a result of past transactions or events.

Liabilities: Probable future sacrifices of economic benefits arising from present obligations of a particular entity to transfer assets or provide services to other entities in the future as a result of past transactions or events.

Equity: Residual interest in the assets of an entity that remains after deducting its liabilities. In a business enterprise, the equity is the ownership interest.

Investments by owners: Increases in net assets of a particular enterprise resulting from transfers to it from other entities of something of value to obtain or increase ownership interests (or equity) in it. Assets are most commonly received as investments by owners, but that which is received may also include services or satisfaction or conversion of liabilities of the enterprise.

Distributions to owners: Decreases in net assets of a particular enterprise resulting from transferring assets, rendering services, or incurring liabilities by the enterprise to owners. Distributions to owners decrease ownership interests (or equity) in an enterprise.

Comprehensive income: Change in equity (net assets) of an entity during a period from transactions and other events and circumstances from nonowner sources. It includes all changes in equity during a period except those resulting from investments by owners and distributions to owners.

Revenues: Inflows or other enhancements of assets of an entity or settlement of its liabilities (or a combination of both) during a period from delivering or producing goods, rendering services, or other activities that constitute the entity's ongoing major or central operations.

Expenses: Outflows or other using up of assets or incurrences of liabilities (or a combination of both) during a period from delivering or producing goods, rendering services, or carrying out other activities that constitute the entity's ongoing major or central operations.

Gains: Increases in equity (net assets) from peripheral or incidental transactions of an entity and from all other transactions and other events and circumstances affecting the entity during a period except those that result from revenues or investments by owners.

Losses: Decreases in equity (net assets) from peripheral or incidental transactions of an entity and from all other transactions and other events and circumstances affecting the entity during a period except those that result from expenses or distributions to owners.

ILLUSTRATION 2-4
BASIC ACCOUNTING ASSUMPTIONS, PRINCIPLES, AND CONSTRAINTS (L.O.6, 7, and 8)

Economic entity assumption: States that economic events can be identified with a particular unit of accountability. The activities of an accounting entity can be and should be kept separate and distinct from its owners and all other accounting entities. The entity concept does not necessarily refer to a legal entity.

Going concern assumption: Assumes that the enterprise will continue in operation long enough to carry out its existing objectives and commitments. Sometimes called the **continuity assumption**, it assumes the entity will continue in operation long enough to recover the cost of its assets. This assumption serves as a basis for basic principles such as the historical cost principle. Because of this assumption, liquidation values of assets are not relevant.

Monetary unit assumption: States that only transaction data capable of being expressed in terms of money should be included in the accounting records of the economic entity. All transactions and events can be measured in terms of a common denominator—units of money. A corollary is the added assumption that the unit of measure remains constant from one period to the next (some people call the corollary the "stable dollar assumption").

Periodicity assumption: Assumes that the economic life of a business can be divided into artificial time periods. Although some companies choose to subdivide the business life into months or quarters, others report financial statements only for an annual period.

Historical cost principle: States that assets should initially be recorded and subsequently accounted for at acquisition cost. The principle also states that cost is measured by the fair market value (cash equivalent value) of the consideration given or the fair market value (cash equivalent value) of the consideration received, whichever is the more objectively determinable. In addition, the cost of an asset includes all costs necessary to acquire the item and get it in the place and condition for its intended use.

Revenue recognition principle: Dictates that revenue should be recognized when (1) **realized** or **realizable** and (2) **earned**. Revenues are **realized** when products (goods or services, merchandise, or other assets) are exchanged for cash or claims to cash. Revenues are **realizable** when assets received or held are readily convertible into cash or claims to cash. Assets are readily convertible when they are salable or interchangeable in an active market at readily determinable prices without significant additional cost. Revenues are considered **earned** when the entity has substantially accomplished what it must do to be entitled to the benefits represented by the revenues. The revenue generating process for most entities includes a number of steps. As a result, revenue is **earned** when the "critical point" in the earnings process is reached. This critical point is different for different circumstances as the following examples illustrate. Examples are: (1) when a sale is involved, the point of sale is the critical event, (2) when long-term construction contracts are involved, progress toward completion is the critical event, (3) when products are salable in an active market at readily determinable prices without significant additional cost, the completion of production is the critical event, and (4) when uncertainty about the collection of receivables exists for credit

ILLUSTRATION 2-4 (Continued)

sales of goods and services, the receipt of cash is the critical event. In example (1), the sales basis is used for revenue recognition. In example (2), the percentage-of-completion method is appropriate for revenue recognition. In example (3), recognition of revenue at the end of production is justified. In example (4), the installment method is used.

Matching principle: Dictates that expenses be matched with revenues whenever it is reasonable and practical to do so. Expenses (efforts) are recognized in the same period as the related revenue (accomplishment) is recognized. Thus, a factory worker's wages are not recognized as an expense when cash is paid or when the work is performed, or when the product is produced; they are recognized as an expense when the labor (service) or the product actually makes its contribution to the revenue generating process (which is when the related product is sold).

Full disclosure principle: Dictates that circumstances and events that make a difference to financial statement users be disclosed. An entity is to disclose through the data contained in the financial statements and the information in the notes that accompany the statements all information necessary to make the statements not misleading. To be recognized in the main body of the financial statements, an item should meet the definition of one of the basic elements, be measurable with sufficient certainty, and be relevant and reliable. The notes to financial statements generally amplify or explain the items presented in the body of the statements. Information in the notes does not have to be quantifiable, nor does it need to qualify as an element.

Cost-benefit relationship: States that the costs of providing the information must be weighed against the benefits that can be derived from using the information. In order to justify requiring a particular measurement or disclosure, the benefits perceived to be derived from it must exceed the costs perceived to be associated with the measurement or disclosure. When the perceived costs exceed the perceived benefits, a measurement or disclosure may be foregone based on its lack of practicality.

Materiality constraint: Dictates that an immaterial item need not be given strict accounting treatment; it can be given expedient treatment. An immaterial item or amount is one that does not make a difference in the decisions that are being made based on an analysis of the financial statements. The point involved here is one of relative size and importance. If the amount involved is significant when compared with other revenues and expenses, assets and liabilities, or net income of the entity, it is a material item and generally acceptable standards should be followed. If the amount is so small that it is quite unimportant when compared with other items, strict treatment is of less importance. The nature of an item may also affect the judgment of its materiality. A misclassification affecting cash has a lower threshold of materiality than the same dollar amount of a misclassification affecting plant assets.

ILLUSTRATION 2-4 (Continued)

Industry practices constraint: States that the peculiar nature of some industries and business concerns sometimes requires departure from what would normally be considered good accounting practice. For example, current assets usually appear first on a balance sheet; however, for a public utility, it is an acceptable industry practice to report plant assets (noncurrent items) first on the balance sheet to highlight the entity's capital-intensive nature.

Conservatism constraint: Dictates that in matters of doubt and uncertainty, the accountant should choose the solution that will be least likely to overstate assets and net income. The axiom "anticipate no gains but provide for all losses" comes from this constraint. There is no virtue, however, in being overconservative. If the accountant is overconservative, other accounting principles such as historical cost, revenue recognition, and matching will be violated.

TIP: Accounting constraints are justifications for departure from the basic accounting principles in certain situations. They are sometimes referred to as "exception principles." For example, the cost of an item that will benefit operations for five years should be initially recorded as an asset and amortized (expensed) over the related five-year period as dictated by the matching principle. However, if the item is a recycling container that cost $20, the amount is deemed to be insignificant and the whole amount is handled with expedience—that is, it is expensed in the period the container is acquired. This departure from the matching principle is justified by the materiality constraint. For another example, if the market value (replacement value) of inventory is below the cost of inventory, the inventory is to be reported at the market value (the lower value). Thus, there is a departure from the historical cost principle with the justification being the conservatism constraint.

CASE 2-2

Purpose: (L.O.6, 7, 8) This exercise will test your comprehension of the essence and significance of basic accounting assumptions, principles, and constraints.

Instructions

For each of the following statements, identify (by letter) the basic accounting assumption, principle or constraint that is **most directly** related to the given phrase. Each code letter may be used more than once.

Assumptions, Principles, and Constraints

a. Economic entity assumption
b. Going concern assumption
c. Monetary unit assumption
d. Periodicity assumption
e. Historical cost principle
f. Revenue recognition principle
g. Matching principle
h. Full disclosure principle
i. Cost-benefit relationship
j. Materiality constraint
k. Industry practices constraint
l. Conservatism constraint

TIP: Before you begin to read and answer the items listed, it would be helpful to briefly think about what you know about each of the assumptions, principles, and constraints. An explanation of each appears in **Illustration 2-4**.

Statements

_____ 1. Revenue should be recognized when it is earned, which is usually at the point of sale.

_____ 2. All information necessary to ensure that the financial statements are not misleading should be reported.

_____ 3. This concept eliminates the "liquidation concept" in viewing business affairs.

_____ 4. Measurement of the standing and progress of entities should be made at regular intervals rather than at the end of the business's life.

_____ 5. Although an item such as a wastebasket may be of service for eight years, the total cost of the item may be expensed when it is purchased, because the amount is too insignificant to warrant the strict treatment of depreciation over the eight years.

_____ 6. The lower-of-cost-or-market rule for inventories is an application of this concept.

_____ 7. The recorded amount of an acquired item should be the fair market value of what was given or the fair market value of what was received in the exchange, whichever can be more objectively determined.

_____ 8. There must be complete and understandable reporting on financial statements.

_____ 9. The president of a business should not loan his spouse the company's credit card for personal gasoline purchases.

_____ 10. In matters of doubt or uncertainty, select the accounting treatment that will result in the lowest figure for net income, assets, and owners' equity.

_____ 11. Expenses should be recognized in the same period that the related revenues are recognized.

_____ 12. This concept is often exemplified by numerous notes to the financial statements.

_____ 13. If revenue is deferred to a future period, the related costs of generating that revenue should be deferred to the same future period.

_____ 14. This concept includes a set of rules concerning when to recognize revenue and how to measure its amount.

_____ 15. All transactions and events are expressed in terms of a common denominator.

_____ 16. Avoid overstatement of net income, assets, and owners' equity, but do not intentionally understate them.

_____ 17. It is assumed that an organization will remain in business long enough to recover the cost of its assets.

_____ 18. Changes in the purchasing power of the dollar are so small from one period to the next that they are ignored in preparing the basic financial statements.

_____ 19. Items whose amounts are very small relative to other amounts on the financial statements may be accounted for in the most expedient manner, rather than requiring strict accounting treatment under GAAP.

_____ 20. The cost of an item should be measured by the amount of the resources expended to acquire it.

_____ 21. Accruals and deferrals are often necessary in order to report expenses in the proper time periods.

_____ 22. Each accounting unit is considered separate and distinct from all other accounting units.

_____ 23. An accountant assumes that a business will continue indefinitely.

_____ 24. Assets which have appreciated in value are not reported at their current worth subsequent to acquisition because of this principle.

_____ 25. Depreciation of a long-term tangible asset is based on the asset's original acquisition cost rather than the asset's current market value.

_____ 26. If an item will not affect any business decisions, it need not be separately reported in the financial statements.

_____ 27. In order to justify requiring a particular measurement or disclosure, the benefits perceived to be derived from it must exceed the costs expected to be associated with it.

_____ 28. Externally acquired intangible assets are capitalized and amortized over the periods benefited.

_____ 29. Repair tools are expensed when purchased even though they may be of use for more than one period.

_____ 30. Brokerage firms use market value for purposes of valuation of all marketable securities. Changes in those market values are recognized in the income statement in the periods the changes occur.

_____ 31. All significant postbalance sheet events are reported in the notes to the financial statements.

_____ 32. Revenue for a retail establishment is recorded at the point of sale.

_____ 33. All important aspects of bond indentures (contracts) are presented in the financial statements.

_____ 34. Reporting must be done at defined time intervals. The time intervals are of equal length.

_____ 35. An allowance for doubtful (uncollectible) accounts is established.

_____ 36. All payments out of petty cash are charged to Miscellaneous Expense, even though some expenditures will benefit the following period. (Do not use conservatism.)

_____ 37. No profits are anticipated but all possible losses are recognized.

_____ 38. A company charges its sales commission costs to expense in the same period that the sale is made.

_____ 39. When the liquidation of an enterprise looks imminent, this assumption is inapplicable and thus, the historical cost principle does not apply. Rather, assets are reported at their net realizable values.

_____ 40. The initial note to financial statements is usually a summary of significant accounting policies.

Solution to Case 2-2

1. f	11. g	21. g	31. h	
2. h	12. h	22. a	32. f	
3. b	13. g	23. b	33. h	
4. d	14. f	24. e	34. d	
5. j	15. c	25. e*	35. g	*An argument could be made for answer "g."
6. l	16. l	26. j	36. j	
7. e	17. b	27. i	37. l	
8. h	18. c	28. g	38. g	
9. a	19. j	29. j	39. b	
10. l	20. e	30. k	40. h	

CASE 2-3

Purpose: (L.O.7) This case is designed to review the three methods of matching expenses with revenues and examples of each.

An unexpired cost represents probable future benefits and hence is accounted for as an asset. An expired cost represents an expiration of benefits and hence is accounted for as an expense or a loss. There are three common bases of expense recognition: (1) cause and effect, (2) systematic and rational allocation, and (3) immediate recognition.

Instructions

Describe each of the three bases of expense recognition and give a few examples of each for a retail establishment.

Solution to Case 2-3

1. **Cause and effect:** When there is a direct association between the expiration of a cost and a particular revenue transaction, the expense recognition should accompany the revenue recognition; that is, the cost is expensed in the same time period that the related specific revenue is recognized.

   Examples: Cost of goods sold, sale commissions, transportation-out.

2. **Systematic and rational allocation:** This basis is used when, although a cost benefits the revenue generating process of two or more accounting periods, the cost cannot be related to particular revenue transactions. Even though a close cause-and-effect relationship between revenue and cost cannot be determined, this relationship is assumed to exist. The cost is thus initially accounted for as an asset and then allocated to the periods benefited (as an expense) in a systematic and rational manner. The allocation method used should appear reasonable to an unbiased observer and should be consistently applied from period to period.

Examples: Depreciation of plant assets, amortization of intangibles, amortization of prepaids (such as rent and insurance).

3. **Immediate recognition:** This basis is used for costs that fall in the following categories:
   (a) Their incurrence during the period provides no discernible future benefits.
   (b) They must be incurred each accounting period, and no build-up of expected future benefits occurs.
   (c) By their nature, they relate to current revenues even though they cannot be directly associated with any specific revenues.
   (d) The amount of cost to be deferred can be measured only in an arbitrary manner or great uncertainty exists regarding the realization of future benefits.
   (e) Uncertainty exists regarding whether allocating them to current and future periods will serve any useful purpose.
   (f) They are measures of asset costs recorded in prior periods from which no future benefits are now discernible.

   Examples: Sales salaries, office salaries, utilities, repairs, advertising, accounting and legal, research and development, postage, write-off of worthless patent.

TIP: Costs incurred by a manufacturing company are often classified into two groups: product costs and period costs. **Product costs** such as material, labor, and manufacturing overhead attach to the product and are carried into future periods (as a balance in inventory) if the product remains unsold at the end of the current period, and, therefore, the revenue recognition is deferred to the period of sale. Product costs are expensed in the period of sale in accordance with the cause and effect basis of expense recognition. **Period costs** such as officers' salaries and other administrative expenses are charged off immediately, even though benefits associated with these costs may occur in the future, because no direct relationship between cost and revenue can be determined and it is highly uncertain what, if any, benefits relate to the future.

TIP: For a manufacturing company, depreciation of the office building is determined and expensed based on a systematic and rational allocation. On the other hand, depreciation of factory machinery is a component of manufacturing overhead; thus, it is an element of product cost. The amount of depreciation that pertains to the products produced during a period is first determined by use of the selected depreciation method. The amount of depreciation that ends up being reflected as an expense on the income statement for the same period depends on the number of products sold (not produced) during the period; it is included as a part of cost of goods sold expense.

ANALYSIS OF MULTIPLE-CHOICE TYPE QUESTIONS

QUESTION

1. (L.O.3) The objectives of financial reporting include all of the following *except* to provide information that:
   a. is useful to the Internal Revenue Service in allocating the tax burden to the business community.
   b. is useful to those making investment and credit decisions.
   c. is helpful in assessing future cash flows.
   d. identifies the economic resources (assets), the claims to those resources (liabilities), and the changes in those resources and claims.

Explanation: Financial reporting is for the use of investors, potential investors, management, and other interested parties. It is not for the IRS. The information required to be reported to the IRS is provided by the reporting entity on tax forms and is referred to as income tax accounting as opposed to financial reporting. (Solution = a)

QUESTION

2. (L.O.4) According to *Statement of Financial Accounting Concepts No. 2*, timeliness is an ingredient of:

	Relevance	Reliability
a.	Yes	Yes
b.	Yes	No
c.	No	No
d.	No	Yes

Approach and Explanation: In answering this question, read the stem and answer "Yes" (true) or "No" (false) when completing the statement with the word **relevance**. Then reread the stem and answer "Yes" or "No" when completing the statement with the word **reliability**. Then look for the corresponding combination of "Yes" and "No" to select your answer. In the diagram of the hierarchy of accounting qualities, timeliness is linked to relevance and not reliability. Therefore, we want to respond "Yes" to the relevance column and "No" to the reliability column. (Solution = b.)

QUESTION

3. (L.O.4) According to *Statement of Financial Accounting Concepts No. 2*, which of the following is considered a pervasive constraint?
   a. Representational faithfulness
   b. Verifiability
   c. Comparability
   d. Costs < Benefits

Approach and Explanation: In visualizing the diagram for a hierarchy of accounting qualities (**Illustration 2-2**), it is an easy task to identify why "costs < benefits" is the pervasive constraint in question and why the other selections can be eliminated in selecting the correct response. Selection "d" is correct because *SFAC No. 2* states that "in order to justify requiring a particular measurement or disclosure, the benefits perceived to be derived from it must exceed the costs perceived to be associated with it." Selections "a" and "b" are incorrect because representational faithfulness and verifiability are both ingredients of primary qualities of accounting information. Selection "c" is incorrect because comparability is a secondary quality of accounting information. (Solution = d.)

QUESTION

4. (L.O.4) If the LIFO inventory method was used last period, it should be used for the current and following periods because of:
   a. materiality.
   b. verifiability.
   c. timeliness.
   d. consistency.

Approach and Explanation: In reading the stem of the question, cover up the answer selections. Anticipate the correct answer by attempting to complete the statement given. This process should yield the answer of "consistency." If you cannot think of the word to complete the statement, then take each answer selection and write down what each means. You should then be able to match up the question with answer selection "d."

Selection "d" is correct because consistency is a secondary quality of accounting information. To be useful, financial statements should reflect consistent application of generally accepted accounting principles. This means that a company should apply the same methods to similar accountable events from period to period. Selection "a" is incorrect because materiality refers to a constraint whereby an item is to be given strict accounting treatment unless it is insignificant. Selection "b" is incorrect because verifiability refers to an ingredient of reliability (it is demonstrated when a high degree of consensus can be secured among independent measurers using the same measurement methods). Selection "c" is incorrect because timeliness is an ingredient of relevance which indicates that for information to be relevant, it must be prepared on a timely basis. (Solution = d.)

QUESTION

5. (L.O.5) The term "articulation" refers to the:
   a. expression of dollar amounts in terms of a foreign currency.
   b. correction of amounts previously reported on the financial statements.
   c. interaction of the elements of financial statements.
   d. degree of preciseness of financial reports.

Approach and Explanation: Define or explain articulation before you read the answer selections. Select the answer that best fits your description. The FASB classifies the elements of financial statements into two distinct groups. The first group of three elements—assets, liabilities, and equity—describes amounts of resources and claims to resources at a **moment in time**. The other seven elements (comprehensive income and its components—revenues, expenses, gains, and losses—as well as investments by owners and distributions to owners) describe transactions, events, and circumstances that affect an enterprise during a **period of time**. The first class—assets, liabilities, and equity—is changed by elements of the second class and at any time is the cumulative result of all changes. This interaction is referred to as "articulation." That is, key figures in one statement (e.g. balance sheet) correspond to balances in another statement (e.g. income statement). (Solution = c.)

QUESTION

6. (L.O.5) Which of the following is *false* with regard to the element "comprehensive income"?
   a. It is more inclusive than the traditional notion of net income.
   b. It includes net income and all other changes in equity exclusive of owners' investments and distributions to owners.
   c. This concept is not yet being applied in practice.
   d. It excludes prior period adjustments (transactions that relate to previous periods, such as corrections of errors).

Explanation: Comprehensive income includes all changes in equity during a period except those resulting from investments by owners and distributions to owners. Prior period adjustments (such as corrections of errors) are included under comprehensive income; they are excluded from the concept of net income (as it is currently applied in practice). (Solution = d.)

QUESTION

7. (L.O.6) The assumption that an enterprise will remain in business indefinitely and will not liquidate in the near future is called the:
   a. economic entity assumption.
   b. going concern assumption.
   c. monetary unit assumption.
   d. periodicity assumption.

Approach and Explanation: Read the stem (while covering up the answer selections) and attempt to complete the statement. Compare your attempt with the selections. Hopefully, you anticipated the correct answer. If your attempt does not match any of the selections given, take each selection and write down the key words in the definitions of the term. This process should lead you to the correct response.

Answer selection "b" is correct because the going concern assumption implies that an enterprise will continue in business and will not liquidate within the foreseeable future. Selection "a" is incorrect because the economic entity assumption indicates that the activities of an accounting entity should be kept separate and distinct from all other accounting entities. Selection "c" is incorrect because the monetary unit assumption indicates that all transactions and events can be measured in terms of a common denominator—units of money. Selection "d" is incorrect because the periodicity assumption indicates that the economic activities of an enterprise can be divided into equally spaced artificial time periods. (Solution = b.)

QUESTION

8. (L.O.7) Pluto Magazine Company sells space to advertisers. The company requires an advertiser to pay for services one month before publication. Advertising revenue should be recognized when:
   a. an advertiser places an order.
   b. a bill is sent to an advertiser.
   c. the related cash is received.
   d. the related ad is published.

Approach and Explanation: Read the last sentence of the stem. We want to know the point at which revenue should be recognized. Write down what you know from the revenue recognition principle. Revenue is generally recognized when (1) realized or realizable, and (2) earned. Read the stem and think of how to apply the revenue recognition principle to the facts given. At the points when an order is placed and a bill is sent to an advertiser, revenue has neither been realized nor earned. At the point when the cash is received in advance of the publication, the revenue is realized but not earned. The revenue is earned when the related ad is published and, thus, should be recognized then. (Solution = d.)

QUESTION

9. (L.O.7) The historical cost principle provides that:
   a. items whose costs are insignificant compared to other amounts on the financial statements may be accounted for in the most expedient manner.
   b. assets and equities be expressed in terms of a common denominator.
   c. the recorded amount of an acquired item should be the fair market value of what is given or the fair market value of what is received in the exchange, whichever is more objectively determinable.
   d. the expenses of generating revenue should be recognized in the same period that the related revenue is recognized.

Approach and Explanation: Briefly define the historical cost principle before you read the answer selections. See **Illustration 2-4**. Answer selection "a" describes the materiality constraint. Selection "b" describes the monetary unit assumption. Selection "d" relates to the matching principle. (Solution = c.)

QUESTION

10. (L.O.7) If revenue is received in the current period, but it is not earned until a future period, the related expenses of generating the revenue should *not* be recognized until that future period. This guideline is an application of the:
    a. revenue recognition principle.
    b. full disclosure principle.
    c. matching principle.
    d. conservatism constraint.

Explanation: The revenue recognition principle dictates that revenue be recognized (recorded and reported) in the period it is realized (or realizable) and earned. The matching principle dictates that expenses be recognized in the same period as the revenue which they helped to generate is recognized. Thus, if revenue is deferred, the related expenses should also be deferred. (Solution = c.)

QUESTION

11. (L.O.8) In matters of doubt and great uncertainty, accounting issues should be resolved by choosing the alternative that has the least favorable effect on net income, assets, and owners' equity. This guidance comes from the:
    a. materiality constraint.
    b. industry practices constraint.
    c. conservatism constraint.
    d. full disclosure principle.

Approach and Explanation: Briefly define each of the answer selections. Choose the item for which your definition most closely agrees with the stem of the question. See **Illustration 2-4**. In matters of doubt and uncertainty, the accountant is conservative and chooses the accounting alternative that is the least likely to cause an overstatement of net income, assets, and owners' equity. (Solution = c.)

CHAPTER 3

THE ACCOUNTING INFORMATION SYSTEM

OVERVIEW

Accounting information must be accumulated and summarized before it can be communicated and analyzed. In this chapter, we will discuss the steps involved in the accounting cycle. We will emphasize the subject of adjusting entries. Adjusting entries are required so that revenues and expenses are reflected on an accrual basis of accounting. Adjusting entries are simply entries required to bring account balances up to date. The failure to record proper adjustments will cause errors on both the income statement and the balance sheet.

SUMMARY OF LEARNING OBJECTIVES

1. **Understand basic accounting terminology.** An understanding of the following eleven terms is important: (1) Event, (2) Transaction, (3) Account, (4) Real and Nominal accounts, (5) Ledger, (6) Journal, (7) Posting, (8) Trial Balances, (9) Adjusting entries, (10) Financial statements, and (11) Closing entries.

2. **Explain double-entry rules.** The left side of an account is the debit side; the right side is the credit side. All asset and expense accounts are increased on the left or debit side and decreased on the right or credit side. Conversely, all liability and revenue accounts are increased on the right or credit side and decreased on the left or debit side. Stockholders' equity accounts, Common Stock and Retained Earnings, are increased on the credit side, whereas the Dividends account is increased on the debit side.

3. **Identify steps in the accounting cycle.** The basic steps in the accounting cycle are (1) identification and measurement of transactions and other events, (2) journalization, (3) posting, (4) unadjusted trial balance, (5) adjustments, (6) adjusted trial balance, (7) statement presentation, and (8) closing.

4. **Record transactions in journals, post to ledger accounts, and prepare a trial balance.** The simplest journal form is a chronological listing of transactions and events expressed in terms of debits and credits to particular accounts. The items entered in a general journal must be transferred to the general ledger; this procedure is called posting. An unadjusted trial balance should be prepared at the end of a given period after the entries have been recorded in the journal and posted to the ledger. A trial balance is a list of all open accounts in the general ledger and their balances; it proves the equality of debits and credits after the recording and posting processes.

5. **Explain the reasons for preparing adjusting entries.** Adjustments are necessary to achieve a proper matching of revenues and expenses so as to determine net income for the current period and to achieve an accurate statement of end-of-the period balances in assets, liabilities, and owners' equity accounts.

6. **Explain how inventory accounts are adjusted at year-end.** When the inventory records are maintained on a periodic inventory system, a Purchases account is used and the Inventory account is unchanged during the period. The Inventory account reflects the beginning inventory amount throughout the period. At the end of the accounting period, the Inventory account must be adjusted by closing out the beginning inventory amount and recording the ending inventory amount. Under a perpetual inventory system, the balance in the Inventory account at the end of the period should reflect the ending inventory amount and no adjusting entries are needed.

7. **Prepare closing entries.** In the closing process, all of the revenue and expense account balances (income statement items) are transferred to a clearing account called Income Summary, which is used only at the end of each accounting period. Revenues and expenses are matched in the Income Summary account and the net result of this matching, which represents the net income or net loss for the period, is then transferred to an owners' equity account (Retained Earnings for a corporation and capital accounts for proprietorships and partnerships.)

8. **Identify adjusting entries that may be reversed.** Reversing entries are most often used to reverse two types of adjusting entries: accrued revenues and accrued expenses. Adjusting entries for prepayments (prepaid expenses and unearned revenues) may also be reversed if the initial entry to record the cash transaction is made to an expense or revenue account.

9. **Prepare a 10-column work sheet.** The 10-column work sheet provides columns for the first (unadjusted) trial balance, adjustments, adjusted trial balance, income statement, and balance sheet. The work sheet does not replace the financial statements. Instead, it is the accountant's informal device for accumulating and sorting information needed for the financial statements. Completing the work sheet provides considerable assurance that all of the details related to the end-of-period accounting procedures and preparation of the financial statements have been properly brought together.

10.* **Differentiate the cash basis of accounting from the accrual basis of accounting.** Accrual basis accounting provides information about cash inflows and outflows associated with earnings activities as soon as these cash flows can be estimated with an acceptable degree of certainty. That is, accrual basis accounting aids in predicting future cash flows by reporting transactions and events with cash consequences at the time the transactions and events occur, rather than when the cash is received and paid.

*This material is covered in Appendix 3-A in the text.

11.** **Identify (a) the use and types of subsidiary ledgers and (b) the use and types of special journals. Subsidiary ledgers** facilitate the recording process by freeing the general ledger from the details of individual entries and balances. Subsidiary ledgers group accounts with common characteristics (e.g., customers' accounts, creditors' accounts, inventory accounts, and equipment accounts). **Special journals** expedite the journalizing and posting processes for frequently occurring transactions. The most common special journals are: sales journal, purchases journal, cash receipts journal, and cash payments journal.

**This material is covered in Appendix 3-B in the text.

TIPS ON CHAPTER TOPICS

TIP: This chapter is an extremely important one. A good understanding of this chapter and an ability to think and work quickly with the concepts incorporated herein are necessary for comprehending subsequent chapters. Although adjusting entries were introduced in your principles course, you are likely to discover new dimensions to this subject in your intermediate accounting course. Pay close attention when studying this chapter!

TIP: When you encounter a transaction, always analyze it in terms of its effects on the elements of the basic accounting equation (or **balance sheet equation**). For your analysis to be complete, it must maintain balance in the basic accounting equation. The **basic accounting equation** is as follows:

ASSETS = LIABILITIES + OWNERS' EQUITY

or

A = L + OE

Assets are economic resources. Liabilities and owners' equities are sources of resources; liabilities are creditor sources, and owners' equity represents owner sources (owner investments and undistributed profits). The basic accounting equation simply states that the total assets at a point in time equal the total liabilities plus total owners' equity at the same point in time.

TIP: **An understanding of the following eleven terms is important.** (1) **Event:** a happening of consequence. An event generally is the source or cause of changes in assets, liabilities, and equity. Events may be external or internal. (2) **Transaction:** an external event involving a transfer or exchange between two or more entities. (3) **Account:** a systematic arrangement that shows the effect of transactions and other events on a specific financial item. A separate account is kept for each type of asset, liability, revenue, and expense, and for capital (owners' equity). (4) **Real and nominal accounts:** real (permanent) accounts are asset, liability, and equity accounts. They appear on the balance sheet. Nominal (temporary) accounts are revenue and expense accounts. They appear on the income statement. Nominal accounts are periodically closed; real accounts are not closed. (5) **Ledger:** the book (or computer system) containing the accounts. (6) **Journal:** the book of original entry where transactions and selected other events are initially recorded. (7) **Posting:** the process of transferring the essential facts and figures from the book of original entry to the ledger accounts. (8) **Trial balance:** a list of all open accounts in the ledger and their balances. (9) **Adjusting entries:** entries made at the end of an accounting period to bring all accounts up to date on an accrual accounting basis so that correct financial statements can be prepared. (10) **Financial statements:** statements that reflect the collection, tabulation, and final summarization of the accounting data. (11) **Closing entries:** the formal process by which all nominal accounts are reduced to zero, and the net income or net loss is determined and transferred to the appropriate owners' equity account.

TIP: **Transactions** are the economic events of an entity recorded by accountants. Some events (happenings of consequence to an entity) are not measurable in terms of money and do not get recorded in the accounting records. Hiring employees, placing an order for supplies, greeting a customer and quoting prices for products are examples of activities that do not by themselves constitute transactions.

TIP: In accordance with the **revenue recognition principle**, revenue is to be recognized (reported) in the period in which it is realized (or realizable) and earned. In accordance with the **matching principle**, the expenses incurred in generating revenues should be recognized in the same period as the revenues they helped to generate. First, the revenue recognition principle is applied to determine in what period(s) to recognize revenue. Then, the matching principle is applied to determine in what period(s) to recognize expense.

TIP: Adjusting entries are often required so that revenues and expenses are reflected on an accrual basis of accounting (revenues recognized when earned and expenses recognized when incurred) rather than on a cash basis of accounting. Therefore, adjusting entries reflect the accruals and deferrals of revenues and expenses and also estimated expenses. Adjusting entries are simply entries required to bring account balances up to date before financial statements can be prepared. The failure to record proper adjustments will cause errors in both the income statement and the balance sheet.

TIP: Notice that **none** of the adjusting entries discussed in Chapter 3 involves the **Cash** account. Therefore, if you are instructed to record **adjusting entries**, double check your work when it is completed. If you have used the Cash account in any adjusting entry, it is very likely in error. (The only time Cash belongs in an adjusting entry is when a bank reconciliation discloses a need to adjust the Cash account—this will be explained in Chapter 7—or when an error has been made that involves the Cash account, in which case a correcting entry is required.)

TIP: Notice that each adjusting entry discussed in this chapter involves a balance sheet account and an income statement account.

TIP: When preparing homework assignments, working through this Self-Study, and answering exam questions, pay careful attention to whether a prepayment situation relates to a **cash inflow** or **cash outflow** for the entity in question. Be sure you then use the proper related account for recording the cash receipt or disbursement and correct terminology in explaining the scenario. If cash is **received** in a rental situation, the amount will be recorded (by a credit) in either an earned rent revenue account or an unearned rent revenue account, **not** in an expense or a prepaid expense account. If cash is **paid** in a rental situation, the amount will be recorded (by a debit) in either an expense or a prepaid expense account.

TIP: In an adjusting entry for an accrual (accrued revenue or accrued expense), the word "accrued" is **not** needed in either account title. If you choose to use the word "accrued" in an account title, it is appropriate to do so **only** in the balance sheet account title. For example, the entry to record accrued salaries of $1,000 is as follows:

Salaries Expense	1,000	
Salaries Payable		1,000

The word "accrued" is not needed in either account title, but it could be used in the liability account title if desired (the account title would then be Accrued Salaries Payable). It would be wrong to insert the word "accrued" in the expense account title. Some people simply call the credit account "Accrued Salaries" but we advise that you include the key word "Payable" and omit the unnecessary word "Accrued."

TIP: An unadjusted trial balance is referred to as either "unadjusted trial balance" or simply "trial balance." An adjusted trial balance is referred to as either "adjusted trial balance" or the "adjusted trial."

TIP: Closing entries are necessary at the end of an accounting period to prepare the nominal accounts (revenues, expenses, gains, and losses) for the recording of transactions for the next accounting period. Closing entries are prepared after the nominal account balances have been used to prepare the income statement. Only nominal accounts are closed. Real accounts are never closed; their balances continue into the next accounting period. **Nominal** accounts are often called **temporary** accounts; **real** accounts are often called **permanent** accounts.

TIP: A nominal account with a credit balance is closed by a debit to that account and a credit to Income Summary. A nominal account with a debit balance is closed by a credit to that account and a debit to Income Summary. The Income Summary account is closed to an owners' equity account (Retained Earnings for a corporation) and is often called the Revenue and Expense Summary.

TIP: If a separate account is used to record owner withdrawals or owner distributions (such as Dividends Declared for a corporation or Owner's Drawings for a proprietorship or partnership), this account is also closed at the end of the accounting period, but it is **not** closed to the Income Summary account because it is not a component of the net income computation. Rather, it is closed directly to Retained Earnings (for a corporation) or to Owner's Capital (for a proprietorship or partnership).

TIP: A **post-closing trial balance** contains only real accounts because the nominal accounts all have a zero balance after the closing process. A post-closing trial balance is prepared to check on the equality of debits and credits after the closing process.

TIP: In preparing a 10-column work sheet, the debit and credit columns for every column pair must be equal before you can proceed to the next column pair. (This pertains to the first three column pairs). All five pairs of columns must balance for a work sheet to be complete.

TIP: You should be able to define the following four terms and describe the related adjusting entry for each; they are:

1. A **prepaid expense** is an expense that has been paid but has not been incurred. An adjusting entry for a deferred expense involves an EXPENSE account and an ASSET (prepaid expense) account.

2. An **unearned revenue** is a revenue that has been collected but has not been earned. An adjusting entry for an unearned revenue involves a LIABILITY (unearned revenue) account and a REVENUE account.

3. An **accrued expense** is an expense that has been incurred but has not been paid. An adjusting entry for an accrued expense involves an EXPENSE account and a LIABILITY (payable account).

4. An **accrued revenue** is a revenue that has been earned but has not been received. An adjusting entry for an accrued revenue involves an ASSET (receivable) account and a REVENUE account.

TIP: A **prepaid expense** may be called a **deferred expense**. A deferred expense is so named because the recognition of expense is being deferred (put-off) to a future period; thus, a debit is carried on the balance sheet now and will be released to the income statement in a future period when the related benefits are consumed (expense is incurred).

TIP: An **unearned revenue** is often called a **deferred revenue** because the recognition of revenue is being deferred to a future period; thus, a credit is carried on the balance sheet now and will be released to the income statement in a future period when the related revenue is earned.

TIP: An adjusting entry for prepaid insurance expense (expense paid but not incurred) involves an expense account and an asset account. The expense account is often called Insurance Expense or Expired Insurance. Possible titles for the asset account include Prepaid Insurance, Deferred Insurance Expense, Prepaid Insurance Expense, Deferred Insurance, and Unexpired Insurance.

TIP: An adjusting entry for deferred rent revenue (revenue collected but not earned) involves a liability account and a revenue account. Possible titles for the liability account include Unearned Rent Revenue, Unearned Rent, Deferred Rent Revenue, Rent Revenue Received in Advance, and Rental Income Collected in Advance. The use of Prepaid Rent Revenue as an account title is **not** appropriate because the term prepaid usually refers to the payment of cash in advance, not the receipt of cash in advance. The revenue account is often called Rent Revenue or Rental Income or Rent Earned.

TIP: In an adjusting entry to record accrued interest revenue (revenue earned but not received), the debit is to an asset account and the credit is to a revenue account. Possible names for that asset account are Interest Receivable and Accrued Interest Receivable. Possible names for the revenue account include Interest Revenue, Interest Income, and Interest Earned.

TIP: In an adjusting entry to record accrued salaries expenses (expense incurred, but not paid) the debit is to an expense account and the credit is to a liability account. The expense account is usually titled Salaries Expense. Possible names for the liability account include Salaries Payable and Accrued Salaries Payable.

ILLUSTRATION 3-1
DOUBLE-ENTRY (DEBIT AND CREDIT) ACCOUNTING SYSTEM (L.O.2)

Asset Accounts

Debit	Credit
+ (increase)	- (decrease)

Liability Accounts

Debit	Credit
- (decrease)	+ (increase)

Expense Accounts

Debit	Credit
+ (increase)	- (decrease)
↑ **Normal Balance**	

Capital/Owners' Equity Accounts

Debit	Credit
- (decrease)	+ (increase)

Revenue Accounts

Debit	Credit
- (decrease)	+ (increase)
	↑ **Normal Balance**

TIP: "Credit" does **not** always mean favorable or unfavorable. In accounting, "debit and "credit" simply mean left and right, respectively. "Debit" is a term that refers to the left side of any account. Thus, the debit side of an account is always the left side. "Credit" is a word that simply refers to the right side of an account. Thus, the credit side of an account is always the right side of the account. The phrase "to debit an account" means to enter an amount on the debit (left) side of an account. Debit can be abbreviated as "Dr." and credit is abbreviated as "Cr."

TIP: A "+" indicates an increase and a "-" indicates a decrease. Therefore, a transaction which causes an increase in an asset is recorded by a debit to the related asset account; a transaction which causes a decrease in the same asset is recorded by a credit to the same account.

TIP: The **normal balance** of an account is the side where increases are recorded. Therefore, the normal balance of an asset account is a debit balance; the normal balance of a liability account is a credit balance.

TIP: A separate account should exist in the general ledger for each item that will appear on the financial statements.

ILLUSTRATION 3-1 (Continued)

TIP: At this stage of your study of accounting, you should be able to quickly and correctly identify the debit and credit rules for any given account. If you are slow at this process, drill on the rules until you improve. If you memorize the rules for an asset account, you can figure out the rules for all other types of accounts by knowing which rules are the opposite of the rules for assets and which are the same. Increases in assets are recorded by debits. Because liabilities and owners' equity are on the other side of the equals sign in the basic accounting equation, they must have debit and credit rules opposite of the rules for assets. Therefore, a liability or an owners' equity account is increased by a credit entry. Revenues earned increase owners' equity (retained earnings for a corporate form of organization) so the rules to record increases in revenue are the same as the rules to record increases in an owners' equity account (increases are recorded by credits). Because expenses and owners' withdrawals reduce owners' equity, they have debit/credit rules which are opposite of the rules for an owners' equity account.

TIP: In the double-entry system of accounting, for every debit there must be a credit(s) of equal amount, and vice versa.

EXERCISE 3-1

Purpose: (L.O.2) This exercise will test your understanding of the debit and credit rules.

Instructions

For each account listed below, put a check mark (√) in the appropriate column to indicate if it is increased by an entry in the debit (left) side of the account or by an entry in the credit (right) side of the account. The first one is done for you.

		Debit	Credit
1.	Cash	√	
2.	Sales Revenue		
3.	Commissions Expense		
4.	Advertising Expense		
5.	Salaries Payable		
6.	Prepaid Insurance		
7.	Property Taxes Payable		
8.	Property Tax Expense		
9.	Dividends Declared		
10.	Interest Revenue		
11.	Salaries Expense		
12.	Commissions Revenue		
13.	Unearned Rent Revenue		

		Debit	Credit
14.	Equipment	_____	_____
15.	Note Payable	_____	_____
16.	Building	_____	_____
17.	Accounts Payable	_____	_____
18.	Land	_____	_____
19.	Accounts Receivable	_____	_____
20.	Common Stock	_____	_____
21.	Retained Earnings	_____	_____

> TIP: In essence, you are being asked to identify the normal balance of each of the accounts listed. The **normal balance** of an account is the side where increases are recorded.

Solution to Exercise 3-1

Approach: Determine the classification of the account (asset, liability, owners' equity, revenue or expense). Think about the debit and credit rules for that classification. Refer to **Illustration 3-1** and the related **TIPS** for those rules.

		Debit	Credit	Classification
1.	Cash	√		Asset
2.	Sales Revenue		√	Revenue
3.	Commissions Expense	√		Expense
4.	Advertising Expense	√		Expense
5.	Salaries Payable		√	Liability
6.	Prepaid Insurance	√		Asset
7.	Property Taxes Payable		√	Liability
8.	Property Tax Expense	√		Expense
9.	Dividends Declared	√		Owners' Equity (Owners' Withdrawals)
10.	Interest Revenue		√	Revenue
11.	Salaries Expense	√		Expense
12.	Commissions Revenue		√	Revenue
13.	Unearned Rent Revenue		√	Liability
14.	Equipment	√		Asset
15.	Note Payable		√	Liability
16.	Building	√		Asset
17.	Accounts Payable		√	Liability
18.	Land	√		Asset
19.	Accounts Receivable	√		Asset
20.	Common Stock		√	Owners' Equity (Owners' Investments)
21.	Retained Earnings		√	Owners' Equity (Earned Capital)

ILLUSTRATION 3-2
SUMMARY OF ADJUSTMENT RELATIONSHIPS AND EXPLANATIONS (L.O.5)

Type of Adjustment	Account Relationship	Reason for Adjustment	Account Balances Before Adjustment	Adjusting Entry
1. Prepaid Expense	Asset and Expense	(a) Prepaid expense initially recorded in asset account has been consumed; or,	Asset overstated Expense understated	Dr. Expense Cr. Asset
		(b) Prepaid expense initially recorded in expense account has not been consumed.	Asset understated Expense overstated	Dr. Asset Cr. Expense
2. Unearned Revenue	Liability and Revenue	(a) Unearned revenue initially recorded in liability account has been earned; or,	Liability overstated Revenue understated	Dr. Liability Cr. Revenue
		(b) Unearned revenue initially recorded in revenue account has not been earned.	Liability understated Revenue overstated	Dr. Revenue Cr. Liability
3. Accrued Expense	Expense and Liability	Expense incurred has not been billed nor paid nor recorded.	Expense understated Liability understated	Dr. Expense Cr. Liability
4. Accrued Revenues	Asset and Revenue	Revenue earned has not been billed nor collected nor recorded.	Asset understated Revenue understated	Dr. Asset Cr. Revenue
5. Estimated Item	Asset and Expense	(a) A previously recorded long-lived asset has now been partially consumed; or,	Asset overstated Expense understated	Dr. Expense Cr. Contra Asset
		(b) An existing asset is not fully realizable.	Asset overstated Expense understated	Dr. Expense Cr. Contra Asset

Explanation:

1. When expenses are paid for before they are incurred, the payment may either be recorded by a debit to an asset account (prepaid expense) or by a debit to an expense account. At the end of the accounting period, the accounts are adjusted as needed. If the prepayment was initially recorded by use of a prepaid (asset) account, the consumed portion is transferred to an expense account in the adjusting entry. Whereas, if the prepayment was initially recorded by use of an expense account, an adjusting entry is required only if a portion of the expense remains prepaid at the end of the accounting period (in which case the unconsumed portion is transferred to an asset account). (See **Illustration 3-3** for an example.)

2. When revenues are received before they are earned, the receipt may either be recorded by a credit to a liability account (unearned revenue) or by a credit to a revenue account. At the end of the accounting period, the accounts are adjusted as needed. If the collection was initially recorded by a credit to a liability account (unearned revenue), the earned portion is transferred to a revenue account in the adjusting entry. Whereas, if the collection was initially recorded by use of a revenue account, an adjusting entry is required only if a portion of the revenue remains unearned at the end of the accounting period (in which case the unearned portion is transferred to a liability account). (See **Illustration 3-3** for an example.)

ILLUSTRATION 3-2 (Continued)

3. Expenses are often incurred before they are paid. An expense incurred but not yet paid is called an **accrued expense**. If at the end of an accounting period this accrued expense has not been recorded (which is often the case because it usually has not been billed yet by the vendor), it must be recorded by way of an adjusting entry. Expense that accrues with the passage of time (such as interest expense) is a good example of a reason to need an accrued expense (or accrued liability) type adjusting entry.
4. Revenues are often earned before they are collected. A revenue earned but not received is called an **accrued revenue**. If at the end of an accounting period this accrued revenue has not been recorded (which is often the case because it usually has not been billed yet), it must be recorded by way of an adjusting entry. Revenue that accrues with the passage of time (such as interest revenue) is a good example of a reason to need an accrued revenue (or accrued asset) type adjusting entry.

TIP: Examine each type of adjustment explained above and notice the logic of the resulting entry. For example, an adjustment to recognize supplies used (when the supplies were recorded in an asset account when purchased) should reduce assets and increase expenses.

TIP: Keep in mind that for accrued items (accrued revenues and accrued expenses), the related cash flow **follows** the period in which the relevant revenue or expense is recognized; whereas, with prepayment type items (unearned revenues and prepaid expenses), the related cash flow **precedes** the period in which the relevant revenue or expense is recognized.

For example, assume the accounting period is the calendar year. Consider an accrued expense such as accrued salaries at the end of 1999. An adjusting entry will be recorded at the end of 1999 so the expense will get reported on the 1999 income statement. The related cash payment to employees will take place in the following accounting period (2000, in this case). For another example, consider a prepaid expense such as the prepayment of rent in December 1999 for January 2000 occupancy. The cash payment occurs in December 1999. The expense is incurred and recognized in the following accounting period (January 2000).

ILLUSTRATION 3-3
ALTERNATIVE TREATMENTS OF PREPAID EXPENSES AND UNEARNED REVENUES (L.O.5)

When a company writes a check to pay for an item that affects expense in at least two different time periods (such as for an insurance premium or a license or dues), the bookkeeper may record the payment in one of two ways. Either as a prepaid expense (asset) or as an expense. The first way is used most often in introductory accounting textbooks; the second is used most often in the real world. Regardless of the way the payment is recorded, an appropriate adjusting entry will be made at the end of the accounting period so that correct balances appear on the income statement and the balance sheet. For example, a $1,200 payment is made on April 1, 1999, for a twelve-month insurance premium covering the time between April 1, 1999 and March 31, 2000. (Assume a calendar year reporting period.) A comparison of the two possible approaches appears below.

Prepayment (Cash Paid) Initially Debited to Asset Account				**OR**	**Prepayment (Cash Paid) Initially Debited to Expense Account**			
4/1	Prepaid Insurance	1,200			4/1	Insurance Expense	1,200	
	Cash		1,200			Cash		1,200
12/31	Insurance Expense	900			12/31	Prepaid Insurance	300	
	Prepaid Insurance		900			Insurance Expense		300

After posting the entries, the accounts appear as follows:

Prepaid Insurance (asset approach)

4/1	1,200	12/31 Adj.	900
12/31 Bal.	300		

Prepaid Insurance (expense approach)

12/31 Adj.	300		

Insurance Expense (asset approach)

12/31 Adj.	900		

Insurance Expense (expense approach)

4/1	1,200	12/31 Adj.	300
12/31 Bal.	900		

Illustration 3-3 (Continued)

Notice that regardless of the path, you end up at the same place—with a balance of $300 in Prepaid Insurance and a balance of $900 in Insurance Expense. That was your objective—to report balances in accordance with the accrual basis of accounting.

TIP: Reversing entries are never required. But if it is company policy to use reversing entries where appropriate, would either or both of the above adjusting entries get reversed? The adjusting entry illustrated in the left column would **not** get reversed since to do so would result in reestablishing an asset amount that the adjusting entry indicated had expired. The adjusting entry illustrated in the right column **can be** reversed since a reversing entry will record $300 of insurance expense in the new accounting period (2000) which is the period we expect the remaining $300 of premium to pertain.

When a company receives cash from a customer in advance of earning the related revenue, the bookkeeper may record the receipt in one of two ways. Either as an unearned revenue (liability) or as an earned revenue. The first way is used most often in introductory accounting textbooks; the second is used most often in the real world. Regardless of the way the receipt is recorded, an appropriate adjusting entry will be made at the end of the accounting period so that correct balances appear on the income statement and the balance sheet. For example, $1,200 is received on May 1, 1999, for a twelve-month magazine subscription covering the time between May 1, 1999 and April 30, 2000. (Assume a calendar year reporting period.) A comparison of the two possible approaches appears below:

Unearned Revenue (Cash Received) Initially Credited to Liability Account				OR	Unearned Revenue (Cash Received) Initially Credited to Revenue Account			
5/1	Cash	1,200			5/1	Cash	1,200	
	Unearned Sub. Rev.		1,200			Sub. Revenue		1,200
12/31	Unearned Sub. Rev.	800			12/31	Sub. Revenue	400	
	Sub. Revenue		800			Unearned Sub. Rev.		400

Illustration 3-3 (Continued)

After posting the entries, the accounts appear as follows:

Unearned Subscription Revenue

12/31 Adj.	800	5/1	1,200
		12/31 Bal.	400

Unearned Subscription Revenue

		12/31 Adj.	400

Subscription Revenue

		12/31 Adj.	800

Subscription Revenue

12/31 Adj.	400	5/1	1,200
		12/31 Bal.	800

Notice that the balances in the accounts are the same regardless of the approach used; that is, Unearned Subscription Revenue is $400, and Subscription Revenue is $800 at December 31, 1999.

TIP: The adjusting entry illustrated in the left column would not be subject to reversal; a reversing entry can be used with the approach illustrated in the right column.

EXERCISE 3-2

Purpose: (L.O.5) This exercise will provide you with examples of adjusting entries for the accrual of expenses and revenues.

The following information relates to the Yuppy Clothing Sales Company at the end of 1999. The accounting period is the calendar year. This is the company's first year of operations.

1. Employees are paid every Friday for the five-day work week ending on that day. Salaries amount to $2,400 per week. The accounting period ends on a Thursday.
2. On October 1, 1999, Yuppy borrowed $8,000 cash by signing a note payable due in one year at 8% interest. Interest is due when the principal is paid.
3. A note for $2,000 was received from a customer in a sales transaction on May 1, 1999. The note matures in one year and bears 12% interest per annum. Interest is due when the principal is due.
4. A portion of Yuppy's parking lot is used by executives of a neighboring company. A person pays $6 per day for each day's use, and the parking fees are due by the fifth business day following the month of use. The fees for December 31, 1999 amount to $1,260.

Instructions

Using the information given above, prepare the necessary adjusting entries at December 31, 1999.

Solution to Exercise 3-2

1.	Salaries Expense	1,920	
	Salaries Payable		1,920
	($2,400 ÷ 5 = $480); ($480 x 4 = $1,920 accrued salaries)		
2.	Interest Expense	160	
	Interest Payable		160
	($8,000 x 8% x 3/12 = $160 accrued interest)		
3.	Interest Receivable	160	
	Interest Revenue		160
	($2,000 x 12% x 8/12 = $160 accrued interest)		
4.	Parking Fees Receivable	1,260	
	Parking Fees Revenue		1,260

Approach and Explanation: Write down the definitions for accrued expense and accrued revenue. Think about what is to be accomplished by each of the adjustments required in this exercise. An **accrued expense** is an expense that has been incurred but not paid. The "incurred" part results in an increase in Expense (debit) and the "not paid" part results in an increase in Payable (credit). An **accrued revenue** is a revenue that has been earned but not received. The "earned" part results in an increase in Revenue (credit) and the "not received" part results in an increase in Receivable (debit).

EXERCISE 3-3

Purpose: (L.O.5) This exercise will provide you with examples of adjusting entries for:

(1) Prepaid expenses when cash payments are recorded in an asset (real) account.

(2) Prepaid expenses when cash payments are recorded in an expense (nominal) account.

(3) Unearned revenues when cash receipts are recorded in a liability (real) account.

(4) Unearned revenues when cash receipts are recorded in a revenue (nominal) account.

Thus, this exercise will review the alternative treatments of prepaid expenses and unearned revenues discussed in **Illustration 3-3**.

Each situation described below is **independent** of the others.

(1) Office supplies are recorded in an asset account when acquired. There were no supplies on hand at the beginning of the period. Cash purchases of office supplies during the period amounted to $900. A count of supplies at the end of the period shows $320 worth to be on hand. The asset account is titled Office Supplies on Hand.

(2) Office supplies are recorded in an expense account when acquired. There were no supplies on hand at the beginning of the period. Cash purchases of office supplies during the period amount to $900. A count of supplies at the end of the period shows $320 worth to be on hand.

(3) Office supplies are recorded in an asset account when acquired. There were $400 of supplies on hand at the beginning of the period. Cash purchases of office supplies during the period amount to $900. A count of supplies at the end of the period shows $320 worth to be on hand.

(4) Office supplies are recorded in an expense account when acquired. There were $400 of supplies on hand at the beginning of the period. Cash purchases of office supplies during the period amount to $900. A count of supplies at the end of the period shows $320 worth to be on hand. No reversing entries are used.

(5) Receipts from customers for magazine subscriptions are recorded as a liability when cash is collected in advance of delivery. There was no beginning balance in the liability account. During the period, $54,000 was received for subscriptions. At the end of the period, it was determined that the balance of the Unearned Subscription Revenue account should be $8,000.

(6) Receipts from customers for magazine subscriptions are recorded as revenue when cash is collected in advance of delivery. There was no balance in the Unearned Subscription Revenue account at the beginning of the period. During the period, $54,000 was received for subscriptions. At the end of the period, it was determined that the balance of the Unearned Subscription Revenue account should be $8,000.

(7) Receipts from customers for magazine subscriptions are recorded as a liability when cash is collected in advance of delivery. The beginning balance in the liability account was $6,700. During the period, $54,000 was received for subscriptions. At the end of the period, it was determined that the balance of the Unearned Subscription Revenue account should be $8,000.

(8) Receipts from customers for magazine subscriptions are recorded as revenue when cash is collected in advance of delivery. The beginning balance in the liability account was $6,700. During the period, $54,000 was received for subscriptions. At the end of the period, it was determined that the balance of the Unearned Subscription Revenue account should be $8,000. No reversing entries are used.

Instructions

For each of the **independent** situations above:

(a) Prepare the appropriate adjusting entry in general journal form.

(b) Indicate the amount of revenue or expense which will appear on the income statement for the period.

(c) Indicate the balance of the applicable asset or liability account at the end of the period.

(d) Indicate the amount of cash received or paid during the period.

(e) Indicate the change in the applicable asset or liability account from the beginning of the period to the end of the period.

TIP: It would be helpful to draw T-accounts for each situation. Enter the information given as it would be, or needs to be, reflected in the accounts. Solve for the adjusting entry that would be necessary to "reconcile" the facts given.

Solution to Exercise 3-3

(1)	a.	Office Supplies Expense	580	
		Office Supplies on Hand		580
	b.	Office Supplies Expense	$580	
	c.	Office Supplies on Hand	$320	
	d.	Cash paid	$900	
	e.	Increase in Office Supplies on Hand	$320	

Approach:

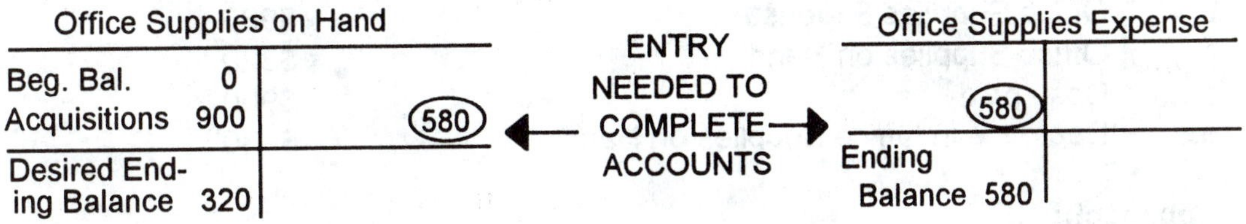

(2)	a.	Office Supplies on Hand	320	
		Office Supplies Expense		320
	b.	Office Supplies Expense	$580	
	c.	Office Supplies on Hand	$320	
	d.	Cash paid	$900	
	e.	Increase in Office Supplies on Hand	$320	

Approach:

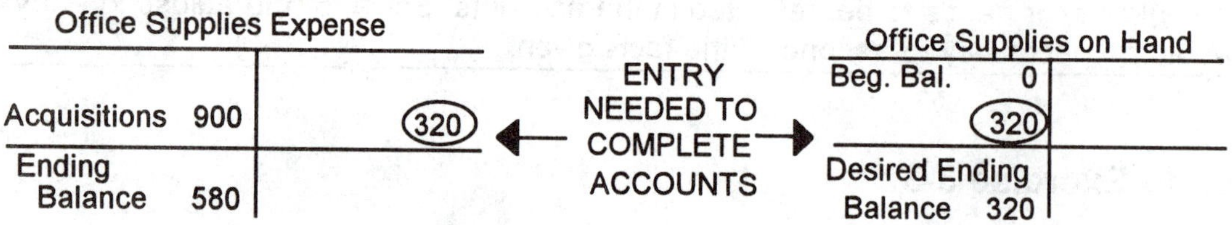

> **TIP:** Compare situation (2) with situation (1). Notice the facts are the same **except** for the account debited for acquisitions of office supplies. The solution is the same **except** for the adjusting entry required.

(3)	a.	Office Supplies Expense	980	
		Office Supplies on Hand		980
	b.	Office Supplies Expense	$980	
	c.	Office Supplies on Hand	$320	
	d.	Cash paid	$900	
	e.	Decrease in Office Supplies on Hand	$ 80	

Approach:

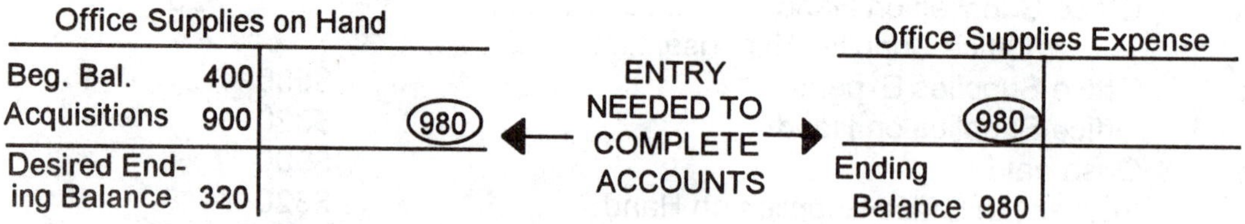

(4)	a.	Office Supplies Expense	80	
		Office Supplies on Hand		80
	b.	Office Supplies Expense	$980	
	c.	Office Supplies on Hand	$320	
	d.	Cash paid	$900	
	e.	Decrease in Office Supplies on Hand	$ 80	

Approach:

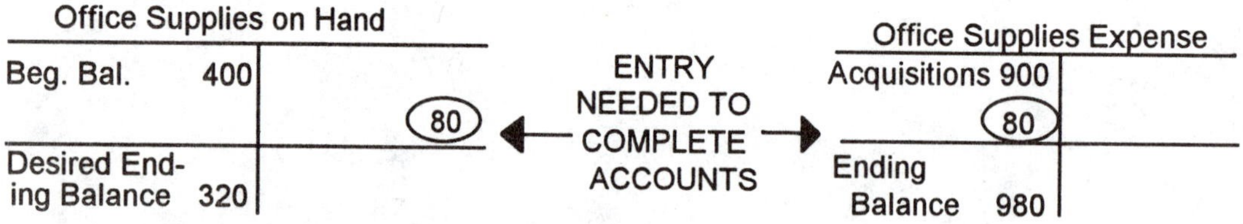

> **TIP:** Compare situation (4) with situation (3). Notice the facts are the same **except** for the account debited for acquisitions of office supplies. The solution is then the same **except** for the adjusting entry required.

(5)	a.	Unearned Subscription Revenue............................	46,000	
		Subscription Revenue.................................		46,000
	b.	Subscription Revenue	$46,000	
	c.	Unearned Subscription Revenue	$ 8,000	
	d.	Cash received	$54,000	
	e.	Increase in Unearned Subscription Revenue	$ 8,000	

Approach:

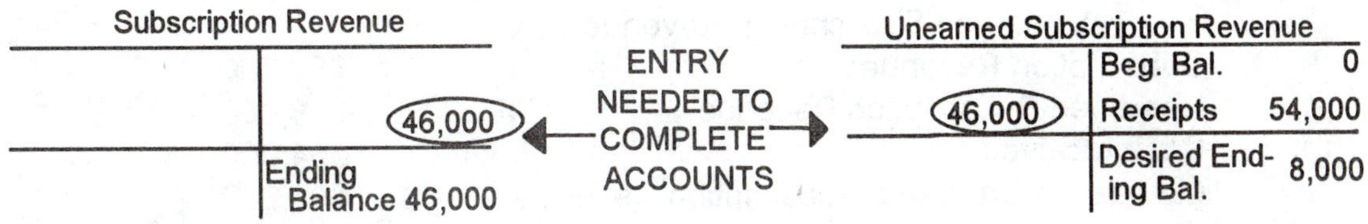

(6)	a.	Subscription Revenue	8,000	
		Unearned Subscription Revenue		8,000
	b.	Subscription Revenue	$46,000	
	c.	Unearned Subscription Revenue	$ 8,000	
	d.	Cash received	$54,000	
	e.	Increase in Unearned Subscription Revenue	$ 8,000	

Approach:

> **TIP:** Compare situation (6) with situation (5). Notice the facts are the same **except** for the account credited for receipt of revenue in advance of the period in which the revenue is earned. The solution is the same **except** for the adjusting entry required.

(7)	a.	Unearned Subscription Revenue............................	52,700	
		Subscription Revenue.................................		52,700
	b.	Subscription Revenue	$52,700	
	c.	Unearned Subscription Revenue	$ 8,000	
	d.	Cash received	$54,000	
	e.	Increase in Unearned Subscription Revenue	$ 1,300	

Approach:

8.	a.	Subscription Revenue	1,300	
		Unearned Subscription Revenue		1,300
	b.	Subscription Revenue	$52,700	
	c.	Unearned Subscription Revenue	$ 8,000	
	d.	Cash received	$54,000	
	e.	Increase in Unearned Subscription Revenue	$ 1,300	

Approach:

TIP: Compare situation (8) with situation (7). Notice the facts are the same **except** for the account credited for receipt of revenue in advance of the period in which the revenue is earned. The solution is the same **except** for the adjusting entry required.

TIP: You should be able to handle what for most students can be the most challenging situations. Refer back to the descriptions of situations (4) and (8.) Redo them, assuming that reversing entries **are** used. Those new solutions should appear as follows.

Assuming reversing entries **are** used.

a.	Office Supplies on Hand	320	
	Office Supplies Expense............................		320
b.	Office Supplies Expense	$980	
c.	Office Supplies on Hand	$320	
d.	Cash paid	$900	
e.	Decrease in Office Supplies on Hand	$ 80	

Approach:

Assuming reversing entries **are** used.

a.	Subscription Revenue	8,000	
	Unearned Subscription Revenue		8,000
b.	Subscription Revenue	$52,700	
c.	Unearned Subscription Revenue	$ 8,000	
d.	Cash received	$54,000	
e.	Increase in Unearned Subscription Revenue	$ 1,300	

Approach:

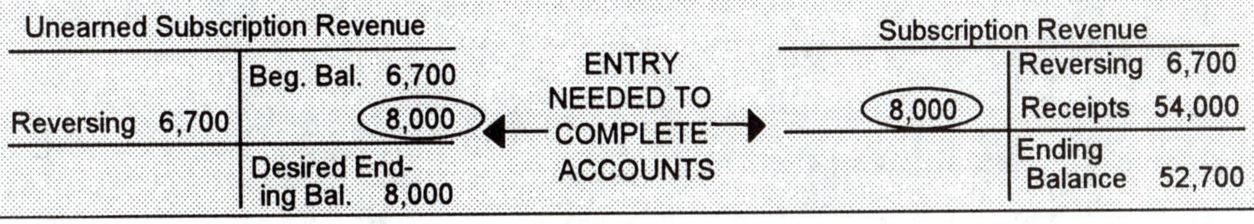

ILLUSTRATION 3-4
REVERSING ENTRIES (COMPARISON OF SYSTEM USING REVERSING ENTRIES WITH SYSTEM WHERE NO REVERSALS ARE USED) (L.O.8)

JOURNAL ENTRIES	Accounting System Where Reversing Entries ARE Used			Accounting System Where Reversing Entries are NOT Used		
(1) During 1998	(1) Interest Expense.......	80,000		(1) Interest Expense...........	80,000	
	Cash.....................		80,000	Cash..........................		80,000
(2) 12/31/98 Adjusting	(2) Interest Expense........	5,500		(2) Interest Expense...........	5,500	
	Interest Payable....		5,500	Interest Payable........		5,500
(3) 12/31/98 Closing	(3) Income Summary......	85,500		(3) Income Summary..........	85,500	
	Interest Expense....		85,500	Interest Expense........		85,500
(4) 1/1/99 Reversing	(4) Interest Payable........	5,500		(4) No entry		
	Interest Expense....		5,500			
(5) 1/1/99 Payment	(5) Interest Expense........	6,000		(5) Interest Expense...........	500	
				Interest Payable...........	5,500	
	Cash.....................		6,000	Cash..........................		6,000

LEDGER ACCOUNT POSTINGS	Interest Expense		Interest Payable		Interest Expense		Interest Payable	
(1) During 1998	80,000				80,000			
(2) 12/31/98 Adjusting	5,500			5,500	5,500			5,500
(3) 12/31/98 Closing		85,500				85,500		
(4) 1/1/99 Reversing		5,500	5,500					
(5) 1/1/99 Payment	6,000				500		5,500	

FINANCIAL STATEMENTS	Reversing Entries ARE Used	Reversing Entries are NOT Used
Interest Expense for the year 1998	$ 85,500	$ 85,500
Interest Paid in 1998	$ 80,000	$ 80,000
Balance of Interest Payable at close of business on 12/31/98	$ 5,500	$ 5,500
Interest Expense for the day 1/1/99	$ 500	$500
Balance of Interest Payable at close of business on 1/1/99	$ 0	$ 0

EXERCISE 3-4

Purpose: (L.O.5,6,8) This exercise will illustrate the preparation of adjusting entries from an unadjusted trial balance and additional data.

The following list of accounts and their balances represents the unadjusted trial balance of Tami Corp. at December 31, 1999.

	Dr.	Cr.
Cash	$ 15,000	
Accounts Receivable	122,500	
Allowance for Doubtful Accounts		$ 1,875
Inventory (January 1, 1999)	145,000	
Prepaid Insurance	7,350	
Prepaid Rent	33,000	
Investment in Lamb Corp. Bonds	45,000	
Land	25,000	
Plant and Equipment	260,000	
Accumulated Depreciation		45,000
Accounts Payable		23,275
Bonds Payable		125,000
Discount on Bonds Payable	3,750	
Capital Stock		250,000
Retained Earnings (January 1, 1999)		201,650
Sales		533,275
Rent Revenue		25,500
Purchases	425,000	
Purchase Discounts		6,000
Transportation-out	22,500	
Transportation-in	8,750	
Salaries and Wages	87,500	
Interest Expense	9,000	
Miscellaneous Expense	2,225	
	$1,211,575	$1,211,575

Additional Information:

1. On March 31, 1999, Tami rented a warehouse for $2,750 per month, paid $33,000 in advance, and debited Prepaid Rent to record the payment.
2. On September 1, 1999, Tami received $25,500 rent from its lessee for a 12-month lease on a parking lot, beginning on that date. The receipt was recorded by a credit to Rent Revenue.
3. Tami estimates that 1% of the credit sales made during 1999 will result in accounts receivable that will ultimately become uncollectible. All sales are made on credit (on account).
4. Prepaid Insurance contains the $7,350 premium cost of a policy that is for a 2-year term and was taken out on May 1, 1999.
5. Tami uses a periodic inventory system. Per a physical count, inventory on hand at December 31, 1999 was $162,500. Record the adjusting entry for inventory by using a Cost of Goods Sold account.

6. On April 1, 1999, Tami issued 125, $1,000, 8% bonds, maturing on April 1, 2009, at 97% of par value. Interest payment dates are April 1 and October 1. The straight-line method is used to amortize any bond premium or discount. Amortization is recorded only at year-end.
7. The regular rate of depreciation is 10% of acquisition cost per year. Acquisitions and retirements during a year are depreciated at half this rate. Assets costing $16,000 were retired during the year. On December 31, 1998, the balance of Plant and Equipment was $230,000.
8. On September 1, 1999, Tami purchased 45, $1,000, 10% Lamb Corp. bonds, at par. The bonds mature on August 31, 2001. Interest is to be received every August 31 and February 28.

Instructions

(a) Prepare the year-end adjusting entries in general journal form using the information above. (Round amounts to the nearest dollar.)

(b) Indicate the adjusting entries that could be reversed.

Solution to Exercise 3-4

(a)	1.	Rent Expense..	24,750	
		Prepaid Rent..		24,750
		($33,000 x 9/12 = $24,750 expired rent)		
	2.	Rent Revenue	17,000	
		Unearned Rent Revenue..............................		17,000
		($25,500 x 8/12 = $17,000 unearned revenue)		
	3.	Bad Debt Expense	5,333	
		Allowance for Doubtful Accounts..................		5,333
		($533,275 x 1% = $5,333 bad debt expense)		

TIP: If the estimate for uncollectible accounts receivable is to be based on a percentage of net sales, the expense figure is a percentage of net sales and any existing balance in the Allowance account will **not** affect the amount of the adjusting entry. If the estimate for uncollectible accounts receivable is to be based on an aging of accounts receivable or a percentage of accounts receivable existing at the balance sheet date, the desired ending balance for the Allowance account is determined and any existing balance in the Allowance account **will** affect the amount of the adjusting entry. (This subject will be more thoroughly reviewed in Chapter 7.)

4.	Insurance Expense	2,450	
	Prepaid Insurance		2,450
	($7,350 x 8/24 = $2,450 expired insurance)		
5.	Inventory (Ending)	162,500	
	Purchase Discounts	6,000	
	Cost of Goods Sold	410,250	
	Inventory (Beginning)		145,000
	Transportation-in		8,750
	Purchases		425,000

TIP: The Cost of Goods Sold account is an expense account; therefore, it is increased by debits and decreased by credits. The normal balance of the Cost of Goods Sold account is a debit balance.

6. a.	Interest Expense	2,500	
	Interest Payable		2,500
	($125,000 x 8% x 3/12 = $2,500 accrued interest)		
b.	Interest Expense	281	
	Discount on Bonds Payable		281
	(125 x $1,000 x 97% = $121,250) [(125 x $1,000) - $121,250 = $3,750] ($3,750 x 9/120 = $281 discount amortization)		
7.	Depreciation Expense	24,500	
	Accumulated Depreciation		24,500
	($230,000 - $16,000 assets retired = $214,000 assets used for full year) ($214,000 x 10% = $21,400 depreciation on assets held for full year) ($16,000 x 10% x 1/2 = $800 depreciation on assets disposed of during the year) ($260,000 - $214,000 = $46,000 assets acquired during the year) ($46,000 x 10% x 1/2 = $2,300 depreciation on assets acquired during the year) ($21,400 + $800 + $2,300 = $24,500 total depreciation for the year)		
8.	Interest Receivable	1,500	
	Interest Revenue		1,500
	($45,000 x 10% x 4/12 = $1,500 accrued interest)		

> **TIP:** An interest rate is an annual rate unless otherwise indicated. For preparing an adjusting entry involving interest, compute interest assuming the rate given is for a whole year, unless it is evident that this is not the case. Also, assume a 360 day year, unless otherwise indicated.

Approach and Explanation: Identify each item as involving: (1) a prepaid expense, (2) an accrued expense, (3) an unearned revenue, (4) an accrued revenue, or (5) an estimated item. From the facts, determine the existing account balances. Read the facts carefully to determine the desired account balances for financial statements in accordance with generally accepted accounting principles (historical cost principle, revenue recognition principle, matching principle, etc.). Determine the adjusting entries necessary to bring existing account balances to the appropriate account balances.

1. This situation involves a prepaid expense. The advance payment was for twelve months and was recorded in an asset account. At December 31, 1999, nine months have passed for which the rent was paid, so the expired portion of the rent must be removed from the Prepaid Rent (asset) account and put into the Rent Expense account.

2. This situation involves unearned revenue. On September 1, 1999, cash was received and recorded as follows:

Cash	25,500	
Rent Revenue		25,500

At December 31, 1999, before adjustment, there is no Unearned Rent Revenue account on the trial balance. We need a balance of $17,000 ($25,500 x 8/12) in Unearned Rent Revenue at the balance sheet date. Therefore, in an adjusting entry, Unearned Rent Revenue is credited for $17,000. The other half of an adjusting entry dealing with Unearned Rent Revenue always has to be Rent Revenue. The debit to Rent Revenue in this exercise will reduce the balance in the earned revenue account to the amount actually earned during 1999 ($8,500).

3. This situation involves an estimated expense. The bad debt expense for the year is estimated to be 1% of credit sales and all sales are on account. Thus, an expense of $5,333 (1% of $533,275 sales) is recorded and a valuation account to Accounts Receivable is credited. The $1,875 balance in that valuation account (Allowance for Doubtful Accounts) before adjustment does **not** affect the amount required in the adjusting entry in this case.

4. This item involves a prepaid expense. Before adjustment, the total cost of the insurance premium is in the Prepaid Insurance account. The expired portion must be taken out of Prepaid Insurance (credit) and put into Insurance Expense (debit).

5. The adjustment of the Inventory account and the recording of cost of goods sold is required. The beginning inventory amount is removed from the Inventory account by a credit (and added to Cost of Goods Sold by a debit). Purchases

and Transportation-in are added to cost of goods sold by transferring the balances of their accounts to the Cost of Goods Sold account. Purchase discounts are deducted from cost of goods sold. The ending inventory is established in the Inventory account and deducted from cost of goods sold by a debit to Inventory and a credit to Cost of Goods Sold. The foregoing is done in one compound entry in the solution shown. The same things could be accomplished by an alternative equivalent set of four entries as follows:

Cost of Goods Sold	145,000	
Inventory		145,000
Cost of Goods Sold	433,750	
Purchases		425,000
Transportation-in		8,750
Purchase Discounts	6,000	
Cost of Goods Sold		6,000
Inventory	162,500	
Cost of Goods Sold		162,500

6. This situation involves an accrued expense and amortization of a related discount. Interest must be accrued since the last interest payment date (October 1) so three months of interest belong in the accrual entry. The discount (3% of the par value) is to be amortized on a straight-line basis from the date of issuance (April 1, 1999) to the date of maturity (April 1, 2009) which is a ten-year period.

7. Of the $260,000 ending balance in Plant and Equipment, $230,000 represents items held during the whole year. There were retirements of $16,000 during the year so we can compute the $46,000 amount of acquisitions. (Acquisitions and retirements are to be depreciated for only one-half of a year—that is, at a 5% rate). A 10% rate of depreciation per year is equivalent to depreciating assets over a 10-year period using the straight-line method.

8. This situation involves an accrued revenue. Interest must be accrued since the last interest payment date, which is four months. The 10% interest rate stated is expressed on an annual basis.

(b) Accrual type adjusting entries can always be reversed. Therefore, items 6a. and 8 can be reversed. Estimated items such as depreciation of plant assets, the recognition of bad debts, and amortization of intangibles and discounts and premiums on receivables and payables should **never** be reversed. Therefore, items 3, 6b, and 7 should **not** be reversed. The entry to adjust the Inventory account and to record cost of goods sold is **never** to be reversed, so item 5 is not reversed. Adjustments involving deferrals can be reversed **if** the original cash entry involved a nominal account (revenue or expense account) rather than a prepaid or unearned account (a real account) and the adjustment **increases** a prepaid expense or unearned revenue account. Therefore, item 2 **can be** reversed but items 1 and 4 should **not** be reversed.

EXERCISE 3-5

Purpose: (L.O.7) This exercise will review the preparation of closing entries.

The adjusted trial balance for the Motorboat Repair Corporation at December 31, 1998 appears as follows:

Motorboat Repair Corporation
ADJUSTED TRIAL BALANCE
December 31, 1998

	Debit	Credit
Cash	$ 2,600	
Accounts Receivable	2,200	
Supplies on Hand	2,100	
Accounts Payable		$ 700
Common Stock		3,000
Retained Earnings (January 1, 1998)		1,300
Service Revenue		4,900
Rent Expense	800	
Advertising Expense	300	
Cleaning Expense	200	
Utilities Expense	80	
Utilities Payable		80
Supplies Expense	1,700	
	$ 9,980	$ 9,980

Instructions

(a) Prepare the appropriate closing entries at December 31, 1998.
(b) Explain why closing entries are necessary.

Solution to Exercise 3-5

		Debit	Credit
(a)	Service Revenue	4,900	
	Income Summary		4,900
	(To close the revenue account to Income Summary)		
	Income Summary	3,080	
	Rent Expense		800
	Advertising Expense		300
	Cleaning Expense		200
	Utilities Expense		80
	Supplies Expense		1,700
	(To close expense accounts to Income Summary)		

Income Summary	1,820	
Retained Earnings...		1,820
(To close Income Summary to Retained Earnings) ($4,900 total revenues - $3,080 total expenses = $1,820 credit balance in Income Summary before closing)		

(b) The major reason closing entries are needed is that they prepare the temporary (nominal) accounts for the recording of transactions of the next accounting period. Closing entries produce a zero balance in each of the temporary accounts so that they can be used to accumulate data pertaining to the next accounting period. Because of closing entries, the revenues of 1999 are not commingled with the revenues of the prior period (1998). A second reason closing entries are needed is that the Retained Earnings account will reflect a true balance only after closing entries have been completed. Closing entries formally recognize in the ledger the transfer of net income (or loss) and dividends declared to retained earnings as indicated in the statement of retained earnings.

TIP: The Income Summary account is used only in the closing process. Before it is closed, the balance in this account must equal the net income or net loss figure for the period.

TIP: Where do you look for the accounts (and their amounts) to be closed? If a work sheet is used, you can use the amounts listed in the Income Statement column pair and the balance of the Dividends Declared (or Owner's Drawing) account. If a work sheet is not used, you must refer to the temporary accounts (after adjustment) in the ledger to determine the balances to be closed.

EXERCISE 3-6

Purpose: (L.O.9) This exercise will allow you to quickly check your knowledge of how items are extended on a 10-column work sheet.

Instructions

The last six columns of an incomplete 10-column work sheet are illustrated below. Place an "X" in the appropriate columns to indicate the proper work sheet treatment of the balance in each of the accounts listed. (The accounts are **not** listed in their usual order, the work sheet is **only partially** illustrated, and the Trial Balance and Adjustments columns have been **omitted**.)

Handy Dandy Hardware
WORK SHEET
For the Year Ended December 31, 1999

Account	Adjusted Trial Balance		Income Statement		Balance Sheet	
	Debit	Credit	Debit	Credit	Debit	Credit
Advertising Expense						
Depreciation Expense						
Land						
Store Equipment						
Wages and Salaries Expense						
Mortgage Payable						
Cash						
Salaries Payable						
Prepaid Insurance						
Delivery Equipment						
Accumulated Depreciation						
Revenue Received in Advance						
Rent Expense						
Sales Revenue						
Prepaid Rent						
Dividends Declared						
Repairs Expense						
Wages Payable						
Interest Receivable						
Accounts Receivable						
Net Income						
Retained Earnings						

Solution to Exercise 3-6

Handy Dandy Hardware
WORK SHEET
For the Year Ended December 31, 1999

Account	Adjusted Trial Balance		Income Statement		Balance Sheet	
	Debit	Credit	Debit	Credit	Debit	Credit
Advertising Expense	X		X			
Depreciation Expense	X		X			
Land	X				X	
Store Equipment	X				X	
Wages and Salaries Expense	X		X			
Mortgage Payable		X				X
Cash	X				X	
Salaries Payable		X				X
Prepaid Insurance	X				X	
Delivery Equipment	X				X	
Accumulated Depreciation		X				X
Revenue Received in Advance		X				X
Rent Expense	X		X			
Sales Revenue		X		X		
Prepaid Rent	X				X	
Dividends Declared	X				X	
Repairs Expense	X		X			
Wages Payable		X				X
Interest Receivable	X				X	
Accounts Receivable	X				X	
Net Income			X			X
Retained Earnings		X				X

TIP: The amount shown for Retained Earnings on the work sheet above is the balance of that account **before** considering dividends declared during the period (determined by the fact that a separate Dividends Declared account appears on the same work sheet) and **before** considering net income for the period.

TIP: Every amount appearing in the Adjusted Trial Balance column pair must be extended to one of the four statement columns. Debit amounts go to a debit column further to the right and credit amounts go to a credit column further to the right of the adjusted trial balance column pair.

TIP: When a dollar amount is added to balance the income statement column pair of columns, the same amount must be added in an opposite debit or credit column in the balance sheet column pair. This amount in a balance sheet column indicates the impact of net income (or net loss) on owners' equity.

EXERCISE 3-7

Purpose: (L.O.8) This exercise will provide practice in determining which adjusting entries may be reversed.

Instructions

The following represent adjusting entries prepared for the Bent Tree Company at December 31, 1999 (end of the accounting period). The company has the policy of using reversing entries when appropriate. For each adjusting entry below, indicate if it would be appropriate to reverse it at the beginning of 2000. Indicate your answer by circling "yes" or "no."

Yes	No	1.	Deferred Advertising Expense	4,500	
			Advertising Expense		4,500
Yes	No	2.	Interest Expense	800	
			Discount on Bonds Payable		800
Yes	No	3.	Interest Receivable	690	
			Interest Revenue		690
Yes	No	4.	Unearned Rental Income	900	
			Rental Income		900
Yes	No	5.	Insurance Expense	1,600	
			Prepaid Insurance		1,600
Yes	No	6.	Salaries Expense	1,100	
			Salaries Payable		1,100

Solution to Exercise 3-7

1.	Yes	3.	Yes	5.	No
2.	No	4.	No	6.	Yes

> **TIP:** A **reversing entry** is an entry made at the very beginning of an accounting period that is the exact opposite of an adjusting entry made at the end of the previous period. The recording of reversing entries is an **optional** step in the accounting cycle. The **purpose** of a reversing entry is to simplify the recording of transactions in the new accounting period. The use of reversing entries does not change the amounts reported in financial statements.

Approach: Write down what the related reversing entry would look like and then (1) think about the effects that the reversing entry would have on the account balances in the accounting period that follows the one for which the adjustment was made, and (2) think about whether those effects are appropriate or not. It is appropriate to reverse an adjusting entry involving a deferral (prepaid expense or unearned revenue) **only if** the adjustment increases (rather than decreases) a balance sheet account. It is **always** appropriate to reverse an adjusting entry involving an accrual. It is **never** appropriate to reverse an adjusting entry for depreciation or amortization or bad debts.

Explanation:

1. An adjustment for a deferred expense can be reversed if the adjustment increases an asset or liability account. This adjustment increases a prepaid expense (asset) account.
2. Never reverse an adjustment for amortization of a discount or premium.
3. An accrual type adjustment can always be reversed.
4. A reversal of this entry would put back into the Unearned Rental Revenue account the amount that the adjustment indicated has been earned.
5. An adjustment for a deferral can be reversed only if it increases a balance sheet account. This adjustment decreases an asset account.
6. An accrual type adjustment can always be reversed. You can tell the adjusting entry is for an accrued expense because the debit is to an expense account and the credit is to a payable account.

EXERCISE 3-8

Purpose: (L.O.3,9) This exercise reviews the procedures involved in the accounting cycle when two optional steps, a work sheet and reversing entries, are employed.

Instructions

Ten steps in the accounting cycle for a company which uses a work sheet and reversing entries are listed below in random order. Arrange the ten procedures carried out in the accounting cycle in the order in which they should be performed by numbering them "1," "2," and so forth in the spaces provided.

_________ a. Journalize and post closing entries.

_________ b. Prepare financial statements from the work sheet.

_________ c. Prepare a post-closing trial balance.

_________ d. Balance the ledger accounts and prepare a trial balance on the work sheet.

_________ e. Journalize and post adjustments made on the work sheet.

_________ f. Record transactions in the journals.

_________ g. Journalize and post reversing entries.

_________ h. Post from journals to the ledgers.

_________ i. Complete the work sheet (adjusting entries, adjusted trial balance, and extend amounts to the appropriate financial statement columns).

_________ j. Identify and analyze business transactions and events.

Solution to Exercise 3-8

a.	8	c.	9	e.	7 (or 6)	g.	10	i.	5
b.	6 (or 7)	d.	4	f.	2	h.	3	j.	1

Approach: As you work through this exercise, concentrate on the logical progression and the flow of information in the data gathering process. Think about the purpose served by each step involved in the process of identifying, recording, classifying, summarizing, reporting, and interpreting transactions and other events relating to enterprises. This process is summarized below, first assuming no work sheet is used. Then differences introduced by use of a work sheet are discussed.

Explanation:

(1) Transactions and other events that are to be recognized (recorded) are first **identified** and **analyzed**. Many happenings (such as interviews of prospective employees and the order for placement of an advertisement in a local newspaper) are not recorded. However, the payment or accrual for salaries to employees and amounts owed to vendors of services are recordable events.

(2) Transactions and other events are **recorded** chronologically in the journal(s). A transaction can be viewed in its entirety in a journal.

(3) Transactions and events are **classified** by posting from the journal(s) to the ledger(s).

(4) All transactions and events affecting individual accounts are **summarized** by balancing the accounts (determining the balances of all accounts).

(5) Adjusting entries are recorded in the general journal and posted to the general ledger to update the accounts for accruals, deferrals, and estimated items. An adjusted trial balance is prepared to prove the maintenance of the equality of total debits and total credits after the adjustments.

(6) The **income statement** is prepared using the balances of accounts for revenues, expenses, gains, and losses (nominal or temporary accounts).

(7) **Closing entries** are recorded in the general journal and posted to the general ledger. Closing entries are necessary to prepare the nominal (temporary) accounts for recordings of the subsequent period. Closing entries also update the balance of the Retained Earnings account for the balance sheet.

(8) The statement of retained earnings is prepared to report the changes in retained earnings during the period. It uses the net income figure as one reason for change.

(9) The **balance sheet** is prepared. It reports the balances of assets, liabilities, and owners' equity.

(10) A **post-closing** trial balance is prepared.

(11) **Reversing entries** may be recorded and posted to facilitate certain recordings in the subsequent period.

(12) Financial statements are **interpreted** by users after careful analysis of all items reported.

TIP: A **work sheet** is usually prepared to facilitate the process of adjusting the accounts and accumulating the balances needed for the financial statements. When a work sheet is employed, the adjusting entries and the adjusted trial balance are entered directly on the work sheet. The adjusted account balances are then sorted on the work sheet and all balances needed for the financial statements are accumulated in one handy place (on the work sheet). The actual journalizing and posting of adjusting entries and closing entries are then normally done after the financial statements are completed.

ILLUSTRATION 3-5
CONVERSION OF CASH BASIS TO ACCRUAL BASIS

Cash Basis ▶	▶	▶ **Accrual Basis**
Receipts from customers	- Beginning accounts receivable + Ending accounts receivable	= Net sales
Rent receipts	+ Beginning unearned rent - Ending unearned rent - Beginning rent receivable + Ending rent receivable	= Rent revenue
Payment for goods	+ Beginning inventory - Ending inventory - Beginning accounts payable + Ending accounts payable	= Cost of goods sold
Payment for expenses	+ Beginning prepaid expenses - Ending prepaid expenses - Beginning accrued expenses + Ending accrued expenses	= Operating expenses (except depreciation and similar write-offs)
Payments for property, plant, and equipment	- Cash payments for property, plant, and equipment + Periodic write-off of the asset cost through some formula(s)	= Depreciation or amortization expense

EXERCISE 3-9

Purpose: (L.O.5,10) This exercise will point out the relationships that exist between cash data and accrual amounts when certain balance sheet accounts increase during the period.

Instructions

Complete each of the blanks below with one of the following, whichever is appropriate:

> symbol for "is greater than"
< symbol for "is less than"
or = symbol for "equals."

1. On a comparative balance sheet, if an accrued receivable increased, then revenue earned _____ cash received so net income on the accrual basis _____ income on a cash basis.

2. On a comparative balance sheet, if an unearned revenue increased, then revenue earned _____ cash received so net income on the accrual basis _____ income on a cash basis.

3. On a comparative balance sheet, if a prepaid expense increased, then expense incurred _____ cash paid so net income on the accrual basis _____ income on a cash basis.

4. On a comparative balance sheet, if an accrued payable increased, then expense incurred _____ cash paid so net income on the accrual basis _____ income on a cash basis.

Solution to Exercise 3-9

1.	>	2.	<	3.	<	4.	>
	>		<		>		<

TIP: Notice that the signs are the **same** in the answers to 1 and 2 but the signs are **different** in the answers to 3 and 4. The reason is that **revenue** is a **positive** component of income and **expense** is a **negative** component of income.

TIP: A comparative balance sheet is a balance sheet with amounts shown for at least two different dates; for example, at the end of the current period (December 31, 1999) and at the end of the prior period (December 31, 1998). The date at the end of the prior period (end of day December 31, 1998) is the same as the date of the beginning of the current period (beginning of day January 1, 1999).

EXERCISE 3-10

Purpose: (L.O.10) This exercise illustrates the different results that are obtained when the accrual and the cash methods of accounting are used.

Annabell's Specialty Service Shop, a proprietorship business, conducted the following transactions during the first week in March.

1. Purchased supplies for $1,800. Paid 20% down; remaining 80% to be paid in 10 days.
2. Paid $30 for newspaper advertising to appear this week.
3. Collected $1,400 from customers on account.
4. Performed services at a $1,620 charge to customers; however, cash payment is not due until next week.
5. Paid $600 rent for the month of March.
6. Performed services for $280 cash.
7. Paid part-time sales clerk $40 wages for the week.
8. Wrote a check for $100 to the owner for her personal use.
9. Consumed supplies of $1,400.

Instructions

(a) Compute the net income for the week, using the cash method of accounting.
(b) Compute the net income for the week, using the accrual method of accounting.
Show your computations in good form.

Solution to Exercise 3-10

(a) **Cash Method:**

Cash Received from Customers ($1,400 + $280)		$1,680
Less: Payment for Supplies ($1,800 x 20%)	$ 360	
Payment for Advertising	30	
Payment for Rent	600	
Payment to Employee	40	1,030
Net Income (cash method)		$ 650

> **TIP:** Using the **cash basis** (method) of accounting, revenues are recognized (reported) in the period in which they are **received** and expenses are recognized in the period in which they are **paid**. The cash basis is **not** in accordance with generally accepted accounting principles.

(b) **Accrual Method:**

Service Revenue ($1,620 + $280)		$ 1,900
Less: Operating Expenses		
Supplies Expense	$1,400	
Advertising Expense	30	
Rent Expense ($600 ÷ 4)	150	
Wages Expense	40	1,620
Net Income (accrual method)		$ 280

> **TIP:** Withdrawals by owner ($100) do **not** enter into the income computations.
>
> **TIP:** Using the **accrual basis** (method) of accounting, revenues are recognized in the period in which they are **earned** and expenses are recognized in the period in which they are **incurred**.

ANALYSIS OF MULTIPLE-CHOICE TYPE QUESTIONS

QUESTION

1. (L.O.1) Which of the following is a nominal account?
   a. Prepaid Insurance
   b. Unearned Revenue
   c. Insurance Expense
   d. Interest Receivable

Approach and Explanation: Read the question. Before looking at the answer selections, write down the meaning of the term "nominal account." Then answer "true" or "false" as you ask whether each answer selection is a nominal account. A nominal account is an account whose balance is closed at the end of an accounting period. Revenue and expense accounts are closed; real accounts (including asset and liability accounts) are never closed. Prepaid Insurance and Interest Receivable are asset accounts. Unearned Revenue is a liability account. Insurance Expense is a nominal account. (Solution = c.)

QUESTION

2. (L.O.4) Which of the following errors will cause an imbalance in the trial balance?
   a. Omission of a transaction in the journal.
   b. Posting an entire journal entry twice to the ledger.
   c. Posting a credit of $720 to Accounts Payable as a credit of $720 to Accounts Receivable.
   d. Listing the balance of an account with a debit balance in the credit column of the trial balance.

Approach and Explanation: Analyze each error (answer selection) and write down whether or not the error will cause the trial balance to be out of balance. Look for the selection which will cause an imbalance (selection "d"). Selections "a," "b," and "c" do not cause an imbalance in the trial balance. (Solution = d.)

QUESTION

3. (L.O.5) Which of the following statements is associated with the accrual basis of accounting?
   a. The timing of cash receipts and disbursements is emphasized.
   b. A minimum amount of record keeping is required.
   c. This method is used less frequently by businesses than the cash method of accounting.
   d. Revenues are recognized in the period they are earned, regardless of the time period the cash is received.

Approach and Explanation: Mentally define the accrual basis of accounting. Write down the key words and phrases of your definition. Compare each answer selection with your definition and choose the one that best matches. Using the **accrual basis of accounting**, events that change a company's financial statements are recorded in the periods in which the events occur. Thus, revenues are recognized in the period in which they are earned, and expenses are recognized in the period in which they are incurred, regardless of when the related cash is received or paid. Answer selections "a" and "b" refer to the cash basis of accounting which is not GAAP. (Solution = d.)

QUESTION

4. (L.O.5) An accrued expense is an expense that:
   a. has been incurred but has not been paid.
   b. has been paid but has not been incurred.
   c. has been incurred for which payment is to be made in installments.
   d. will never be paid.

Approach and Explanation: Write down a definition for accrued expense. Compare each answer selection with your definition and choose the best match. Expenses may be paid for in the same period in which they are incurred or they may be paid for in the period before or in the period after the one in which they are incurred. An **accrued expense** refers to an expense that has been incurred but has not yet been paid. It will be paid for in a period subsequent to the period in which it was incurred. (Solution = a.)

QUESTION

5. (L.O.5) In reviewing some adjusting entries, you observe an entry which contains a debit to Prepaid Insurance and a credit to Insurance Expense. The purpose of this journal entry is to record a(n):
   a. accrued expense.
   b. deferred expense.
   c. expired cost.
   d. prepaid revenue.

Approach and Explanation: Write down the entry so you can see what the entry does. Notice the entry records a prepaid expense (an asset). Then examine each answer selection one at a time. A debit to Prepaid Insurance records an increase in a prepaid expense. A prepaid expense is an expense that has been paid but has not been incurred. Another name for a prepaid expense is deferred expense. A deferred expense is an expense whose recognition is being deferred (put off) until a future period. An accrued expense is an expense incurred, but not paid. An expired cost is an expense or a loss. Prepaid revenue is a bad term for unearned revenue (or deferred revenue). (Solution = b.)

QUESTION

6. (L.O.5) The failure to properly record an adjusting entry to accrue an expense will result in an:
   a. understatement of expenses and an understatement of liabilities.
   b. understatement of expenses and an overstatement of liabilities.
   c. understatement of expenses and an overstatement of assets.
   d. overstatement of expenses and an understatement of assets.

Approach and Explanation: Write down the adjusting entry to record an accrued expense. Analyze the effects of the entry. This will help you to determine the effects of the failure to properly make that entry. (Solution = a.)

Dr.	Expenses	xx	
Cr.	Liabilities		xx

This entry increases expenses and liabilities. Therefore, the failure to make this entry would result in an understatement of expenses and an understatement of liabilities.

QUESTION

7. (L.O.5,8) The Office Supplies on Hand account had a balance at the beginning of year 3 of $1,600. Payments for acquisitions of office supplies during year 3 amounted to $10,000 and were recorded as expense. A physical count at the end of year 3 revealed supplies costing $1,900 were on hand. Reversing entries are used by this company. The required adjusting entry at the end of year 3 will include a debit to:
   a. Office Supplies Expense for $300.
   b. Office Supplies on Hand for $300.
   c. Office Supplies Expense for $9,700.
   d. Office Supplies on Hand for $1,900.

Approach and Explanation: Draw T-accounts. Enter the data given and solve for the adjusting entry. Compare each alternative answer to the adjusting entry you have sketched in the accounts. (Solution = d.)

Office Supplies Expense

Reversing 1,600	
Acqstns. 10,000	(1,900)
Ending Bal. 9,700	

ENTRY NEEDED TO COMPLETE ACCOUNTS

Office Supplies on Hand

Beg. Bal. 1,600	
(1,900)	Reversing 1,600
Desired Ending Bal. 1,900	

> **TIP:** If reversing entries were **not** used, the adjusting entry would include a debit to Office Supplies on Hand for $300 and a credit to Office Supplies Expense for $300.

QUESTION

8. (L.O.7) The purpose of recording closing entries is to:
   a. reduce the number of nominal accounts.
   b. enable the accountant to prepare financial statements at the end of an accounting period.
   c. prepare revenue and expense accounts for the recording of the next period's revenues and expenses.
   d. establish new balances in some asset and liability accounts.

Approach and Explanation: Cover up the answer selections while you read the question. Attempt to complete the statement started by the stem of the question. Think about when closing entries are made and what they do. Then go through the selections using a process of elimination approach. Closing entries clear out the balances of revenue and expense accounts so that the accounts are ready to accumulate data for a new accounting period. Selection "c" is correct. Selection "a" is incorrect; closing entries do not change the number of accounts. Selection "b" is incorrect; financial statements are prepared before closing entries are done. If closing entries were posted first, the income statement would include nothing but zero amounts. Selection "d" is incorrect, closing entries will affect only nominal accounts and owners' equity. (Solution = c.)

QUESTION

9. (L.O.10) If ending accounts receivable exceeds the beginning accounts receivable:
   a. cash collections during the period exceed the amount of revenue earned.
   b. net income for the period is less than the amount of cash basis income.
   c. no cash was collected during the period.
   d. cash collections during the year are less than the amount of revenue earned.

Approach and Explanation: Write down the format for reconciling the amount of cash receipts to the amount of revenue earned.

Cash receipts	$	
Beginning accounts receivable	( )	
Ending accounts receivable	+	
Revenue earned		

Fill in what you know from the question.

Cash receipts	$ X	
Beginning accounts receivable	( )	
Ending accounts receivable	+	More than beginning receivable
Revenue earned	$	Greater than X

An increase in accounts receivable indicates that the amount of revenue earned (and recognized) exceeds the amount of cash collected. Thus, net income for the period exceeds the amount of cash basis income. (Solution = d.)

QUESTION

10. (L.O.11) When special journals are used, the return of merchandise to a supplier for credit is usually recorded in the:
   a. sales journal.
   b. purchases journal.
   c. cash receipts journal.
   d. cash payments journal.
   e. general journal.

Approach and Explanation: List the four special journals listed as the answer selections and briefly describe their function. Also describe the general journal's function.

1. **Sales journal:** all sales of merchandise on account.
2. **Cash receipts journal:** all receipts of cash (including cash sales).
3. **Purchases journal:** all purchases of merchandise on account.
4. **Cash payments journal:** all payments of cash (including cash purchases).
5. **General journal:** all transactions that do not appropriately fit in a special journal (including adjustments and closing entries.)

The transaction described does not fit the description of any of the four special journals. Thus, it goes into the general journal. (Solution = e.)

QUESTION

11. (L.O.11) Each of the following likely appears as a column heading in the cash receipts journal **except:**
    a. Accounts Receivable Cr.
    b. Sales Dr.
    c. Sales Discounts Dr.
    d. Other Accounts Cr.

Approach and Explanation: Think about the purpose of the cash receipts journal—to record all transactions involving a receipt of cash. A receipt of cash is recorded by a debit to Cash; therefore, the rest of the entry involves a credit to a noncash account. The credit is (1) to Sales for a cash sale of merchandise, or (2) to Accounts Receivable for a collection on a customer's account, or (3) to some other account (such as Equipment for a sale of equipment or Interest Revenue for interest earned on money loaned to others).

If a merchandiser offers a cash discount on sales for timely payment of the customer's account, the collection of the account receivable within the discount period results in recording a debit to Sales Discounts (a contra sales account). Thus, a special column in the cash receipts journal for Sales Discounts Dr. is needed to accommodate the recording of this frequent transaction. Debits are made to the Sales account only to (1) correct erroneous credit entries to the same account, and (2) close the balance of the Sales account to Income Summary at the end of the period. Therefore, "Sales Dr." does not appear as a column heading in any special journal. (Solution = b.)

QUESTION

12. (L.O.11) When special journals are used, the most likely source of a debit posting to the Accounts Receivable account in the general ledger is the:
    a. Sales journal.
    b. Purchases journal.
    c. Cash receipts journal.
    d. Cash payments journal.
    e. General journal.

Approach and Explanation: Identify the most common reason for debits to Accounts Receivable—sales on account (on credit). Mentally review the special journals and the transactions recorded therein. All sales on account are recorded in the sales journal. (Solution = a.)

QUESTION

13. (L.O. 11) When special journals are used, the payment to a supplier for merchandise which had previously been purchased on account is usually recorded in the:
    a. Sales journal.
    b. Purchases journal.
    c. Cash receipts journal.
    d. Cash disbursements journal.
    e. General journal.

Approach and Explanation: Mentally review the types of journals and their functions. All cash payments are recorded in the cash payments journal which is often called the cash disbursements journal. (Solution = d.)

CHAPTER 4

INCOME STATEMENT AND RELATED INFORMATION

OVERVIEW

An income statement reports on the results of operations of an entity for a period of time. It is important to classify revenues, expenses, gains, and losses properly on the income statement. In this chapter, we discuss the income statement classifications and the content of the statement of retained earnings along with related disclosure issues. It is imperative that charges and credits that represent elements of income determination be properly reflected in the financial statements. Errors in the determination of income cause errors on the income statement, statement of retained earnings, and balance sheet.

SUMMARY OF LEARNING OBJECTIVES

1. **Identify the uses and limitations of an income statement.** The income statement provides investors and creditors with information that helps them predict the amount, timing and uncertainty of future cash flows. Also, the income statement helps users determine the risk (level of uncertainty) of not achieving particular cash flows. The limitations of an income statement are: (1) the income statement does not include many items that contribute to general growth and well-being of an enterprise; and (2) income numbers are often affected by the accounting methods employed.

   The capital maintenance approach takes the net assets or "capital values" based on some valuation and measures income by the difference in capital values at two points in time. The **transaction approach** focuses on the activities that have occurred during a given period; instead of presenting only a net change in net assets, it discloses the components of the change. The transaction approach to income measurement requires the use of revenue, expense, gain, and loss accounts.

2. **Prepare a single-step income statement.** In a **single-step income statement**, just two groupings exist: revenues and expenses. Expenses are deducted from revenues to arrive at net income or net loss. The expression "single-step" is derived from the single subtraction necessary to arrive at net income. Frequently, however, income taxes are reported separately as the last item before net income to indicate their direct relationship to income before taxes.

3. **Prepare a multiple-step income statement.** A **multiple-step income statement** shows two further classifications: (1) a separation of operating results from those obtained through the subordinate or nonoperating activities of the company; and (2) a classification of expenses by functions, such as merchandising or manufacturing, selling, and administration.

4. **Explain how irregular items are reported.** Irregular gains or losses or nonrecurring items are generally closed to Income Summary and are included in the income statement. These are treated in the income statement as follows: (1) Discontinued operations of a segment of a business is classified as a separate item, after continuing operations; (2) The unusual, material, nonrecurring items that are significantly different from the typical or customary business

activities are shown in a separate section for "extraordinary items," below discontinued operations; (3) Other items of a material amount that are of an unusual or nonrecurring nature and are not considered extraordinary are separately disclosed as components of income from continuing operations; and (4) The cumulative adjustment that occurs when a change in accounting principle is reported in the income statement is disclosed as a separate item, just before net income.

5. **Explain intraperiod tax allocation.** The tax expense for the year should be related, where possible, to specific items on the income statement to provide a more informative disclosure to statement users. This procedure is called **intraperiod tax allocation**, that is, allocation within a period. Its main purpose is to relate the income tax expense for the fiscal period to the following items that affect the amount of the tax provisions: (1) income from continuing operations, (2) discontinued operations, (3) extraordinary items, and (4) changes in accounting principles.

6. **Explain where earnings per share information is reported.** Because of the inherent dangers of focusing attention solely on earnings per share, the profession concluded that earnings per share must be disclosed on the face of the income statement. A company that reports a discontinued operation, an extraordinary, or the cumulative effect of a change in accounting principle, must report per share amounts for these line items either on the face of the income statement or in the notes to financial statements.

7. **Prepare a retained earnings statement.** The statement of retained earnings should disclose net income (loss), dividends, prior period adjustments, and transfers to and from unrestricted retained earnings (appropriations).

8. **Explain how other comprehensive income is reported.** The components of other comprehensive income are reported in a second income statement, a combined statement of comprehensive income, or in a statement of stockholders' equity.

9.* **Measure and report gains and losses from discontinued operations.** The (1) results of operations (income or loss) of a discontinued segment of business and (2) gain or loss on disposal of the discontinued segment are reported net of tax in a separate income statement category after income from continuing operations and before extraordinary items. The accountant may be required to report gains and losses from discontinued operations (sale or abandonment of a segment of the business) under three different situations: (1) no phase-out period, (2) a phase-out period, or (3) an extended phase-out period. The gain or loss on disposal of a segment involves the sum of (1) income or loss from operations **after** the measurement date (the phase-out period) and (2) the gain or loss on disposal of the assets of the discontinued segment.

*This material is covered in Appendix 4-A in the text.

TIPS ON CHAPTER TOPICS

TIP: The **income statement** or **statement of income** is often referred to as the statement of operations or the operating statement because it reports on the results of operations for a period of time. Other names include the "earnings statement," "statement of earnings," and "profit and loss statement" (or "P&L statement").

TIP: The income statement is often referred to as a link between balance sheets because it explains one major reason why the balance of owners' equity changed during the period. Owners' equity (net assets) at the beginning of the period can be reconciled with ending owners' equity as follows:

	Owners' equity at the beginning of the period
+	Additional owner investments during the period
-	Owner withdrawals during the period
±	Results of operations for the period (net income or net loss)
=	Owners' equity at the end of the period

TIP: A **contra revenue** item has the same effect on net income as that of an expense; it decreases net income. Contra revenue accounts include Sales Discounts and Sales Returns and Allowances.

TIP: It is often helpful to form an acronym when attempting to remember a list of items. In looking at the order of the things that can appear after the "Income from Continuing Operations" line on an income statement, you might come up with **DEC** to help you to remember the exact order of these items:

Discontinued operations
Extraordinary items
Cumulative effect of changes in accounting principles

TIP: The income tax consequences of all items appearing above the line "Income from continuing operations before income taxes" are summarized in the line "Income taxes." Revenues cause an increase in income taxes and expenses cause a decrease in income taxes. The income tax consequences of items appearing below the "income from continuing operations" line are reported right along with the items (hence, these items are reported "net of tax"). This procedure of allocating income taxes within a period is referred to as **intraperiod tax allocation**.

TIP: An extraordinary item is reported "net of tax" by deducting the tax effect from the related gain or loss. For example, if the tax rate is 30%, an extraordinary gain of $400,000 will be reported at $280,000 net of tax. Likewise, an extraordinary loss of $400,000 will be reported at $280,000 net of tax. The gain situation increases net income, whereas the loss reduces it.

TIP: Corrections for errors in the reporting of revenues and expenses in prior periods are accounted for as prior period adjustments. A **prior period adjustment** is reported as an adjustment (debit or credit, whichever is applicable) to the opening balance of Retained Earnings on the statement of retained earnings for the current period (period in which the adjustment is made) and is shown net of any related income tax effect.

TIP: Net income minus preferred stock dividend requirements (i.e., income applicable to common stockholders) is divided by the weighted average of common stock shares outstanding to arrive at **earnings per share (EPS)**. This is a key ratio in financial analysis and must be disclosed on the face of the income statement. A per share amount must **always** be disclosed for "net income." Also, the following holds true:

(1) A company that reports discontinued operations must report a per share amount for that item.

(2) A company that reports an extraordinary item must report a per share amount for the extraordinary item.

(3) A company that reports a change in accounting principle must report a per share amount for the cumulative effect of a change in accounting principle.

TIP: In the EPS calculation, preferred dividends are deducted from net income if they were declared; however, if the preferred stock is cumulative, the preferred dividend preference for the current period is deducted whether or not the dividends were declared. Dividends declared on common stock have no effect on the EPS calculation.

EXERCISE 4-1

Purpose: (L.O.1) This exercise reviews the basic accounting formula (Assets = Liabilities + Owners' Equity) and the connection between the income statement and the balance sheet (which is a change in owners' equity due to the net income or net loss for the period). This exercise focuses on the capital maintenance (or change in equity) approach to income determination.

The following data were extracted from the records of Dora Loesing's Cookies, a sole proprietorship:

Total assets, beginning of the period	$100,000
Total liabilities, beginning of the period	36,000
Owner withdrawals during the period	30,000
Total assets, end of the period	108,000
Total liabilities, end of the period	38,000
Owner's contributions during the period	10,000

Instructions

Compute the amount of net income (or loss) for the period. Show computations.

Solution to Exercise 4-1

Beginning owner's equity	$ 64,000[a]
Additional owner contributions	10,000
Owner withdrawals during the period	(30,000)
Subtotal	44,000
Net income (loss) for the period	+ X
Ending owner's equity	$ 70,000[b]
Solving for X, net income =	$ 26,000

[a]A = L + OE
$100,000 = $36,000 + ?
Beginning owner's equity = $64,000

[b]A = L + OE
$108,000 = $38,000 + ?
Ending owner's equity = $70,000

Approach: The question asks you to solve for net income; however, no information is given regarding revenues and expenses for the period. Only balance sheet data and transactions affecting owner's equity are given. Net income (or net loss) for a period is one reason for a change in the balance of owner's equity. Write down the items that reconcile the beginning owner's equity balance with the ending owner's equity balance, enter the amounts known, compute beginning and ending owner's equity balances by use of the basic accounting equation, and then solve for the amount of net income. Recall that assets - liabilities = net assets; that is, assets - liabilities = owner's equity at a point in time.

TIP: The basic accounting equation (A = L + OE) is applied at a specific point in time. When you have the facts for the equation components at two different points in time for the same entity (such as amounts as of the beginning of a year and amounts as of the end of a year), you can modify the basic accounting equation to reflect that total changes in assets equals total changes in liabilities + total changes in owners' equity. Using the symbol Δ to designate change, the following equation also holds true:

$$\Delta A = \Delta L + \Delta OE$$

Reasons for changes in owners' equity include:
(1) additional owner investments,
(2) owner withdrawals, and
(3) results of operations (net income or net loss).

TIP: When using the **capital maintenance** (or **change in equity**) approach, the amount of owners' equity is determined at the beginning and at the end of the period (using the same valuation method). The difference between these two amounts, adjusted for owner withdrawals and additional owner investments during the same period, is the measure of net income for the period.

TIP: Net income (or net loss) is the change in owners' equity for a period of time, other than from capital transactions. Capital transactions are those that involve owners acting in their capacity of being owners of the entity.

ILLUSTRATION 4-1
ELEMENTS OF THE INCOME STATEMENT (L.O.1)

REVENUES. Inflows or other enhancements of assets of an entity or settlements of its liabilities during a period from delivering or producing goods, rendering services, or other activities that constitute the entity's ongoing major or central operations.

EXPENSES. Outflows or other using-up of assets or incurrences of liabilities during a period from delivering or producing goods, rendering services, or carrying out other activities that constitute the entity's ongoing major or central operations.

GAINS. Increases in equity (net assets) from peripheral or incidental transactions of an entity except those that result from revenues or investments by owners.

LOSSES. Decreases in equity (net assets) from peripheral or incidental transactions of an entity except those that result from expenses or distributions to owners.

Revenues take many forms, such as sales revenue, fees earned, dividend income, and rents earned. Expenses also take many forms, such as cost of goods sold, rent, salaries, depreciation, interest, and taxes.

Revenues and gains are similar (they both increase net income), and expenses and losses are similar (they both decrease net income). However, these terms are dissimilar in the fact that they convey significantly different information about an enterprise's performance. Revenues and expenses result from an entity's ongoing major or central operations and activities—that is, from activities such as producing or delivering goods, rendering services, lending, insuring, investing, and financing. In contrast, gains and losses result from incidental or peripheral transactions of an enterprise with other entities and from other events and circumstances affecting it. Gains and losses often arise from the sale of investments; disposal of plant assets; settlement of liabilities for an amount other than their book value; and write-offs of assets due to obsolescence, casualty, or theft.

Revenues and expenses are commonly displayed as **gross** inflows or outflows of net assets; while gains and losses are usually displayed as **net** inflows or outflows. For example, assume a company buys an inventory item for $6,000, sells it for $10,000, and pays a sales representative a $1,000 commission. Further, the same company sells for $20,000 a plant asset with a book value (carrying value) of $15,000 and pays an outside agency $2,100 for finding the buyer. The various flows associated with the first transaction (the company's major activity) will be reported gross on its income statement and the various elements of the second transaction (a peripheral transaction) will be reported net. Assuming these were the only two transactions completed during the period and ignoring income taxes, the income statement would reflect the following:

Sales revenue	$ 10,000
Cost of goods sold expense	6,000
Gross profit	4,000
Selling expense (sales commission)	1,000
Income from operations	3,000
Gain on sale of plant asset	2,900[a]
Net income	$ 5,900

[a]$20,000 proceeds - $15,000 book value - $2,100 finders fee = $2,900 gain on sale.

ILLUSTRATION 4-2
SECTIONS OF A MULTIPLE-STEP INCOME STATEMENT (L.O.3)

1. **OPERATING SECTION.** A report of the revenues and expenses of the company's principal operations. (This section may or may not be presented on a departmental basis.)
   (a) **SALES OR REVENUE SECTION.** A subsection presenting sales, discounts, allowances, returns, and other related information. Its purpose is to arrive at the net amount of sales revenue.
   (b) **COST OF GOODS SOLD SECTION.** A subsection that shows the cost of goods that were sold to produce the sales.
   (c) **SELLING EXPENSES.** A subsection that lists expenses resulting from the company's efforts to make sales.
   (d) **ADMINISTRATIVE OR GENERAL EXPENSES.** A subsection reporting expenses of general administration.

2. **NONOPERATING SECTION.** A report of revenues and expenses resulting from secondary or auxiliary activities of the company. In addition, special gains and losses that are infrequent or unusual, but not both, are normally reported in this section. Generally these items break down into two main subsections:
   (a) **OTHER REVENUES AND GAINS.** A list of the revenues earned or gains incurred, generally net of related expenses, from nonoperating transactions.
   (b) **OTHER EXPENSES AND LOSSES.** A list of the expenses or losses incurred, generally net of any related incomes, from nonoperating transactions.

3. **INCOME TAXES.** A short section reporting federal and state taxes levied on income from continuing operations.

4. **DISCONTINUED OPERATIONS.** Material gains or losses resulting from the disposal of a segment of the business.

5. **EXTRAORDINARY ITEMS.** Unusual and infrequent material gains and losses.

6. **CUMULATIVE EFFECT OF A CHANGE IN ACCOUNTING PRINCIPLE.**

7. **EARNINGS PER SHARE.**

EXERCISE 4-2

Purpose: (L.O.2,3,6) This exercise will allow you to contrast the multiple-step format and the single-step format for the income statement.

The accountant for Bubble Bath Products, Inc. has compiled the following information from the company's records as a basis for an income statement for the year ended December 31, 1999. (There was no change during the year in the 12,000 shares of common stock outstanding.)

Net sales	$ 970,000
Depreciation on plant assets (60% selling, 40% administrative)	70,000
Dividends declared	14,400
Rent revenue	30,000
Interest on notes payable	17,000
Market appreciation on land held as an investment	44,000
Merchandise purchases	421,000
Transportation-in—merchandise	37,000
Merchandise inventory, January 1, 1999	82,000
Merchandise inventory, December 31, 1999	81,000
Purchase returns and allowances	11,000
Wages and salaries—sales	95,000
Materials and supplies—sales	11,400
Income taxes	45,000
Wages and salaries—administrative	135,900
Other administrative expenses	46,700
Advertising expense	20,000
Express mail	6,000

Instructions

(a) Prepare a multiple-step income statement.

(b) Prepare a single-step income statement.

Solution to Exercise 4-2

(a)

Bubble Bath Products, Inc.
INCOME STATEMENT
For the Year Ending December 31, 1999

Sales Revenue			
Net sales revenue			$970,000
Cost of Goods Sold			
Merchandise inventory, Jan. 1		$ 82,000	
Purchases	$ 421,000		
Less purchase returns & allowances	11,000		
Net purchases	410,000		
Transportation-in	37,000	447,000	
Total merchandise available for sale		529,000	
Less merchandise inventory, Dec. 31		81,000	
Cost of goods sold			448,000
Gross profit			522,000
Operating Expenses			
Selling expenses			
Wages and salaries	95,000		
Advertising	20,000		
Materials and supplies	11,400		
Depreciation (60% x $70,000)	42,000		
Express mail	6,000	174,400	
Administrative expenses			
Wages and salaries	135,900		
Depreciation (40% x $70,000)	28,000		
Other administrative expenses	46,700	210,600	385,000
Income from operations			137,000
Other Revenues and Gains			
Rent revenue			30,000
			167,000
Other Expenses and Losses			
Interest expense			17,000
Income before taxes			150,000
Income taxes			45,000
Net income			$105,000
Earnings per share ($105,000 ÷ 12,000)			$8.75

TIP: Dividends declared do not appear on the income statement. They are a distribution of corporate income—**not** a determinant of net income. Increases in the market value of assets held (such as plant assets, inventory, and most investments) are not recognized in the accounts until they are realized through the sale of the assets. Hence, the market appreciation on the land held as an investment does **not** appear on the income statement.

(b)

Bubble Bath Products, Inc.
INCOME STATEMENT
For the Year Ending December 31, 1999

Revenues	
Net sales	$ 970,000
Rent revenue	30,000
Total revenue	1,000,000
Expenses	
Cost of goods sold	448,000
Selling expenses	174,400
Administrative expenses	210,600
Interest expense	17,000
Total expenses	850,000
Income before taxes	150,000
Income taxes	45,000
Net income	$ 105,000
Earnings per share	$8.75

TIP: In the single-step income statement, just two groupings exist: revenues and expenses. Expenses are deducted from revenues to arrive at net income or loss. The expression "single-step" is derived from the single subtraction necessary to arrive at net income. Frequently, however, income taxes are reported separately to indicate their direct relationship to income before income taxes.

TIP: In the multiple-step income statement, there are three major subtotals presented before arriving at net income. They are: net sales revenue, gross profit, and income from operations. These subtotals emphasize (1) a classification of expenses by function, such as merchandising or manufacturing (cost of goods sold), selling, and administration, and (2) a separation of operating and subordinate or nonoperating activities of the company. The "other revenues and gains" and "other expenses and losses" sections include (1) investing and financing revenues and expenses such as interest revenue, dividend revenue (from dividends received), and interest expense, and (2) the results of nonoperating items such as the sale of plant assets and investments.

TIP: The nature of an entity's typical operations is critical in determining whether the results of a transaction should be classified as an operating or a nonoperating revenue, gain, expense, or loss. For example, consider rental activities. A business specializing in equipment rentals will classify rent revenue as an operating revenue. Whereas, a retail establishment that occasionally rents its temporarily idle assets to others will classify rent revenue as a nonoperating (other) revenue. For a second example, consider the sale of an investment. An investment dealer will report the revenue from a sale as an operating revenue. Whereas, a retail entity that occasionally sells an investment will report the difference between the proceeds from the sale and the investment's carrying value as a nonoperating gain or loss.

TIP: There is no specific order in which the individual selling expenses and administrative expenses are to be listed in the multiple-step income statement. Very often, they appear in order of decreasing magnitude.

TIP: Some accountants prefer to use a multiple-step income statement format because it discloses the amount of income from operations. Thus, by this disclosure, the difference between regular and irregular or incidental activities is highlighted. Irregular activities encompass transactions and other events that are derived from developments outside the normal operations of the business. Thus, they may not be expected to continue at the same level in future periods.

EXERCISE 4-3

Purpose: (L.O.2,7) This exercise will give you practice in identifying components of net income and the order of items appearing on a single-step version of a combined statement of income and retained earnings.

Presented below is the adjusted trial balance of the Toby Keith Corporation at December 31, 1999. The account titles and balances are **not** in the customary order.

Toby Keith Corporation
ADJUSTED TRIAL BALANCE
December 31, 1999

	Debits	Credits
Sales		$ 958,500
Notes Receivable	$ 80,000	
Investments	88,500	
Accounts Payable		51,000
Accumulated Depreciation—Equipment		31,000
Sales Discounts	10,500	
Sales Returns	17,500	
Purchase Discounts		8,000
Cash	190,000	
Accounts Receivable	95,000	
Rent Revenue		14,000
Retained Earnings		240,000
Salaries Payable		22,000
Notes Payable		75,000
Common Stock, $15 par		300,000
Income Tax Expense	68,000	
Cash Dividends Declared	70,000	
Allowance for Doubtful Accounts		6,500
Supplies on Hand	11,000	
Freight-In	16,000	
Selling Expenses	212,000	
Administrative Expenses	114,000	
Land	65,000	
Equipment	130,000	
Merchandise Inventory	79,000	
Building	104,000	
Purchases	500,000	
Dividend Income		10,000
Loss on Sale of Investment	13,000	
Interest Revenue		9,000
Interest Expense	12,500	
Bonds Payable		100,000
Gain on Sale of Land		24,500
Accumulated Depreciation—Building		26,500
Totals	$ 1,876,000	$ 1,876,000

A physical count of inventory on December 31 resulted in an inventory amount of $100,000.

Instructions

Prepare a combined statement of income and retained earnings using the single-step form. Assume that the only changes in retained earnings during the current year were from net income and dividends. Twenty thousand shares of common stock were outstanding the entire year.

Solution to Exercise 4-3

Toby Keith Corporation
COMBINED STATEMENT OF INCOME AND RETAINED EARNINGS
For the Year Ending December 31, 1999

Revenues	
Net sales *	$ 930,500
Gain on sale of land	24,500
Rent revenue	14,000
Dividend income	10,000
Interest revenue	9,000
Total revenues	988,000
Expenses	
Cost of goods sold**	487,000
Selling expenses	212,000
Administrative expenses	114,000
Loss on sale of investment	13,000
Interest expense	12,500
Total expenses	838,500
Income before taxes	149,500
Income taxes	68,000
Net income (per common share, $4.08)	81,500
Retained earnings at beginning of the year	240,000
	321,500
Cash dividends declared and paid	70,000
Retained earnings at end of the year	$ 251,500

*Net sales:

Sales			$ 958,500
Less:	Sales discounts	$ 10,500	
	Sales returns	17,500	28,000
	Net sales		$ 930,500

**Cost of goods sold:

Merchandise inventory, Jan. 1		$ 79,000
Purchases	$ 500,000	
Less purchase discounts	8,000	
Net purchases		492,000
Add freight-in		16,000
Merchandise available for sale		587,000
Less merchandise inventory, Dec. 31		100,000
Cost of merchandise sold		$ 487,000

Approach:

(1) Go through the adjusted trial balance and lightly cross through any account title that does **not** pertain to the computation of net income. With the exception of the balance of Merchandise Inventory, balance sheet account balances are not used in determining net income.

(2) Compute intermediate subtotals for items such as (a) net sales, (b) cost of goods sold, (c) selling expenses, and (d) administrative expenses. Show your computations for these subtotals. (In this particular exercise, selling expenses and administrative expenses are already summarized.)

(3) Identify revenue and gain items.

(4) Identify expense and loss items.

(5) Identify income taxes for the period.

(6) Identify any discontinued operations, extraordinary items, and cumulative effect on prior periods of a change in accounting principle (none of these appear in this exercise).

(7) Compute net income.

(8) Add beginning retained earnings.

(9) Include any prior period adjustments (none identified in this exercise).

(10) Deduct dividends declared.

(11) Arrive at ending retained earnings.

> **TIP:** The account balances in the adjusted trial balance that are **not** used for the solution requested are as follows: Notes Receivable, Investments, Accounts Payable, Accumulated Depreciation—Equipment, Cash, Accounts Receivable, Salaries Payable, Notes Payable, Common Stock, Allowance for Doubtful Accounts, Supplies on Hand, Land, Equipment, Building, Bonds Payable, and Accumulated Depreciation—Building.

EXERCISE 4-4

Purpose: (L.O.3,4,5,6,7) This exercise is designed to give you practice in preparing a condensed multiple-step income statement and a separate retained earnings statement.

Presented below is information related to Silk Trees Corp., for the year 1999.

Net sales	$ 650,000
Cost of goods sold	400,000
Selling expenses	32,000
Administrative expenses	24,000
Dividend revenue	10,000
Interest revenue	7,000
Interest expense	15,000
Write-off of goodwill due to impairment	25,000
Depreciation expense omitted in 1997	35,000
Uninsured loss due to flood (unusual and infrequent)	60,000
Dividends declared	42,000
Retained earnings at December 31, 1998	1,800,000
Cumulative effect on prior years of change in accounting principle (credit)	75,000
Federal tax rate of 30% on all items	

Instructions

(a) Prepare a multiple-step income statement for 1999. Assume that 50,000 shares of common stock were outstanding during 1999.

(b) Prepare a separate retained earnings statement for 1999.

Solution to Exercise 4-4

(a)

Silk Trees Corp.
INCOME STATEMENT
For the Year Ended December 31, 1999

Net sales		$ 650,000
Cost of goods sold		400,000
Gross profit		250,000
Operating expenses		
Selling expenses	$ 32,000	
Administrative expenses	24,000	56,000
Income from operations		194,000
Other revenues and gains		
Dividend revenue	10,000	
Interest revenue	7,000	17,000
		211,000
Other expenses and losses		
Interest expense	15,000	
Loss due to write-off of goodwill	25,000	40,000
Income before taxes and extraordinary item and cumulative effect of change in accounting principle		171,000
Income taxes		51,300
Income before extraordinary item and cumulative effect of change in accounting principle		119,700
Extraordinary item—loss from flood	60,000	
Less applicable income tax effect	18,000	42,000
Cumulative effect on prior years of change in accounting principle	75,000	
Less applicable income tax effect	22,500	52,500
Net income		$ 130,200

Per share of common stock:	
Income before extraordinary item and cumulative effect of change in accounting principle ($119,700 ÷ 50,000)	$2.39
Extraordinary item (net of tax) ($42,000 ÷ 50,000)	(.84)
Cumulative effect of accounting change (net of tax) ($52,500 ÷ 50,000)	1.05
Net income ($130,200 ÷ 50,000)	$2.60

TIP: The total income taxes pertaining to 1999 for this company was $33,300. This amount resulted from a tax bill of $51,300 that relates to the tax consequences of all items reportable on the 1999 tax return **before** considering the casualty loss of $60,000. This casualty loss caused a tax savings of $18,000. Because the casualty loss is reported as an extraordinary item on the income statement, the requirement for a net-of-tax presentation calls for the $18,000 tax reduction to be reported along with the extraordinary loss, leaving income taxes of $51,300 to be matched with income before extraordinary items. The income tax effect of the accounting change involves deferred income taxes which are discussed in Chapter 20.

TIP: In this case, the change in accounting principle caused an increase in the reported amount of net income for 1999 (because it was a credit). Sometimes the cumulative effect of a change in accounting principle is a charge (debit) to the current income statement which reduces net income.

(b)

Silk Trees Corp.
RETAINED EARNINGS STATEMENT
For the Year Ended December 31, 1999

Retained earnings, Jan. 1, 1999, as previously reported	$ 1,800,000
Correction of an error in depreciation in prior period (net of $10,500 income tax effect)	(24,500)
Adjusted balance of retained earnings at Jan. 1, 1999	1,775,500
Net income	130,200
	1,905,700
Dividends declared	42,000
Retained earnings, December 31, 1999	$ 1,863,700

ILLUSTRATION 4-3
TREATMENT OF IRREGULAR ITEMS (L.O.4)

1. **DISCONTINUED OPERATIONS.** The (1) results of operations (income or loss) of a segment of business that has been or will be disposed of, and (2) gain or loss on disposal of the discontinued segment are reported in a separate income statement category called "Discontinued operations." This category appears **after** continuing operations but **before** extraordinary items. Each of the possible two components of this category is reported net of the related income tax effect.

2. **EXTRAORDINARY ITEMS.** Extraordinary items are reported individually in a separate category (immediately after discontinued operations, if any) net of any related income tax effect. Extraordinary items are defined as nonrecurring (infrequent) material items that differ significantly from the entity's typical business activities. In addition to being material in amount, a transaction or event must meet **both** of the following criteria to be classified as extraordinary:
   (a) **UNUSUAL NATURE.** The underlying event or transaction should possess a high degree or abnormality and be of a type clearly unrelated to, or only incidentally related to, the ordinary and typical activities of the entity, taking into account the environment in which the entity operates.
   (b) **INFREQUENCY OF OCCURRENCE.** The underlying event or transaction should be of a type that would not reasonably be expected to recur in the foreseeable future, taking into account the environment in which the entity operates.

   Examples of items that are **not** classified as extraordinary:
   (a) Writedown or writeoff of receivables, inventories, equipment leased to others, deferred research and development costs, or other intangible assets.
   (b) Gains or losses from exchange or translation of foreign currencies, including those relating to major devaluations and revaluations.
   (c) Gains or losses on disposal of a segment of a business.
   (d) Other gains or losses from sale or abandonment of property, plant, or equipment used in the business.
   (e) Effects of a strike, including those against competitors and major suppliers.
   (f) Adjustment of accruals on long-term contracts.

   Examples of items that **are** classified as extraordinary:
   An event or transaction that clearly meets both criteria (unusual in nature and infrequent in occurrence) and gives rise to a gain or loss from the writedown or writeoff of assets or to a gain or loss from disposal of assets and is a **direct result** of one of the following:
   (a) A **major casualty** (such as an earthquake, tornado, hurricane, flood, or hail storm).
   (b) An **expropriation** (such as the confiscation of assets by a government or the exercise of eminent domain or condemnation).
   (c) A **prohibition** under a newly enacted law or regulation.

ILLUSTRATION 4-3 (Continued)

> **TIP:** Material gains and losses from extinguishment of debt should be reported as extraordinary items even though these gains or losses often do not meet the normal two criteria.

3. **UNUSUAL GAINS AND LOSSES.** A gain or loss that arises from a transaction that is unusual or infrequent, but not both, should be reported in the income statement as part of "income from continuing operations" (or "income before extraordinary items"). If the amount is material, it should be separately disclosed; if the amount is immaterial, it may be combined with other items on the income statement. In a multiple-step income statement, unusual gains and losses normally are classified in the "other revenues and gains" or "other expenses and losses" section, although a separate unusual items section may be displayed. Unusual gains and losses are **not** to be reported net of tax; rather, the tax consequences of these items are combined with the tax effects of all other components of income from continuing operations in the line called "income taxes."

4. **CHANGES IN ACCOUNTING PRINCIPLE.** A change in accounting principle occurs when a company changes from one generally accepted method to another generally accepted method. Because such a change violates consistency and, therefore, reduces or destroys comparability of successive financial statements, a change in principle should only be made when the newly adopted principle is preferable (e.g., for better matching of revenues and expenses). A change in accounting principle is generally recognized by including the cumulative effect of the change (net of the related income tax effect) as a separate item following extraordinary items in the income statement. This cumulative effect is based on a retroactive computation. That is, the effect on prior periods of using the old method is compared to the effect that would have occurred if the new method had been used for all prior periods; the difference is the cumulative effect of the change on all prior periods. (This subject is more thoroughly discussed in Chapter 23.)

5. **CHANGES IN ACCOUNTING ESTIMATE (Normal Recurring Corrections and Adjustments).** A change from one good faith estimate to another good faith estimate because of new information or experience constitutes a change in accounting estimate. A change in an estimate will affect the amount of related revenue or expense reported in the period of change if the change affects only that period, or in the period of change (called the current period) and future periods if the change affects both. Examples are a change in the estimate of uncollectible accounts receivable (bad debts expense) and a change in the estimated service life of a plant (fixed) asset (depreciation expense). A change in estimate is **not** considered a correction of an error (prior period adjustment); therefore, it is **not** handled retroactively.

EXERCISE 4-5

Purpose: (L.O.4) This exercise will test your knowledge of the elements and arrangement of the major sections of the income statement.

Instructions

The following list represents captions that would appear on an income statement (single-step format) for a company reporting an extraordinary gain, losses from discontinued operations, and a change in depreciation method, as well as the results of continuing operations for the period. You are to "unscramble" the list and prepare a skeleton income statement using the captions given. (If you do not wish to write out each caption above, you may still test your knowledge by listing the appropriate letters in the correct order.)

(a) Income before extraordinary item and cumulative effect of a change in accounting principle
(b) Revenues
(c) Cumulative effect on prior years of a change in depreciation method (net of tax)
(d) Income taxes
(e) Discontinued operations:
(f) Extraordinary gain (net of tax)
(g) Expenses
(h) Loss from disposal of discontinued segment of business (net of tax)
(i) Net income
(j) Income from continuing operations before income taxes
(k) Loss from operations of discontinued segment of business (net of tax)
(l) Income from continuing operations

Solution to Exercise 4-5

Company Name
INCOME STATEMENT
For the Year Ended December 31, 19XX

(b) Revenues
(g) Expenses
(j) Income from continuing operations before income taxes
(d) Income taxes
(l) Income from continuing operations
(e) Discontinued operations:
(k) Loss from operations of discontinued segment of business (net of tax)
(h) Loss from disposal of discontinued segment of business (net of tax)
(a) Income before extraordinary item and cumulative effect of a change in accounting principle
(f) Extraordinary gain (net of tax)
(c) Cumulative effect on prior years of a change in depreciation method (net of tax)
(i) Net income

TIP: The **current operating performance concept** would call for all irregular gains and losses and corrections of revenues and expenses of prior periods to be taken directly into the Retained Earnings account, rather than reported in the current period's income statement. Whereas, the **all-inclusive concept** would call for these items to all be reported in the current period's income statement. Generally accepted accounting principles in the United States currently require a **modified all-inclusive concept**. This means the corrections of revenues and expenses of prior periods go directly to Retained Earnings and, with minor exceptions, all other items (such as unusual gains and losses, discontinued operations, extraordinary items, and the effects of accounting changes) are reported on the income statement.

EXERCISE 4-6

Purpose: (L.O.3,4,5,6,7) This exercise will enable you to practice identifying the proper classification for items on an income statement. It will also give you an example of how the tax effects of various items are reflected in the income statement.

Margaret Moylan had the following selected transactions and events occur during 1999. The corporation is subject to a 30% tax rate on all items. All amounts are material. The corporation is engaged in the sale of energy products.

1. The corporation experienced an uninsured flood loss in the amount of $60,000 during the year. A flood is unusual and infrequent in the region where the corporation resides.

2. At the beginning of 1997, the corporation purchased an office machine for $108,000 (salvage value of $18,000) that has a useful life of six years. The bookkeeper used straight-line depreciation for 1997 and 1998, but failed to deduct the salvage value in computing the depreciable base. The same depreciation calculations were used for tax purposes.

3. Sale of securities held as a part of Moylan's portfolio resulted in a loss of $62,200 (pretax).

4. When its president died, the corporation realized $100,000 from an insurance policy. The cash surrender value of this policy had been carried on the books as an investment in the amount of $34,000 (the gain is nontaxable).

5. The corporation disposed of a segment of business at a loss of $140,000 before taxes. Assume that this transaction meets the criteria for being classified as discontinued operations. There were no results of operations for this division during 1999.

6. The corporation decided to change its method of inventory pricing from average cost to the FIFO method. The effect of this change on prior years would be to increase 1997 income by $64,000 and decrease 1998 income by $20,000 before taxes. The FIFO method has been used for 1999.

Instructions:

Describe how each of the items above will be reported in a multiple-step income statement for 1999. Indicate the amount that will be reported and the section of the income statement in which the amount will appear.

Solution to Exercise 4-6:

1. A loss of $42,000 ($60,000 minus 30% of $60,000) will be reported in the extraordinary items section of the income statement.

2. Depreciation expense of $15,000 [($108,000 - $18,000) ÷ 6 years] will appear in the administrative expense (an operating expense) section of the 1999 income statement. The correction of prior periods' depreciation (a prior period adjustment) will **not** appear on the income statement. Rather, a credit of $4,200 will appear on the statement of retained earnings for 1999 as an adjustment to the beginning balance of retained earnings. The prior period adjustment is reported net of tax. Computations:
   $108,000 ÷ 6 = $18,000 depreciation taken in 1997.
   $108,000 ÷ 6 = $18,000 depreciation taken in 1998.
   ($108,000 - $18,000) ÷ 6 = $15,000 correct annual depreciation.
   $15,000 x 2 = $30,000 correct depreciation for 1997 & 1998.
   ($18,000 + $18,000) - $30,000 = $6,000 overstated expense in prior years.
   $6,000 - 30%($6,000) = $4,200 addition to retained earnings.

3. A loss of $62,200 will be reported in the other expenses and losses section of the income statement. It is **not** reported net of tax.

4. A gain of $66,000 ($100,000 - $34,000) will appear in the other revenues and gains section of the income statement. It is **not** reported net of tax (in this case, it had no tax effect anyway). A good caption for this item is "Gain from proceeds of life insurance policy."

5. A loss of $98,000 ($140,000 minus 30% of $140,000) will appear as a "loss on disposal of assets of discontinued segment" in the discontinued operations section of the income statement.

6. A cumulative effect on prior periods of a change in accounting principle will appear as a $30,800 credit on the 1999 income statement. This is the last item shown on the statement before arriving at net income. Computations:

$64,000	credit (increase in prior period income)
20,000	debit (decrease in prior period income)
44,000	credit (net catch-up adjustment needed)
70%	net of tax rate
$30,800	credit (cumulative effect, net of tax)

ILLUSTRATION 4-4
NET INCOME AND COMPREHENSIVE INCOME (L.O.9)

Comprehensive income includes all changes in stockholders' equity except those resulting from investments by owners and distributions to owners. Comprehensive income therefore includes all revenues, gains, expenses, and losses reported in net income. In addition, it includes gains and losses that bypass net income but are included as part of comprehensive income. These gains and losses are referred to as **other comprehensive income.**

An example of a gain or loss that is reported as other comprehensive income is an unrealized gain or loss on available-for-sale securities held as an investment. Excluding this type of gain or loss from net income and disclosing it separately reduces the volatility of net income due to changes in fair value yet informs the financial statement user of the gain or loss that would occur if the securities were sold at fair value. This subject is discussed further in Chapter 18. Other examples of other comprehensive items are translation gains and losses on foreign currency (a subject in an advanced accounting text) and excess of additional pension liability over unrecognized prior service cost (a subject of Chaper 21).

The FASB requires that components of other comprehensive income be reported in one of three ways: (1) in a separate (second) income statement, (2) in a combined statement of comprehensive income, or (3) as a part of the statement of stockholders' equity. To illustrate these three presentation formats, assume Rosie O'Donnell Inc. reports the following information for 1999: sales revenues, $1,600,000, cost of goods sold $1,200,000, operating expenses $180,000, and an unrealized holding gain on available-for-sale securities of $60,000.

The first approach is to provide information in a two income statement format. It is shown below:

Rosie O'Donnell Inc.
Income Statement
For the Year Ended December 31, 1999

Sales revenue	$1,600,000
Cost of goods sold	1,200,000
Gross profit	400,000
Operating expenses	180,000
Net income	$ 220,000

Rosie O'Donnell Inc.
Comprehensive Income Statement
For the Year Ended December 31, 1999

Net income	$220,000
Other comprehensive income	
Unrealized holding gains	60,000
Comprehensive income	$280,000

ILLUSTRATION 4-4 (Continued)

Reporting comprehensive income in a separate statement indicates that the gains and losses identified as other comprehensive income do not have the same status as traditional gains and losses. In addition, the relationship of the traditional income statement to the new statement is apparent because net income is the starting point in the new statement.

The second approach is to provide a combined statement. It is shown below:

Rosie O'Donnell Inc.
Combined Statement of Comprehensive Income
For the Year Ended December 31, 1999

Sales revenue	$1,600,000
Cost of goods sold	1,200,000
Gross profit	400,000
Operating expenses	180,000
Net income	220,000
Unrealized holding gains, net of tax	60,000
Comprehensive income	$ 280,000

The combined statement has the advantage of not requiring the creation of a new financial statement. However, burying the traditional net income figure as a subtotal on the statement is a disadvantage.

A third approach is to report other comprehensive income items in a statement of stockholders' equity. This statement reports the changes in each stockholders' equity account and in total stockholders' equity during the year. The statement of stockholders' equity is prepared in columnar form with columns for each account and for total stockholders' equity. A statement of stockholders' equity for Rosie O'Donnell Inc. is shown below:

Rosie O'Donnell Inc.
Statement of Stockholders' Equity
For the Year Ended December 31, 1999

	Total	Comprehensive Income	Retained Earnings	Accumulated Other Comprehensive Income	Common Stock
Beginning balance	$ 820,000		$100,000	$120,000	$600,000
Issuance of stock	150,000				150,000
Net income	220,000	$220,000	220,000		
Other comprehensive income	60,000	60,000		60,000	
Ending balance	$1,250,000	$280,000	$320,000	$180,000	$750,000

The net income for a period of time is closed to Retained Earnings (a component of stockholders' equity). Other comprehensive income for a period is closed to Accumulated Other Comprehensive Income (a separate component of stockholders' equity). The accumulated other comprehensive income is reported in the stockholders' equity section of the balance sheet as follows:

ILLUSTRATION 4-4 (Continued)

Rosie O'Donnell Inc.
Balance Sheet (Partial)
As of December 31, 1999

Stockholders' equity	
Common stock	$ 750,000
Retained earnings	320,000
Accumulated other comprehensive income	180,000
Total stockholders' equity	$1,250,000

TIP: By providing a comprehensive income statement and a stockholders' equity statement, the company reports information about all changes in net assets (owners' equity). With this information, users will be better able to understand the quality of the company's earnings. This information should help users to predict the amount, timing, and uncertainty of future cash flows.

TIP: The **statement of stockholders' equity** is often called the **statement of changes in stockholders' equity** or **stockholders' equity statement.**

TIP: If a company chooses to report the components of other comprehensive income in a statement of stockholders' equity, that statement must be displayed as a primary financial statement.

TIP: A company is required to display the components of other comprehensive income either (1) net of related tax effects or (2) before related tax effects with one amount shown for the aggregate amount of tax related to the total amount of other comprehensive income. Under either alternative, each component of other comprehensive income must be shown, net of related taxes, either on the face of the statement or in the notes.

EXERCISE 4-7

Purpose: (L.O.9) This exercise will give you examples of the various situations possible [realized gains (losses) and expected gains (losses)] when you have an extended phase-out period for discontinued operations.

Koon Company has discontinued operations. The basic facts are as follows:
Measurement date: October 1, 1999.
Disposal is expected to be completed by May 1, 2000.
Accounting period ends December 31, 1999.

Instructions

For each of the following independent cases, indicate the amount of "gain (loss) on disposal of segment" to be reported on the 1999 and 2000 income statements by filling in the blanks provided. Assume all amounts are net of tax.

Case	Realized Income (Loss) from Operations Oct. 1, 1999-Dec. 31, 1999	Realized Gain (Loss) on Sale of Assets Oct. 1, 1999-Dec. 31, 1999	Expected Income (Loss) from Operations Jan. 1, 2000-May 1, 2000	Expected Gain (Loss) on Sale of Assets Jan. 1, 2000-May 1, 2000	Gain (Loss) on Disposal of Segment
1	(144,000)	(52,500)	(117,600)	(88,200)	1999 ______ 2000 ______
2	300,000	(52,500)	(117,600)	(88,200)	1999 ______ 2000 ______
3	(144,000)	(52,500)	324,000	(88,200)	1999 ______ 2000 ______
4	(144,000)	(52,500)	(117,600)	360,000	1999 ______ 2000 ______
5	300,000	(52,500)	324,000	(88,200)	1999 ______ 2000 ______

Solution to Exercise 4-7

	1999	2000
Case 1	(402,300)	-0-
Case 2	41,700	-0-
Case 3	-0-	39,300
Case 4	-0-	45,900
Case 5	247,500	235,800

Approach and Explanation: To compute the amount to report as the gain or loss on disposal of a segment:

(1) Compute the net realized items.

(2) Compute the net estimated items.

(3) Follow the rules for handling the income (loss) on operations and the gains and losses on disposal of assets estimated in the phase-out of discontinued operations, which are as follows:

- (a) If the estimated items net to a loss, accrue the net estimated losses in total to the period of the date of measurement.
- (b) If the estimated items net to a gain and the realized items net to a gain, defer recognition of all of the estimated items to the period these gains are realized (period of date of disposal).
- (c) If the estimated items net to a gain and the realized items net to a loss, use the net estimated gain (or portion thereof) to offset the net realized loss in the period of the date of measurement. Defer the recognition of any excess of net estimated gains over net realized losses.

Case	Net Realized Items	Net Estimated Items	Treatment
1	($196,500)	$(205,800)	Accrue net estimated losses to 1999 (See "a" above).
2	$247,500	$(205,800)	Accrue net estimated losses to 1999 (see "a" above).
3	$(196,500)	$235,800	Use some estimated gains to offset net realized losses in 1999; defer the rest to 2000 (see "c" above).
4	$(196,500)	$242,400	Use some estimated gains to offset net realized losses in 1999; defer the rest to 2000 (see "c" above).
5	$247,500	$235,800	Do not reflect any estimated gains in 1999; there are no realized losses to offset. Defer all estimated gains to period realized (2000) (see "b" above).

TIP: To qualify for treatment as discontinued operations, the assets, results of operations, and activities of a segment of business must be clearly distinguishable, physically and operationally, from the other assets, results of operations, and activities of the entity. The **measurement date** is the date that management commits itself to a formal plan to dispose of a segment of business. The **disposal date** is the date of closing the sale if the disposal is by sale or the date that operations cease if the disposal is by abandonment. The period of time between the measurement date and the disposal date is called the **phase-out period**.

TIP: Discontinued operations are reported in a separate section of the income statement, net of tax. There are two components to this section of the income statement: (1) income or loss from operations of the discontinued segment, and (2) gain or loss on disposal of the discontinued segment. The first component reflects the results of operations (revenues and expenses) of the discontinued segment from the beginning of the year (period) **up to the measurement date**. Included in the second component are the results of operations of the discontinued segment **after the measurement date** (the phase-out period) and the gain or loss on disposal of the assets of the discontinued segment.

TIP: An extended phase-out period for discontinued operations refers to a situation where the disposal of the discontinued segment of business occurs in the reporting period following the reporting period in which the date of measurement occurs. Thus, at the date financial statements are to be prepared, estimates must be made for the (1) income (loss) from operations of the discontinued segment during the phase-out period, and (2) ultimate gain or loss on disposal of the assets of the discontinued segment.

ANALYSIS OF MULTIPLE-CHOICE TYPE QUESTIONS

QUESTION

1. (L.O.4) A loss from the disposal of a segment of business should be reported in the income statement:
   a. after extraordinary items and before cumulative effect of an accounting change.
   b. before extraordinary items and after cumulative effect of an accounting change.
   c. after extraordinary items and cumulative effect of an accounting change.
   d. before extraordinary items and cumulative effect of an accounting change.

Approach and Explanation: Keep in mind the acronym **DEC**. Write the items down in the proper order. Read each answer response to see if it properly describes the order in which you have listed the items.

The correct order of the items involved in the question is as follows:

(1) Discontinued operations
(2) Extraordinary items
(3) Cumulative effect of a change in accounting principle (Solution = d.)

QUESTION

2. (L.O.4) A material loss should be presented separately as a component of income from continuing operations when it is:
   a. unusual in nature and infrequent in occurrence.
   b. unusual in nature but **not** infrequent in occurrence.
   c. an extraordinary loss.
   d. a cumulative effect of a change in accounting principle.

Approach and Explanation: Visualize an income statement and mentally identify the section that reports income from continuing operations. Read one answer at a time and determine if it correctly describes how the statement in the question stem can be completed. A material loss that is (1) unusual in nature **and** (2) infrequent in occurrence should be reported as an extraordinary item. A loss that meets one of the criteria for being classified as extraordinary, but not both, should be separately disclosed as a component of income from continuing operations. An extraordinary item and a cumulative effect of a change in accounting principle are to be reported **after** (and not part of) income from continuing operations. (Solution = b.)

QUESTION

3. (L.O.3) The following expenses and loss were among those incurred by Mitzer Company during 1999:

Rent for office space	$ 660,000
Loss on sale of office furniture	55,000
Interest	132,000
Accounting and legal fees	352,000
Freight-out	70,000

One-half of the rented premises is occupied by the sales department. How much of the items listed above should be classified as general and administrative expenses in Mitzer's income statement for 1999?

a. $682,000
b. $869,000
c. $884,000
d. $939,000

Approach and Explanation: For each item listed, identify where it is reported. Then collect together the ones that you identify as general and administrative (G&A) expenses.

Rent for office space:	One-half selling; one-half G&A
Loss on sale of equipment:	Other expenses and losses
Interest:	Other expenses and losses
Accounting and legal fees:	G&A expenses
Freight-out:	Selling expenses

One-half of office space (.5 x $660,000)	$330,000	
Accounting and legal fees	352,000	
General and administrative expenses	$682,000	(Solution = a.)

QUESTION

4. (L.O.4) During the year ended December 31, 1999, Schmelya Corporation incurred the following infrequent losses:
   1. A factory was shutdown during a major strike by employees; costs were $120,000.
   2. A loss of $50,000 was incurred on the abandonment of computer equipment used in the business.
   3. A loss of $82,000 was incurred as a result of flood damage to a warehouse.

   How much total loss should Schmelya report in the extraordinary item section of its 1999 income statement?

a. $82,000
b. $120,000
c. $202,000
d. $252,000

Approach and Explanation: It is wise to review the list of items that are not extraordinary items (see **Illustration 4-3**) until you can readily recognize items that appear in the list. In the question at hand, the first two items are on the list of items that are **not** extraordinary. Therefore, the only possible one being extraordinary is the loss from flood damage. A flood would be considered infrequent in some locations but not others. The stem of the question indicates it is deemed infrequent for Schmelya. To be classified as extraordinary, an item needs to be unusual in nature and infrequent in occurrence. However, there are certain items that do **not** constitute extraordinary items. (Solution = a.)

QUESTION

5. (L.O.3) Which of the following is **not** a selling expense?
   a. Advertising expense
   b. Office salaries expense
   c. Freight-out
   d. Store supplies consumed

Approach and Explanation: Take each account and determine its classification. Items "a," "c," and "d" are selling expenses because they are associated with the sales function. Office salaries are related to normal operations, but they are not related to the sales function of the business. Therefore, they are not classified as a selling expense. (Solution = b.)

QUESTION

6. (L.O.3) The accountant for the Orion Sales Company is preparing the income statement for 1999 and the balance sheet at December 31, 1999. The January 1, 1999 merchandise inventory balance will appear:
   a. only as an asset on the balance sheet.
   b. only in the cost of goods sold section of the income statement.
   c. as a deduction in the cost of goods sold section of the income statement and as a current asset on the balance sheet.
   d. as an addition in the cost of goods sold section of the income statement and as a current asset on the balance sheet.

Explanation: The January 1, 1999 inventory amount is the beginning inventory figure. Beginning inventory is a component of the cost of goods available for sale for the period which is a component of cost of goods sold. (Solution = b.)

TIP: If the question asked about the December 31, 1999 merchandise inventory balance (ending inventory) rather than the beginning inventory balance, the correct answer would have been "c" (as a deduction in computing cost of sales and as a current asset).

QUESTION

7. (L.O.2,3) The following amounts relate to the current year for the Ira Company:

Beginning inventory	$ 20,000
Ending inventory	28,000
Purchases	166,000
Purchase returns	4,800
Transportation-out	6,000

The amount of cost of goods sold for the period is:

a. $169,200.
b. $162,800.
c. $153,200.
d. $147,200.

Approach and Explanation: Write down the computation model for cost of goods sold. Enter the amounts given and solve for the unknown.

$ 20,000		Beginning Inventory	
+ 166,000	+	Purchases	
- 4,800	-	Purchase Returns and Allowances	
	-	Purchase Discounts	
	+	Freight-in	
181,200	=	Cost of Goods Available for Sale	
- 28,000	-	Ending Inventory	
$ 153,200	=	Cost of Goods Sold	(Solution = c.)

TIP: Transportation-out is classified as a selling expense, not a component of cost of goods sold. "Transportation-out" is often called "freight-out; "transportation-in" is another name for "freight-in."

QUESTION

8. (L.O.7) A correction of an error in prior periods' income will be reported:

	In the income statement	Net of tax
a.	Yes	Yes
b.	No	No
c.	Yes	No
d.	No	Yes

Approach and Explanation: Write down what you know about the accounting for a correction of an error in computing income in a prior period. Then answer "yes" or "no" to each question posed at the top of the appropriate column. Find the combination that matches yours. A correction of an error is a prior period adjustment; it is reported net of tax as an adjustment to the beginning retained earnings balance on the statement of retained earnings in the period the error is corrected. (Solution = d.)

QUESTION

9. (L.O.9) When a segment of a business has been discontinued during the year, that segment's operating losses of the current year after the measurement date should be included in the:
   a. income statement as part of the income (loss) from operations of the discontinued segment.
   b. income statement as part of the gain (loss) on disposal of the discontinued segment.
   c. income statement as part of the income (loss) from continuing operations.
   d. statement of retained earnings as a direct decrease in retained earnings.

Approach and Explanation: Read the question and write down the two captions used to report discontinued operations and also write down a brief description of what goes in each category. Read each answer selection and answer **True** or **False** as to whether or not it correctly completes the statement in the stem. There are two lines in the "discontinued operations" section of the income statement: (1) income (loss) from operations of discontinued segment, and (2) gain or loss on disposal of discontinued segment. The results of operations of the discontinued segment from the beginning of the year up to the measurement date are to be reported in the first line. The results of operations of the discontinued segment after the measurement date go in the second line, along with the gain or loss in disposal of the assets of the discontinued segment. (Solution = b.)

CHAPTER 5

BALANCE SHEET AND STATEMENT OF CASH FLOWS

OVERVIEW

A balance sheet reports on the financial position of an entity at a point in time. A statement of cash flows reports reasons for cash receipts and cash payments during the period. In this chapter, we discuss the classifications of a balance sheet and a statement of cash flows along with related disclosure issues. It is extremely important that items are properly classified. Errors in classification will result in incorrect ratio analyses which can lead to misinterpretations of the meaning of the information conveyed. This can affect the decisions that are being made based on that information.

SUMMARY OF LEARNING OBJECTIVES

1. **Identify the uses and limitations of a balance sheet.** The balance sheet provides information about the nature and amounts of investments in enterprise resources, obligations to enterprise creditors, and the owners' equity in resources. The balance sheet contributes to financial reporting by providing a basis for: (1) computing rates of return, (2) evaluating the capital structure of the enterprise, and (3) assessing the liquidity and financial flexibility of the enterprise. The limitations of a balance sheet are: (1) the balance sheet does not reflect current value because accountants have adopted a historical cost basis in valuing and reporting assets and liabilities; (2) judgments and estimates must be used in preparing a balance sheet (the collectibility of receivables, the salability of inventory, and the useful life of long-term tangible and intangible assets are difficult to determine); and (3) the balance sheet necessarily omits many items that are of financial value to the business but cannot be recorded objectively, for example, human resources, customer base, managerial skills, research superiority, and reputation.

2. **Identify the major classifications of the balance sheet.** The general elements of the balance sheet are assets, liabilities, and equity. The major classifications within the balance sheet on the asset side are current assets; long-term investments; property, plant, and equipment; intangible assets; and other assets. The major classifications of liabilities are current liabilities and long-term liabilities. In a corporation, owners' equity is generally classified as capital stock, additional paid-in capital, and retained earnings.

3. **Prepare a classified balance sheet using the report and account formats.** The report form lists liabilities and stockholders' equity directly below assets on the same page. The account form lists assets on the left side and liabilities and stockholders' equity on the right side.

4. **Identify balance sheet information requiring supplemental disclosure.** Four types of information normally are supplemental to account titles and amounts presented in the balance sheet: (1) **Contingencies:** material events that have an uncertain outcome; (2) **Valuations and accounting policies:** explanations of the valuation methods used or the basic assumptions

made concerning inventory valuation, depreciation methods, investments in subsidiaries, etc.; (3) **Contractual situations:** explanations of certain restrictions or covenants attached to specific assets or, more likely, to liabilities; (4) **Post-balance sheet disclosures:** disclosures of certain events that have occurred after the balance sheet date but before the financial statements have been issued.

5. **Identify major disclosure techniques for the balance sheet.** There are four methods of disclosing pertinent information in the balance sheet: (1) **Parenthetical explanations:** additional information or description is often provided by parenthetical explanation following the item; (2) **Notes:** notes are used if additional explanations or descriptions cannot be shown conveniently as parenthetical explanations; (3) **Cross reference and contra items:** a direct relationship between an asset and a liability is "cross referenced" on the balance sheet; (4) **Supporting schedules:** often a separate schedule is needed to present more detailed information about certain assets or liabilities, because the balance sheet provides just a single summary item.

6. **Indicate the purpose of the statement of cash flows.** The primary purpose of a statement of cash flows is to provide relevant information about the cash receipts and cash payments of an enterprise during a period. Reporting the sources, uses, and net increase or decrease in cash is useful because investors, creditors, and others want to know what is happening to a company's most liquid resource.

7. **Identify the content of the statement of cash flows.** Cash receipts and cash payments during a period are classified in the statement of cash flows in three different activities: (1) **Operating activities** include all transactions and other events that are not defined as investing or financing activities. Operating activities generally involve producing and delivering goods and providing services. Cash flows from operating activities are generally the cash effects of transactions that enter into the determination of net income. (2) **Investing activities** include making and collecting loans and acquiring and disposing of investments (both debt and equity) and property, plant, and equipment. (3) **Financing activities** include (a) obtaining resources from owners and providing them with a return on and a return of their investment, (b) borrowing money from creditors and repaying the amounts borrowed, and (c) obtaining and paying for other resources obtained from creditors.

8. **Prepare a statement of cash flows.** The information to prepare a statement of cash flows usually comes from (1) comparative balance sheets, (2) the current income statement, and (3) selected transaction data. Preparing the statement of cash flows from these sources involves the following steps: (1) determine the net cash provided by operating activities, (2) determine the net cash provided by or used in investing activities, (3) determine the net cash provided by or used in financing activities, (4) determine the net change (increase or decrease) in cash during the period, and (5) reconcile the net change in cash with the beginning and the ending cash balances.

9. **Understand the usefulness of the statement of cash flows.** Creditors examine the cash flow statement carefully because they are concerned about being paid. The amount and trend of net cash flow provided by operating activities in relation to the company's liabilities is helpful in making the assessment. In addition, measures such as a free cash flow analysis provide creditors and stockholders with a better picture of the company's financial flexibility.

10. **Identify the major types of financial ratios and what they measure.** Ratios express the mathematical relationship between one quantity and another, in terms of a percentage, a rate, or a proportion. Liquidity ratios measure the short-run ability to pay maturing obligations. Activity ratios measure the effectiveness of asset usage. Profitability ratios measure the success or failure of an enterprise. Coverage ratios measure the degree of protection for long-term creditors and investors.

*This material is covered in Appendix 5-A in the text.

TIPS ON CHAPTER TOPICS

TIP: Memorize the definition of current assets. **Current assets** are cash and other assets that are expected to be converted into cash, sold, or consumed within the year or operating cycle that immediately follows the balance sheet date, whichever is longer. Think about how various examples of current assets meet this definition. Accounts receivable are current assets because they will be converted to cash shortly after the balance sheet date; inventory is a current asset because it will be sold within the year that follows the balance sheet date; prepaid insurance is a current asset because it will be consumed (used up) within the next year.

TIP: A normal **operating cycle** is the length of time required to go from cash back to cash. That is, for an entity which sells products, the operating cycle is the time required to take cash out to buy (or to manufacture) inventory then sell the inventory and receive cash (either from a cash sale or the collection of an account receivable stemming from a credit sale). Thus, the length of an entity's operating cycle depends on the nature of its business. Unless otherwise indicated, always assume the operating cycle for an entity is less than a year so that the one-year test is used as the cutoff between current and noncurrent.

TIP: Memorize the definition of current liabilities. **Current liabilities** are obligations which are expected to require the use of current assets or the incurrence of other current liabilities. A liability may be due within a year of the balance sheet and **not** be a current liability. An example is a debt due in six months that will be liquidated by use of a noncurrent asset.

TIP: In a classified balance sheet, any asset that is not classified as a current asset is a noncurrent asset. There are four noncurrent asset classifications: long-term investments; property, plant and equipment; intangible assets; and other assets.

TIP: In a classified balance sheet, liabilities are classified either as current or noncurrent liabilities. The noncurrent liabilities are usually titled "long-term liabilities" or "long-term debt."

TIP: It is extremely important that items are properly classified on a balance sheet. Errors in classification can result in incorrect ratio analyses (to be discussed in Chapter 25) which may lead to misrepresentations of the meaning of the information conveyed and can effect decisions that are based on those analyses.

TIP: Current assets are listed in the order of their liquidity, with the most liquid ones being listed first. Current liabilities are not listed in any prescribed order; however, notes payable (short-term) is usually listed first followed by accounts payable (and the remainder of the current liabilities are often listed in descending order of amount). Property, plant and equipment items are listed in order of length of life, with the longest life first.

TIP: "**Short-term**" is synonymous with "**current**," and "**long-term**" is synonymous with "**noncurrent**." Therefore, "short-term debt" can be used to refer to "current liabilities." Asset classifications are typically titled current and noncurrent; whereas, liability classifications are typically titled current and long-term.

TIP: All noncurrent assets (assets in classifications other than "current assets") are resources that are not expected to be converted into cash or fully consumed in operations within one year or the operating cycle, whichever is longer.

TIP: An investment may be classified as a current asset (if it is a short-term investment) or as a noncurrent asset (if it is a long-term investment). For an investment to be classified as current: (1) it should be readily marketable, and (2) there should be a lack of management intent to hold it for a long-term purpose.

TIP: If an account title starts with "Allowance for...," then it generally is a contra balance sheet account.

TIP: If an account title starts with "Provision for...," it is generally an income statement account.

TIP: The balance of liabilities and the balance of owners' equity at a point in time simply serve as scorecards of the total amounts of unspecified assets which have come about from creditor sources (liabilities) and owner sources (owners' equity). Thus, you can **not** determine the amount of cash (or any other specific asset) held by an entity by looking at the balance of owners' equity or liabilities. You must look at the listing of individual assets on the balance sheet to determine the amount of cash owned.

TIP: An appropriation of retained earnings is a positive component of total retained earnings. An appropriation of retained earnings refers to a portion of retained earnings which for one reason or another is restricted, which simply means it cannot be used as a basis for the declaration of dividends.

TIP: A **valuation account** is an account whose balance is needed to properly value the item to which the valuation account relates. A **contra account** is a valuation account whose normal balance (debit versus credit) is opposite of the normal balance of the account to which the valuation account relates. An **adjunct account** is a valuation account whose normal balance is the same as the normal balance of the account to which it relates.

TIP: Interest on debt is due annually or more frequently (semiannually or monthly, for example). Therefore, interest accrued on long-term debt is generally classified as a current liability. Likewise, interest receivable stemming from the accrual of interest on long-term receivables is generally classified as a current asset.

TIP: A fund can consist of restricted cash or noncash assets such as stocks and bonds of other companies. Funds are reported in the long-term investment classification.

TIP: In answering questions regarding the classification of items on a balance sheet, always assume an individual item is material unless it is apparent otherwise.

ILLUSTRATION 5-1
BALANCE SHEET CLASSIFICATIONS (L.O.2)

CURRENT ASSETS: includes cash and items which are expected to be converted to cash or sold or consumed within the next year or operating cycle, whichever is longer.

LONG-TERM INVESTMENTS: includes long-term receivables, restricted funds, investments in stocks and bonds of others, and land held for future plant site.

PROPERTY, PLANT AND EQUIPMENT: includes long-lived tangible assets (land, building, equipment, and machinery) that are currently being used in operations (used to produce goods and services for customers). Two items that do not meet this criteria but are included in property, plant and equipment are Plant Under Construction and Deposits on Equipment. Assets in this category are often referred to as plant assets or fixed assets. They are not held for resale.

INTANGIBLE ASSETS: includes assets that lack physical substance, such as a patent, copyright, franchise, trademark, or trade names that give the holder exclusive right of use for a specified period of time. Their value to a company is generally derived from the rights or privileges granted by governmental or other authority.

OTHER ASSETS: includes assets that by common practice are not classified elsewhere.

CURRENT LIABILITIES: obligations that are due within a year and are expected to require the use of current assets or the incurrence of other current liabilities to liquidate them.

LONG-TERM LIABILITIES: obligations that do not meet the criteria to be classified as current liabilities.

CAPITAL STOCK: the par or stated value of shares issued or about to be issued.

ADDITIONAL PAID-IN CAPITAL: the excess of the issuance price over the par or stated value of stock issued or about to be issued.

RETAINED EARNINGS: Excess of net incomes over net losses and dividend distributions since inception of the business. An appropriation of retained earnings is a restricted portion of the total retained earnings figure.

EXERCISE 5-1

Purpose: (L.O.2) This exercise lists examples of balance sheet accounts and enables you to practice determining where they are classified.

Instructions

Indicate which balance sheet classification is the most appropriate for reporting each account listed below by selecting the abbreviation of the corresponding section.

CA	Current Assets	CL	Current Liabilities
INV	Long-term Investments	LTL	Long-term Liabilities
PPE	Property, Plant, and Equipment	CS	Capital Stock
ITG	Intangible Assets	APC	Additional Paid-in Capital
OA	Other Assets	RE	Retained Earnings

If the account is a contra account, indicate that fact by putting the abbreviation in parenthesis. If the exact classification depends on facts which are not given, indicate your answer of "depends on" by the abbreviation **DEP** and the possible classifications. If the account is reported on the income statement rather than the balance sheet, indicate that fact with an **IS**. Assume all items are material.

Classification	Account	Classification	Account
________	1. Accounts Payable.	________	11. Advances to Vendors.
________	2. Accounts Receivable.	________	12. Advertising Expense.
________	3. Accrued Interest Receivable on Long-term Investments.	________	13. Allowance for Bad Debts.
________	4. Accrued Interest Payable.	________	14. Allowance for Depreciation.
________	5. Accrued Taxes Payable.	________	15. Allowance for Doubtful Accounts.
________	6. Accumulated Depreciation—Building.	________	16. Allowance for Excess of Cost Over Market Value of Inventory.
________	7. Accumulated Depreciation—Machinery.	________	17. Allowance for Inventory Price Declines.
________	8. Mineral Reserves.	________	18. Allowance for Purchase Discounts.
________	9. Advances by Customers.	________	19. Allowance for Sales Discounts.
________	10. Advances to Affiliates.	________	20. Allowance for Uncollectible Accts.

Classification	Account
______	21. Appropriation for Bond Sinking Fund.
______	22. Appropriation for Contingencies.
______	23. Appropriation for Future Plant Expansion.
______	24. Appropriation for Treasury Stock Purchased.
______	25. Bank Overdraft.
______	26. Bond Interest Payable.
______	27. Bond Interest Receivable.
______	28. Bond Sinking Fund.
______	29. Building.
______	30. Cash.
______	31. Cash in Preferred Stock Redemption Fund.
______	32. Cash Surrender Value of Life Insurance.
______	33. Certificate of Deposit.
______	34. Common Stock.
______	35. Construction in Process (entity's new plant under construction).
______	36. Creditor's accounts with debit balances.
______	37. Current Maturities of Bonds Payable (to be paid from Bond Sinking Fund).
______	38. Current Maturities of Bonds Payable (to be paid from general cash account).

Classification	Account
______	39. Current Portion of Mortgage Payable.
______	40. Current Portion of Long-term Debt.
______	41. Customers' accounts with credit balances.
______	42. Customers' Deposits.
______	43. Deferred Income Tax Asset.
______	44. Deferred Income Tax Liability.
______	45. Deferred Property Tax Expense.
______	46. Deferred Office Supplies.
______	47. Deferred Rental Income.
______	48. Deferred Subscription Revenue.
______	49. Deferred Service Contract Revenue.
______	50. Deposits on Equipment Purchases.
______	51. Depreciation of Equipment.
______	52. Discount on Bonds Payable.
______	53. Discount on Common Stock.
______	54. Discount on Notes Payable.
______	55. Discount on Notes Receivable.
______	56. Dishonored Notes Receivable.
______	57. Dividend Payable in Cash.
______	58. Dividend Payable in Common Stock.
______	59. Earned Rental Revenue.
______	60. Accrued Pension Liability.

Classification	Account
________	61. Estimated Liability for Income Taxes.
________	62. Estimated Liability for Warranties.
________	63. Estimated Premium Claims Outstanding.
________	64. Factory Supplies.
________	65. Finished Goods Inventory.
________	66. Furniture and Fixtures.
________	67. Gain on Sale of Equipment.
________	68. General and Administrative Expenses.
________	69. Goodwill.
________	70. Income Tax Payable.
________	71. Income Tax Refund Receivable.
________	72. Income Tax Withheld (from employees).
________	73. Interest Payable.
________	74. Interest Receivable.
________	75. Interest Revenue.
________	76. Investment in General Motors Stock.
________	77. Investment in U.S. Gov. Bonds.
________	78. Investment in Unconsolidated Subsidiary.
________	79. Land.
________	80. Land Held for Future Plant Site.

Classification	Account
________	81. Land Used for Parking Lot.
________	82. Leasehold Improvements.
________	83. Leasehold Costs.
________	84. Loss on Sale of Marketable Securities.
________	85. Machinery and Equipment.
________	86. Machinery and Equip. Sitting Idle.
________	87. Marketable Securities.
________	88. Merchandise Inventory.
________	89. Mortgage Payable.
________	90. Notes Payable.
________	91. Notes Payable to Banks.
________	92. Notes Receivable.
________	93. Notes Receivable Discounted.
________	94. Office Supplies on Hand.
________	95. Office Supplies Prepaid.
________	96. Office Supplies Used.
________	97. Organization Costs.
________	98. Patents.
________	99. Petty Cash Fund.
________	100. Plant and Equipment.
________	101. Preferred Stock Redemption Fund.
________	102. Premium on Bonds Payable.
________	103. Premium on Common Stock.

Classification	Account
______	104. Prepaid Advertising.
______	105. Prepaid Insurance.
______	106. Prepaid Insurance Expense.
______	107. Prepaid Office Supplies.
______	108. Prepaid Royalty Payments.
______	109. Prepaid Property Taxes.
______	110. Provision for Bad Debts.
______	111. Provision for Income Taxes.
______	112. Rent Revenue.
______	113. Salaries Payable.
______	114. Sales Discounts and Allowances.
______	115. Selling Expense Control.
______	116. Stock Dividends Distributable.
______	117. Stock Dividends Payable.
______	118. Store Supplies.
______	119. Store Supplies Used.
______	120. Tools and Dies (5-year life).
______	121. Tools and Dies (6-mos. life).
______	122. Treasury Stock Common (at cost).
______	123. Unamortized Bond Issue Costs.
______	124. Unamortized Organization Costs.
______	125. Unearned Rental Income.
______	126. Unearned Royalties.
______	127. Unearned Subscription Income.
______	128. Unexpired Insurance.
______	129. Vacation Pay Payable.
______	130. Vouchers Payable.
______	131. Work in Process.

Solution to Exercise 5-1

Solution	Explanation and/or Comment
CL	1. These are trade payables usually due within 30 or 60 days.
CA	2. These are trade receivables usually due within 30 or 60 days.
CA	3. Interest is usually due annually or more frequently.
CL	4. A better title is simply Interest Payable (item 73).
CL	5. A better title is simply Taxes Payable.
(PPE)	6. This is a contra account. It is another title for item 14 (item 6 is used more frequently).
(PPE)	7. This is a contra account and an alternative title for item 14.
PPE	8. Tracks of natural resources are classified in PPE.
DEP: CL or LTL	9. These advances refer to revenue amounts received in advance from customers.
DEP: CA or INV or OA	10. These advances are loans.
DEP: CA or INV or OA	11. These advances can be prepayments or loans.

Solution		Explanation and/or Comment
IS	12.	This is a selling expense.
(CA)	13.	This is another title for Allowance for Doubtful Accounts.
(PPE)	14.	This is another title for Accumulated Depreciation (items 6 & 7).
(CA)	15.	This is contra to Accounts Receivable.
(CA)	16.	This account arises because of the use of the lower of cost or market rule. It is contra to Inventory.
(CA)	17.	This is contra to Inventory; it is another title for item 16.
(CL)	18.	This account reflects amounts included in Accounts Payable that will not be paid because of purchase discounts to be taken.
(CA)	19.	This account reflects amounts included in Accounts Receivable that will not be collected because of sales discounts allowed.
(CA)	20.	This is another title for Allowance for Doubtful Accounts.
RE	21.	This is a restriction on retained earnings (portion of total retained earnings).
RE	22.	This is a restriction on retained earnings (portion of total retained earnings).
RE	23.	This is a restriction on retained earnings (portion of total retained earnings).
RE	24.	This is a restriction on retained earnings (portion of total retained earnings).
CL	25.	When the item exists, it is usually listed as the first item under current liabilities.
CL	26.	
CA	27.	
INV	28.	A fund can be comprised of restricted cash or securities.
PPE	29.	
CA	30.	This is unrestricted cash.
INV	31.	This cash is restricted for a long-term purpose.
INV or OA	32.	The assumption is that the entity will continue the insurance coverage rather than take the cash surrender value.
DEP: CA or INV	33.	Some CDs are for 90 days, 180 days, 30 months, or 60 months.
CS	34.	This reflects the par or stated value of issued shares.
PPE	35.	This is one of two exceptions to the general guidelines for items to be included in the PPE classification.
CA	36.	A creditor has been overpaid or items purchased on account have been returned for credit after payment of account has been made.
LTL	37.	This answer assumes that the Bond Sinking Fund is classified under long-term investments.
CL	38.	This item will require current assets to settle the debt.
CL	39.	"Current portion" refers to the portion that is coming due within a year of the balance sheet date.
CL	40.	Some accountants list this item first in the list of current liabilities, others list it last.
CL	41.	This arises when customers overpay or return goods after full payment is made.
DEP: CL or LTL	42.	A deposit may be an advance payment for goods and services or a security deposit.
DEP: CA or OA	43.	Deferred tax consequences of transactions reflected in the financial statements.
DEP: CL or LTL	44.	Deferred tax consequences of transactions reflected in the financial statements.

Solution		Explanation and/or Comment
CA	45.	This is another title for item 109, Prepaid Property Taxes.
CA	46.	This is another title for items 94, 95, and 107.
DEP: CL or LTL	47.	This is another title for item 125, Unearned Rental Income.
DEP: CL or LTL	48.	Some subscriptions are for one year, others are for two or more years. This is another title for item 127, Unearned Subscription Revenue.
DEP: CL or LTL	49.	A service contract often covers two or more years; revenue has been collected but not earned.
PPE	50.	This is the second of two exceptions to the general guidelines for items to be included in the PPE classification.
IS	51.	This refers to the depreciation charges for the current period.
(LTL)	52.	In the rare instance where the bonds payable are classified as current, the discount would be current also.
(CS)	53.	It is rare that common stock is sold below par.
DEP: (CL) or (LTL)	54.	A discount occurs when the effective rate exceeds the stated rate.
DEP: (CA) or (INV)	55.	A discount results when the note is issued below par.
CA	56.	A dishonored note receivable is one that has reached its maturity date and remains uncollected.
CL	57.	A dividend is usually paid approximately three to four weeks after it is declared.
CS	58.	This is a bad title for Stock Dividend Distributable. This is the same as items 116 and 117.
IS	59.	This is another title for Rent Revenue.
LTL	60.	This item will be explained in Chapter 21.
CL	61.	This is another title for Income Tax Payable.
DEP: CL or LTL	62.	Some warranties are for more than one year.
DEP: CL or LTL	63.	Premiums in this context are similar to prizes.
CA	64.	This item is similar to a prepaid expense; these supplies will be part of factory overhead (hence, work in process inventory) when used.
CA	65.	This is one of three inventory accounts for a manufacturer.
PPE	66.	
IS	67.	
IS	68.	
ITG	69.	This is referred to as an unidentifiable intangible asset with an indefinite life.
CL	70.	
CA	71.	
CL	72.	
CL	73.	This is another title for item 4 (item 73 is the preferable title).
CA	74.	
IS	75.	
CA	76.	This answer assumes there is no reason to hold the stock for a long-term purpose.
DEP: CA or INV	77.	
INV	78.	The fact that the investee is a subsidiary means there is an intention to hold the investee's stock for a long-term purpose.
PPE	79.	
INV	80.	
PPE	81.	

Solution		Explanation and/or Comment
PPE	82.	Some textbooks suggest classifying Leasehold Improvements as intangible assets.
ITG	83.	These are costs incurred in obtaining a lease.
IS	84.	
PPE	85.	
OA	86.	
CA or INV	87.	This is a title often used to refer to short-term investments; it can also refer to securities (stocks and/or bonds of other entities) held for long-term purposes.
CA	88.	This is another title for Inventory for a retailer.
LTL	89.	The portion of this balance due within the next year will be reclassified and reported as a current liability.
DEP: CL or LTL	90.	
DEP: CL or LTL	91.	
DEP: CA or INV	92.	
DEP: (CA) or (INV)	93.	
CA	94.	This is another title for items 46, 95, and 107.
CA	95.	This is another title for items 46, 94, and 107.
IS	96.	This is another title for Office Supplies Expense.
ITG	97.	This is another title for item 124 (item 97 is the more commonly used title).
ITG	98.	
CA	99.	
PPE	100.	
INV	101.	
LTL	102.	This is an adjunct type valuation account. If the related bonds payable are classified as a current liability, this valuation account will also be in current liabilities.
APC	103.	This is an adjunct type valuation account.
CA	104.	This is a prepaid expense.
CA	105.	This is another title for items 106 and 128.
CA	106.	This is another title for items 105 and 128.
CA	107.	This is another title for items 46, 94, and 95.
CA	108.	This is a prepaid expense.
CA	109.	This is another title for item 45.
IS	110.	This is another title for Uncollectible Accounts Expense or Bad Debt Expense.
IS	111.	This is another title for Income Tax expense.
IS	112.	
CL	113.	This is another title for Accrued Salaries or Accrued Salaries Payable. Salaries Payable is the preferred title.
IS	114.	This is a contra sales revenue item.
IS	115.	A control account is an account in the general ledger for which the details appear in a subsidiary ledger.
CS	116.	This is another title for items 58 and 117. The title in item 116 is the preferred title.
CS	117.	This is another title for items 58 and 116. This is a misleading title because the word "payable" suggests a liability, which a stock dividend is not.

Solution		Explanation and/or Comment
CA	118.	This answer assumes the supplies are on hand rather than used.
IS	119.	This item refers to Store Supplies Expense.
PPE	120.	
IS	121.	The service life is so short that the benefits yielded do not extend beyond one year. Therefore, the expenditure is not capitalized.
(CS + APC + RE)	122.	Treasury Stock is contra to the total of all other stockholder equity items when the cost method is used to account for it.
OA	123.	This is usually called Bond Issue Costs.
ITG	124.	This is usually called Organization Costs. It is the same as item 97.
DEP: CL or LTL	125.	This is another title for item 47.
DEP: CL or LTL	126.	Revenue has been received, but not earned; hence, an obligation exists to provide a service or good or a refund.
DEP: CL or LTL	127.	This is another title for item 48.
CA	128.	This is another title for items 105 and 106.
CL	129.	This is an accrued liability.
CL	130.	This is another title for Accounts Payable when a voucher system is in use.
CA	131.	This is an inventory account for a manufacturer.

Approach: For each balance sheet classification, write down a definition or description of what is to be reported in that classification. Refer to those notes as you go down the list of items to be classified. Your notes should contain the guidelines summarized in **Illustration 5-1**.

EXERCISE 5-2

Purpose: (L.O.3) This exercise will enable you to practice identifying errors and other deficiencies in a balance sheet.

Lee Cockrell Company has decided to expand its operations. The bookkeeper recently completed the balance sheet presented below to submit to the bank in order to obtain additional funds for expansion.

Lee Cockrell Company
BALANCE SHEET
For the Year Ended 1999

Current assets	
Cash (net of bank overdraft of $15,000)	$ 180,000
Accounts receivable (net)	380,000
Inventories, at lower of FIFO cost or market	435,000
Marketable securities—at cost (fair value $110,000)	90,000
Property, plant, and equipment	
Building (net)	590,000
Office equipment (net)	180,000
Land held for future use	75,000
Intangible assets	
Franchise	90,000
Cash surrender value of life insurance	80,000
Prepaid insurance	6,000
Current liabilities	
Salaries payable	18,000
Accounts payable	85,000
Note payable, due June 30, 2001	100,000
Pension obligation	92,000
Taxes payable	40,000
Note payable, due October 1, 2000	25,000
Discount on bonds payable	50,000
Long-term liabilities	
Bonds payable, 8%, due May 1, 2003	400,000
Stockholders' equity	
Common stock, $1 par, authorized 500,000 shares, issued 310,000 shares	310,000
Additional paid-in capital	279,000
Retained earnings	?

Instructions

Prepare a revised balance sheet in good form. Correct any errors and weaknesses you find in the presentation above. Assume that the accumulated depreciation balance for the building is $150,000 and for the office equipment, $105,000. Marketable securities are classified as trading securities. The allowance for doubtful accounts has a balance of $20,000. The pension obligation is considered to be a long-term liability.

Solution to Exercise 5-2

Lee Cockrell Company
BALANCE SHEET
December 31, 1999

Assets

Current Assets			
Cash			$ 195,000
Trading securities, at fair value (cost is $90,000)			110,000
Accounts receivable		$ 400,000	
Less allowance for doubtful accounts		20,000	380,000
Inventories, at lower of FIFO cost or market			435,000
Prepaid insurance			6,000
Total current assets			1,126,000
Long-term Investments			
Land held for future use		75,000	
Cash surrender value of life insurance		80,000	
Total long-term investments			155,000
Property, Plant, and Equipment			
Building	$ 740,000		
Less accumulated depreciation—building	150,000	590,000	
Office equipment	285,000		
Less accumulated depreciation—office equipment	105,000	180,000	
Total property, plant, and equipment			770,000
Intangible Assets			
Franchise			90,000
Total assets			$ 2,141,000

Liabilities and Stockholders' Equity

Current Liabilities			
Bank overdraft			$ 15,000
Note payable, due October 1, 2000			25,000
Accounts payable			85,000
Taxes payable			40,000
Salaries payable			18,000
Total current liabilities			183,000
Long-term Liabilities			
Note payable, due June 30, 2001		$ 100,000	
8% Bonds payable, due May 1, 2003	$ 400,000		
Less discount on bonds payable	50,000	350,000	
Pension obligation		92,000	
Total long-term liabilities			542,000
Total liabilities			725,000
Stockholders' equity			
Paid-in capital			
Common stock, $1 par, authorized 500,000 shares, issued and outstanding 310,000 shares	310,000		
Additional paid-in capital	279,000	589,000	
Retained earnings		827,000	
Total stockholders' equity			1,416,000
Total liabilities and stockholders' equity			$ 2,141,000

Explanation:

1. A bank overdraft in one bank account should not be reflected as an offset to positive cash items (such as a positive balance in another account). A bank overdraft must be reported as a current liability. (The one exception to this rule is as follows: if an account with a positive balance exists in the same bank as the overdraft, the overdraft can be reflected as an offset to the extent of that positive balance.)

2. Marketable securities in a trading portfolio are to be reported on the balance sheet at their fair value. The difference between cost and fair value has been included as an element of income and is therefore reflected in the balance of Retained Earnings at the balance sheet date. (This topic will be more fully explained in Chapter 18.)

3. Land held for future use is not to be classified in the property, plant, and equipment section because the land is not currently being used in operations.

4. Cash surrender value of life insurance is an intangible item in a legal sense (because it lacks physical substance), but it is classified as a long-term investment for accounting purposes.

5. Prepaid expenses such as prepaid insurance represent prepayments that relate to benefits that are expected to be consumed within the year that follows the balance sheet date. Hence, they are current assets.

6. A pension obligation is generally not expected to become due in the near future and, therefore, is not expected to require the use of current assets within a year of the balance sheet date. Hence, it is a long-term liability.

7. Discount on Bonds Payable is a contra type valuation account. A valuation account should always be reported with the account to which it relates.

8. Bonds payable are always assumed to be a long-term liability unless the facts make them appear to meet the definition for a current liability.

9. The balance of retained earnings for this exercise can be derived by determining the amount needed to cause total liabilities and stockholders' equity to equal total assets.

EXERCISE 5-3

Purpose: (L.O.3) This exercise will enable you to practice identifying errors and other deficiencies in a balance sheet.

Presented below is a balance sheet for the Gabby Corporation.

Gabby Corporation
BALANCE SHEET
December 31, 1999

Current assets	$ 520,000	Current liabilities	$ 365,000
Investments	700,000	Long-term liabilities	920,000
Property, plant, & equip.	2,185,000	Stockholders' equity	2,690,000
Intangible assets	570,000		
	$ 3,975,000		$ 3,975,000

The following information is available:

1. The current asset section includes: cash $120,000, accounts receivable $190,000 less $10,000 for allowance for doubtful accounts, inventories $230,000, and unearned revenue $10,000 (credit balance). Inventories are stated at their replacement cost; original cost on a FIFO basis is $200,000.

2. The investments section includes the cash surrender value of a life insurance contract $60,000; investments in common stock, short-term $70,000 and long-term $160,000; bond sinking fund $220,000; organizational costs $70,000; and land upon which a new plant is being constructed $120,000. Investments are all classified as available for sale and have fair values equal to their cost.

3. Property, plant, and equipment includes buildings $1,600,000 less accumulated depreciation $375,000; equipment $400,000 less accumulated depreciation $240,000; land $500,000; and land held for future use $300,000. The building is stated at a recent appraisal value of $1,600,000; original cost was $1,250,000.

4. Intangible assets include a franchise $140,000, goodwill $80,000, discount on bonds payable $30,000, and construction in process $320,000 (a new plant is under construction and will be ready for operations within nine months).

5. Current liabilities include accounts payable $80,000, notes payable—short-term $110,000, notes payable—long-term $150,000, and salaries payable $25,000. It does not include any amount for loss contingencies. The company's attorney states that it is probable the company will have to pay $60,000 in 2000 due to litigation pending at the balance sheet date.

6. Long-term liabilities are composed of 10% bonds payable (due June 1, 2007) $800,000 and pension obligation $120,000.

7. Stockholders' equity includes preferred stock, no par or stated value, 200,000 shares authorized with 70,000 shares issued for $450,000; and common stock, $2 par value, 300,000 shares authorized with 100,000 shares issued at an average price of $10. In addition, the corporation has retained earnings of $1,240,000.

Instructions

Prepare a corrected balance sheet in good form.

Solution to Exercise 5-3

Gabby Corporation
BALANCE SHEET
December 31, 1999

Assets

Current Assets			
Cash			$ 120,000
Available-for-sale securities—at fair value			70,000
Accounts receivable		$ 190,000	
Less allowance for doubtful accounts		10,000	180,000
Inventories, at lower of FIFO cost or market			200,000
Total current assets			570,000
Investments			
Available-for-sale securities—at fair value		160,000	
Bond sinking fund		220,000	
Cash surrender value of life insurance		60,000	
Land held for future use		300,000	
Total long-term investments			740,000
Property, Plant, and Equipment			
Land		620,000	
Buildings	$ 1,250,000		
Less accumulated depreciation—building	375,000	875,000	
Construction in process		320,000	
Equipment	400,000		
Less accumulated depreciation—equip.	240,000	160,000	
Total property, plant, and equipment			1,975,000
Intangible Assets			
Organization costs		70,000	
Franchise		140,000	
Goodwill		80,000	
Total intangible assets			290,000
Total assets			$ 3,575,000

Gabby Corporation
BALANCE SHEET
December 31, 1999
(Continued)

Liabilities and Stockholders' Equity

Current Liabilities			
Notes payable			$ 110,000
Accounts payable			80,000
Estimated litigation obligation			60,000
Salaries payable			25,000
Unearned revenue			10,000
Total current liabilities			285,000
Long-term Liabilities			
Notes payable		$ 150,000	
10% bonds payable, due June 1, 2007	$ 800,000		
Less discount on bonds payable	30,000	770,000	
Pension obligation		120,000	
Total long-term liabilities			1,040,000
Total liabilities			1,325,000
Stockholders' Equity			
Paid-in capital			
Preferred stock, no par value; 200,000 shares authorized, 70,000 issued and outstanding	450,000		
Common stock, $2 par value; 300,000 shares authorized, 100,000 issued and outstanding	200,000		
Paid-in capital in excess of par on common stock	800,000*	1,450,000	
Retained earnings		800,000**	
Total stockholders' equity			2,250,000
Total Liabilities and Stockholders' Equity			$ 3,575,000

*100,000 shares x ($10 - $2) = $800,000.

**The corrected balance for the Retained Earnings account can be reconciled with the before corrected amount as follows:

Retained Earnings, before corrections	$ 1,240,000
Overstatement of inventory	(30,000)
Overstatement of buildings	(350,000)
Understatement of litigation liability	(60,000)
Corrected Retained Earnings balance	$ 800,000

The errors that Gabby had on the balance sheet affected some income statement accounts (which were closed to Retained Earnings) or directly affected the Retained Earnings account.

TIP: The $620,000 reported amount for land is comprised of land $500,000 plus land upon which a new plant is being constructed $120,000.

EXERCISE 5-4

Purpose: (L.O.7) The exercise enables you to practice identifying investing and financing activities.

Instructions

Place the appropriate code in the blanks to identify each of the following transactions as giving rise to an:

Code	
II	inflow of cash due to an investing activity, or
IO	outflow of cash due to an investing activity, or
FI	inflow of cash due to a financing activity, or
FO	outflow of cash due to a financing activity.

_____ 1. Sell common stock to new stockholders.

_____ 2. Purchase treasury stock.

_____ 3. Borrow money from bank by issuance of short-term note.

_____ 4. Repay money borrowed from bank.

_____ 5. Purchase bonds as an investment.

_____ 6. Sell investment in real estate.

_____ 7. Loan money to an affiliate.

_____ 8. Collect on loan to affiliate.

_____ 9. Buy equipment.

_____ 10. Sell a plant asset.

_____ 11. Pay cash dividends to stockholders.

Solution to Exercise 5-4

1.	FI	4.	FO	7.	IO	10.	II
2.	FO	5.	IO	8.	II	11.	FO
3.	FI	6.	II	9.	IO		

Approach:

1. Reconstruct journal entries for the transactions. Examine each entry to identify if there is an inflow of cash (debit to Cash) or an outflow of cash (credit to Cash).

2. Write down the definitions for investing activities and financing activities (see below). Analyze each transaction to see if it fits one of these definitions.

   a) **Investing activities**—include (1) making and collecting loans, (2) acquiring and disposing of investments in debt and equity instruments, and (3) acquiring and disposing of property, plant, and equipment and other productive assets.

b) **Financing activities**—include (1) obtaining capital from owners and providing them with a return on and a return of their investment, and (2) borrowing money from creditors and repaying the amounts borrowed, and (3) obtaining and paying for other resources obtained from creditors.

3. Assume purchases and sales of items are for cash, unless otherwise indicated.

TIP: The journal entry to record a transaction that is an investing activity which results in a cash flow will involve: (1) Cash and (2) an asset account other than Cash, such as Investments (short-term or long-term), Land, Building, Equipment, Patent, Franchise, etc.

TIP: The journal entry to record a transaction that is a financing activity which results in a cash flow will involve: (1) Cash and (2) a liability account or an owners' equity account, such as Bonds Payable, Note Payable, Dividends Payable, Common Stock, Additional Paid-in Capital, Treasury Stock, etc.

EXERCISE 5-5

Purpose: (L.O.8) This exercise will enable you to practice reconciling net income with net cash provided by operating activities.

The following data relate to the L. Heckenmueller Co. for 1999.

Net income	$ 75,000
Increase in accounts receivable	7,000
Decrease in prepaid expenses	3,200
Increase in accounts payable	5,000
Decrease in taxes payable	900
Gain on sale of investment	1,700
Depreciation	3,500
Loss on sale of equipment	600

Instructions
Compute the net cash provided by operating activities for 1999.

Solution to Exercise 5-5

Net income	$ 75,000
Increase in accounts receivable	(7,000)
Decrease in prepaid expenses	3,200
Increase in accounts payable	5,000
Decrease in taxes payable	(900)
Gain on sale of investment	(1,700)
Depreciation	3,500
Loss on sale of equipment	600
Net cash provided by operating activities	$ 77,700

Explanation:

1. Net income is a summary of all revenues earned, all expenses incurred, and all gains and losses recognized for a period. Most revenues earned during the year result in a cash inflow during the same period but there may be some cash and/or revenue flows that do not correspond. Most expenses incurred during the year result in a cash outflow during the same period but there may be some cash and/or expense flows that do not correspond.

2. An increase in accounts receivable indicates that revenues earned exceed cash collected from customers and, therefore, net income exceeds net cash provided by operating activities.

3. A decrease in prepaid expenses indicates that expenses incurred exceed cash paid and, therefore, net income is less than net cash provided by operating activities.

4. An increase in accounts payable indicates that expenses incurred exceed cash paid and, therefore, net income is less than net cash provided by operating activities.

5. A decrease in taxes payable indicates expenses incurred are less than the cash paid, and, therefore, net income is greater than net cash provided by operating activities.

6. When an investment is sold, the entire proceeds are to be displayed as an investing activity on the statement of cash flows. The gain included in net income must, therefore, be deducted from net income to arrive at the net cash provided by operating activities. If this adjustment was not made, there would be double counting for the gain amount. For example: An investment with a carrying value of $4,000 is sold for $7,000. The entire $7,000 proceeds is an investing inflow; the $7,000 includes the gain of $3,000 and a recovery of the investment's $4,000 carrying value; the $3,000 gain will be deducted from net income to arrive at the net cash from operating activities figure.

7. Depreciation is a noncash charge (debit) against income. It must be added to net income to arrive at the amount of net cash provided by operating activities.

8. A loss on the sale of equipment does not cause a cash outlay so it is added back to net income to arrive at the amount of net cash provided by operating activities. The cash proceeds from the sale of equipment are shown as a cash inflow from an investing activity.

ILLUSTRATION 5-2
A SUMMARY OF FINANCIAL RATIOS (L.O.10)

Ratio	Formula for Computation	Purpose or Use
I. Liquidity		
1. Current ratio	Current assets / Current liabilities	Measures short-term debt-paying ability.
2. Quick or acid-test ratio	Cash, marketable securities, and receivables (net) / Current liabilities	Measures immediate short-term liquidity.
3. Current cash debt ratio	Net cash provided by operating activities / Average current liabilities	Measures the company's ability to pay off its current liabilities out of its operations for a given year.
II. Activity		
4. Receivable turnover	Net sales / Average trade receivables (net)	Measures liquidity of receivables
5. Inventory turnover	Cost of goods sold / Average inventory	Measures liquidity of inventory.
6. Asset turnover	Net sales / Average total assets	Measures how efficiently assets are used to generate sales.
III. Profitability		
7. Profit margin on sales	Net income / Net sales	Measures net income generated by each dollar of sales.
8. Rate of return on assets	Net income / Average total assets	Measures overall profitability of assets.
9. Rate of return on common stock equity	Net income minus preferred dividends / Average common stockholders' equity	Measures profitability of owners' investment.

ILLUSTRATION 25-1 (Continued)

Ratio	Formula for Computation	Purpose or Use
10. Earnings per share	Net income minus preferred dividends / Weighted shares outstanding	Measures net income earned on each share of common stock.
11. Price earnings ratio	Market price of stock / Earnings per share	Measures the ratio of the market price per share to earnings per share.
12. Payout ratio	Cash dividends / Net income	Measures percentage of earnings distributed in the form of cash dividends.
IV. Coverage		
13. Debt to total assets	Total debt / Total assets or equities	Measures the percentage of total assets provided by creditors.
14. Times interest earned	Income before interest charges and taxes / Interest charges	Measures ability to meet interest payments as they come due.
15. Cash debt coverage ratio	Net cash provided by operating activities / Average total liabilities	Measures a company's ability to repay its total liabilities in a given year out of its operations.
16. Book value per share	Common stock-holders' equity / Outstanding shares	Measures the amount each share of common stock would receive if the company were liquidated at the amounts reported on the balance sheet.

TIP: Throughout the remainder of the textbook, ratios are provided to help understand and interpret the information provided. In Chapter 25, an extensive discussion of financial statement analysis, of which ratio analysis is only a part, is presented. Above, we provide you with the ratios that will be used throughout the text. You should find the chart helpful as you examine these ratios in more detail in the following chapters.

ANALYSIS OF MULTIPLE-CHOICE TYPE QUESTIONS

QUESTION

1. (L.O.2) The Heather Miller Company has the following obligations at December 31, 1999:

I.	Accounts payable	$ 72,000
II.	Taxes payable	60,000
III.	Notes payable issued November 1, 1999, due October 31, 2000	80,000
IV.	Bonds payable issued December 1, 1990, due November 30, 2000 (to be paid by use of a sinking fund)	100,000

The amount that should be reported for total current liabilities at December 31, 1999 is:

a. $312,000.
b. $212,000.
c. $132,000.
d. $72,000.

Approach and Explanation: Write down the definition (or key phrases therein) for a current liability. (A **current liability** is an obligation which is coming due within a year of the balance sheet date and is expected to require the use of current assets or the incurrence of another current liability to liquidate it.) Analyze each of the obligations listed to see if it meets the criteria for being classified as current.

Accounts payable and taxes payable will both be due shortly after the balance sheet date and will require cash to liquidate the debts. The notes payable are due within a year of the balance sheet date and there is no evidence to indicate that assets other than current assets will be used for settlement; thus, the notes payable are a current liability. The bonds payable are coming due within a year, but they will **not** require the use of current assets to liquidate the debt because a sinking fund (restricted cash or securities classified as a long-term investment) is to be used to extinguish that debt: $72,000 + $60,000 + $80,000 = $212,000. (Solution = b.)

QUESTION

2. (L.O.2) Land held for a future plant site should be classified in the section for:

a. current assets.
b. long-term investments.
c. property, plant, and equipment.
d. intangible assets.

Approach and Explanation: Quickly review in your mind the descriptions of what goes in each of the asset classifications. Then read each answer selection and respond **True** or **False** if the selection answers the question. The land is not being used in operations, so it doesn't belong in property, plant, and equipment. It is not lacking physical existence, so it can't be an intangible asset. The land is not expected to be converted to cash or sold or consumed within the next year, so it is not a current asset. The land properly belongs in long-term investments. (Solution = b.)

QUESTION

3. (L.O.4) A loss contingency that has a level of likelihood rated as reasonably possible and an amount that can be reasonably estimated should be:

	Accrued	Disclosed
a.	Yes	Yes
b.	Yes	No
c.	No	Yes
d.	No	No

Approach and Explanation: Read the stem and write down how you would complete the statement in the stem. Then look at the answer selections one at a time to find the one that corresponds with your anticipated response. A loss contingency that is probable and estimable should be accrued. A loss contingency that is reasonably possible should be disclosed only in the notes (and not be accrued). A loss contingency that is only remotely possible can usually be ignored and not accrued or disclosed. (Solution = c.)

QUESTION

4. (L.O.3) Which of the following is a contra account?
   a. Premium on bonds payable
   b. Unearned revenue
   c. Patents
   d. Accumulated depreciation

Approach and Explanation: After reading the stem and before reading the answer selections, write down the description of the term "contra account". (A **contra account** is a valuation account whose normal balance is opposite of the balance of the account to which it relates.) Then take each answer selection and answer **True** or **False** whether it meets that description. Premium on bonds payable is a valuation account, but it is an adjunct type (its normal balance is the same as the normal balance of the account to which it relates). Unearned Revenue and Patents are not valuation accounts. Accumulated Depreciation is a valuation account for property, plant, and equipment. The normal balance of the Accumulated Depreciation account is a credit and the normal balance of a property, plant, and equipment account is a debit. Hence, Accumulated Depreciation is a contra account. (Solution = d.)

QUESTION

5. (L.O.7) Which of the following should be classified as an inflow of cash in the investing section of a statement of cash flows?
   a. Cash sale of merchandise inventory
   b. Sale of delivery equipment at book value
   c. Sale of common stock
   d. Issuance of a note payable to a bank

Approach and Explanation: Read the stem and, before reading the answer selections, write down the items that appear in the definition of investing activities. (**Investing activities** include making and collecting loans to others, acquiring and disposing of stocks and bonds of other entities, acquiring and disposing of property, plant, and equipment and other productive assets.) Think of the items included in that definition that would produce a cash inflow (collecting loans, disposing of investments and property, plant, and equipment). Look for the answer selection that fits that analysis. As you analyze each answer selection, indicate what kind of activity it represents. A cash sale of merchandise inventory is an operating activity. The sale of common stock is a financing activity. The issuance of a note payable is a financing activity. A sale of equipment is an investing activity. (Solution = b.)

QUESTION

6. (L.O.4) Events that occur after the December 31, 1999 balance sheet date (but before the balance sheet is issued) and provide additional evidence about conditions that existed at the balance sheet date and affect the realizability of accounts receivable should be:
   a. discussed only in the MD&A (Management's Discussion and Analysis) section of the annual report.
   b. disclosed only in the Notes to the Financial Statements.
   c. used to record an adjustment to Bad Debt Expense for the year ending December 31, 1999.
   d. used to record an adjustment directly to the Retained Earnings account.

Approach and Explanation: There are two types of subsequent events. The one described in the question encompasses information that would have been recorded in the accounts had it been available at the balance sheet date. This type requires adjustments to be made before the financial statements are issued. The second type involves events that provide evidence about conditions that did not exist at the balance sheet date but arise subsequent to that date.

The financial statements should not be adjusted for subsequent events of the second type; however, some of these events may have to be disclosed to keep the financial statements from being misleading. (Solution = c.)

QUESTION

7. (L.O.7) An example of a cash flow from an operating activity is:
   a. payment to employees for services.
   b. payment of dividends to stockholders.
   c. receipt of proceeds from the sale of an investment.
   d. receipt of proceeds from the sale of common stock to stockholders.

Explanation: Operating activities include the cash effects of transactions that ultimately create revenues and expenses and thus enter into the determination of net income. Operating activities include collections from customers, collections of interest and dividends, payments for merchandise and other goods and services, and payments for interest and taxes. The payment of dividends is a financing activity. The sale of an investment is an investing activity. The sale of common stock is a financing activity. (Solution = a.)

QUESTION

8. (L.O.8) Net cash flow from operating activities for 1999 for Graham Corporation was $75,000. The following items are reported on the financial statements for 1999:

Depreciation and amortization	5,000
Cash dividends paid on common stock	3,000
Increase in accrued receivables	6,000

Based only on the information above, Graham's net income for 1999 was:

a. $64,000.
b. $66,000.
c. $74,000.
d. $76,000.
e. None of the above.

Approach and Explanation: Write down the format for the reconciliation of net income to net cash flow from operating activities. Fill in the information given. Solve for the unknown.

Net income	$ X
Depreciation and amortization	5,000
Increase in accrued receivables	(6,000)
Net cash flow from operating activities	$ 75,000

Solving for X, net income = $76,000. Cash dividends paid on common stock have no effect on this computation because cash dividends paid is not a component of net income and not an operating activity. Cash dividends paid is classified as a financing activity. (Solution = d.)

QUESTION

9. (L.O.9) Free cash flow is:

a. net cash provided by operating activities minus capital expenditures and dividends.
b. net cash provided by operating activities minus retirement of debt and purchases of treasury stock.
c. the amount of cash obtained from donations.
d. the amount of net cash increase during the period.

Explanation: One method of examining a company's financial flexibility is to develop a free cash flow analysis. This analysis starts with net cash provided by operating activities and ends with free cash flow which is calculated as net cash provided by operating activities less capital expenditures and dividends. Free cash flow is the amount of discretionary cash flow a company has for purchasing additional investments, retiring its debt, purchasing treasury stock, or simply adding to its liquidity. This measure indicates a company's level of financial flexibility. (Solution = a.)

QUESTION

10. (L.O.10) Activity ratios measure the effectiveness of asset usage. One of the activity ratios is the:
    a. inventory turnover ratio.
    b. current ratio.
    c. acid-test ratio.
    d. rate of return on assets.

Explanation: The activity ratios include the (1) receivable turnover ratio, (2) inventory turnover ratio, and (3) asset turnover ratio. The current ratio and acid-test (or quick) ratio are both liquidity ratios. The rate of return on assets ratio is a profitability ratio. (Solution = a.)

CHAPTER 6

ACCOUNTING AND THE TIME VALUE OF MONEY

OVERVIEW

Due to the time value of money, a certain sum today is not equal to the same sum at a future point in time. We must consider the compound interest factor for the time between two given dates in order to determine what amount in the future is equivalent to a given sum today or what amount today is equivalent to a given sum in the future. We compound the dollar amount forward in time in the former case and discount the dollar amount from the future to the present time in the latter case. In this chapter we discuss both of these procedures for a single sum and the appropriate procedures for compounding and discounting annuities. Interest tables appear at the end of this chapter.

SUMMARY OF LEARNING OBJECTIVES

1. **Identify accounting topics where the time value of money is relevant.** Some of the applications of present-value-based measurements to accounting topics are: (1) notes, (2) leases, (3) amortization of premiums and discounts, (4) pensions and other postretirement benefits, (5) capital assets, (6) sinking funds, (7) business combinations, (8) disclosures, and (9) installment contracts.

2. **Distinguish between simple and compound interest.** Interest is a payment for the use of money. It is the excess cash received or repaid over and above the amount lent (invested) or borrowed (principal). Simple interest is interest that is computed on the amount of the principal only. It is the return on (or growth of) the principal for one time period. Simple interest is commonly expressed as follows:

$$\text{Interest} = p \times i \times n$$

where: p = principal
i = rate of interest for a single period
n = number of periods

Compound interest is computed on principal **and** on any interest earned to date on that principal that has not been paid or withdrawn.

3. **Learn how to use appropriate compound interest tables.** In order to identify the appropriate compound interest table to use of the five given, you must identify whether you are solving for (1) the future value of a single sum, (2) the present value of a single sum, (3) the future value of a series of sums, or (4) the present value of a series of sums. In addition, when a series of equal payments or receipts that occur at equal intervals of time (an annuity) is involved, you must identify whether these sums are received or paid (1) at the **beginning** of each period (annuity due) or (2) at the **end** of each period (ordinary annuity).

4. **Identify variables fundamental to solving interest problems.** The following four variables are fundamental to all compound interest problems: (1) **Rate of interest:** unless otherwise stated, an annual rate that must be adjusted to reflect the length of the compounding period if less than a year. (2) **Number of time periods:** the number of compounding periods (a period may be equal to or less than a year). (3) **Future value:** the value at a future date of a given sum or sums invested assuming compound interest. (4) **Present value:** the value now (present time) of a future sum or sums discounted back to the present assuming compound interest.

5. **Solve future and present value of 1 problems.** The future value (or future amount) of a single sum is the value at a future point in time of a given amount to be deposited (or invested) today using compound interest. The present value of a single sum is the current worth of a given future sum. In determining the future value, we move forward in time using a process of accumulation; in determining present value, we move backward in time using a process of discounting. The present value is always a smaller amount than a known future amount because interest will be earned and accumulated on the present value to the future date.

6. **Solve future value of ordinary and annuity due problems.** The future value of an annuity is the future value (accumulated total) of a series of equal deposits at regular intervals at compound interest. Both deposits and interest increase the accumulation. Thus, the future value of an annuity is the sum of all the rents plus the accumulated compound interest on them.

7. **Solve present value of ordinary and annuity due problems.** The present value of an annuity is the present value (worth) of a series of equal rents due in the future, all discounted at compound interest; in other words, it is the sum when invested today at compound interest that will permit a series of equal withdrawals at regular intervals.

TIPS ON CHAPTER TOPICS

TIP: The **future value of 1** (a single sum) is often referred to as the **future amount of 1**, and the **future value of an annuity** is often called the **future amount of an annuity**.

TIP: Anytime you have a present value or a future value problem to solve, it is wise to draw a time diagram (or time line). This picture will help you to determine:
1. if you are given present value or future value data or both.
2. if you are dealing with a single sum or an annuity situation.
3. what you are to solve for—present value, future value, *n* (number of periods), *i* (interest rate) or rent.

TIP: The present value of a single sum is based on three variables: (1) the dollar amount to be received or paid (future value), (2) the length of time until the amount is received or paid (number of periods), and (3) the interest rate (the discount rate). The process of determining the present value is referred to as discounting the future value. The relationship of these fundamental variables is depicted in the following diagram.

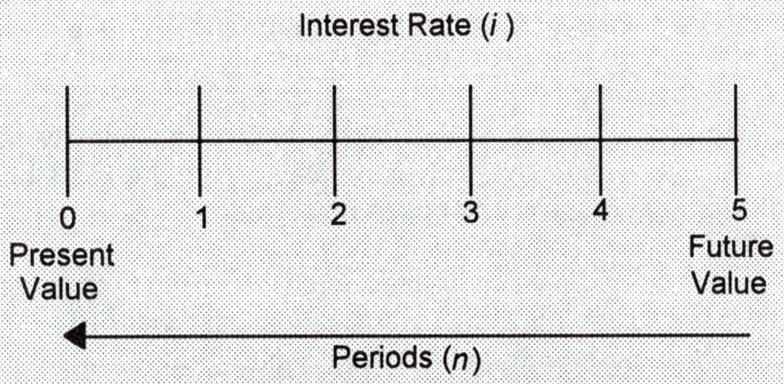

Unless otherwise indicated, an interest rate is stated on an annual basis. To convert an annual interest rate into a compounding period interest rate, divide the annual rate by the number of compounding periods per year. The total number of periods is determined by multiplying the number of years involved by the number of compounding periods per year.

TIP: The **interest rate** is often referred to as the **discount rate** in computing present value. The **higher** the discount rate (interest rate) is, the **lower** the present value will be.

TIP: The factor for the "present value of 1" is the reciprocal (inverse) of the factor for the "future value of 1." Thus, if you are given the factor from the Future Value of 1 Table for $n = 3$, $i = 8\%$ which is 1.25971, you can compute the factor for the "present value of 1" for $n = 3$, $i = 8\%$ by dividing 1 by 1.25971. This division yields a factor of .79383, which does agree with the factor for $n = 3$, $i = 8\%$ in the Present Value of 1 Table.

TIP: The factor for the present value of an ordinary annuity of 1 for *n* periods is the sum of factors for the present value of 1 for each of the *n* periods. For example, the factor for the present value of an ordinary annuity of 1 for $n = 3$, $i = 8\%$ (which is 2.57710) is equal to sum of the factors from the 8% column of the Present Value of 1 Table for $n = 1$, $n = 2$, $n = 3$ (.92593 + .85734 + .79383 = 2.57710).

TIP: One payment (or receipt) involved in an annuity is called a **rent**.

TIP: The factor for the future value of an ordinary annuity of 1 for $n = 3$, $i = 8\%$ is 3.24640. It reflects interest on the first rent for two periods, interest on the second rent for one period, and no interest on the third rent. The factor for the future value of an annuity due of 1 for $n = 3$, $i = 8\%$ is 3.50611. It reflects interest on the first rent for three periods, interest on the second rent for two periods, and interest for one period on the third rent. Thus, for a given *n* and *i*, the factor for an annuity due is greater than the factor for an ordinary annuity.

TIP: Referring to the TIP immediately above, we can see that the future value of an annuity due factor can be found by multiplying the future value of an ordinary annuity factor by 1 plus the interest rate. Likewise, the present value of an annuity due factor can be found by multiplying the present value of an ordinary annuity factor by 1 plus the interest rate.

TIP: A deferred annuity is an annuity in which the rents begin after a specified number of periods. A deferred annuity does not begin to produce rents until two or more periods have expired.

TIP: A factor for the present value or the future value of an annuity reflects one rent per period. Therefore, if an annuity involves a delay before the rents begin, the factor for *n* must be adjusted before the problem can be solved.

TIP: Any present value or future value problem is an application (or variation) of one or more of the following formulas: (parentheses indicate multiplication)

Future Value of an Amount = Present Value (Future Value of 1 Factor)
Present Value of an Amount = Future Value (Present Value of 1 Factor)
Future Value of an Annuity = Rent (Future Value of an Annuity Factor)
Present Value of an Annuity = Rent (Present Value of an Annuity Factor)

ILLUSTRATION 6-1
STEPS IN SOLVING FUTURE VALUE AND PRESENT VALUE PROBLEMS (L.O.5,6,7)

Step 1: Classify the problem into one of six types:

a. Future value of a single sum.
b. Present value of a single sum.
c. Future value of an ordinary annuity.
d. Present value of an ordinary annuity.
e. Future value of an annuity due.
f. Present value of an annuity due.

Step 2: Determine *n*, the number of compounding periods, and *i*, the interest rate per period.

a. Draw a time diagram. This is helpful when the number of periods or number of rents must be figured out from the dates given in the problem.
b. If interest is compounded more than once a year:
   1) To find *n*: **multiply** the number of years by the number of compounding periods per year.
   2) To find *i*: **divide** the annual interest rate by the number of compounding periods per year.

Step 3: Use *n* and *i* (if known) to choose the proper interest factor from the interest table indicated in Step 1.

Step 4: Solve for the missing quantity. A summary of the possibilities appears in **Illustration 6-2**. Abbreviations used in that summary are explained at the end of the summary.

ILLUSTRATION 6-2
SUMMARY OF SIX TYPES OF FUTURE VALUE AND PRESENT VALUE PROBLEMS (L.O.5,6,7)

1. Future Value of a Single Sum

a. Future Value = Present Value x $FVF_{n,i}$

b. $FVF_{n,i}$ = $\frac{\text{Future Value}}{\text{Present Value}}$

(1) "i" unknown and "n" known, or — Trace solved factor to Table 6-1.
(2) "n" unknown and "i" known — Trace solved factor to Table 6-1.

TIP: The present value amount is sometimes called the **principal.**

2. Present Value of a Single Sum

a. Present Value = Future Value x $PVF_{n,i}$

b. $PVF_{n,i}$ = $\frac{\text{Present Value}}{\text{Future Value}}$

(1) "i" unknown and "n" known, or — Trace solved factor to Table 6-2.
(2) "n" unknown and "i" known — Trace solved factor to Table 6-2.

3. Future Value of an Ordinary Annuity

a. Future Value of an Ordinary Annuity = Rent x $FVF\text{-}OA_{n,i}$

b. Rent = $\frac{\text{Future Value of an Ordinary Annuity}}{FVF\text{-}OA_{n,i}}$

c. $FVF\text{-}OA_{n,i}$ = $\frac{\text{Future Value of an Ordinary Annuity}}{\text{Rent}}$

(1) "i" unknown and "n" known, or — Trace solved factor to Table 6-3.
(2) "n" unknown and "i" known — Trace solved factor to Table 6-3.

4. Present Value of an Ordinary Annuity

a. Present Value of an Ordinary Annuity = Rent x $PVF\text{-}OA_{n,i}$

b. Rent = $\frac{\text{Present Value of an Ordinary Annuity}}{PVF\text{-}OA_{n,i}}$

c. $PVF\text{-}OA_{n,i}$ = $\frac{\text{Present Value of an Ordinary Annuity}}{\text{Rent}}$

(1) "i" unknown and "n" known, or — Trace solved factor to Table 6-4.
(2) "n" unknown and "i" known — Trace solved factor to Table 6-4.

ILLUSTRATION 6-2 (Continued)

5. Future Value of an Annuity Due

a. Future Value of an Annuity Due = Rent x $FVF\text{-}AD_{n,i}$

b. Rent = $\dfrac{\text{Future Value of an Annuity Due}}{FVF\text{-}AD_{n,i}}$

> **TIP:** There is no table in this book for Future Value of an Annuity Due, so ordinary annuity factors must be modified as follows:
>
> $FVF\text{-}AD_{n,i} = FVF\text{-}OA_{n,i} \times (1 + i)$ **OR** $FVF\text{-}AD_{n,i} = FVF\text{-}OA_{n+1,i} - 1.00000$

6. Present Value of an Annuity Due

a. Present Value of an Annuity Due = Rent x $PVF\text{-}AD_{n,i}$

b. Rent = $\dfrac{\text{Present Value of an Annuity Due}}{PVF\text{-}AD_{n,i}}$

c. $PVF\text{-}AD_{n,i}$ = $\dfrac{\text{Present Value of an Annuity Due}}{\text{Rent}}$

(1) "*i*" unknown and "*n*" known, or — Trace solved factor to Table 6-5.
(2) "*n*" unknown and "*i*" known — Trace solved factor to Table 6-5.

> **TIP:** Factors for the present value of an annuity due can be derived by adjusting factors from the Table for Present Value of an Ordinary Annuity as follows:
>
> $PVF\text{-}AD_{n,i} = PVF\text{-}OA_{n,i} \times (1 + i)$ **OR** $PVF\text{-}AD_{n,i} = PVF\text{-}OA_{n-1,i} + 1.00000$

Abbreviations:

i	=	Interest Rate
n	=	Number of Periods or Rents
$FVF_{n,i}$	=	Future Value of 1 Factor for *n* periods at *i* interest
$PVF_{n,i}$	=	Present Value of 1 Factor for *n* periods at *i* interest
$FVF\text{-}OA_{n,i}$	=	Future Amount of an Ordinary Annuity of 1 Factor for *n* periods at *i* interest
$PVF\text{-}OA_{n,i}$	=	Present Value of an Ordinary Annuity of 1 Factor for *n* periods at *i* interest
$FVF\text{-}OA_{n,i}$	=	Future Amount of an Annuity Due of 1 Factor for *n* periods at *i* interest
$PVF\text{-}OA_{n,i}$	=	Present Value of an Annuity Due of 1 Factor for *n* periods at *i* interest

ILLUSTRATION 6-3
STEPS IN SOLVING FUTURE VALUE AND PRESENT VALUE PROBLEMS ILLUSTRATED (L.O.5,6,7)

The steps in solving future value and present value problems (listed in **Illustration 6-1** on page **6-4**) are illustrated below and on the following pages:

1. **If $10,000 is deposited in the bank today at 8% interest compounded annually, what will be the balance in 5 years?**

Step 1: This is a future value of a single sum problem.
Step 2: $n = 5$; $i = 8\%$

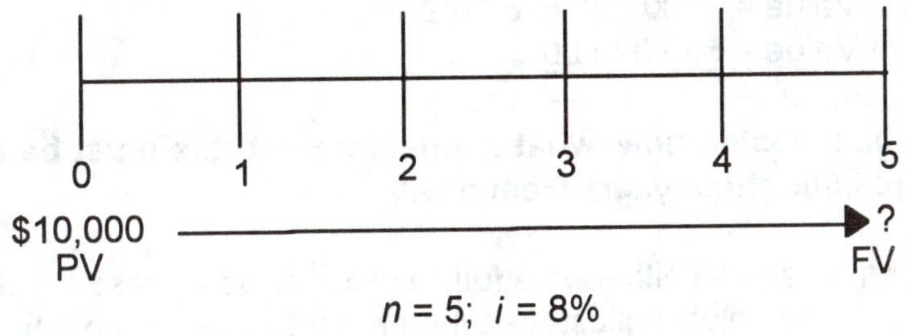

Step 3: The interest factor from Table 6-1 is 1.46933.
Step 4: Future Value = Present Value x $FVF_{n,i}$
Future Value = $10,000 x 1.46933
Future Value = $14,693.30

2. **A company needs $100,000 to retire debt when the debt matures two years from now. What amount must be deposited on January 1, 1999 at 8% interest compounded quarterly in order to accumulate the desired sum by January 1, 2001?**

Step 1: This is a present value of a single sum problem.
Step 2: It is 2 years from 1/1/99 to 1/1/01. The annual interest rate is 8%. $n = 2 \times 4 = 8$; $i = 8\% \div 4 = 2\%$.

ILLUSTRATION 6-3 (Continued)

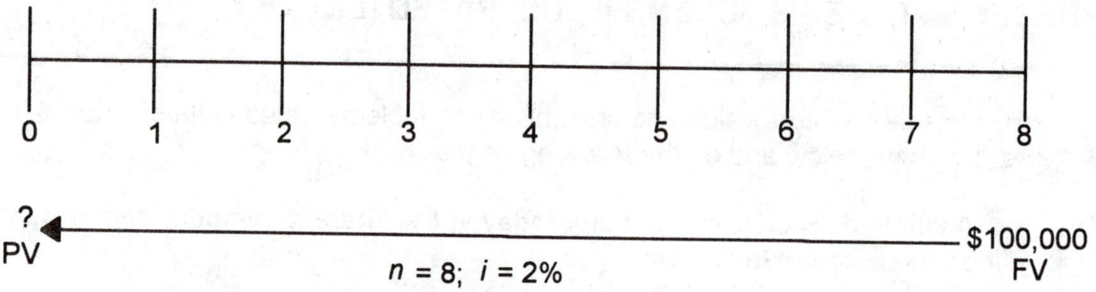

Step 3: The interest factor from Table 6-2 is .85349.
Step 4: Present Value = Future Value x $PVF_{n,i}$
Present Value = $100,000 x .85349
Present Value = <u>$85,349.00</u>

3. If $71,178 can be invested now, what annual interest rate must be earned in order to accumulate $100,000 three years from now?

Step 1: This can be solved either as a future value or as a present value of a single sum problem. This solution illustrates the present value approach.
Step 2: *n* = 3; *i* must be solved for.

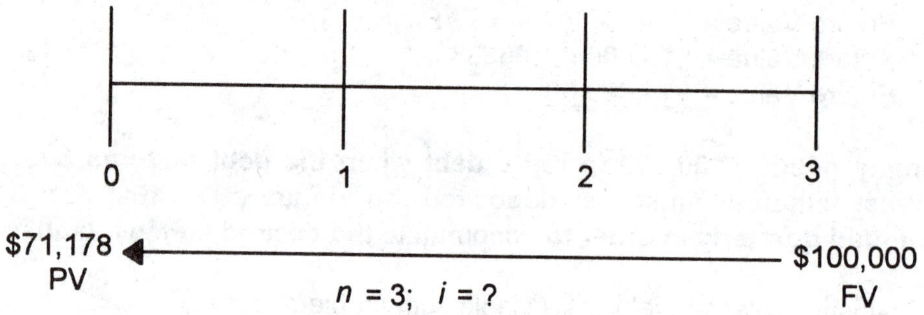

Step 3: *i* must be solved for.
Step 4: Present Value = Future Value x $PVF_{n,i}$
$71,178 = $100,000 x $PVF_{n,i}$
$71,178 ÷ $100,000 = $PVF_{n,i}$
.71178 = $PVF_{n,i}$
Refer to Table 6-2 in the 3 period row.
<u>i = 12%</u>

ILLUSTRATION 6-3 (Continued)

4. **If $1,000 is deposited into an account at the end of every year for six years, what will be the balance in the account after the sixth deposit if all amounts on deposit earn 6% interest?**

Step 1: This is a future value of an ordinary annuity problem.
Step 2: $n = 6$; $i = 6\%$

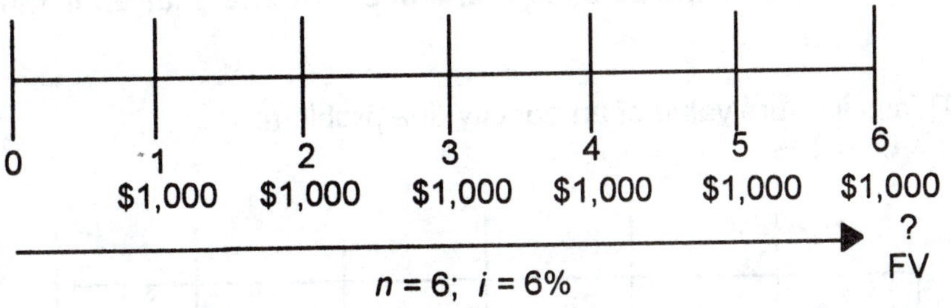

Step 3: The interest factor from Table 6-3 is 6.97532.
Step 4: Future Value of an Ordinary Annuity = Rent x FVF-OA$_{n,i}$
Future Value of an Ordinary Annuity = $1,000 x 6.97532
Future Value of an Ordinary Annuity = $6,975.32

5. **What amount must be deposited at 10% in an account on January 1, 1999 if it is desired to make equal annual withdrawals of $10,000 each, beginning on January 1, 2000 and ending on January 1, 2003?**

Step 1: This is a present value of an ordinary annuity problem.
Step 2: The time diagram shows 4 withdrawals. $n = 4$; $i = 10\%$

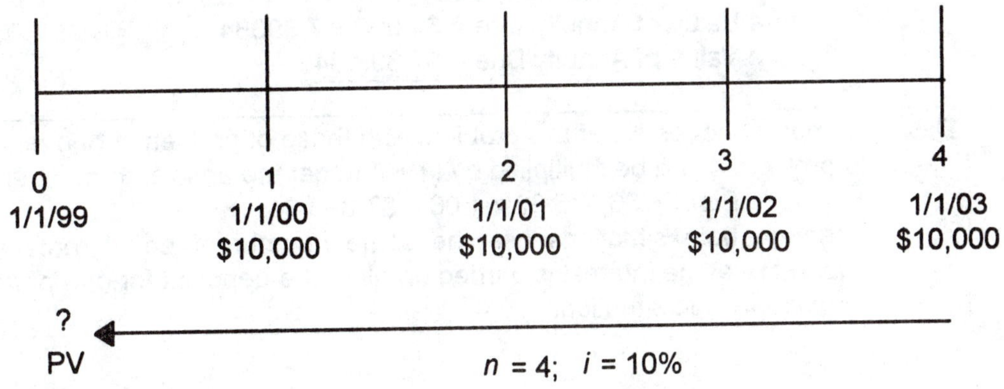

ILLUSTRATION 6-3 (Continued)

Step 3: The interest factor from Table 6-4 is 3.16986.
Step 4: Present Value of an Ordinary Annuity = Rent x PVF-OA$_{n,i}$
Present Value of an Ordinary Annuity = $10,000 x 3.16986
Present Value of an Ordinary Annuity = <u>$31,698.60</u>

6. **Beginning today, six annual deposits of $1,000 each will be made into an account paying 6%. What will be the balance in the account one year after the sixth deposit is made?**

Step 1: This is a future value of an annuity due problem.
Step 2: $n = 6$; $i = 6\%$.

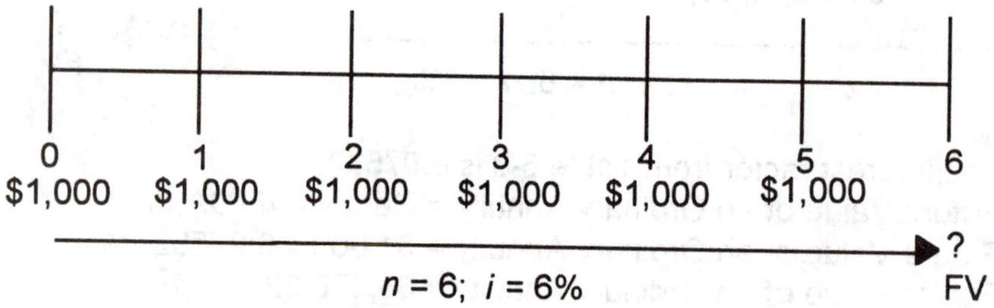

Step 3: Table 6-3 with factors for future value of an ordinary annuity (FVF-OA$_{n,i}$) can be used to derive the factor needed here for future value of an annuity due (FVF-AD$_{n,i}$). The process is as follows:

FVF-OA for $n = 6$, $i = 6\%$	6.97532
Multiplied by $1 + i$	1.06
FVF-AD for $n = 6$, $i = 6\%$	7.39384

Step 4: Future Value of an Annuity Due = Rent x FVF-AD$_{n,i}$
Future Value of Annuity Due = $1,000 x 7.39384
Future Value of Annuity Due = <u>$7,393.84</u>

> **TIP:** Compare the results of this problem with those of problem 4 above. The solution to problem 4 can be multiplied by $(1 + i)$ to get the answer to number 6.
> Proof: $6,975.32 x 1.06 = $7,393.84.
> Although both situations use the same number of equal rents and the same interest rate, the interest is earned on all of the deposits for one period more under the annuity due situation.

ILLUSTRATION 6-3 (Continued)

7. What is the present value of four annual payments of $10,000 each if interest is 10% and the first payment is made today?

Step 1: This is a present value of an annuity due problem.
Step 2: $n = 4$; $i = 10\%$.

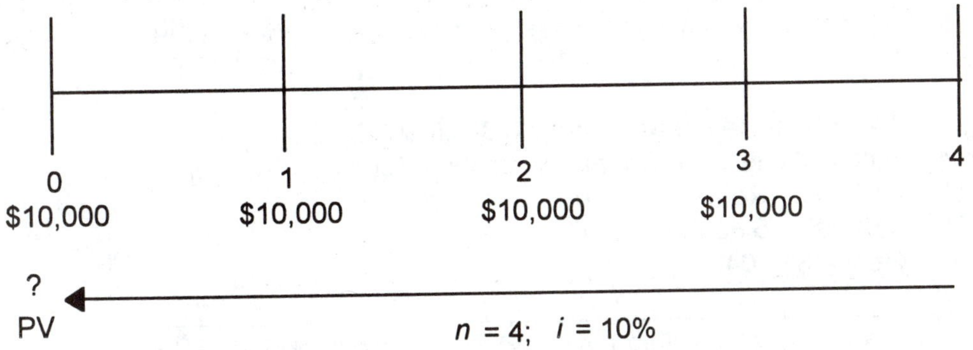

Step 3: The interest factor from Table 6-5 is 3.48685.
This factor can also be derived by using the present value of an ordinary annuity table (Table 6-4) as follows:

PVF-OA for $n = 4$, $i = 10\%$	3.16986
Multiplied by $1 + i$	1.10
PVF-AD for $n = 4$, $i = 10\%$	3.48685

Step 4: Present Value of an Annuity Due = Rent x PVF-$AD_{n,i}$
Present Value of an Annuity Due = $10,000 x 3.48685
Present Value of an Annuity Due = $34,868.50

> **TIP:** Compare the results of this problem with those of problem 5 above. The solution to problem 5 can be multiplied by $(1 + i)$ to get the answer to number 7.
> Proof: $31,698.60 x 1.10 = $34,868.46
> (Difference of $.04 is due to the rounding of the factors.)
> Although both situations use the same number of equal rents and the same interest rate, the discounting is done on all of the deposits for one period less under the annuity due situation.

8. What amount must be deposited at the end of each year in an account paying 8% interest if it is desired to have $10,000 at the end of the fifth year?

Step 1: This is a future value of an ordinary annuity problem.
Step 2: $n = 5$; $i = 8\%$.

ILLUSTRATION 6-3 (Continued)

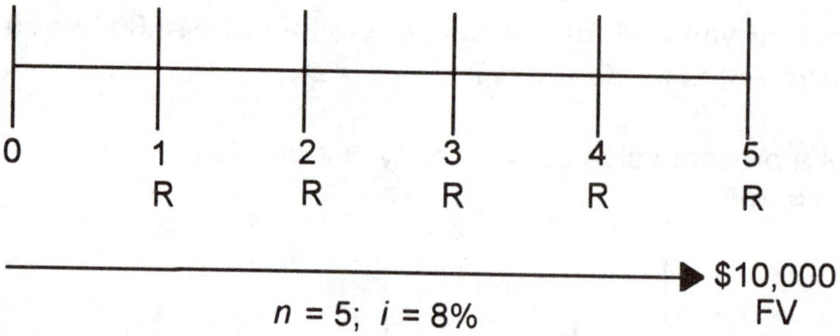

Step 3: The interest factor from Table 6-3 is 5.86660.
Step 4: Future Value of an Ordinary Annuity = Rent x $FVF\text{-}OA_{n,i}$
$10,000 = Rent x 5.86660
$10,000 ÷ 5.86660 = Rent
Rent = $1,704.56

TIP: You can prove this solution by: $1,704.56 x 5.86660 = $9,999.97
The difference of $.03 is due to rounding.

EXERCISE 6-1

Purpose: (L.O.3) This exercise will test your knowledge of the applicability of the five compound interest tables discussed in this chapter.

Instructions

For each independent situation below, (1) indicate which table you would need to use in order to locate the appropriate factor to solve for the figure requested, and (2) indicate if you divide (D) or multiply (M) by that factor to solve for the figure requested. Use the appropriate numerals and letters to indicate your answer for each.

I. Future Value of 1
II. Present Value of 1
III. Future Value of an Ordinary Annuity of 1
IV. Present Value of an Ordinary Annuity of 1
V. Present Value of an Annuity Due of 1

TIP: There are two approaches to solving problems involving present value or future value of a single sum; there is only one approach available for solving annuity problems.

(1)	(2)		
_____	_____	1.	$1,000 is put on deposit today to earn 6% interest, compounded annually. How much will be on deposit at the end of 8 years?
_____	_____	2.	What amount today is equivalent to receiving $600 at the end of every year for 6 years, assuming interest is compounded annually at the rate of 5%?
_____	_____	3.	If you wish to be able to withdraw the sum of $8,000 at the end of 12 years, how much do you have to deposit today, assuming interest is compounded annually at the rate of 6%?
_____	_____	4.	If $400 is put in a savings account at the end of every year for 5 years, how much will be accumulated in the account if all amounts that remain on deposit earn 6% interest, compounded annually?
_____	_____	5.	What amount today is equivalent to receiving $1,000 ten years from now if interest of 7% is compounded annually?
_____	_____	6.	What amount today is equivalent to receiving $1,000 at the end of each year for ten years if interest of 7% is compounded annually?
_____	_____	7.	How much must be deposited today to allow for the withdrawal of $1,000 at the end of each year for ten years if interest of 7% is compounded annually?
_____	_____	8.	What is the present value of $500 due in 8 years at 6% compounded interest?
_____	_____	9.	What is the future value of an ordinary annuity of $100 per period for 6 years at 7% compounded interest?
_____	_____	10.	How much money must be deposited today to be able to withdraw $700 at the end of 7 years, assuming 7% compounded interest?
_____	_____	11.	How much money must be deposited today to be able to withdraw $700 at the beginning of each of 7 years, assuming 7% compounded interest?
_____	_____	12.	What is the discounted value of $700 due in 7 years at a 7% compounded interest rate?
_____	_____	13.	What is the future value of $700 put on deposit now for 7 years at 7% compounded interest?
_____	_____	14.	What is the future value in seven years of $700 put on deposit at the end of each of 7 years if all amounts on deposit earn 7% compound interest?

_____ _____ 15. How much can be withdrawn at the end of 5 years if $1,000 is deposited now at a 6% compound interest rate?

_____ _____ 16. What amount can be withdrawn at the end of each period for five years if $1,000 is deposited now and all amounts on deposit earn 6% interest compounded annually?

_____ _____ 17. If a debt of $5,000 is to be repaid in five equal beginning-of-year installments, what is the amount of each installment if interest at 7% is charged on the unpaid balance?

_____ _____ 18. What amount must be deposited at the end of each of four years to accumulate a fund of $7,000 at the end of the fourth year, assuming interest at a rate of 6% compounded annually?

Solution to Exercise 6-1

1.	I	M	or	II	D
2.	IV	M			
3.	II	M	or	I	D
4.	III	M			
5.	II	M	or	I	D
6.	IV	M			
7.	IV	M			
8.	II	M	or	I	D
9.	III	M			
10.	II	M	or	I	D
11.	V	M			
12.	II	M	or	I	D
13.	I	M	or	II	D
14.	III	M			
15.	I	M	or	II	D
16.	IV	D			
17.	V	D			
18.	III	D			

Approach and Explanation: Draw a time diagram and place each fact given in the appropriate position on the diagram. Determine what is to be solved for in the question. Think about the content of each of the five compound interest tables included at the end of this chapter. Review the use of the interest factors as summarized in **Illustration 6-2**. The titles and the contents of the five interest tables are as follows:

1. **Future Value of 1 Table.** Contains the amount to which $1 will accumulate if deposited now at a specified rate of interest and left for a specified number of periods (Table 6-1).
2. **Present Value of 1 Table.** Contains the amount that must be deposited now at a specified rate of interest to equal $1 at the end of a specified number of periods (Table 6-2).

3. **Future Value of an Ordinary Annuity of 1 Table.** Contains the amount to which periodic rents of $1 will accumulate if the payments (rents) are invested at the **end** of each period at a specified rate of interest for a specified number of periods (Table 6-3).
4. **Present Value of an Ordinary Annuity of 1 Table.** Contains the amount that must be deposited now at a specified rate of interest to permit withdrawals of $1 at the **end** of regular periodic intervals for the specified number of periods (Table 6-4).
5. **Present Value of an Annuity Due of 1 Table.** Contains the amount that must be deposited now at a specified rate of interest to permit withdrawals of $1 at the **beginning** of regular periodic intervals for the specified number of periods (Table 6-5).

EXERCISE 6-2

Purpose: (L.O.5,6,7) This exercise will illustrate some key concepts such as (1) the more frequently interest is compounded, the more interest will accumulate; (2) the greater the interest rate, the lower the present value will be; and (3) there is more interest reflected in an annuity due situation than in an ordinary annuity situation.

Instructions

Answer each of the questions below following the steps outlined in **Illustration 6-1**. Interest tables are included at the end of this chapter. Use the appropriate factors where needed.

There are a wide variety of situations in which present value and/or future value concepts must be applied. A few of them are illustrated in the questions that follow.

1. If $1,000 is put on deposit today to earn 6% interest, how much will be on deposit at the end of 10 years if interest is compounded annually?

2. If $1,000 is put on deposit today to earn 6% interest, how much will be on deposit at the end of 10 years if interest is compounded semiannually?

3. In comparing questions 1 and 2, which answer would you expect to be the larger? Why?

4. What is the value today of $1,000 due 10 years in the future if the time value of money is 6% and interest is compounded once annually?

5. What is the value today of $1,000 due 10 years in the future if the time value of money is 6% and interest is compounded semiannually?

6. In comparing questions 4 and 5, which answer would you expect to be the larger? Why?

7. What is the present value of $1,000 due in 10 years if interest is compounded annually at 10%?

8. What is the present value of $1,000 due in 10 years if interest is compounded annually at 8%?

9. In comparing questions 7 and 8, which answer would you expect to be the larger? Why?

10. If $1,000 is deposited at the end of each year for 10 years and all amounts on deposit draw 6% interest compounded annually, how much will be on deposit at the end of 10 years?

11. If $1,000 is deposited at the beginning of each year for 10 years and all amounts on deposit draw 6% interest compounded annually, how much will be on deposit at the end of 10 years?

12. In comparing questions 10 and 11, which answer would you expect to be the larger? Why?

Solution to Exercise 6-2

1. (1) This is a future value of a single sum problem.
   (2) $n = 10$; $i = 6\%$.

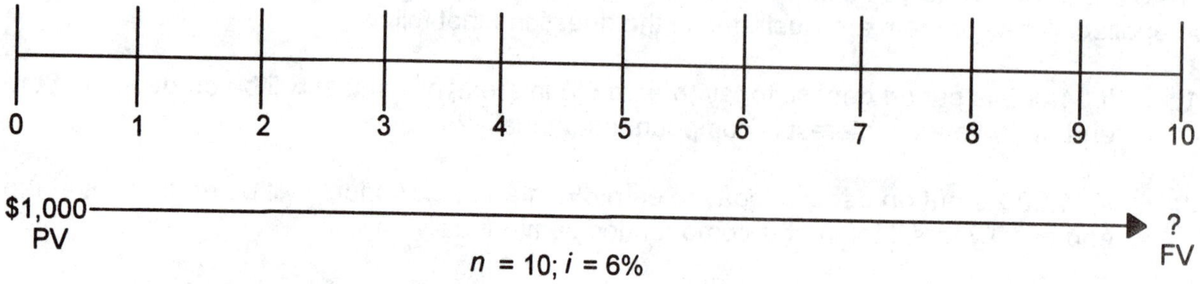

   (3) The interest factor from Table 6-1 is 1.79085.
   (4) Future Value = Present Value x $FVF_{n,i}$
   Future Value = $1,000 x 1.79085
   Future Value = $1,790.85

2. (1) This is a future value of a single sum problem.
   (2) $n = 10 \times 2 = 20$; $i = 6\% \div 2 = 3\%$

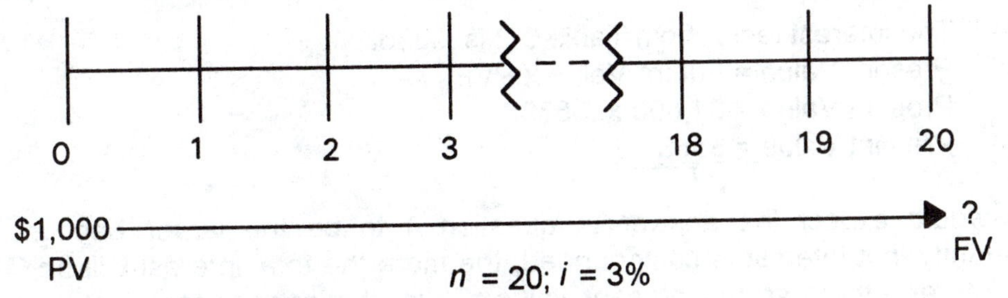

(3) The interest factor from Table 6-1 is 1.80611.
(4) Future Value = Present Value x $FVF_{n,i}$
Future Value = $1,000 x 1.80611
Future Value = $1,806.11

3. We would expect the answer to question 2 to be a little larger than the answer to question 1 because the interest is compounded more frequently in question 2 which means there will be a larger amount of accumulated interest by the end of year 10 in this scenario.

4. (1) This is a present value of a single sum problem.
(2) $n = 10$; $i = 6\%$.

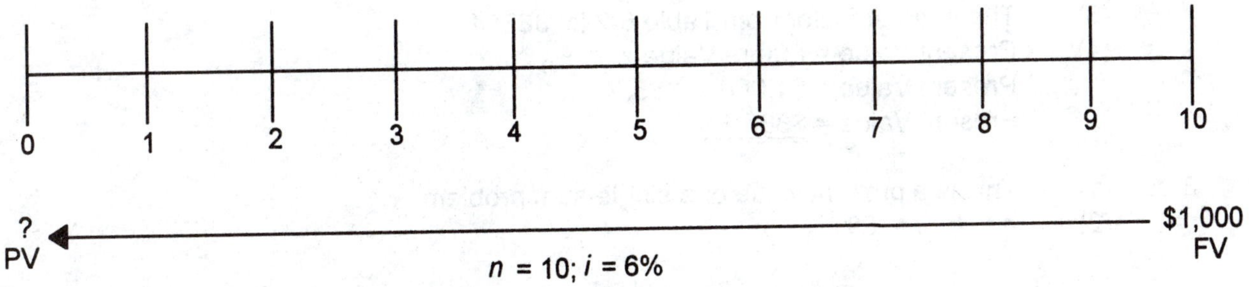

(3) The interest factor from Table 6-2 is .55839.
(4) Present Value = Future Value x $PVF_{n,i}$
Present Value = $1,000 x .55839
Present Value = $558.39

5. (1) This is a present value of single sum problem.
(2) $n = 10 \times 2 = 20$; $i = 6\% \div 2 = 3\%$

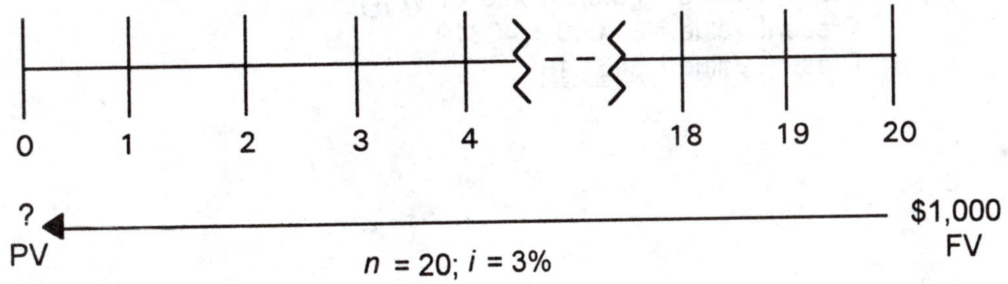

(3) The interest factor from Table 6-2 is .55368.

(4) Present Value = Future Value x $PVF_{n,i}$

Present Value = $1,000 x .55368

Present Value = <u>$553.68</u>

6. We would expect the answer to question 4 to be the larger because the more frequently that interest is compounded, the more the total interest will be. The greater the interest, the less the present value. Thus, the answer to question 5 has more interest reflected and a lesser present value figure.

7. (1) This is a present value of a single-sum problem.

(2) *n* = 10; *i* = 10%

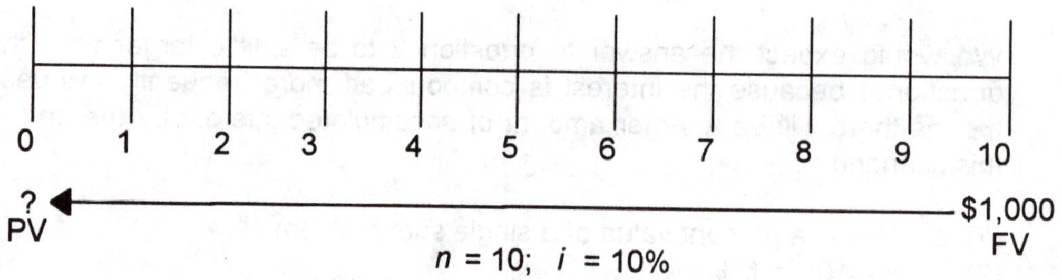

(3) The interest factor from Table 6-2 is .38554.

(4) Present Value = Future Value x $PVF_{n,i}$

Present Value = $1,000 x .38554

Present Value = <u>$385.54</u>

8. (1) This is a present value of a single-sum problem.

(2) *n* = 10; *i* = 8%

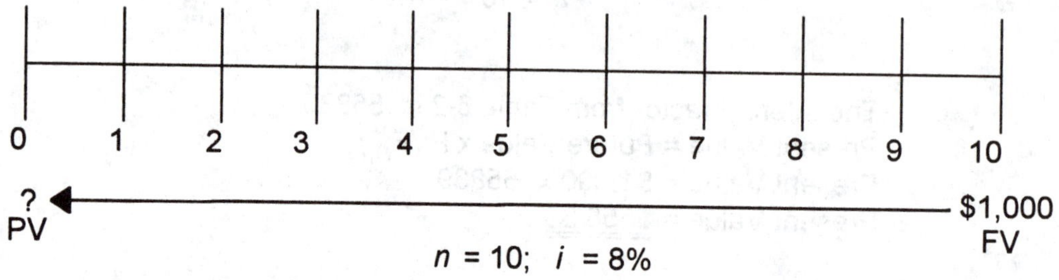

(3) The interest factor from Table 6-2 is .46319.

(4) Present Value = Future Value x $PVF_{n,i}$

Present Value = $1,000 x .46319

Present Value = <u>$463.19</u>

9. We would expect the answer to question 8 to be the larger because the smaller the discount rate, the larger the present value. This is the case because the interest amount is smaller. The less the interest, the greater the present value figure.

10. (1) This is a future value of an ordinary annuity problem.
(2) $n = 10$; $i = 6\%$

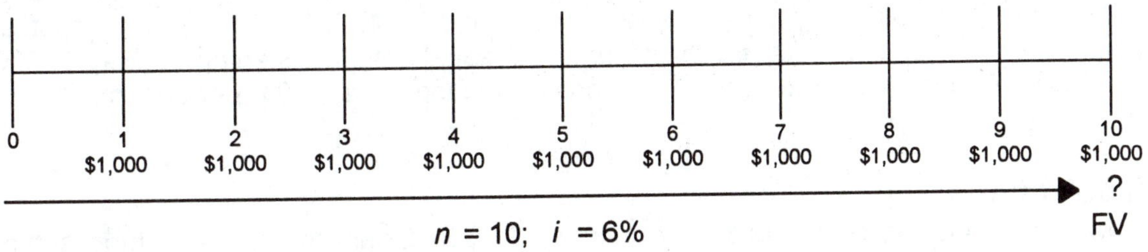

(3) The interest factor from Table 6-3 is 13.18079.
(4) Future Value of an Ordinary Annuity = Rent x FVF-OA$_{n,i}$
Future Value of an Ordinary Annuity = $1,000 x 13.18079
Future Value of an Ordinary Annuity = $13,180.79

11. (1) This is a future value of an annuity due problem.
(2) $n = 10$; $i = 6\%$

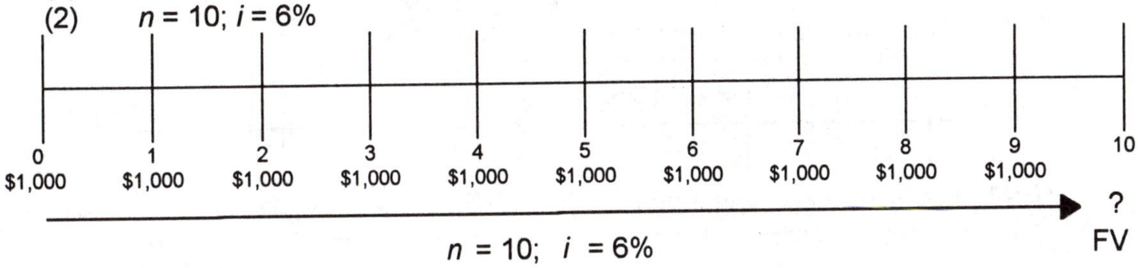

(3) The interest factor can be derived as follows:

FVF-OA for $n = 10$, $i = 6\%$	13.18079
Multiply by $(1 + i)$	x 1.06
FVF-AD for $n = 10$, i = 6%	13.97164

(4) Future Value of an Annuity Due = Rent x FVF-AD$_{n,i}$
Future Value of an Annuity Due = $1,000 x 13.97164
Future Value of an Annuity Due = $13,971.64

12. We would expect the answer to question 11 to be the larger because there is one more interest period reflected in the annuity due arrangement. The number of rents are the same, the interest rate is the same, but the rents begin earlier in the annuity due setup so there is one more interest period reflected.

TIP: In computing the **future amount** of an **ordinary annuity**, the number of compounding periods is **one less** than the number of rents. In computing the **future amount** of an **annuity due**, the number of compounding periods is the **same** as the number of rents. On the other hand, in computing the **present value** of an **ordinary annuity**, the final rent is discounted back the **same** number of periods that there are rents. In computing the **present value** of an **annuity due**, there is **one less** discount period than there are rents.

EXERCISE 6-3

Purpose: (L.O.5,6) This exercise will exemplify a situation that requires a two-part solution.

Judson Green borrowed $90,000 on May 1, 1999. This amount plus accrued interest at 12% compounded semiannually is to be repaid in total on May 1, 2009. To retire this debt, Judson plans to contribute to a debt retirement fund four equal amounts starting on May 1, 2005 and continuing for the next three years. The fund is expected to earn 10% per annum.

Instructions

How much must be contributed each year by Judson Green to provide a fund sufficient to retire the debt on May 1, 2009?

Solution to Exercise 6-3

Amount to be repaid on May 1, 2009:
Time diagram:

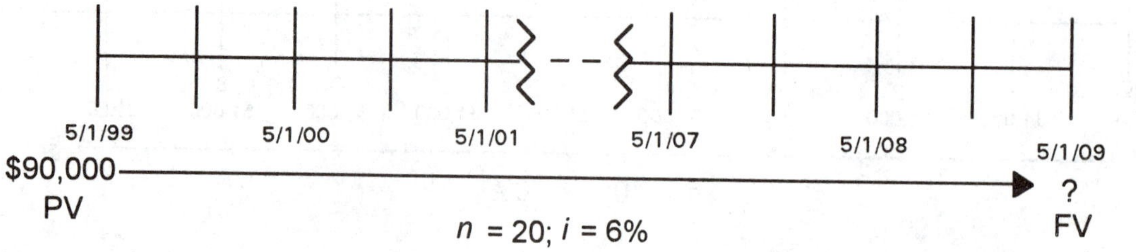

Future Value = $90,000 x $FVF_{n,i}$
Future Value = $90,000 x 3.20714
Future Value = $288,642.60

Amount of annual contribution to retirement fund:
Time diagram:

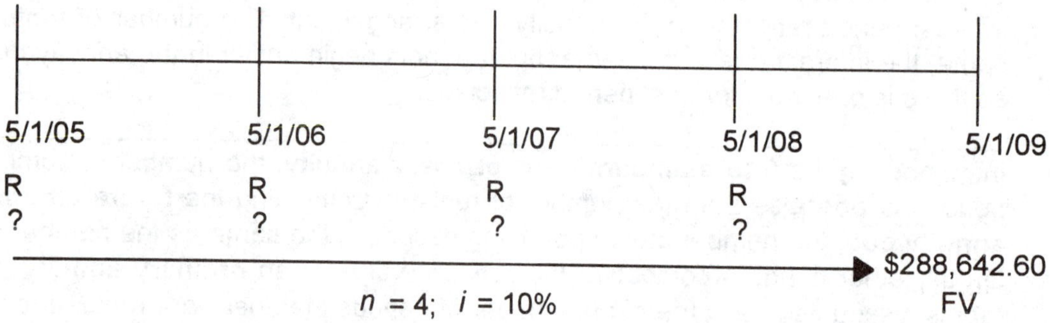

R = rent; FV = future value

Future value of ordinary annuity of 1 for 4 periods at 10%	4.64100
Multiplied by (1 + *i*)	x 1.10
Future value of annuity due of 1 for 4 periods at 10%	5.10510

Future value of an annuity due = Rent x FVF-$AD_{n,i}$
\$288,642.60 = Rent x 5.10510
\$288,642.60 ÷ 5.10510 = Rent
Rent = \$56,540.05

Approach: First solve for the future value of a single sum. This future amount is \$288,642.60. Then solve for the rent reflected in the future value of an ordinary annuity. The rent is \$56,540.05. The solution to the first part establishes the future value of an ordinary annuity for which the rent must be determined in the second part of the problem.

EXERCISE 6-4

Purpose: (L.O.5,6,7) This exercise will illustrate how to solve present value problems that require the computation of the rent in an annuity or the number of periods or the interest rate.

Instructions

Using the appropriate interest table, provide the solution to each of the following four questions by computing the unknowns.

(a) Jimmy Gunshanan has \$5,000 to invest today at 5% to pay a debt of \$7,387. How many years will it take him to accumulate enough to liquidate the debt if interest is compounded once annually?

(b) Jimmy's friend Nathan has a \$6,312.40 debt that he wishes to repay four years from today. He intends to invest \$5,000.00 for four years and use the accumulated funds to liquidate the debt. What rate of interest will he need to earn annually in order to accumulate enough to pay the debt if interest is compounded annually?

(c) Jason Zahner wishes to accumulate \$35,000 to use for a trip around the world. He plans to gather the designated sum by depositing payments into an account at Sun Bank which pays 4% interest, compounded annually. What is the amount of each payment that Jason must make at the end of each of six years to accumulate a fund balance of \$35,000 by the end of the sixth year?

(d) Your sister is twenty years old today and she wishes to accumulate \$900,000 by her fifty-fifth birthday so she can retire to her summer place on Lake Tahoe. She wishes to accumulate the \$900,000 by making annual deposits on her twentieth through her fifty-fourth birthdays. What annual deposit must your sister make if the fund will earn 8% interest compounded annually?

Solution to Exercise 6-4

(a) Time diagram:

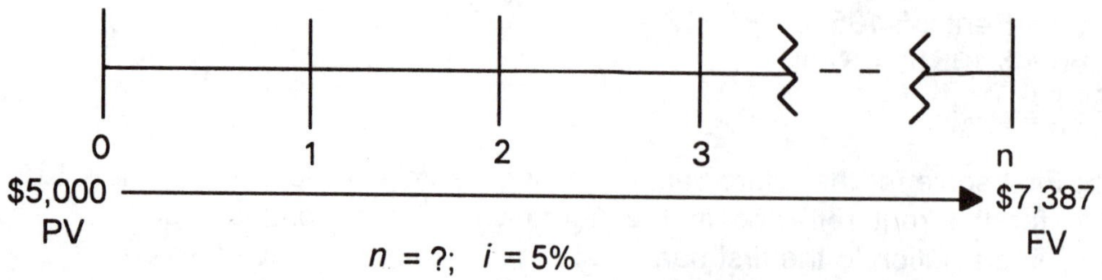

Future Value Approach
Future value = Present value x $FVF_{n,i}$
$7,387.00 = $5,000 x $FVF_{n,i}$
1.4774 = FV factor for i = 5%, n = ?
By reference to Table 6-1, 1.47746 is the FV factor for i = 5%, n = 8
n = 8 years

OR

Present Value Approach
Present value = Future value x $PVF_{n,i}$
$5,000.00 = $7,387 x $PVF_{n,i}$
.67686 = PV factor for i = 5%, n = ?
By reference to Table 6-2, .67684 is the PV factor for i = 5%, n = 8
n = 8 years

(b) Time diagram:

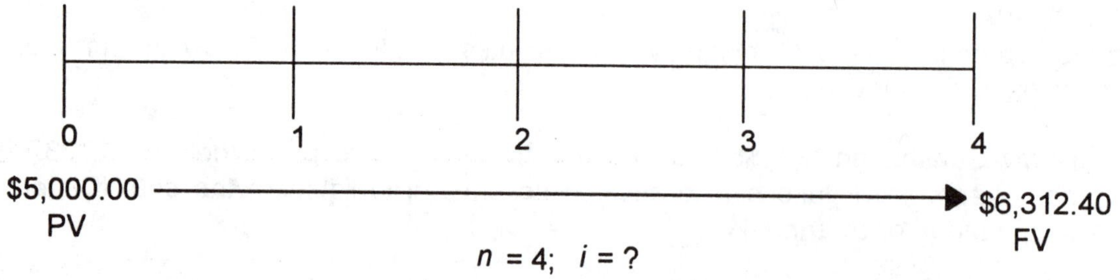

Future Value Approach
Future value = Present value x $FVF_{n,i}$
$6,312.40 = $5,000.00 x $FVF_{n,i}$
1.26248 = FV factor for n = 4, i = ?
By reference to Table 6-1, 1.26248 is the FV factor for n = 4, i = 6%.
i = 6%

OR

Present Value Approach
Present value = Future value x PVFn,i
$5,000.00 = $6,312.40 x PVF$n,i$
.79209 = PV factor for n = 4, i = ?
By reference to Table 6-2, .79209 is the PV factor for n = 4, i = 6%.
i = 6%

(c) Time diagram:

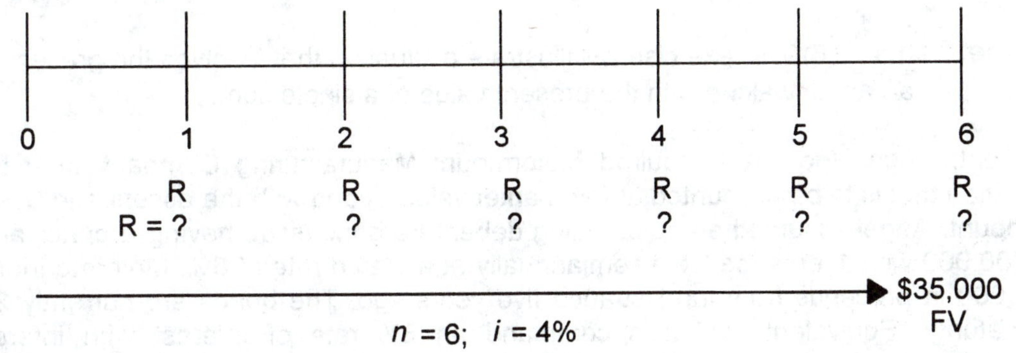

Future Value = Rent x FVF-OA$_{n,i}$
$35,000 = Rent x 6.63298
$35,000 ÷ 6.63298 = Rent
$5,276.66 = Rent

(d) Time diagram:

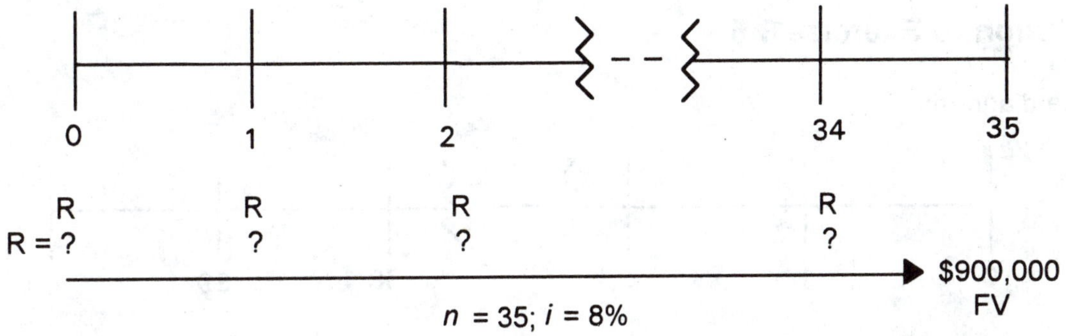

Future value of an ordinary annuity due of 1 for 35 periods at 8%	172.31680
Multiplied by (1 + i)	x 1.08
Future value of annuity due of 1 for 35 periods at 8%	186.10214

Future value of annuity due = Rent x FVF-AD$n,i$
$900,000 = Rent x 186.10214
$900,000 ÷ 186.10214 = Rent
$4,836.05 = Rent

EXERCISE 6-5

Purpose: (L.O.5,6) This exercise will illustrate a situation that involves the present value of an annuity along with the present value of a single sum.

Your client, Angel, Inc., has acquired Motormount Manufacturing Company in a business combination that is to be accounted at fair market value. Along with the assets and business of Motormount, Angel assumed an outstanding debenture bond issue having a principal amount of $5,000,000 with interest payable semiannually at a stated rate of 6%. Motormount received $5,800,000 in proceeds from the issuance five years ago. The bonds are currently 20 years from maturity. Equivalent securities command an 8% rate of interest with interest paid semiannually.

Instructions

Your client requests your advice regarding the amount to record as the fair value (present value) of the acquired bond issue.

Solution to Exercise 6-5

Time diagram:

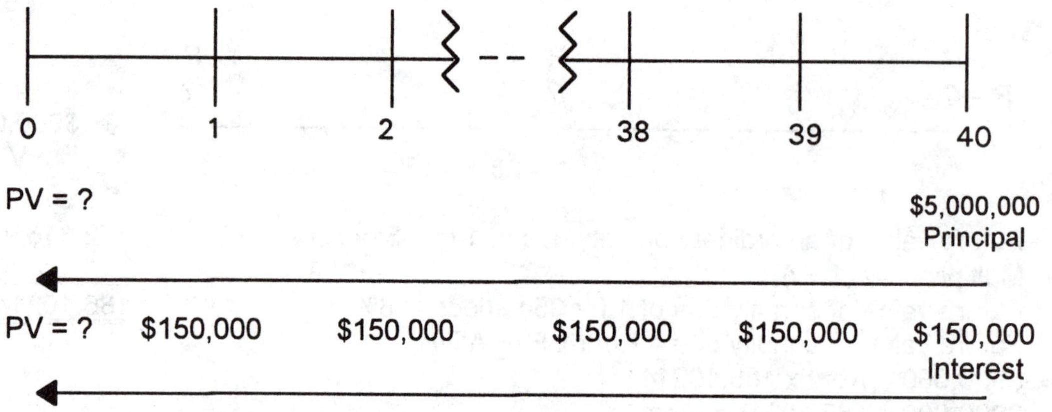

n = 40 six-month periods; *i* = 4% per six-month period

Present value of the principal = $5,000,000 x .20829	$ 1,041,450.00
Present value of the interest payments = $150,000 x 19.79277	2,968,915.50
Total present value of bond liability	$ 4,010,365.50

Approach and Explanation: Draw a time diagram and enter all future cash flows where they belong. The fair value of the bond liability being acquired by Angel is determined by discounting all of the future cash flows related to the bond issue back to the present date using the current market rate of interest (4% per six-month interest period). The face amount of the bonds ($5,000,000) is a single sum due in 20 years (40 semiannual periods). The interest payments constitute an ordinary annuity for forty semiannual periods. Each interest payment is computed by multiplying the stated rate (3% per interest period) by the face amount of the bonds ($5,000,000).

ANALYSIS OF MULTIPLE-CHOICE TYPE QUESTIONS

QUESTION

1. (L.O.3,7) A grandfather wishes to set up a fund today that will allow his grandson to withdraw $5,000 from the fund at the beginning of each year for four years to pay for college expenses. The first withdrawal is to occur later today. How should grandpa compute the required investment if the fund is to earn 6% interest compounded annually and the fund is to be exhausted by his last withdrawal?
   a. $5,000 multiplied by the factor for the present value of an annuity due of 1 where $n = 4$, $i = 6\%$.
   b. $5,000 divided by the factor for the present value of an annuity due of 1 where $n = 4$, $i = 6\%$.
   c. $5,000 multiplied by the factor for the future amount of an annuity due of 1 where $n = 4$, $i = 6\%$.
   d. $5,000 divided by the factor for the future amount of an annuity due of 1 where $n = 4$, $i = 6\%$.

Approach and Explanation: Follow the steps in solving future value and present value problems:

1. This is a present value of an annuity due problem.
2. Time diagram:

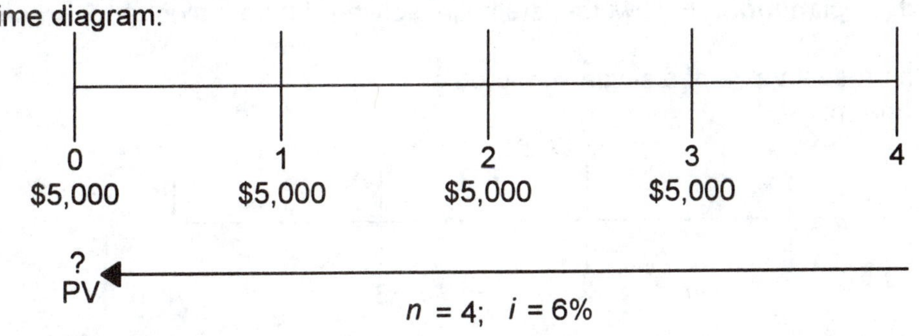

3. The factor for present value of annuity due for $n = 4$, $i = 6\%$ can be found in Table 5; it can also be derived by multiplying the factor for $n = 4$, $i = 6\%$ from the table for present value of an ordinary annuity times $1 + i$.
4. Present Value of an Annuity Due = Rent x Present Value of an Annuity Due Factor.

Therefore, the present value of the annuity due equals $5,000 multiplied by the factor for present value of an annuity due for $n = 4$, $i = 6\%$. (Solution = a.)

Questions 2 and 3 use the following present value table. Given below are the present value factors for $1.00 discounted at 9% for one to five periods.

Periods	Present Value of $1 i = 9?
1	.91743
2	.84168
3	.77218
4	.70843
5	.64993

QUESTION

2. (L.O.3,5) What amount should be deposited in a bank account today if a balance of $1,000 is desired four years from today and the prevailing interest rate is 9%?
   a. $1,000 x .91743 x 4
   b. $1,000 x .70843
   c. $1,000 ÷ .70843
   d. $1,000 x (.91743 + .84168 + .77218 + .70843)

Approach and Explanation: Follow the steps in solving future value and present value problems:

1. This is a present value of a single sum problem.
2. Time diagram:

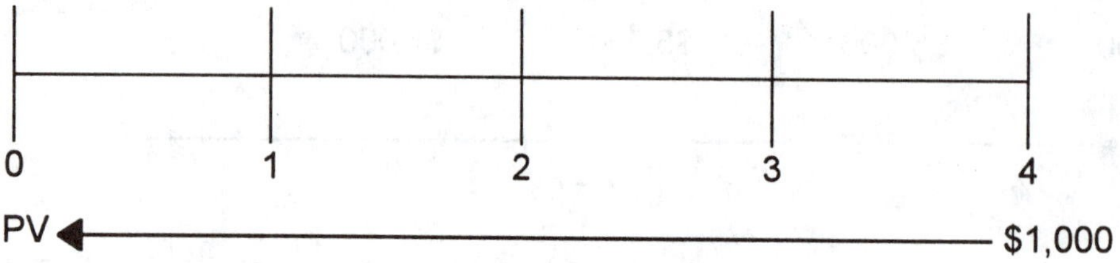

n = 4; i = 9%

3. The present value factor is .70843 for n = 4, i = 9%.
4. Present Value = Future Value x PV Factor
   Present Value = $1,000 x .70843 (Solution = b.)

QUESTION

3. (L.O.3,5) If $1,000 is deposited today to earn 9% interest compounded annually, how much will be on deposit at the end of three years?
   a. $1,000 x .77218
   b. $1,000 ÷ .77218
   c. ($1,000 ÷ .91743) x 3
   d. ($1,000 ÷ .77218) x 3

Approach and Explanation:

1. This is a future value of a single sum problem.
2. Time diagram:

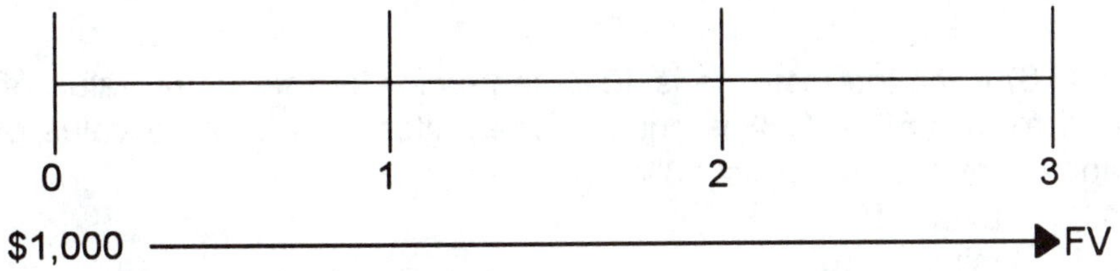

$n = 3$; $i = 9\%$

3. The future value factor is not given; however, for a single sum, the future value factor is the inverse of the present value factor. Therefore, 1.00000 divided by the present value factor for $n = 3$, $i = 9\%$ equals the future value factor for $n = 3$, $i = 9\%$.
4. Future Value = Present Value x FV Factor
   Future Value = $1,000 x (1 ÷ .77218)
   Future Value = $1,000 ÷ .77218 (Solution = b.)

> **TIP:** By looking at the time diagram, you can reason out that the amount on deposit at the end of three years should be greater than $1,000 but less than $1,500 (three years of 9% simple interest would give a balance of $1,270 and the compounding process would yield a little higher figure). In looking at the alternative answers, you can see that selection "a" will yield a result that is less than $1,000; selection "b" will give a result close to $1,300; selection "c" will give a result close to $3,200; and selection "d" will yield a result that is close to $3,900. Therefore, a reasonableness test would show that answer selection "b" must be the correct choice.

QUESTION

4. (L.O.4) In the time diagram below, which concept is being depicted?

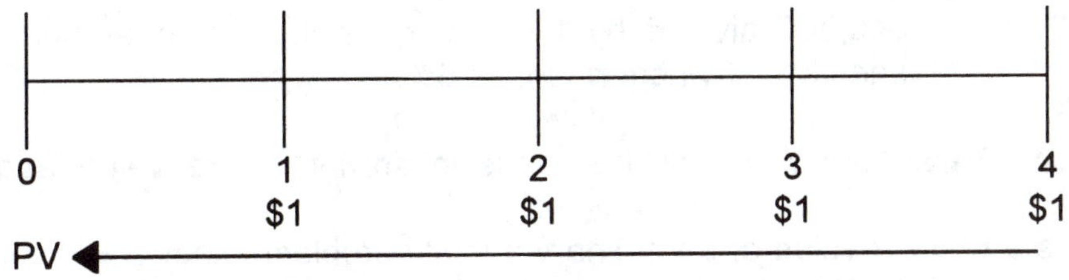

a. Present value of an ordinary annuity
b. Present value of an annuity due
c. Future value of an ordinary annuity
d. Future value of an annuity due

Explanation: It is an annuity since there is a series of equal periodic payments or receipts. The annuity is an ordinary one because the payments are due at the **end** (not the beginning) of each period. The arrow is drawn so that it is headed back to the present rather than forward to the future. Thus, we have a present value problem. (Solution = a.)

QUESTION

5. (L.O.6) If the interest rate is 10%, the factor for the future value of annuity due of 1 for n = 5, i = 10% is equal to the factor for the future value of an ordinary annuity of 1 for n = 5, i = 10%:
   a. plus 1.10.
   b. minus 1.10.
   c. multiplied by 1.10.
   d. divided by 1.10.

Explanation: All amounts involved in an annuity due come in exactly one period earlier than for an ordinary annuity. Therefore, all of the rents and accumulated interest are allowed to generate interest for one more period in the annuity due case. (Solution = c.)

QUESTION

6. (L.O.7) A grandmother is setting up a savings account to help fund her granddaughter's college expenses. She is putting $40,000 in an account today that will earn 6% interest compounded annually. How much may Josey, the granddaughter, withdraw at the beginning of each of four years of college if her first withdrawal is to be one year from today and her last withdrawal is to exhaust the fund? The answer would be determined by which one of the following?
   a. $40,000 multiplied by the factor for the present value of an ordinary annuity of 1 where n = 4, i = 6%.
   b. $40,000 divided by the factor for the present value of an ordinary annuity of 1 where n = 4, i = 6%.
   c. $40,000 multiplied by the factor for the future amount of an ordinary annuity of 1 where n = 4, i = 6%.
   d. $40,000 divided by the factor for the future amount of an ordinary annuity of 1 where n = 4, i = 6%.

Approach and Explanation: Follow the steps in solving future value and present value problems.

1. This is a present value of an ordinary annuity problem although by the wording of the question it could easily be confused with an annuity due situation. There are four rents and the first one is to be received a year from today.

2. Time diagram:

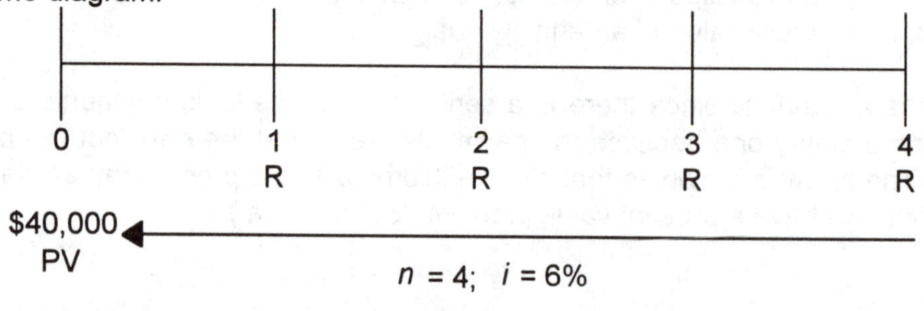

3. The factor for present value of an ordinary annuity for n = 4, i = 6% would be obtained from Table 6-4.
4. Present Value of an Ordinary Annuity = Rent x Present Value of an Ordinary Annuity Factor. The Rent would be determined by dividing both sides of the equation by the factor. Therefore, the rent would equal the $40,000 divided by the factor for the present value of an ordinary annuity of 1. (Solution = b.)

QUESTION

7. (L.O.4) On December 1, 1999, Michael Hess Company sold some machinery to Shawn Keling Company. The two companies entered into an installment sales contract at a predetermined interest rate. The contract required four equal annual payments with the first payment due on December 1, 1999, the date of the sale. What present value concept is appropriate for this situation?
   a. Future amount of an annuity of 1 for four periods
   b. Future amount of 1 for four periods
   c. Present value of an ordinary annuity of 1 for four periods
   d. Present value of an annuity due of 1 for four periods.

Explanation: There is a series of equal payments due at the first of each period (year) because the first payment is due at the date of the sale (December 1, 1999); hence, this is an annuity due. The relevant amount to solve for would be the present value of the annuity; this present value would be involved in the determination of the sale (or purchase) price of the machinery. (Solution = d.)

QUESTION

8. (L.O.4) On May 1, 1999, a company purchased a new machine that it does not have to pay for until May 1, 2001. The total payment on May 1, 2001 will include both principal and accumulated interest. Assuming interest is computed at a 10% rate compounded annually, the total payment due will be the price of the machine multiplied by what time value of money factor?
   a. Future value of 1
   b. Future value of an ordinary annuity of 1
   c. Present value of 1
   d. Present value of an ordinary annuity of 1

Explanation: The total payment due will be the price today (present value) plus the interest that will accumulate in two years. In computing the future value of a given amount today, the given amount is multiplied by a future value of 1 factor. (Solution = a.)

QUESTION

9. (L.O.3) A series of equal receipts at equal intervals of time when each receipt is received at the beginning of each time period is called an:
   a. ordinary annuity.
   b. annuity in arrears.
   c. annuity due.
   d. unearned receipt.

Explanation: A series of equal receipts or payments at equal intervals is called an annuity. An ordinary annuity is an annuity where the rents (receipts or payments) occur at the **end** of each period; another name for an **ordinary annuity** is an **annuity in arrears**. An annuity due is one where the first rent occurs at the **beginning** of the first period; another name for an **annuity due** is an **annuity in advance**. (Solution = c.)

QUESTION

10. (L.O.5) Which of the following statements is **true**?
    a. The higher the discount rate, the higher the present value.
    b. The process of accumulating interest on interest is referred to as discounting.
    c. If money is worth 10% compounded annually, $1,100 due one year from today is equivalent to $1,000 today.
    d. If a single sum is due on December 31, 2002, the present value of that sum decreases as the date draws closer to December 31, 2002.

Explanation: Selection "a" is false because the higher the discount rate the lower the present value. Selection "b" is false because the process of accumulating interest on interest is referred to as compounding; discounting refers to the process of computing present value. Selection "d" is false because the present value of a single sum increases over time due to the time value of money (accumulation of interest). Selection "c" is correct because 10% of $1,000 is $100 interest; $1,000 today plus interest of $100 for one year means $1,100 one year from today is equivalent to $1,000 today if money is worth 10%. (Solution = c.)

Table 6-1 FUTURE VALUE OF 1 (FUTURE VALUE OF A SINGLE SUM)

$$FVF_{n,i} = (1 + i)^n$$

(n) Periods	2%	2-1/2%	3%	4%	5%	6%
1	1.02000	1.02500	1.03000	1.04000	1.05000	1.06000
2	1.04040	1.05063	1.06090	1.08160	1.10250	1.12360
3	1.06121	1.07689	1.09273	1.12486	1.15763	1.19102
4	1.08243	1.10381	1.12551	1.16986	1.21551	1.26248
5	1.10408	1.13141	1.15927	1.21665	1.27628	1.33823
6	1.12616	1.15969	1.19405	1.26532	1.34010	1.41852
7	1.14869	1.18869	1.22987	1.31593	1.40710	1.50363
8	1.17166	1.21840	1.26677	1.36857	1.47746	1.59385
9	1.19509	1.24886	1.30477	1.42331	1.55133	1.68948
10	1.21899	1.28008	1.34392	1.48024	1.62889	1.79085
11	1.24337	1.31209	1.38423	1.53945	1.71034	1.89830
12	1.26824	1.34489	1.42576	1.60103	1.79586	2.01220
13	1.29361	1.37851	1.46853	1.66507	1.88565	2.13293
14	1.31948	1.41297	1.51259	1.73168	1.97993	2.26090
15	1.34587	1.44830	1.55797	1.80094	2.07893	2.39656
16	1.37279	1.48451	1.60471	1.87298	2.18287	2.54035
17	1.40024	1.52162	1.65285	1.94790	2.29202	2.69277
18	1.42825	1.55966	1.70243	2.02582	2.40662	2.85434
19	1.45681	1.59865	1.75351	2.10685	2.52695	3.02560
20	1.48595	1.63862	1.80611	2.19112	2.65330	3.20714
21	1.51567	1.67958	1.86029	2.27877	2.78596	3.39956
22	1.54598	1.72157	1.91610	2.36992	2.92526	3.60354
23	1.57690	1.76461	1.97359	2.46472	3.07152	3.81975
24	1.60844	1.80873	2.03279	2.56330	3.22510	4.04893
25	1.64061	1.85394	2.09378	2.66584	3.38635	4.29187
26	1.67342	1.90029	2.15659	2.77247	3.55567	4.54938
27	1.70689	1.94780	2.22129	2.88337	3.73346	4.82235
28	1.74102	1.99650	2.28793	2.99870	3.92013	5.11169
29	1.77584	2.04641	2.35657	3.11865	4.11614	5.41839
30	1.81136	2.09757	2.42726	3.24340	4.32194	5.74349
31	1.84759	2.15001	2.50008	3.37313	4.53804	6.08810
32	1.88454	2.20376	2.57508	3.50806	4.76494	6.45339
33	1.92223	2.25885	2.65234	3.64838	5.00319	6.84059
34	1.96068	2.31532	2.73191	3.79432	5.25335	7.25103
35	1.99989	2.37321	2.81386	3.94609	5.51602	7.68609
36	2.03989	2.43254	2.89828	4.10393	5.79182	8.14725
37	2.08069	2.49335	2.98523	4.26809	6.08141	8.63609
38	2.12230	2.55568	3.07478	4.43881	6.38548	9.15425
39	2.16474	2.61957	3.16703	4.61637	6.70475	9.70351
40	2.20804	2.68506	3.26204	4.80102	7.03999	10.28572

8%	9%	10%	11%	12%	15%	(n) Periods
1.08000	1.09000	1.10000	1.11000	1.12000	1.15000	1
1.16640	1.18810	1.21000	1.23210	1.25440	1.32250	2
1.25971	1.29503	1.33100	1.36763	1.40493	1.52088	3
1.36049	1.41158	1.46410	1.51807	1.57352	1.74901	4
1.46933	1.53862	1.61051	1.68506	1.76234	2.01136	5
1.58687	1.67710	1.77156	1.87041	1.97382	2.31306	6
1.71382	1.82804	1.94872	2.07616	2.21068	2.66002	7
1.85093	1.99256	2.14359	2.30454	2.47596	3.05902	8
1.99900	2.17189	2.35795	2.55803	2.77308	3.51788	9
2.15892	2.36736	2.59374	2.83942	3.10585	4.04556	10
2.33164	2.58043	2.85312	3.15176	3.47855	4.65239	11
2.51817	2.81267	3.13843	3.49845	3.89598	5.35025	12
2.71962	3.06581	3.45227	3.88328	4.36349	6.15279	13
2.93719	3.34173	3.79750	4.31044	4.88711	7.07571	14
3.17217	3.64248	4.17725	4.78459	5.47357	8.13706	15
3.42594	3.97031	4.59497	5.31089	6.13039	9.35762	16
3.70002	4.32763	5.05447	5.89509	6.86604	10.76162	17
3.99602	4.71712	5.55992	6.54355	7.68997	12.37545	18
4.31570	5.14166	6.11591	7.26334	8.61276	14.23177	19
4.66096	5.60441	6.72750	8.06231	9.64629	16.36654	20
5.03383	6.10881	7.40025	8.94917	10.80385	18.82152	21
5.43654	6.65860	8.14028	9.93357	12.10031	21.64475	22
5.87146	7.25787	8.95430	11.02627	13.55235	24.89146	23
6.34118	7.91108	9.84973	12.23916	15.17863	28.62518	24
6.84847	8.62308	10.83471	13.58546	17.00000	32.91895	25
7.39635	9.39916	11.91818	15.07986	19.04007	37.85680	26
7.98806	10.24508	13.10999	16.73865	21.32488	43.53532	27
8.62711	11.16714	14.42099	18.57990	23.88387	50.06561	28
9.31727	12.17218	15.86309	20.62369	26.74993	57.57545	29
10.06266	13.26768	17.44940	22.89230	29.95992	66.21177	30
10.86767	14.46177	19.19434	25.41045	33.55511	76.14354	31
11.73708	15.76333	21.11378	28.20560	37.58173	87.56507	32
12.67605	17.18203	23.22515	31.30821	42.09153	100.69983	33
13.69013	18.72841	25.54767	34.75212	47.14252	115.80480	34
14.78534	20.41397	28.10244	38.57485	52.79962	133.17552	35
15.96817	22.25123	30.91268	42.81808	59.13557	153.15185	36
17.24563	24.25384	34.00395	47.52807	66.23184	176.12463	37
18.62528	26.43668	37.40434	52.75616	74.17966	202.54332	38
20.11530	28.81598	41.14479	58.55934	83.08122	232.92482	39
21.72452	31.40942	45.25926	65.00087	93.05097	267.86355	40

Table 6-2 PRESENT VALUE OF 1 (PRESENT VALUE OF A SINGLE SUM)

$$PVF_{n,i} = \frac{1}{(1+i)^n} = (1+i)^{-n}$$

(n) Periods	2%	2-1/2%	3%	4%	5%	6%
1	.98039	.97561	.97087	.96154	.95238	.94340
2	.96117	.95181	.94260	.92456	.90703	.89000
3	.94232	.92860	.91514	.88900	.86384	.83962
4	.92385	.90595	.88949	.85480	.82270	.79209
5	.90573	.88385	.86261	.82193	.78353	.74726
6	.88797	.86230	.83748	.79031	.74622	.70496
7	.87056	.84127	.81309	.75992	.71068	.66506
8	.85349	.82075	.78941	.73069	.67684	.62741
9	.83676	.80073	.76642	.70259	.64461	.59190
10	.82035	.78120	.74409	.67556	.61391	.55839
11	.80426	.76214	.72242	.64958	.58468	.52679
12	.78849	.74356	.70138	.62460	.55684	.49697
13	.77303	.72542	.68095	.60057	.53032	.46884
14	.75788	.70773	.66112	.57748	.50507	.44230
15	.74301	.69047	.64186	.55526	.48102	.41727
16	.72845	.67362	.62317	.53391	.45811	.39365
17	.71416	.65720	.60502	.51337	.43630	.37136
18	.70016	.64117	.58739	.49363	.41552	.35034
19	.68643	.62553	.57029	.47464	.39573	.33051
20	.67297	.61027	.55368	.45639	.37689	.31180
21	.65978	.59539	.53755	.43883	.35894	.29416
22	.64684	.58086	.52189	.42196	.34185	.27751
23	.63416	.56670	.50669	.40573	.32557	.26180
24	.62172	.55288	.49193	.39012	.31007	.24698
25	.60593	.53939	.47761	.37512	.29530	.23300
26	.59758	.52623	.46369	.36069	.28124	.21981
27	.58586	.51340	.45019	.34682	.26785	.20737
28	.57437	.50088	.43708	.33348	.25509	.19563
29	.56311	.48866	.42435	.32065	.24295	.18456
30	.55207	.47674	.41199	.30832	.23138	.17411
31	.54125	.46511	.39999	.29646	.22036	.16425
32	.53063	.45377	.38834	.28506	.20987	.15496
33	.52023	.44270	.37703	.27409	.19987	.14619
34	.51003	.43191	.36604	.26355	.19035	.13791
35	.50003	.42137	.35538	.25342	.18129	.13011
36	.49022	.41109	.34503	.24367	.17266	.12274
37	.48061	.40107	.33498	.23430	.16444	.11579
38	.47119	.39128	.32523	.22529	.15661	.10924
39	.46195	.38174	.31575	.21662	.14915	.10306
40	.45289	.37243	.30656	.20829	.14205	.09722

8%	9%	10%	11%	12%	15%	(n) Periods
.92593	.91743	.90909	.90090	.89286	.86957	1
.85734	.84168	.82645	.81162	.79719	.75614	2
.79383	.77218	.75132	.73119	.71178	.65752	3
.73503	.70843	.68301	.65873	.63552	.57175	4
.68058	.64993	.62092	.59345	.56743	.49718	5
.63017	.59627	.56447	.53464	.50663	.43233	6
.58349	.54703	.51316	.48166	.45235	.37594	7
.54027	.50187	.46651	.43393	.40388	.32690	8
.50025	.46043	.42410	.39092	.36061	.28426	9
.46319	.42241	.38554	.35218	.32197	.24719	10
.42888	.38753	.35049	.31728	.28748	.21494	11
.39711	.35554	.31863	.28584	.25668	.18691	12
.36770	.32618	.28966	.25751	.22917	.16253	13
.34046	.29925	.26333	.23199	.20462	.14133	14
.31524	.27454	.23939	.20900	.18270	.12289	15
.29189	.25187	.21763	.18829	.16312	.10687	16
.27027	.23107	.19785	.16963	.14564	.09293	17
.25025	.21199	.17986	.15282	.13004	.08081	18
.23171	.19449	.16351	.13768	.11611	.07027	19
.21455	.17843	.14864	.12403	.10367	.06110	20
.19866	.16370	.13513	.11174	.09256	.05313	21
.18394	.15018	.12285	.10067	.08264	.04620	22
.17032	.13778	.11168	.09069	.07379	.04017	23
.15770	.12641	.10153	.08170	.06588	.03493	24
.14602	.11597	.09230	.07361	.05882	.03038	25
.13520	.10639	.08391	.06631	.05252	.02642	26
.12519	.09761	.07628	.05974	.04689	.02297	27
.11591	.08955	.06934	.05382	.04187	.01997	28
.10733	.08216	.06304	.04849	.03738	.01737	29
.09938	.07537	.05731	.04368	.03338	.01510	30
.09202	.06915	.05210	.03935	.02980	.01313	31
.08520	.06344	.04736	.03545	.02661	.01142	32
.07889	.05820	.04306	.03194	.02376	.00993	33
.07305	.05340	.03914	.02878	.02121	.00864	34
.06763	.04899	.03558	.02592	.01894	.00751	35
.06262	.04494	.03235	.02335	.01691	.00653	36
.05799	.04123	.02941	.02104	.01510	.00568	37
.05369	.03783	.02674	.01896	.01348	.00494	38
.04971	.03470	.02430	.01708	.01204	.00429	39
.04603	.03184	.02210	.01538	.01075	.00373	40

Table 6-3 FUTURE VALUE OF AN ORDINARY ANNUITY OF 1

$$FVF\text{-}OA_{n,i} = \frac{(1+i)^n - 1}{i}$$

(n) Periods	2%	2-1/2%	3%	4%	5%	6%
1	1.00000	1.00000	1.00000	1.00000	1.00000	1.00000
2	2.02000	2.02500	2.03000	2.04000	2.05000	2.06000
3	3.06040	3.07563	3.09090	3.12160	3.15250	3.18360
4	4.12161	4.15252	4.18363	4.24646	4.31013	4.37462
5	5.20404	5.25633	5.30914	5.41632	5.52563	5.63709
6	6.30812	6.38774	6.46841	6.63298	6.80191	6.97532
7	7.43428	7.54743	7.66246	7.89829	8.14201	8.39384
8	8.58297	8.73612	8.89234	9.21423	9.54911	9.89747
9	9.75463	9.95452	10.15911	10.58280	11.02656	11.49132
10	10.94972	11.20338	11.46338	12.00611	12.57789	13.18079
11	12.16872	12.48347	12.80780	13.48635	14.20679	14.97164
12	13.41209	13.79555	14.19203	15.02581	15.91713	16.86994
13	14.68033	15.14044	15.61779	16.62684	17.71298	18.88214
14	15.97394	16.51895	17.08632	18.29191	19.59863	21.01507
15	17.29342	17.93193	18.59891	20.02359	21.57856	23.27597
16	18.63929	19.38022	20.15688	21.82453	23.65749	25.67253
17	20.01207	20.86473	21.76159	23.69751	25.84037	28.21288
18	21.41231	22.38635	23.41444	25.64541	28.13238	30.90565
19	22.84056	23.94601	25.11687	27.67123	30.53900	33.75999
20	24.29737	25.54466	26.87037	29.77808	33.06595	36.78559
21	25.78332	27.18327	28.67649	31.96920	35.71925	39.99273
22	27.29898	28.86286	30.53678	34.24797	38.50521	43.39229
23	28.84496	30.58443	32.45288	36.61789	41.43048	46.99583
24	30.42186	32.34904	34.42647	39.08260	44.50200	50.81558
25	32.03030	34.15776	36.45926	41.64591	47.72710	54.86451
26	33.67091	36.01171	38.55304	44.31174	51.11345	59.15638
27	35.34432	37.91200	40.70963	47.08421	54.66913	63.70577
28	37.05121	39.85980	42.93092	49.96758	58.40258	68.52811
29	38.79223	41.85630	45.21885	52.96629	62.32271	73.63980
30	40.56808	43.90270	47.57542	56.08494	66.43885	79.05819
31	42.37944	46.00027	50.00268	59.32834	70.76079	84.80168
32	44.22703	48.15028	52.50276	62.70147	75.29883	90.88978
33	46.11157	50.35403	55.07784	66.20953	80.06377	97.34316
34	48.03380	52.61289	57.73018	69.85791	85.06696	104.18376
35	49.99448	54.92821	60.46208	73.65222	90.32031	111.43478
36	51.99437	57.30141	63.27594	77.59831	95.83632	119.12087
37	54.03425	59.73395	66.17422	81.70225	101.62814	127.26812
38	56.11494	62.22730	69.15945	85.97034	107.70955	135.90421
39	58.23724	64.78298	72.23423	90.40915	114.09502	145.05846
40	60.40198	67.40255	75.40126	95.02552	120.79977	154.76197

8%	9%	10%	11%	12%	15%	(n) Periods
1.00000	1.00000	1.00000	1.00000	1.00000	1.00000	1
2.08000	2.09000	2.10000	2.11000	2.12000	2.15000	2
3.24640	3.27810	3.31000	3.34210	3.37440	3.47250	3
4.50611	4.57313	4.64100	4.70973	4.77933	4.99338	4
5.86660	5.98471	6.10510	6.22780	6.35285	6.74238	5
7.33592	7.52334	7.71561	7.91286	8.11519	8.75374	6
8.92280	9.20044	9.48717	9.78327	10.08901	11.06680	7
10.63663	11.02847	11.43589	11.85943	12.29969	13.72682	8
12.48756	13.02104	13.57948	14.16397	14.77566	16.78584	9
14.48656	15.19293	15.93743	16.72201	17.54874	20.30372	10
16.64549	17.56029	18.53117	19.56143	20.65458	24.34928	11
18.97713	20.14072	21.38428	22.71319	24.13313	29.00167	12
21.49530	22.95339	24.52271	26.21164	28.02911	34.35192	13
24.21492	26.01919	27.97498	30.09492	32.39260	40.50471	14
27.15211	29.36092	31.77248	34.40536	37.27972	47.58041	15
30.32428	33.00340	35.94973	39.18995	42.75328	55.71747	16
33.75023	36.97371	40.54470	44.50084	48.88367	65.07509	17
37.45024	41.30134	45.59917	50.39593	55.74972	75.83636	18
41.44626	46.01846	51.15909	56.93949	63.43968	88.21181	19
45.76196	51.16012	57.27500	64.20283	72.05244	102.44358	20
50.42292	56.76453	64.00250	72.26514	81.69874	118.81012	21
55.45676	62.87334	71.40275	81.21431	92.50258	137.63164	22
60.89330	69.53194	79.54302	91.14788	104.60289	159.27638	23
66.76476	76.78981	88.49733	102.17415	118.15524	184.16784	24
73.10594	84.70090	98.34706	114.41331	133.33387	212.79302	25
79.95442	93.32398	109.18177	127.99877	150.33393	245.71197	26
87.35077	102.72314	121.09994	143.07864	169.37401	283.56877	27
95.33883	112.96822	134.20994	159.81729	190.69889	327.10408	28
103.96594	124.13536	148.63093	178.39719	214.58275	377.16969	29
113.28231	136.30754	164.49402	199.02088	241.33268	434.74515	30
123.34587	149.57522	181.94343	221.91317	271.29261	500.95692	31
134.21354	164.03699	201.13777	247.32362	304.84772	577.10046	32
145.95062	179.80032	222.25154	275.52922	342.42945	644.66553	33
158.62667	196.98234	245.47670	306.83744	384.52098	765.36535	34
172.31680	215.71076	271.02437	341.58955	431.66350	881.17016	35
187.10215	236.12472	299.12681	380.16441	484.46312	1014.34568	36
203.07032	258.37595	330.03949	422.98249	543.59869	1167.49753	37
220.31595	282.62978	364.04343	470.51056	609.83053	1343.62216	38
238.94122	309.06646	401.44778	523.26673	684.01020	1546.16549	39
259.05652	337.88245	442.59256	581.82607	767.09142	1779.09031	40

Table 6-4 PRESENT VALUE OF AN ORDINARY ANNUITY OF 1

$$PVF\text{-}OA_{n,i} = \frac{1 - \dfrac{1}{(1+i)^n}}{i}$$

(n) Periods	2%	2-1/2%	3%	4%	5%	6%
1	.98039	.97561	.97087	.96154	.95238	.94340
2	1.94156	1.92742	1.91347	1.88609	1.85941	1.83339
3	2.88388	2.85602	2.82861	2.77509	2.72325	2.67301
4	3.80773	3.76197	3.71710	3.62990	3.54595	3.46511
5	4.71346	4.64583	4.57971	4.45182	4.32948	4.21236
6	5.60143	5.50813	5.41719	5.24214	5.07569	4.91732
7	6.47199	6.34939	6.23028	6.00205	5.78637	5.58238
8	7.32548	7.17014	7.01969	6.73274	6.46321	6.20979
9	8.16224	7.97087	7.78611	7.43533	7.10782	6.80169
10	8.98259	8.75206	8.53020	8.11090	7.72173	7.36009
11	9.78685	9.51421	9.25262	8.76048	8.30641	7.88687
12	10.57534	10.25776	9.95400	9.38507	8.86325	8.38384
13	11.34837	10.98319	10.63496	9.98565	9.39357	8.85268
14	12.10625	11.69091	11.29607	10.56312	9.89864	9.29498
15	12.84926	12.38138	11.93794	11.11839	10.37966	9.71225
16	13.57771	13.05500	12.56110	11.65230	10.83777	10.10590
17	14.29187	13.71220	13.16612	12.16567	11.27407	10.47726
18	14.99203	14.35336	13.75351	12.65930	11.68959	10.82760
19	15.67846	14.97889	14.32380	13.13394	12.08532	11.15812
20	16.35143	15.58916	14.87747	13.59033	12.46221	11.46992
21	17.01121	16.18455	15.41502	14.02916	12.82115	11.76408
22	17.65805	16.76541	15.93692	14.45112	13.16300	12.04158
23	18.29220	17.33211	16.44361	14.85684	13.48857	12.30338
24	18.91393	17.88499	16.93554	15.24696	13.79864	12.55036
25	19.52346	18.42438	17.41315	15.62208	14.09394	12.78336
26	20.12104	18.95061	17.87684	15.98277	14.37519	13.00317
27	20.70690	19.46401	18.32703	16.32959	14.64303	13.21053
28	21.28127	19.96489	18.76411	16.66306	14.89813	13.40616
29	21.84438	20.45355	19.18845	16.98371	15.14107	13.59072
30	22.39646	20.93029	19.60044	17.29203	15.37245	13.76483
31	22.93770	21.39541	20.00043	17.58849	15.59281	13.92909
32	23.46833	21.84918	20.38877	17.87355	15.80268	14.08404
33	23.98856	22.29188	20.76579	18.14765	16.00255	14.23023
34	24.49859	22.72379	21.13184	18.41120	16.19290	14.36814
35	24.99862	23.14516	21.48722	18.66461	16.37419	14.49825
36	25.48884	23.55625	21.83225	18.90828	16.54685	14.62099
37	25.96945	23.95732	22.16724	19.14258	16.71129	14.73678
38	26.44064	24.34860	22.49246	19.36786	16.86789	14.84602
39	26.90259	24.73034	22.80822	19.58448	17.01704	14.94907
40	27.35548	25.10278	23.11477	19.79277	17.15909	15.04630

8%	9%	10%	11%	12%	15%	(n) Periods
.92593	.91743	.90909	.90090	.89286	.86957	1
1.78326	1.75911	1.73554	1.71252	1.69005	1.62571	2
2.57710	2.53130	2.48685	2.44371	2.40183	2.28323	3
3.31213	3.23972	3.16986	3.10245	3.03735	2.85498	4
3.99271	3.88965	3.79079	3.69590	3.60478	3.35216	5
4.62288	4.48592	4.35526	4.23054	4.11141	3.78448	6
5.20637	5.03295	4.86842	4.71220	4.56376	4.16042	7
5.74664	5.53482	5.33493	5.14612	4.96764	4.48732	8
6.24689	5.99525	5.75902	5.53705	5.32825	4.77158	9
6.71008	6.41766	6.14457	5.88923	5.65022	5.01877	10
7.13896	6.80519	6.49506	6.20652	5.93770	5.23371	11
7.53608	7.16073	6.81369	6.49236	6.19437	5.42062	12
7.90378	7.48690	7.10336	6.74987	6.42355	5.58315	13
8.24424	7.78615	7.36669	6.98187	6.62817	5.72448	14
8.55948	8.06069	7.60608	7.19087	6.81086	5.84737	15
8.85137	8.31256	7.82371	7.37916	6.97399	5.95424	16
9.12164	8.54363	8.02155	7.54879	7.11963	6.04716	17
9.37189	8.75563	8.20141	7.70162	7.24967	6.12797	18
9.60360	8.95012	8.36492	7.83929	7.36578	6.19823	19
9.81815	9.12855	8.51356	7.96333	7.46944	6.25933	20
10.01680	9.29224	8.64869	8.07507	7.56200	6.31246	21
10.20074	9.44243	8.77154	8.17574	7.64465	6.35866	22
10.37106	9.58021	8.88322	8.26643	7.71843	6.39884	23
10.52876	9.70661	8.98474	8.34814	7.78432	6.43377	24
10.67478	9.82258	9.07704	8.42174	7.84314	6.46415	25
10.80998	9.92897	9.16095	8.48806	7.89566	6.49056	26
10.93516	10.02658	9.23722	8.54780	7.94255	6.51353	27
11.05108	10.11613	9.30657	8.60162	7.98442	6.53351	28
11.15841	10.19828	9.36961	8.65011	8.02181	6.55088	29
11.25778	10.27365	9.42691	8.69379	8.05518	6.56598	30
11.34980	10.34280	9.47901	8.73315	8.08499	6.57911	31
11.43500	10.40624	9.52638	8.76860	8.11159	6.59053	32
11.51389	10.46444	9.56943	8.80054	8.13535	6.60046	33
11.58693	10.51784	9.60858	8.82932	8.15656	6.60910	34
11.65457	10.56682	9.64416	8.85524	8.17550	6.61661	35
11.71719	10.61176	9.67651	8.87859	8.19241	6.62314	36
11.77518	10.65299	9.70592	8.89963	8.20751	6.62882	37
11.82887	10.69082	9.73265	8.91859	8.22099	6.63375	38
11.87858	10.72552	9.75697	8.93567	8.23303	6.63805	39
11.92461	10.75736	9.77905	8.95105	8.24378	6.64178	40

Table 6-5 PRESENT VALUE OF AN ANNUITY DUE OF 1

$$PVF\text{-}AD_{n,i} = 1 + \frac{1 - \dfrac{1}{(1+i)^{n-1}}}{i}$$

(n) Periods	2%	2-1/2%	3%	4%	5%	6%
1	1.00000	1.00000	1.00000	1.00000	1.00000	1.00000
2	1.98039	1.97561	1.97087	1.96154	1.95238	1.94340
3	2.94156	2.92742	2.91347	2.88609	2.85941	2.83339
4	3.88388	3.85602	3.82861	3.77509	3.72325	3.67301
5	4.80773	4.76197	4.71710	4.62990	4.54595	4.46511
6	5.71346	5.64583	5.57971	5.45182	5.32948	5.21236
7	6.60143	6.50813	6.41719	6.24214	6.07569	5.91732
8	7.47199	7.34939	7.23028	7.00205	6.78637	6.58238
9	8.32548	8.17014	8.01969	7.73274	7.46321	7.20979
10	9.16224	8.97087	8.78611	8.43533	8.10782	7.80169
11	9.98259	9.75206	9.53020	9.11090	8.72173	8.36009
12	10.78685	10.51421	10.25262	9.76048	9.30641	8.88687
13	11.57534	11.25776	10.95400	10.38507	9.86325	9.38384
14	12.34837	11.98319	11.63496	10.98565	10.39357	9.85268
15	13.10625	12.69091	12.29607	11.56312	10.89864	10.29498
16	13.84926	13.38138	12.93794	12.11839	11.37966	10.71225
17	14.57771	14.05500	13.56110	12.65230	11.83777	11.10590
18	15.29187	14.71220	14.16612	13.16567	12.27407	11.47726
19	15.99203	15.35336	14.75351	13.65930	12.68959	11.82760
20	16.67846	15.97889	15.32380	14.13394	13.08532	12.15812
21	17.35143	16.58916	15.87747	14.59033	13.46221	12.46992
22	18.01121	17.18455	16.41502	15.02916	13.82115	12.76408
23	18.65805	17.76541	16.93692	15.45112	14.16300	13.04158
24	19.29220	18.33211	17.44361	15.85684	14.48857	13.30338
25	19.91393	18.88499	17.93554	16.24696	14.79864	13.55036
26	20.52346	19.42438	18.41315	16.62208	15.09394	13.78336
27	21.12104	19.95061	18.87684	16.98277	15.37519	14.00317
28	21.70690	20.46401	19.32703	17.32959	15.64303	14.21053
29	22.28127	20.96489	19.76411	17.66306	15.89813	14.40616
30	22.84438	21.45355	20.18845	17.98371	16.14107	14.59072
31	23.39646	21.93029	20.60044	18.29203	16.37245	14.76483
32	23.93770	22.39541	21.00043	18.58849	16.59281	14.92909
33	24.46833	22.84918	21.38877	18.87355	16.80268	15.08404
34	24.98856	23.29188	21.76579	19.14765	17.00255	15.23023
35	25.49859	23.72379	22.13184	19.41120	17.19290	15.36814
36	25.99862	24.14516	22.48722	19.66461	17.37419	15.49825
37	26.48884	24.55625	22.83225	19.90828	17.54685	15.62099
38	26.96945	24.95732	23.16724	20.14258	17.71129	15.73678
39	27.44064	25.34860	23.49246	20.36786	17.86789	15.84602
40	27.90259	25.73034	23.80822	20.58448	18.01704	15.94907

8%	9%	10%	11%	12%	15%	(n) Periods
1.00000	1.00000	1.00000	1.00000	1.00000	1.00000	1
1.92593	1.91743	1.90909	1.90090	1.89286	1.86957	2
2.78326	2.75911	2.73554	2.71252	2.69005	2.62571	3
3.57710	3.53130	3.48685	3.44371	3.40183	3.28323	4
4.31213	4.23972	4.16986	4.10245	4.03735	3.85498	5
4.99271	4.88965	4.79079	4.69590	4.60478	4.35216	6
5.62288	5.48592	5.35526	5.23054	5.11141	4.78448	7
6.20637	6.03295	5.86842	5.71220	5.56376	5.16042	8
6.74664	6.53482	6.33493	6.14612	5.96764	5.48732	9
7.24689	6.99525	6.75902	6.53705	6.32825	5.77158	10
7.71008	7.41766	7.14457	6.88923	6.65022	6.01877	11
8.13896	7.80519	7.49506	7.20652	6.93770	6.23371	12
8.53608	8.16073	7.18369	7.49236	7.19437	6.42062	13
8.90378	8.48690	8.10336	7.74987	7.42355	6.58315	14
9.24424	8.78615	8.36669	7.98187	7.62817	6.72448	15
9.55948	9.06069	8.60608	8.19087	7.81086	6.84737	16
9.85137	9.31256	8.82371	8.37916	7.97399	6.95424	17
10.12164	9.54363	9.02155	8.54879	8.11963	7.04716	18
10.37189	9.75563	9.20141	8.70162	8.24967	7.12797	19
10.60360	9.95012	9.36492	8.83929	8.36578	7.19823	20
10.81815	10.12855	9.51356	8.96333	8.46944	7.25933	21
11.01680	10.29224	9.64869	9.07507	8.56200	7.31246	22
11.20074	10.44243	9.77154	9.17574	8.64465	7.35866	23
11.37106	10.58021	9.88322	9.26643	8.71843	7.39884	24
11.52876	10.70661	9.98474	9.34814	8.78432	7.43377	25
11.67478	10.82258	10.07704	9.42174	8.84314	7.46415	26
11.80998	10.92897	10.16095	9.48806	8.89566	7.49056	27
11.93518	11.02658	10.23722	9.54780	8.94255	7.51353	28
12.05108	11.11613	10.30657	9.60162	8.98442	7.53351	29
12.15841	11.19828	10.36961	9.65011	9.02181	7.55088	30
12.25778	11.27365	10.42691	9.69379	9.05518	7.56598	31
12.34980	11.34280	10.47901	9.73315	9.08499	7.57911	32
12.43500	11.40624	10.52638	9.76860	9.11159	7.59053	33
12.51389	11.46444	10.56943	9.80054	9.13535	7.60046	34
12.58693	11.51784	10.60858	9.82932	9.15656	7.60910	35
12.65457	11.56682	10.64416	9.85524	9.17550	7.61661	36
12.71719	11.61176	10.67651	9.87859	9.19241	7.62314	37
12.77518	11.65299	10.70592	9.89963	9.20751	7.62882	38
12.82887	11.69082	10.73265	9.91859	9.22099	7.63375	39
12.87858	11.72552	10.75697	9.93567	9.23303	7.63805	40

CHAPTER 7

CASH AND RECEIVABLES

OVERVIEW

In previous chapters, you learned the basic formats for general purpose financial statements. In this chapter you begin your in-depth study of accounting for items appearing on the balance sheet: (1) what is to be included in an item classification, (2) related internal control procedures, (3) rules for determining the dollar amount to be reported, (4) disclosure requirements, and (5) special accounting procedures which may be required. In this chapter, you will learn what is to be included under the cash caption on the balance sheet and some key internal controls which should be employed for business activities involving cash. Also discussed are the methods of accounting for accounts receivable and notes receivable.

Many businesses grant credit to customers. They know that when making sales "on account," a risk exists because some accounts will never be collected. However, the cost of these bad debts is more than offset by the profit from the extra sales made due to the attraction of granting credit. The collections department may make many attempts to collect an account before "writing-off" a bad debtor. Frequently an account is deemed to be uncollectible a year or more after the date of the credit sale. In this chapter, we will discuss the allowance method of accounting for bad debts. The allowance method permits the accountant to estimate the amount of bad debt expense that should be matched with current revenues rather than waiting to book expense at the time of an actual write-off.

SUMMARY OF LEARNING OBJECTIVES

1. **Identify items considered cash.** To be reported as "cash," an asset must be readily available for the payment of current obligations and free from contractual restrictions that limit its use in satisfying debts. Cash consists of coin, currency, and available funds on deposit at the bank. Negotiable instruments such as money orders, certified checks, cashier's checks, personal checks, and bank drafts are also viewed as cash. Savings accounts are usually classified as cash.

2. **Indicate how cash and related items are reported.** Cash is reported as a current asset in the balance sheet. The reporting of other related items are: (1) **Restricted cash:** The SEC recommends that legally restricted deposits held as compensating balances against short-term borrowing be stated separately among the "cash and cash equivalent items" in Current Assets. Restricted deposits held against long-term borrowing arrangements should be separately classified as noncurrent assets in either the Investments or Other Assets sections. (2) **Bank overdrafts:** They should be reported separately in the Current Liabilities section of the balance sheet. (3) **Cash equivalents:** This item is often reported together with cash as "cash and cash equivalents." Cash equivalents are short-term, highly liquid investments that are both (a) readily convertible to known amounts of cash, and (b) so near their maturity that they present insignificant risk of changes in interest rates. Generally, only investments with original maturities of three months or less qualify under this definition. Examples of cash equivalents are treasury bills, commercial paper, and money market funds.

3. **Define receivables and identify the different types of receivables.** Receivables are claims held against customers and others for money, goods, or services. The receivables are classified into three types: (1) current or noncurrent, (2) trade or nontrade, and (3) accounts receivable or notes receivable.

4. **Explain accounting issues related to the recognition of accounts receivable.** Two issues that may complicate the measurement of accounts receivable are: (1) the availability of discounts (trade and cash discounts) and (2) the length of time between the sale and the payment due dates (the interest element). Ideally, receivables should be measured in terms of their present value—that is, the discounted value of the cash to be received in the future. The profession specifically excludes from the present value considerations receivables arising from normal business transactions that are due in customary trade terms within approximately one year.

5. **Explain accounting issues related to the valuation of accounts receivable.** Short-term receivables are valued and reported at net realizable value—the net amount expected to be received in cash, which is not necessarily the amount legally receivable. Determining net realizable value requires an estimation of both uncollectible receivables and any returns or allowances.

6. **Explain accounting issues related to the recognition of notes receivable.** Short-term notes are recorded at face value. Long-term notes receivable are recorded at the present value of the cash expected to be collected. When the interest stated on an interest-bearing note is equal to the effective (market) rate of interest, the note is recorded at face value. When the stated rate is different from the effective rate and the note is exchanged for something other than cash, either a discount or premium is recorded.

7. **Explain accounting issues related to the valuation of notes receivable.** Like accounts receivable, short-term notes receivable are recorded and reported at their net realizable value. The same is true of long-term receivables. Special issues relate to impairments and notes receivable past due.

8. **Explain accounting issues related to disposition of accounts and notes receivable.** To accelerate the receipt of cash from receivables, the owner may transfer the receivables to another company for cash. The transfer of receivables to a third party for cash may be accomplished in one of two ways: (1) **Secured borrowing:** A creditor often requires that the debtor designate or pledge receivables as security for a loan. (2) **Sales (factoring) of receivables:** Factors are finance companies or banks that buy receivables from businesses and then collect the remittances directly from the customers. In many cases, transferors may have some continuing involvement with the receivables sold. A financial components approach is used to record this type of transaction.

9. **Explain how receivables are reported and analyzed.** Disclosure of receivables requires valuation accounts be appropriately offset against receivables, receivables be appropriately classifed as current or noncurrent, pledged or designated receivables be identified, and concentrations of risks arising from receivables be identified. Receivables may be analyzed relative to turnover and the days outstanding.

*10. **Explain common techniques employed to control cash.** The common techniques employed to control cash are: (1) **Using bank accounts:** a company can vary the number and location of banks and the types of accounts to obtain desired control objectives. (2) **The imprest petty cash system:** It may be impractical to require small amounts of various expenses to be paid by check, yet some control over them is important. (3) **Physical protection of cash balances:** Adequate control of receipts and disbursements is a part of the protection of cash balances. Every effort should be made to minimize the cash on hand in the office. (4) **Reconciliation of**

bank balances: Cash on deposit is not available for count and is proved by preparing a bank reconciliation.

*This material is covered in Appendix 7-A in the text.

11. **Prepare a proof of cash (four-column bank reconciliation). The proof of cash reconciles four items per the bank statement to four items per the company's books: (1) the beginning-of-the-period cash balances, (2) the current period cash receipts, (3) the current period cash disbursements, and (4) the end-of-the-period cash balances.

**This material appears in Appendix 7-B in the text.

TIPS ON CHAPTER TOPICS

TIP: Trade accounts receivable result from the sale of products or services to customers. Nontrade accounts receivable (amounts that are due from nontrade customers who do not buy goods or services in the normal course of the company's main business activity) should be listed separately on the balance sheet from the trade accounts receivable balance.

TIP: In the event that a customer's account has a credit balance on the balance sheet date, it should be classified as a current liability and not offset against other accounts receivable with debit balances.

TIP: The net realizable value of accounts receivable is the amount of the receivables expected to be ultimately converted to cash.

TIP: Whenever you want to analyze the effect of (1) recording bad debt expense, (2) writing off an individual customer's account receivable, and/or (3) the collection of an account receivable that was previously written off, write down the related journal entry(ies) and analyze each debit and credit separately. (See **Illustration 7-1** for examples.)

TIP: There are two methods of accounting for bad debts; they are:

1. **Direct Write-Off Method:** No entry is made until a specific account has definitely been established as uncollectible. Then the loss is recorded by crediting Accounts Receivable and debiting Bad Debt Expense.
2. **Allowance Method:** An estimate is made of the expected uncollectible accounts from all sales made on account or from the total of outstanding receivables. This estimate is entered as an expense and an indirect reduction in accounts receivable (via an increase in the allowance account) in the period in which the sale is recorded.

The direct write-off method is not a generally accepted method for an entity having a material amount of bad debts because it fails to properly match bad debt expense with the related revenue (in the period the credit sale was recognized) and it overstates Accounts Receivable as to their net realizable value.

TIP: A note receivable is considered to be **impaired** when it is probable that the creditor will be unable to collect all amounts due (both principal and interest) according to the contractual terms of the loan. In that case, the present value of the expected future cash flows is determined by discounting those flows at the historical effective rate. This present value amount is deducted from the carrying amount of the receivable to measure the loss.

TIP: The objective of a bank reconciliation is to explain all reasons why the bank balance differs from the book balance and to identify errors and omissions in the bank's records and in the book records. In the context of a bank reconciliation, "per bank" refers to the records of the bank pertaining to the depositor's account and "per books" refers to the depositor's records of the same bank account.

TIP: Total receipts per bank for a month include all deposits made by the depositor during the month plus any bank credit memos (such as for interest credited by the bank or a customer's note receivable collected by the bank).

TIP: Total disbursements per bank for a month include all the depositor's checks which cleared the banking system during the month plus any bank debit memos originating during the month (such as for bank service charges or a customer's NSF check).

TIP: Beginning cash balance per bank plus total receipts for the month per bank minus total disbursements for the month per bank equals ending cash balance per bank.

TIP: Beginning cash balance per books plus total receipts for the month per books minus total disbursements for the month per books equals ending cash balance per books.

EXERCISE 7-1

Purpose: (L.O.1) This exercise will review the items which are included in the "Cash" caption on a balance sheet.

In auditing the balance sheet at December 31, 1999 for the Maxwell Vermulen Company, you find the following:

(a) Coins and currency for change funds.
(b) Coins and currency which are from the current day's receipts which have not yet been deposited in the bank.
(c) Petty cash.
(d) General checking account at First Union Bank.
(e) General checking account at Sun Trust Bank.
(f) Unused stamps.
(g) Deposit in transit.
(h) Customer's NSF check (returned with bank statement).
(i) Postdated checks from customers.
(j) Certificate of deposit--60 day CD purchased on December 1, 1999.
(k) Certificate of deposit--5 year CD purchased 2 years ago.
(l) 100 shares of General Motors stock (intention is to sell in one year or less).
(m) Cash to be used to retire long-term debt.
(n) Travel advances made to executives for business purposes.

Instructions

Select the items from the list above that should be included in the "Cash" caption on the balance sheet as of December 31, 1999. For any item not included in "Cash", indicate the proper classification.

Solution to Exercise 7-1

Items to be **included** as "Cash" on the balance sheet include:

(a) Coins and currency for change funds.
(b) Coins and currency which are from the current day's receipts which have not yet been deposited in the bank—this is said to be "cash on hand" or could be considered a "deposit in transit."
(c) Petty cash.
(d) General checking account at First Union Bank—the amount included should be the "adjusted cash balance" per a bank reconciliation.
(e) General checking account at Sun Trust Bank—the amount included should be the "adjusted cash balance" per a bank reconciliation.
(g) Deposit in transit—this amount is already reflected in the "balance per books" and will be reflected in the "adjusted cash balance" per the bank reconciliation.

Items to be **excluded** from "Cash" include:

(f) Unused stamps—report as prepaid expense.
(h) Customer's NSF check—classify as a receivable.
(i) Postdated checks from customers—accounts receivable.
(j) Certificate of deposit--60 day--original maturity date was 3 months or less—cash equivalent. Some entities include cash equivalents with cash; others report them as short-term (temporary) investments.
(k) Certificate of deposit--original maturity date not 3 months or less—short-term investment.
(l) 100 shares of General Motors Stock—short-term investment because there is a lack of intent to hold for a long-term purpose and is readily marketable.
(m) Cash to be used to retire long-term debt—long-term investment (assuming the related debt is classified as long-term).
(n) Travel advances made to executives for business purposes—prepaid expense.

ILLUSTRATION 7-1
ENTRIES FOR THE ALLOWANCE METHOD (L.O.5)

Journal Entry			Effect on Net Income	Effect on Working Capital	Effect on Allowance Account	Effect on Net Receivables
Entry to record bad debt expense, $1,000						
Bad Debt Expense	1,000		Decrease $1,000	No effect	No effect	No effect
Allowance for Doubtful Accounts		1,000	No effect	Decrease $1,000	Increase $1,000	Decrease $1,000
Net effect of entry			Decrease $1,000	Decrease $1,000	Increase $1,000	Decrease $1,000
Entry to write-off a customer's account, $200						
Allowance for Doubtful Accounts	200		No effect	Increase $200	Decrease $200	Increase $200
Accounts Receivable		200	No effect	Decrease $200	No effect	Decrease $200
Net effect of entry			No effect	No effect	Decrease $200	No effect
Entries to record collection of account receivable previously written off, $120						
Accounts Receivable	120		No effect	Increase $120	No effect	Increase $120
Allowance for Doubtful Accounts		120	No effect	Decrease $120	Increase $120	Decrease $120
Cash	120		No effect	Increase $120	No effect	No effect
Accounts Receivable		120	No effect	Decrease $120	No effect	Decrease $120
Net effect of entries			No effect	No effect	Increase $120	Decrease $120

TIP: Be careful to distinguish the entry to write-off a customer account from the entry to record bad debt expense. The journal entry to record the estimated bad debt expense for a period and to adjust the corresponding allowance for doubtful accounts involves a debit to Bad Debt Expense and a credit to Allowance for Doubtful Accounts. The entry to write off an individual customer's account (an actual bad debt) involves a debit to Allowance for Doubtful Accounts and a credit to Accounts Receivable.

TIP: Two entries are necessary to record the recovery of an account that was previously written off:

1. An entry to record the reinstatement of the account receivable (debit Accounts Receivable and credit Allowance for Doubtful Accounts). This is simply a reverse of the write-off entry.
2. An entry to record the collection of the receivable (debit Cash and credit Accounts Receivable).

TIP: Allowance for Doubtful Accounts is often called Allowance for Uncollectible Accounts. Bad Debt Expense is often called Uncollectible Accounts Expense **or** Doubtful Accounts Expense.

TIP: Notice that the entry to record bad debts reduces current assets and reduces net income. The entry to record the write-off of an individual account has **no** net effect on the amount of current assets nor does it affect income. It merely reduces Accounts Receivable and the Allowance for Doubtful Accounts account (which is a contra item) so the entry has no **net** effect on the net realizable value of accounts receivable. Thus, it is the entry to record the bad debt expense that impacts **both** the income statement and the balance sheet.

ILLUSTRATION 7-1 (Continued)

TIP: The normal balance of the Allowance for Doubtful Accounts is a credit. Therefore, a debit balance in this account indicates an abnormal balance. It is not uncommon to have a debit balance in the allowance account before adjusting entries are prepared because individual accounts may be written off at various times during a period and the entry to adjust the allowance account is prepared at the end of the period before financial statements are prepared. After adjustment, the allowance account should have a credit balance.

TIP: When using the allowance method of accounting for bad debts, there are two methods available for determining the amount of the adjusting entry to record bad debts expense and to adjust the allowance account. Each method has adaptations.

1. By estimating bad debt expense:
   a. The average percentage relationship between actual bad debt losses and net credit sales is ascertained from prior experience. This percentage, adjusted for current conditions, is then applied to the actual net credit sales of the period to determine the amount of expense for the period.
   b. Use of the same procedure as in "a" above, except the percentage of bad debts to total sales is used. This method is not as logical as "a" because cash sales will not result in bad debts, and, if the relationship between cash sales and credit sales shifts, that change will necessitate revision of the percentage being used to estimate bad debts.
2. By estimating the net realizable value of the existing receivables:
   a. From experience, the average percentage relationship between uncollectible accounts receivable and outstanding accounts receivable is determined. This percentage, adjusted for current conditions, is applied each period to the ending balance in accounts receivable to determine the desired balance of the allowance account.
   b. Total uncollectible accounts at the end of an accounting period is determined by an aging analysis. The balance in the allowance account is then adjusted so that it equals the total amount of the estimated uncollectible accounts. This aging method is preferable to "2a" because it takes into consideration the age of a receivable. (The older the age, the lower the probability of collection.)

Both methods (and their variations) listed above are acceptable. The first method discussed, estimation of bad debt expense based on credit sales, focuses on matching current bad debt expense with revenues of the current period and thus emphasizes the income statement. The second method, estimation of the net realizable value of existing receivables, focuses on an evaluation of the net realizable value of all accounts receivable and thus emphasizes the balance sheet. It only incidentally measures bad debt expense; the expense reported may not be directly related to the credit sales of the current period, thus violating the matching principle. If this method is to be used, the aging technique is preferable to the use of a simple percentage times total accounts receivable.

ILLUSTRATION 7-1 (Continued)

TIP: When using the allowance method and estimating bad debt expense as a percentage of credit sales for the period, the amount of bad debt expense is simply calculated and recorded; a by-product of this approach is the increasing of the allowance account. When using the allowance method and estimating the net realizable value of accounts receivable (such as by an aging analysis), the amount of uncollectible accounts calculated represents the new ending balance of the allowance account. The adjusting entry records the amount necessary to increase (or decrease) the current allowance account balance to equal the newly computed one. A by-product of this approach is the increasing of bad debt expense for the period.

TIP: Very often, an entity may use the percentage-of-sales method to account for bad debts for interim periods and then use the aging method to adjust the allowance account at year-end for annual reporting purposes.

EXERCISE 7-2

Purpose: (L.O.5,8) This exercise will require you to record: (1) the adjusting entry to recognize bad debt expense and adjust the Allowance for Doubtful Accounts account, and (2) the transfer of accounts receivable with recourse.

The trial balance before adjustment at December 31, 1999 for the Liz Company shows the following balances:

	Dr.	Cr.
Accounts Receivable	$ 90,000	
Allowance for Doubtful Accounts	2,120	
Sales (all on credit)		$ 500,000
Sales Returns and Allowances	7,600	

Instructions

Using the data above, give the journal entries required to record each of the following cases (each situation is **independent**):

1. The company wants to maintain the Allowance for Doubtful Accounts at 4% of gross accounts receivable.
2. The company wishes to increase the allowance by 1.5% of net credit sales.
3. Liz performs an aging analysis at December 31, 1999 which indicates an estimate of $6,000 of uncollectible accounts.
4. To obtain additional cash, Liz factors, without recourse, $20,000 of accounts receivable with Fleetwood Finance. The finance charge is 10% of the amount factored.

Solution to Exercise 7-2

1.

Bad Debt Expense	5,720	
Allowance for Doubtful Accounts [($90,000 x 4%) + $2,120]		5,720

Explanation: This entry is to adjust the allowance account. A by-product of the entry is the recognition of uncollectible accounts expense. Because an appropriate balance for the valuation account is determined to be a percentage of the receivable balance at the balance sheet date, the existing balance ($2,120 debit) in the allowance account must be considered in computing the necessary adjustment.

2.

Bad Debt Expense [($500,000 - $7,600) x 1.5%]	7,386	
Allowance for Doubtful Accounts		7,386

Explanation: The percentage of net credit sales approach to applying the allowance method of accounting for bad debts focuses on determining an appropriate expense figure. The existing balance in the allowance account is **not** relevant in the computation.

3.

Bad Debt Expense	8,120	
Allowance for Doubtful Accounts ($6,000 + $2,120)		8,120

Explanation: An aging analysis provides the best estimate of the net realizable value of accounts receivable. By using the results of the aging to adjust the allowance account, the amount reported for net receivables on the balance sheet is the net realizable value of accounts receivable. It is important to notice that the balance of the allowance account before adjustment is a determinant in the adjustment required. The following T-account reflects the facts used to determine the necessary adjustment:

Allowance for Doubtful Accounts

Unadjusted balance	2,120	Adjustment needed	8,120
		Desired balance at 12/31/99	6,000

4.

Cash	18,000	
Loss on Sale of Receivables ($20,000 x 10%)	2,000	
Accounts Receivable		20,000

Explanation: The factoring of accounts receivable without recourse is accounted for as a sale of accounts receivable; hence, the receivables are removed from the accounts, cash is recorded, and a loss is recognized for the excess of the face value of the receivables over the proceeds received.

EXERCISE 7-3

Purpose: (L.O.6) This exercise will illustrate the accounting for two situations involving the exchange of a noncash asset or service for a promissory note: (1) the exchange of land for a promissory note where the fair value of the land is known, and (2) the exchange of services for a note where the fair value of the services are not known.

General Host's annual accounting period ends on December 31. Reversing entries are used when appropriate. On July 1, 1999, General Host Company made two sales:

1. It sold land having a fair market value of $700,000 in exchange for a four-year noninterest-bearing promissory note in the face amount of $1,101,460. The land is carried on General Host Company's books at a cost of $620,000.
2. It rendered services in exchange for a 3%, 8-year promissory note having a face value of $300,000 with interest payable annually. General Host company recently had to pay 8% interest for money that it borrowed from Arizona National Bank. The customer in this transaction has a credit rating that requires them to borrow money at 12% interest.

Instructions

(a) Prepare the two journal entries that should be recorded by General Host company for the sales transactions above.

(b) Prepare the amortization schedule for the note receivable accepted in the first transaction [Note (1)].

(c) Prepare the amortization schedule for the note receivable accepted in the second transaction [Note (2)].

(d) Prepare the necessary journal entries at December 31, 1999 and December 31, 2000 that relate to the first transaction.

(e) Prepare the necessary journal entries at December 31, 1999, January 1, 2000 (reversing entry), June 30, 2000, and December 31, 2000 that relate to the second transaction. Assume the customer makes the scheduled interest payments on time. Also, assume amortization is recorded only at year-end.

Solution to Exercise 7-3

(a) (1) Timeline:

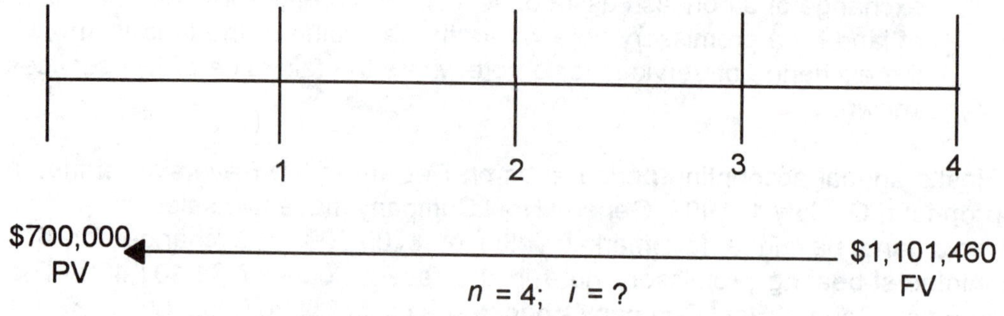

7/1/99	Notes Receivable [Note (1)]	1,101,460.00	
	Discount on Notes Receivable		401,460.00
	Land		620,000.00
	Gain on Sale of Land ($700,000 - $620,000)		80,000.00

The exchange price is equal to the fair market value of the property (which is $700,000). The interest rate implicit in this price is therefore calculated by:

$700,000 = $1,101,460 x PV Factor

$700,000 ÷ $1,101,460 = .63552

By reference to Table 6-2 (Present Value of 1 Table), .63552 is the PV factor for n = 4, i = 12%.

(2) Timeline:

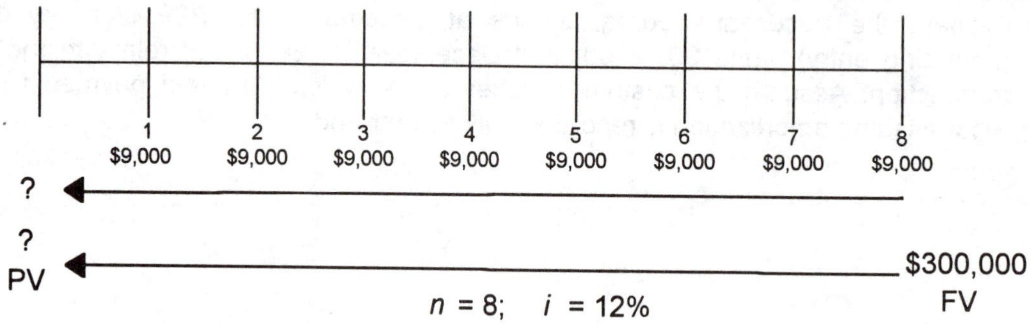

7/1/99	Notes Receivable [Note (2)]	300,000.00	
	Discount on Notes Receivable		134,127.24
	Service Revenue		165,872.76

Use the market rate of interest to compute the present value of the note which is then used to establish the exchange price in the transaction. The market rate of interest should be the rate the borrower normally would have to pay to borrow money for similar activities.

Computation of the present value of the note:		
Maturity value		$300,000.00
Present value of $300,000 due in 8 years at 12% ($300,000 x .40388)	$121,164.00	
Present value of $9,000 payable annually for 8 years at 12% ($9,000 x 4.96764)	44,708.76	
Present value of the note and interest		165,872.76
Discount on note receivable		$134,127.24

(b) **Amortization Schedule for Note (1)**

Date	0% Stated Interest	12% Effective Interest	Amortization of Discount	PV Balance
7/01/99				$ 700,000.00
6/30/00	$0	$ 84,000.00[a]	$ 84,000.00	784,000.00
6/30/01	0	94,080.00	94,080.00	878,080.00
6/30/02	0	105,369.60	105,369.60	983,449.60
6/30/03	0	118,010.40[1]	118,010.40	1,101,460.00
Totals	$0	$401,460.00	$ 401,460.00	

[a]$700,000.00 x 12% = $84,000.00.
[1]Includes rounding error of $3.55.

(c) **Amortization Schedule for Note (2)**

Date	3% Stated Interest	12% Effective Interest	Amortization of Discount	PV Balance
7/01/99				$ 165,872.76
6/30/00	$ 9,000.00[a]	$ 19,904.73[b]	$ 10,904.73[c]	176,777.49[d]
6/30/01	9,000.00	21,213.30	12,213.30	188,990.79
6/30/02	9,000.00	22,678.89	13,678.89	202,669.68
6/30/03	9,000.00	24,320.36	15,320.36	217,990.04
6/30/04	9,000.00	26,158.80	17,158.80	235,148.84
6/30/05	9,000.00	28,217.86	19,217.86	254,366.70
6/30/06	9,000.00	30,524.00	21,524.00	275,890.70
6/30/07	9,000.00	33,109.30[1]	24,109.30	300,000.00
Totals	$72,000.00	$206,127.24	$ 134,127.24	

[a]$300,000.00 face value x 3% stated interest rate = $9,000.00 stated interest.
[b]$165,872.76 present value x 12% effective interest rate = $19,904.73 effective interest.
[c]$19,904.73 effective interest - $9,000.00 stated interest = $10,904.73 discount amortization.
[d]$165,872.76 PV balance 7/01/99 + $10,904.73 discount amortization for 12 months = $176,777.49 PV balance 6/30/00.
[1]Includes rounding error of $2.42.

(d)	12/31/99	Discount on Notes Receivable	42,000.00	
		Interest Revenue		42,000.00
		(1/2 x $84,000 = $42,000)		
	12/31/00	Discount on Notes Receivable	89,040.00	
		Interest Revenue		89,040.00
		(1/2 x $84,000 = $42,000; 1/2 x $94,080 = $47,040; $42,000 + $47,040 = $89,040)		
(e)	12/31/99	Interest Receivable	4,500.00	
		Discount on Notes Receivable	5,452.37	
		Interest Revenue		9,952.37
		(1/2 x $9,000 = $4,500; 1/2 x $19,904.73 = $9,952.37)		
	1/1/00	Interest Revenue	4,500.00	
		Interest Receivable		4,500.00
		(To reverse last period's accrual)		
	6/30/00	Cash	9,000.00	
		Interest Revenue		9,000.00
	12/31/00	Interest Receivable	4,500.00[a]	
		Discount on Notes Receivable	11,559.01[b]	
		Interest Revenue		16,059.01[c]

[a]1/2 x $9,000.00 = $4,500.00 interest receivable at 12/31/00.
[b]1/2 x $19,904.73 = $9,952.36 interest earned 1/1/00 thru 6/30/00; 1/2 x $21,213.30 = $10,606.65 interest earned 7/1/00 thru 12/31/00; $9,952.36 + $10,606.65 = $20,559.01 total interest earned in 2000; $20,559.01 effective interest for 2000 - $9,000.00 stated interest for 2000 = $11,559.01 discount amortization for 2000.
[c]$20,559.01 total interest for 2000 - $4,500.00 balance in Interest Revenue account before adjustment = $16,059.01 interest to record at 12/31/00.

Explanation: When a note is received in exchange for property, goods, or services in a bargained transaction entered into at arms length, the stated interest rate is assumed to be fair and is thus used to compute interest revenue unless:

1. No interest rate is stated, or
2. The stated interest rate is unreasonable, or
3. The face amount of the note is materially different from the current cash sales price for the same or similar items or from the current market value of the debt instrument.

In these circumstances, the present value of the note is measured by the fair value of the property, goods, or services. (General Host received a note in exchange for land, and the fair value of the land was known to be $700,000; thus, the fair value of the land was used to establish the present value of the note.) If the fair value of the property, goods, or services is not readily determinable, the market value of the note is used to establish the present value of the note. If the note has no ready market, the present value of the note is approximated by discounting all of the related future cash receipts (for interest and principal) on the note at the market rate of interest. This rate is referred to as an imputed rate and should be equal to the borrower's incremental borrowing rate (that is, the rate of interest the maker of the note would currently have to pay if it borrowed money from another source for this same purpose). General Host received a second note in exchange for services. No information was given about the fair value of the services or the market value of the note. Thus, 12% was used to impute interest and determine the note's present value.

ILLUSTRATION 7-2
ACCOUNTING FOR TRANSFERS OF RECEIVABLES (L.O.8)

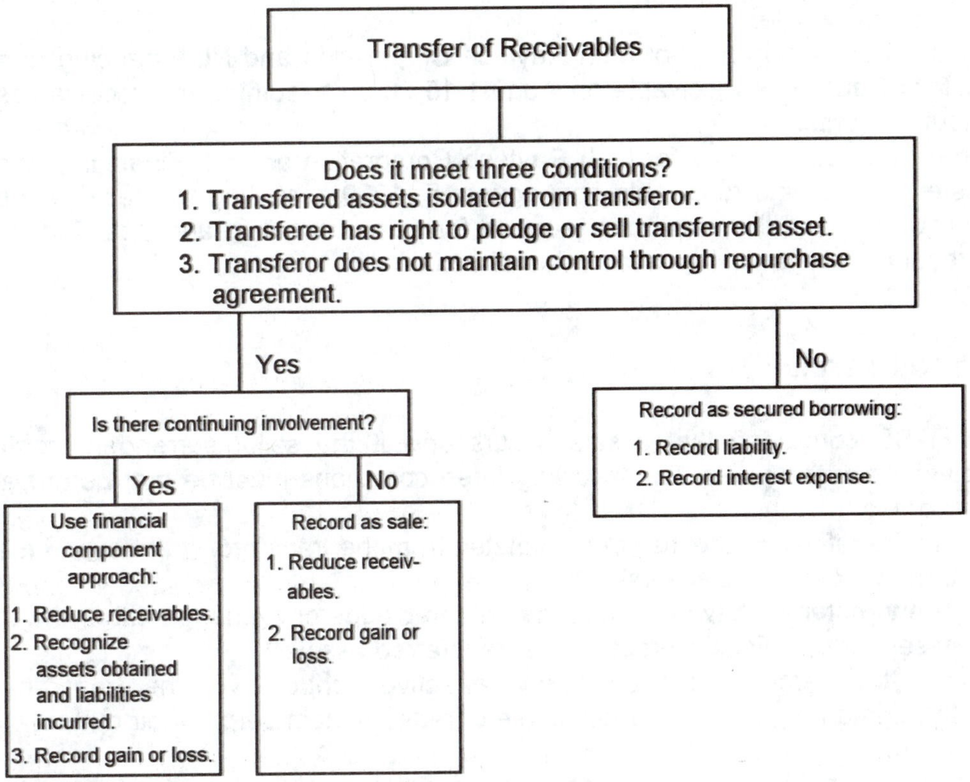

TIP: If there is continuing involvement in a sale transaction, the assets obtained and liabilities incurred must be recorded at fair value.

EXERCISE 7-4

Purpose: (L.O.8) This exercise will help you to compare two possible ways of structuring a sale of accounts receivable (1) without recourse, or (2) with recourse.

Raytech Corporation factors $90,000 of accounts receivable with NL Financing, Inc. NL Financing will collect the receivables. The receivable records are transferred to NL Financing on August 15, 1999. NL Financing assesses a finance charge of 4% of the amount of accounts receivable and also retains an amount equal to 6% of accounts receivable to cover probable adjustments.

Instructions

(a) Explain the conditions that must be met for a transfer of receivables with recourse to be accounted for as a sale.

(b) Explain when the financial components approach is used in accounting for a transfer of accounts receivable.

(c) Prepare the journal entry for both Raytech Corporation and NL Financing to record the transfer of accounts receivable on August 15, 1999 assuming the receivables are sold without recourse.

(d) Prepare the journal entry for both Raytech Corporation and NL Financing to record the transfer of accounts receivable on August 15, 1999 assuming the receivables are sold with recourse and the conditions required for sale accounting are met. Further, assume the recourse obligation has a fair value of $2,000.

Solution to Exercise 7-4

(a) The FASB concluded that a sale occurs only if the seller surrenders control of the receivables to the buyer. The following three conditions must be met before a sale can be recorded:

1. The transferred asset has been isolated from the transferor (put beyond reach of the transferor and its creditors).
2. The transferees have obtained the right to pledge or exchange either the transferred assets or beneficial interests in the transferred assets.
3. The transferor does not maintain effective control over the transferred assets through an agreement to repurchase or redeem them before their maturity.

If the three conditions are met, a sale occurs. Otherwise, the transferor should record the transfer as a secured borrowing. If sale accounting is appropriate, it is still necessary to consider assets obtained and liabilities incurred in the transaction. If there is continuing involvement in a sale transaction, the assets obtained and liabilities incurred must be recorded at fair value.

(b) A **financial components approach** is used to account for a transfer of accounts receivable with recourse whenever the transfer arrangement meets the conditions necessary for the transfer to be accounted for as a sale (see answer (a) above). If receivables are sold (factored) with recourse, the seller guarantees payment to the purchaser in the event the debtor fails to pay. Under the financial components approach, each party to the sale recognizes the assets and liabilities that it controls after the sale and no longer recognizes the assets and liabilities that were sold or extinguished.

(c) Sale of receivables without recourse:

Raytech Corp.

Cash	81,000	
Due from Factor	5,400*	
Loss on Sale of Receivables	3,600**	
Accounts Receivable		90,000

NL Financing

Accounts Receivable	90,000	
Due to Raytech		5,400
Financing Revenue		3,600
Cash		81,000

*$90,000 X 6% = $5,400
**$90,000 X 4% = $3,600

TIP: The factor's profit will be the difference between the financing revenue of $3,600 and the amount of any uncollectible receivables.

(d) Sale of receivables with recourse:

Raytech Corp.

Cash	81,000	
Due from Factor	5,400	
Loss on Sale of Receivables	5,600*	
Accounts Receivable		90,000
Recourse Liability		2,000

NL Financing

Accounts Receivable	90,000	
Due to Raytech		5,400
Financing Revenue		3,600
Cash		81,000

*Cash received	$81,000
Due from factor	5,400
Subtotal	86,400
Resource obligation	(2,000)
Net proceeds expected	$84,400
Carrying (book) value	$90,000
Net proceeds	(84,400)
Loss on sale of receivables	$ 5,600

TIP: In this case, a liability of $2,000 is recorded by Raytech to indicate the probable payment to NL Financing for uncollectible receivables. If all the receivables are collected, Raytech would eliminate its recourse liability and increase net income. NL Financing's profit is the financing revenue of $3,600 because it will have no bad debts related to these receivables.

EXERCISE 7-5

Purpose: (L.O.8) This exercise will illustrate the computations and entries involved in accounting for the transfer of receivables that is treated as a secured borrowing transaction.

Ashton Winery transfers $350,000 of its accounts receivable to First Union Bank as collateral for a $250,000 note on September 1, 1999. Ashton will continue to collect the accounts receivable; the account debtors are not notified of the arrangement. First Union Bank assesses a finance charge of 1% of the accounts receivable and interest on the note of 12%. Settlement by Ashton Winery to the bank is made monthly for all cash collected on the receivables.

Instructions

Prepare the journal entries for both Ashton Winery and First Union Bank to record the following:

(a) Transfer of accounts receivable and issuance of the note on September 1, 1999.
(b) Collection in September of $220,000 of the transferred accounts receivable less cash discounts of $3,000. In addition, sales returns of $7,000 were processed.
(c) Remittance by Ashton of September collections plus accrued interest to the bank on October 1.
(d) Collection in October of the balance of the transferred accounts receivable less $1,000 written off as uncollectible.
(e) Remittance by Ashton of the balance due of $33,000 ($250,000 - $217,000) on the note plus interest on November 1.

Solution to Exercise 7-5

(a)

Ashton Winery			First Union Bank		
Cash	246,500		Notes Receivable	250,000	
Finance Charge	3,500*		Finance Revenue		3,500*
Notes Payable		250,000	Cash		246,500

*1% X $350,000 = $3,500

(b)

Ashton Winery			First Union Bank
Cash	217,000		(No Entry)
Sales Discounts	3,000		
Sales Returns	7,000		
Accounts Receivable		227,000*	

*$220,000 + $7,000 = $227,000

(c)

Ashton Winery			First Union Bank		
Interest Expense	2,500*		Cash	219,500	
Notes Payable	217,000		Interest Revenue		2,500*
Cash		219,500	Notes Receivable		217,000

*$250,000 X .12 X. 1/12 = $2,500

(d)

Cash	122,000		(No Entry)		
Allowance for Doubtful Accounts	1,000				
Accounts Receivable		123,000*			

*$350,000 - $227,000 = $123,000

(e)

Interest Expense	330*		Cash	33,330	
Notes Payable	33,000		Interest Revenue		330*
Cash		33,330	Notes Receivable		33,000

*$33,000 X .12 X 1/12

TIP: Receivables are often used as collateral in a borrowing transaction. A creditor often requires that the debtor designate or pledge receivables as security for the loan. If the loan is not paid when due, the creditor has the right to convert the collateral to cash—that is, to collect the receivables. (If the receivables are transferred to the transferee for custodial purposes, the custodial arrangement is often referred to as a **pledge**.) **Factors** are finance companies or banks that buy receivables from businesses for a fee and then collect remittances directly from the customers. This exercise **(Exercise 7-5)** illustrates a borrowing transaction whereas **Exercise 7-4** illustrates a sales transaction.

ILLUSTRATION 7-3
TWO FORMATS FOR BANK RECONCILIATIONS (L.O.10)

First One:

Balance per bank
- Add positive items per books not on bank's records.
- Deduct negative items per books not on bank's records.
- Add or deduct, whichever is applicable, bank error in recording receipts or disbursements.

Correct cash balance

Balance per books
- Add positive items per bank not on books.
- Deduct negative items per bank not on books.
- Add or deduct, whichever is applicable, depositor error in recording receipts or disbursements.

Correct cash balance

Second One:

Balance per bank
- Add positive items per books not on bank's records.
- Deduct negative items per books not on bank's records.
- Add or deduct, whichever is applicable, bank error in recording receipts or disbursements.
- Deduct positive items per bank not on books.
- Add negative items per bank not on books.
- Add or deduct, whichever is applicable, depositor error in recording receipts or disbursements.

Balance per books

Examples of reconciling items:

Positive item per books not on bank's records:
- Deposit in transit

Negative item per books not on bank's records:
- Outstanding check

Positive item per bank not on books:
- Note collected by bank
- Interest paid by bank to depositor on account balance

Negative item per bank not on books:
- Bank service charge
- Customer's NSF check returned by bank
- Note paid by bank

Error by bank:
- In recording receipt
- In recording disbursement

Error by depositor:
- In recording receipt
- In recording disbursement

ILLUSTRATION 7-3 (Continued)

TIP: If you have a checking account, look at the back of your bank statement. A bank often includes a form to assist you in reconciling your bank account. Very often that form reconciles the cash balance per bank to the cash balance per books rather than reconciling both the bank cash balance and the book cash balance to the correct (adjusted) cash balance.

TIP: The "Balance per bank" caption on a bank reconciliation is often replaced with "Balance per bank statement," and "Balance per books" is often titled "Balance per ledger."

TIP: The "Correct cash balance" caption on a bank reconciliation is often replaced with "Adjusted cash balance." The adjusted cash balance as determined by the bank reconciliation will be the amount used to report for cash on the balance sheet. (The Cash account in the general ledger often includes cash on hand and cash in the bank, although separate ledger accounts such as Cash in Bank and Cash on Hand may be used. The balance of this account and any other unrestricted cash accounts, such as the Petty Cash account, are added together to report cash on the balance sheet.)

TIP: Some items in a bank reconciliation will require adjustments either on the depositor's books or in the bank's records, while the others will not. When the balance per bank to correct cash balance format is used in preparing a single-column bank reconciliation, all of the reconciling items appearing in the lower half of the reconciliation (balance per books to correct cash balance) require adjustment on the depositor's books. All of the reconciling items appearing in the upper half of the reconciliation **except** for deposits in transit and outstanding checks require adjustment on the bank's books.

TIP: Unless otherwise indicated, an NSF check is assumed to be a customer's NSF check; that is, an NSF check is considered to be from a customer of the depositor, rather than a depositor's NSF check.

TIP: A depositor's checking account is a liability on the bank's books, so a bank debit memo decreases the depositor's cash balance and a bank credit memo increases the depositor's cash balance. On the bank statement, debits appear as a result of checks that have cleared during the month or bank debit memos for items such as bank service charges (BSC). Credits on the bank statement represent deposits or bank credit memos.

EXERCISE 7-6

Purpose: (L.O.10) This exercise will help you review situations that give rise to reconciling items on a bank reconciliation and identify those which require adjusting entries on the depositor's books.

A sketch of the bank reconciliation at July 31, 1999 for the Ace Electric Company and a list of possible reconciling items appear below.

Ace Electric Co.
BANK RECONCILIATION
July 31, 1999

Balance per bank statement, July 31		$X,XXX
A. Add:	$XXX	
	XXX	X,XXX
		X,XXX
B. Deduct:		X,XXX
Correct cash balance, July 31		$X,XXX
Balance per books, July 31		$ X,XXX
C. Add:	$XXX	
	XXX	X,XXX
		X,XXX
D. Deduct:	XXX	
	XXX	
	XXX	
	XXX	X,XXX
Correct cash balance, July 31		$X,XXX

_____ 1. Deposits of July 30 amounting to $1,482 have not reached the bank as of July 31.

_____ 2. A customer's check for $40 that was deposited on July 20 was returned NSF by the bank; return has not been recorded by Ace.

_____ 3. Bank service charge for July amounts to $3.

_____ 4. Included with the bank statement was check No. 422 for $702 as payment of an account payable. In comparing the check with the cash disbursement records, it was discovered that the check was incorrectly entered in the cash disbursements journal for $720.

_____ 5. Outstanding checks at July 31 amount to $1,927.

_____ 6. The bank improperly charged a check of the Ace Plumbing Co. for $25 to Ace Electric Co.'s account.

_____ 7. The bank charged $8 during July for printing checks.

_____ 8. During July, the bank collected a customer's note receivable for the Ace Electric Co.; face amount $1,000, interest $20, and the bank charged a $2 collection fee. This transaction has not been recorded by Ace.

_____ 9. A check written by Ace in June for $180 cleared the bank during July.

_____ 10. Deposits of June 30 for $1,200 were recorded by the company on June 30 but were not recorded by the bank until July 2.

Instructions

(a) Indicate how each of the 10 items listed above would be handled on the bank reconciliation by placing the proper code letter in the space provided. The applicable code letters appear in the sketch of the bank reconciliation. Use the code "NR" for any item which is not a reconciling item on July 31.

(b) Assume that the July 31 balance per bank statement was $4,332. Complete the bank reconciliation using the items given and answer the questions that follow:

1. What is the adjusted (correct) cash balance at July 31? $______________

2. What is the balance per books **before** adjustment at July 31? $______________

3. What reconciling items require an adjusting entry on Ace Electric Company's books? (Identify by item numbers.) ______________________________

4. What item(s) requires a special entry on the bank's records to correct an error(s)? ______________________________

Solution to Exercise 7-6

(a)

1.	A	6.	A
2.	D	7.	D
3.	D	8.	C, D
4.	C	9.	NR
5.	B	10.	NR

> TIP: Items 9 and 10 would have been reconciling items of cash balances on the June 30 bank reconciliation (the prior month).

(b)
1. $3,912* ($4,332 + $1,482 + $25 - $1,927 = $3,912)
2. $2,927* [X + $18 + $1,020 - $40 - $3 - $8 - $2 = $3,912 (answer to question 1)]
   X = $2,927
3. 2; 3; 4; 7; 8
4. 6

*See the completed bank reconciliation on the following page.

Approach to part (b) 2: You can compute the correct cash balance by completing the top half of the bank reconciliation (balance per bank to correct cash balance). The correct cash balance can then be entered on the last line of the bottom half of the reconciliation and used along with certain reconciling items to "work backwards" to compute the $2,927 cash balance per books before adjustment.

Ace Electric Co.
BANK RECONCILIATION
July 31, 1999

Balance per bank statement, July 31		$ 4,332
Add: Deposits in transit on July 31	$1,482	
Check improperly charged by bank	25	1,507
		5,839
Deduct: Checks outstanding as of July 31		1,927
Correct cash balance at July 31		$3,912
Balance per books, July 31		$2,927
Add: Error in recording check No. 422	$ 18	
Collection of customer's note receivable and interest by bank	1,020	1,038
		3,965
Deduct: Customer's NSF check	40	
Bank service charge for July	3	
Cost of printing checks	8	
Bank collection fee	2	53
Correct cash balance at July 31		$3,912

TIP: The required adjusting entries on the depositor's books would be:

Cash	18	
Accounts Payable		18
(To correct error in recording check No. 422)		
Cash	1,020	
Note Receivable		1,000
Interest Revenue		20
(To record collection of note receivable by bank)		
Accounts Receivable	40	
Cash		40
(To record customer's NSF check)		
Miscellaneous Expense	13	
Cash		13
(To record bank service charges: [$3 + $8 + $2 = $13])		

TIP: The above entries can be combined into one compound entry.

EXERCISE 7-7

Purpose: (L.O.10) This exercise will illustrate how to determine deposits in transit and outstanding checks.

Shown below for Molly's Folly are the:

(1) bank reconciliation at September 30, 1999.
(2) listing of deposits for October per the bank statement.
(3) listing of deposits for October per the books.
(4) listing of checks paid by the bank during October.
(5) listing of checks written by the depositor during October.

Molly's Folly
BANK RECONCILIATION
September 30, 1999

Balance per bank statement		$ 15,000
Add: Deposits in transit		
September 29	$ 2,000	
September 30	1,600	3,600
		18,600
Deduct: Outstanding checks		
No. 514	650	
No. 516	410	
No. 520	560	
No. 521	740	
No. 522	1,000	3,360
Correct cash balance		$ 15,240
Balance per books		$ 15,690
Deduct: Customer's NSF check	$ 400	
Bank service charge	50	450
Correct cash balance		$ 15,240

Bank Statement for October—Deposits

Date	Amount	Date	Amount	Date	Amount
10/1	$ 2,000	10/11	$ 1,200	10/25	$ 100
10/2	1,600	10/15	200	10/27	600
10/3	500	10/18	400	10/28	800
10/5	300	10/21	700	10/29	1,300
10/11	1,100	10/22	900	Total	$ 11,700

Cash Receipts Journal

Date	Amount	Date	Amount	Date	Amount
10/1	$ 500	10/20	$ 700	10/29	$ 1,400
10/4	300	10/21	900	10/30	1,500
10/8	1,100	10/23	100	10/31	550
10/10	1,200	10/25	600	Total	$ 11,550
10/13	200	10/27	800		
10/16	400	10/28	1,300		

Bank Statement for October—Checks Paid and Debit Memos

Date	Check #	Amount	Date	Check #	Amount
10/1	514	$ 650	10/13	534	$ 220
10/1	520	560	10/14	535	240
10/4	521	740	10/18	538	380
10/4	522	1,000	10/18	536	250
10/5	525	120	10/18	537	320
10/5	526	140	10/18	539	430
10/6	528	230	10/19	540	510
10/8	529	310	10/23	541	330
10/8	527	210	10/25	542	340
10/8	530	420	10/29	545	540
10/11	532	160	10/29	546	470
10/11	531	130	10/31	DM	30
10/12	533	190	Total		$ 8,920

Cash Payments Journal—Checks Issued

Date	Check #	Amount	Date	Check #	Amount
10/1	525	$ 120	10/14	538	$ 380
10/1	526	140	10/15	539	430
10/3	527	210	10/17	540	510
10/4	528	230	10/20	541	330
10/5	529	310	10/23	542	340
10/5	530	420	10/25	543	110
10/7	531	130	10/26	544	160
10/7	532	106	10/27	545	540
10/7	533	190	10/28	546	470
10/11	534	220	10/31	547	590
10/11	535	240	10/31	548	640
10/12	536	250	Total		$ 7,386
10/14	537	320			

Instructions

(a) Prepare a list of deposits in transit at October 31, 1999.
(b) Prepare a list of outstanding checks at October 31, 1999.
(c) Locate any errors per books, assuming that the information recorded in the bank's records is correct.
(d) Locate any bank memoranda that will need to be recorded on the books.

Solution to Exercise 7-7

(a) Deposits in transit at October 31, 1999:

October 29	$ 1,400
October 30	1,500
October 31	550
Total	$ 3,450

(b) Outstanding checks at October 31, 1999:

No.	Amount
516	$ 410
543	110
544	160
547	590
548	640
	$ 1,910

(c) Check No. 532 was recorded on the depositor's books for $106 when it should have been recorded for the correct amount of $160.

(d) The DM for $30 on October 31 will need to be recorded on the depositor's books. (The DM is likely for bank service charges for October.)

Approach and Explanation:

(a) To identify the deposits in transit at October 31:

(1) Compare the deposits in transit at September 30 (per the company's bank reconciliation at that date) with the October bank statement. If the deposit did not get recorded by the bank during October it is to be considered a deposit in transit at October 31. (It would be extremely rare for a particular deposit to be listed as a deposit in transit on **two** successive bank reconciliations because it would indicate the deposit was lost in the mail or lost in the bank's facilities or a victim of some strange fate.)

For Molly's Folly, the $2,000 and $1,600 items deposited at the end of September (deposits in transit at September 30, 1999) both were recorded by the bank in early October as expected.

(2) Compare the deposits made during October per company records with the October deposits per the bank's records. Deposits not recorded by the bank represent **deposits in transit**. As can be expected, the receipts recorded on the books at the very end of October have not had enough time to be processed by the bank by the end of the day on October 31. These include the deposits made by Molly's Folly on October 29 ($1,400), October 30 ($1,500), and October 31 ($550).

(b) To identify the outstanding checks at October 31, 1999:

(1) Compare the checks outstanding at September 30, 1999 (per the September 30th bank reconciliation) with the checks clearing the bank as shown on the October bank statement. If a September check remains unpaid at the end of October, it is an outstanding check at October 31. For Molly's Folly, check numbers 514, 520, 521, and 522 all cleared the bank during October, but check number 516 ($410) remains unpaid at October 31, 1999. (The check could be lost in the mail or lost in the banking system. More likely, the check is still in the hands of the payee, who for some reason has not yet deposited it to his account.)

(2) Compare the checks written by Molly's Folly during October with the checks paid by the bank. Issued checks that have not been paid by the bank represent **outstanding checks**.

For Molly's Folly, October check numbers 543 ($110), 544 ($160), 547 ($590), and 548 ($640) were written during October and are outstanding at October 31.

(c) To identify errors on either the bank's records or the depositor's books, compare all of the figures on the October bank statement with their source on the depositor's records. If there are any discrepancies, determine which is in error. For Molly's Folly, check number 532 correctly cleared the bank for $160 but was entered in the cash payments journal as $106. (The facts of the problem state that the bank's records are correct.) This transposition-type error caused the depositor's bank balance per ledger to be overstated by $54 ($160 $106 = $54).

TIP: Note that a transposition error (reversing the order of numbers) will cause a difference that is divisible by 9.

EXERCISE 7-8

Purpose: (L.O.10) This exercise will allow you to practice preparing a bank reconciliation.

A bank reconciliation should be prepared by a depositor every month.

The cash balance per bank at October 31 is $17,780, and the cash balance per Molly's Folly's books at October 31 is $19,404.

Instructions

(a) Using the data in **Exercise 7-7** and the solution to that exercise, prepare a bank reconciliation for Molly's Folly at October 31, 1999.

(b) Prepare the adjusting entries at October 31 for the depositor's books. Assume check No. 532 was issued to the power company for utilities.

Solution to Exercise 7-8

(a)

Molly's Folly
BANK RECONCILIATION
October 31, 1999

Balance per bank statement		$ 17,780*
Add: Deposits in transit [Answer (a) Exercise 7-7]		3,450
		21,230
Deduct: Outstanding checks [Answer (b) Exercise 7-7]		1,910
Correct cash balance		$ 19,320
Balance per books		$ 19,404**
Deduct: Bank service charge	$ 30	
Error in recording check No. 532	54	84
Correct cash balance		$ 19,320

*To add to the complexity of this exercise, you could be asked to solve for the $17,780 cash balance per bank statement. The computation would be as follows:

Balance per bank statement at September 30, 1999	$ 15,000
Add: Deposits recorded during October and credit memoranda	11,700
Deduct: Checks paid during October and debit memoranda	8,920
Balance per bank statement at October 30, 1999	$ 17,780

**To add to the complexity of this exercise, you could be asked to solve for the $19,404 cash balance per books at October 31, 1999. The computation would be as follows:

Balance per books at September 30, 1999 before adjustment	$ 15,690
Deduct: NSF check recorded by an adjusting entry	400
Deduct: Bank service charge for September recorded by an adjusting entry	50
Correct cash balance at September 30	15,240
Add: Deposits made during October	11,550
Deduct: Checks written (issued) during October	7,386
Balance per books at October 31, 1999	$ 19,404

An alternate approach to solving for the balance per books before adjustment is illustrated in the **Solution to Exercise 7-6** part (b) 2.

TIP: Keep in mind that deposits in transit and outstanding checks are reconciling items but do **not** require adjusting entries on either the bank's books or the depositor's books.

(b)	Oct. 31	Miscellaneous Expense	30	
		Cash		30
		(To record the bank service charges for Oct.)		
	Oct. 31	Utilities Expense	54	
		Cash		54
		(To correct error in recording check no. 532)		

EXERCISE 7-9

Purpose: (L.O.10) This exercise reviews the journal entries involved with establishing and maintaining a petty cash fund.

The Kirmani Corporation makes most expenditures by check. The following transactions relate to an imprest fund established by the Kirmani Corporation to handle small expenditures on an expedient basis.

		Transactions
May	4	Wrote a $100 check to establish the petty cash fund.
	6	Paid taxi $2 to deliver papers to a branch office.
	6	Purchased stamps, $13.
	8	Paid $15 for advertising posters.
	12	Paid $6 for mail received with "postage due."
	12	Paid $8 for coffee supplies.
	13	Paid $17 for office supplies.
	14	Paid bus charges of $18 to ship goods to a customer.
	15	Counted the remaining coins and currency in the fund, $20. Wrote a check to replenish the fund.

Instructions

(a) Record the transactions in general journal form.

(b) Answer the questions that follow:

1. How much coin and currency should have been in the petty cash box at the end of the day on May 12? $________
2. How much coin and currency should have been in the petty cash box on May 15 before replenishment? $______
3. What was the balance in the Petty Cash ledger account on May 12? $______

4. What was the balance in the Petty Cash ledger account at the end of the day, May 15? $______

TIP: In order to answer the last two questions, it would be helpful to post the journal entries to a T-account for Petty Cash.

Solution to Exercise 7-9

(a)

			Debit	Credit
May 4	Petty Cash		100	
	Cash			100
	(To establish a petty cash fund)			
May 15	Miscellaneous Expense ($2 + $8)		10	
	Postage Expense ($13 + $6)		19	
	Advertising Expense		15	
	Office Supplies		17	
	Transportation-out		18	
	Cash Over and Short		1	
	Cash			80
	(To replenish the petty cash fund)			

(b)

1. There should have been $56 in coin and currency in the fund at the end of the day on May 12. ($100 - $2 - $13 - $15 - $6 - $8 = $56)
2. There should have been $21 in coin and currency in the fund on May 15 before replenishment. ($100 - $2 - $13 - $15 - $6 - $8 - $17 - $18 = $21)

TIP: Because only $20 was found in the fund at that date, there was a shortage of $1, which must be recorded by a debit to the Cash Over and Short account.

3. $100
4. $100

TIP: The balance of the Petty Cash account changes **only** when the fund is established or the size of the fund is increased or decreased. The Petty Cash account balance is **not** affected by expenditures from the fund nor replenishments. (No journal entry is made at the time an expenditure is made. Expenditures from the fund are accounted for at the date of replenishment.)

TIP: Petty Cash is not normally reported separately on the balance sheet. The balance of the Petty Cash account is generally lumped together with all other cash items when a balance sheet is prepared.

EXERCISE 7-10

Purpose: (L.O.11) This exercise will allow you to practice preparing a proof of cash under both of the alternative formats.

The following data pertain to the Burghard Company for 1999:

1. Per the bank statement for February: January 31 balance, $20,000; February receipts, $22,000; February disbursements, $24,000; February 28 balance, $18,000.

2. Per the books: January 31 unadjusted balance, $16,020; February receipts, $19,410; February disbursements, $21,505, February 28 balance, $13,925.

3. Bank service charge of $20 for January is included in book disbursements for February.

4. Bank service charge of $35 for February is included on the bank statement for February.

5. The first deposit shown on the February bank statement was $5,000 and was included in January's cash receipts per books.

6. $7,000 of checks written in February have not cleared the bank by February 28.

7. A check written for office supplies in February for $970 was incorrectly recorded in the cash disbursements journal and in the check register as $790. This check cleared the bank in February for $970. Office supplies are charged to Office Supplies Expense when purchased.

8. The bank credited the firm's account in error for $500 in February for another firm's deposit.

9. The bank collected a $1,000 note receivable for the company in February plus $90 interest. The company has not yet recorded this transaction.

10. Cash receipts for February 28 of $4,000 did not reach the bank until March 2.

11. All $9,000 of checks outstanding at January 31 cleared the banking system during February.

12. A customer's NSF check in the amount of $300 was returned with the February bank statement. This check was redeposited in March. As of the end of February, Burghard has not yet made an entry for the return of this check by the bank.

Instructions

(a) Prepare a proof of cash using the format that reconciles balance per bank to balance per books for the Burghard Co. for February.

(b) Prepare a proof of cash using the format that reconciles both the bank and book balances to correct balances.

(c) Prepare any adjusting entry(ies) required for the books.

TIP: A four-column bank reconciliation is simply a single column reconciliation of cash balances (bank to books or bank to correct and books to correct) at one date and a single-column reconciliation of cash balances at another date plus a reconciliation of total cash receipts and total cash disbursements for the period between those two different dates.

TIP: On a **proof of cash** (another name for a **four-column bank reconciliation**), a reconciling item will appear in two of the four columns:

1. Usually a reconciling item on a proof of cash will appear in one outside column and one inside column. In such instances: If the two columns in which it appears are adjacent, the mathematical signs are opposite of each other; if the two columns in which it appears are nonadjacent, the mathematical signs are the same.
2. Although it is rare, a reconciling item on a proof of cash may appear in both of the center two columns. In such an instance, the mathematical signs are the same. An example of a reconciling item which appears only in the inside columns and not in either of the outside columns is: A customer's check was deposited during February and recorded as a receipt on the books and by the bank. The check was returned NSF by the bank during February and considered by the bank to be a disbursement; however, this action was not recorded on the depositor's books. The returned check was redeposited during February and therefore considered another deposit per the bank's records but was not considered an additional receipt per books. The check then cleared. Thus, the customer's check appears twice in the receipts per bank and once in the disbursements per bank. This differs from the treatment per books as this same check appears only once in the receipts per books and does not appear at all in the disbursements per books.

Solution to Exercise 7-10

(a)

Burghard Company
PROOF OF CASH
For February 1999

	Balance Jan. 31	February Receipts	February Disburse-ments	Balance Feb. 28
Per bank	$20,000	$ 22,000	$ 24,000	$ 18,000
Bank service charge—Jan.	20		20	
Bank service charge—Feb.			(35)	35
Deposits in transit—1/31	5,000	(5,000)		
Outstanding checks—2/28			7,000	(7,000)
Co. error in recording check			(180)	180
Bank error in entering receipt		(500)		(500)
Collection of note by bank		(1,090)		(1,090)
Deposit in transit—2/28		4,000		4,000
Outstanding checks—1/31	(9,000)		(9,000)	
Customer NSF check			(300)	300
Per books	$ 16,020	$ 19,410	$ 21,505	$ 13,925

(b)

Burghard Company
PROOF OF CASH
For February 1999

	Balance Jan. 31	February Receipts	February Disburse-ments	Balance Feb. 28
Per bank	$ 20,000	$ 22,000	$ 24,000	$ 18,000
Deposit in transit—1/31	5,000	(5,000)		
Outstanding checks—2/28			7,000	(7,000)
Bank error in entering receipt		(500)		(500)
Deposit in transit—2/28		4,000		4,000
Outstanding checks—1/31	(9,000)		(9,000)	
Correct amounts	$ 16,000	$ 20,500	$ 22,000	$ 14,500
Per books	$ 16,020	$ 19,410	$ 21,505	$ 13,925
Bank service charge—Jan.	(20)		(20)	
Bank service charge—Feb.			35	(35)
Co. error in recording check			180	(180)
Collection of note by bank		1,090		1,090
Customer NSF check			300	(300)
Correct amounts	$ 16,000	$ 20,500	$ 22,000	$ 14,500

(c)	Office Expenses—Bank Charges	35	
	Cash		35
	Office Supplies Expense	180	
	Cash		180
	Cash	1,090	
	Note Receivable		1,000
	Interest Revenue		90
	Accounts Receivable	300	
	Cash		300

ANALYSIS OF MULTIPLE-CHOICE TYPE QUESTIONS

QUESTION

1. (L.O.1) Which of the following items should **not** be included in the Cash caption on the balance sheet?
   a. Coins and currency in the cash register
   b. Checks from other parties presently in the cash register
   c. Amounts on deposit in checking account at the bank
   d. Postage stamps on hand

Explanation: Cash on hand, cash in banks, and petty cash are often combined and reported simply as Cash. Undeposited checks from other parties is a component of cash on hand. Postage stamps on hand are classified as a prepaid expense. (Solution = d.)

QUESTION

2. (L.O.2) The SEC recommends that legally restricted deposits held at a bank as compensating balances against long-term borrowing arrangements should be:
   a. used to reduce the amount reported as long-term debt on the balance sheet.
   b. reported separately among the "cash and cash equivalent items" in Current Assets on the balance sheet.
   c. separately classified as noncurrent assets in either the Investments or Other Assets sections of the balance sheet.
   d. used to reduce the amount reported as short-term debt on the balance sheet.

Explanation: The SEC recommends that legally restricted deposits held as compensating balances against short-term borrowing arrangements be stated separately among the "cash and cash equivalent items" in Current Assets. Restricted deposits held as compensating balances against long-term borrowing arrangements should be separately classified as noncurrent assets in either the Investments or Other Assets sections, using a caption such as "Cash on Deposit Maintained as Compensating Balance." To use the asset balance to directly reduce a debt (answer selections "a" and "d" would be "offsetting assets against liabilities" which violates a rule against offsetting or setoff. Only in rare circumstances is it permissable to offset assets and liabilities.) (Solution = c.)

QUESTION

3. (L.O.5) Gatorland recorded uncollectible accounts expense of $30,000 and wrote off accounts receivable of $25,000 during the year. The net effect of these two transactions on working capital was a decrease of:
   a. $55,000.
   b. $30,000.
   c. $25,000.
   d. $5,000.

Approach and Explanation: Reconstruct both entries referred to in the question. Then analyze each debit and each credit separately as to its effect on working capital (total current assets minus total current liabilities). (Refer to **Illustration 7-1**.)

			Effect on Working Capital
Uncollectible Accounts Expense	30,000		None
Allow. for Uncollectible Accounts		30,000	Decrease 30,000
Allowance for Uncollectible Accounts	25,000		Increase 25,000
Accounts Receivable		25,000	Decrease 25,000
Net Effect			Decrease 30,000
			(Solution = b.)

QUESTION

4. (L.O.5) Chelser Corporation performed an analysis and an aging of its accounts receivable at December 31, 1999, which disclosed the following:

Accounts receivable balance	$ 100,000
Allowance for uncollectible accounts balance	5,000
Accounts deemed uncollectible	7,400

The net realizable value of the accounts receivable at December 31 is:
   a. $87,600.
   b. $92,600.
   c. $95,000.
   d. $97,600.

Approach and Explanation: Read the last sentence of the question: "The net realizable value of the accounts receivable at December 31 is..." Underline "net realizable value of accounts receivable." Write down the definition of net realizable value of accounts receivable—amount of accounts receivable ultimately expected to be converted into cash. Read the details of the question. If an aging shows $7,400 of the $100,000 accounts are deemed uncollectible, then the remaining $92,600 are expected to be converted into cash. (Because the balance of the allowance account does not agree with the amount of uncollectibles per the aging, the allowance for uncollectible accounts balance must be the unadjusted balance or the percentage of sales method is being used to determine the amount to record as bad debt expense.) (Solution = b.)

QUESTION

5. (L.O.5) The following data are available for 1999:

Sales, cash	$ 200,000
Sales, credit	500,000
Accounts Receivable, January 1	80,000
Accounts Receivable, December 31	72,000
Allowance for Doubtful Accounts, January 1	4,000
Accounts written off during 1999	4,600

The journal entry to record bad debt expense for the period and to adjust the allowance account is to be based on an estimate of 1% of credit sales. The entry to record the uncollectible accounts expense for 1999 would include a debit to the Bad Debt Expense account for:

a. $7,200.
b. $5,600.
c. $4,400.
d. $5,000.

Approach and Explanation: Think about the emphasis of the entry when the percentage-of-sales basis is used. This method emphasizes the income statement. Therefore, 1% times credit sales equals bad debt expense ($500,000 x 1% = $5,000). The balance of the allowance account before adjustment does **not** affect this computation or entry. (Solution = d.)

QUESTION

6. (L.O.5) The following data are available for 1999:

Sales, cash	$ 200,000
Sales, credit	500,000
Accounts Receivable, January 1	80,000
Accounts Receivable, December 31	72,000
Allowance for Doubtful Accounts, January 1	4,000
Accounts written off during 1999	4,600

The journal entry to record bad debt expense for the period and to adjust the allowance account is to be based on an aging analysis of accounts receivable. The aging analysis of accounts receivable at December 31, 1999, reveals that $5,200 of existing accounts receivable are estimated to be uncollectible. The entry to record the uncollectible accounts expense for 1999 will involve a debit to the Bad Debt Expense account for:

a. $9,800.
b. $5,800.
c. $5,200.
d. $4,600.

Approach and Explanation: An aging analysis is performed to determine the best figure to represent the cash (net) realizable value of the accounts receivable in the balance sheet. Thus, $5,200 is the desired balance for the allowance account at the reporting date. Determine the existing balance in the allowance account and the adjusting entry needed to arrive at the desired ending balance.

Allowance for Doubtful Accounts

Write-offs, 1999	4,600	Balance, 1/1/99	4,000	**Entry**
Balance before adjustment	600	Adjustment needed	X	**←Needed.**
		Desired balance at 12/31/99	5,200	

Solving for X: X - \$600 = \$5,200
X = \$5,200 + \$600
X = <u>\$5,800</u> (Solution = b.)

QUESTION

7. (L.O.9) The accounts receivable turnover ratio measures the:
   a. number of times the average balance of accounts receivable is collected during the period.
   b. percentage of accounts receivable turnover over to a collection agency during the period.
   c. percentage of accounts receivable arising during certain seasons.
   d. number of times the average balance of inventory is sold during the period.

Approach and Explanation: Write down the components of the accounts receivable turnover ratio. Think about why it is computed. The computation is as follows:

$$\text{Accounts Receivable Turnover Ratio} = \frac{\text{Net Sales}}{\text{Average trade receivables (net)}}$$

Because cash sales do not go through the Accounts Receivable account, only net credit sales belong in the numerator; however, very often that information is not available. The accounts receivable ratio measures the number of times, on average, the accounts receivable balance was collected during the period. This ratio is used to assess the liquidity of the receivables. This ratio can be divided into 365 days to obtain the average days to collect accounts receivable (Solution = a.)

QUESTION

8. (L.O.10) The term "outstanding checks" refers to:
   a. checks that have been lost in the mail or for some other reason have been misplaced.
   b. depositor checks which have been processed by the bank but have not yet been recorded by the depositor.
   c. customer checks which have been returned by the bank because the customer's bank would not honor them.
   d. depositor checks which have not yet cleared the banking system.

Explanation: There is a lag time between the date a check is issued and the date the check clears the banking system. During the time between these two dates, the checks are referred to as "outstanding checks." Checks written by the enterprise but not mailed until **after** the balance sheet date should not be included with outstanding checks. Rather, they should be added back to the cash balance and reported as accounts payable. (Solution = d.)

QUESTION

9. (L.O.10) The following information pertains to Cruiser Co. at December 31, 1999:

Bank statement balance	$20,000
Checkbook balance	28,200
Deposit in transit	10,000
Outstanding checks	2,000
Bank service charges for December 200	

In Cruiser's balance sheet at December 31, 1999, cash should be reported as:

a. $18,000.
b. $20,000.
c. $28,000.
d. $30,000.

Approach and Explanation: When a question relates to data used in a bank reconciliation, you should sketch out the format for a bank reconciliation, put in the information given, and solve for the unknown piece.

Balance per bank statement	$ 20,000
Deposit in transit	10,000
Outstanding checks	(2,000)
Correct cash balance	$ 28,000
Balance per books	$ 28,200
Bank service charges	(200)
Correct cash balance	$ 28,000

In this particular question, the completion of either the top half or the bottom half of the reconciliation using the bank-to-correct balance method would be enough to solve for the answer requested. (Solution = c.)

QUESTION

10. (L.O.10) The following data relate to the bank account of Springfield Cleaners:

Cash balance, September 30, 1999 per bank	$ 10,000
Cash balance, October 31, 1999 per bank	21,500
Checks paid during October by bank	5,900
Checks written during October per books	6,800
Cash balance, October 31, 1999 per books	22,200
Bank service charges for October, not recorded on books	100
Deposits per books for October	19,000

The amount of deposits recorded by the bank in October is:

a. $19,000.
b. $17,500.
c. $11,500.
d. $5,700.

Approach and Explanation: Think about how deposits recorded by the bank affect the cash balance per bank and other items that cause that balance to change. Plug in the figures given and solve for the unknown.

Balance per bank, September 30	$ 10,000
Deposits per bank during October	X
Bank credit memoranda	-0-
Checks paid by bank during October	(5,900)
Bank service charge for October and other bank debit memoranda	(100)
Balance per bank, October 31	$ 21,500

Solving for X:

$10,000 + X - $5,900 - $100 = $21,500
X = $21,500 - $10,000 + $5,900 + $100
X = $17,500 (Solution = b.)

QUESTION

11. (L.O.10) The following information pertains to Tommy-Jer Corporation at December 31, 1999:

Balance per bank	$ 10,000
Deposit in transit	3,000
Outstanding checks	8,000
Bank service charges for December	200
Bank erroneously charged Tommy-Jer's account for Sonny-Ber's check written for $700. As of Dec. 31, the bank had not corrected this error	700

Tommy-Jer's cash balance per ledger (books) before adjustment at December 31, 1999 is:

a. $14,100.
b. $5,900.
c. $5,500.
d. $4,100.

Approach and Explanation: The balance per books (before adjustment) can easily be computed by putting the data into the format for a bank reconciliation. Either format (balance per bank to balance per books or balance per bank to correct balance) can be used. Each approach is illustrated below: (Solution = b.)

Balance per bank statement	$ 10,000
Deposit in transit	3,000
Outstanding checks	(8,000)
Bank service charges	200
Bank error in charge for check	700
Balance per ledger	$ 5,900

Balance per bank statement	$ 10,000
Deposit in transit	3,000
Outstanding checks	(8,000)
Bank error in charge for check	700
Correct cash balance	$ 5,700

Balance per books (ledger)	$ X
Bank service charge	(200)
Correct cash balance	$ 5,700

X = $5,900

CHAPTER 8

VALUATION OF INVENTORIES: A COST BASIS APPROACH

OVERVIEW

In accounting, the term inventory refers to a stock of goods held for sale in the ordinary course of business or goods that will be used or consumed in the production of goods to be sold. A number of questions regarding inventory are addressed in this chapter; these include: (1) How will the selection of a particular cost flow assumption affect the income statement and balance sheet? (2) What goods should be included in inventory? (3) How do inventory errors affect the financial statements? (4) How does a periodic inventory system differ from a perpetual system? (5) How do you compute the various layers of inventory when the dollar-value LIFO method is used?

SUMMARY OF LEARNING OBJECTIVES

1. **Identify major classifications of inventory.** Only one inventory account, Merchandise Inventory, appears in the financial statements of a merchandising concern. A manufacturer normally has three inventory accounts: Raw Materials, Work in Process, and Finished Goods. The cost assigned to goods and materials on hand but not yet placed into production is reported as raw materials inventory. The cost of the raw materials on which production has been started but not completed, plus the direct labor cost applied specifically to this material and a ratable share of manufacturing overhead costs, constitute the work in process inventory. The costs identified with the completed but unsold units on hand at the end of the fiscal period are reported as finished goods inventory.

2. **Distinguish between the perpetual and periodic inventory systems.** Under a perpetual inventory system, a continuous record of changes in inventory is maintained in the Inventory account. That is, all purchases and sales (issues) of goods are recorded directly in the Inventory account as they occur. Under a periodic inventory system, the quantity of inventory on hand is determined only periodically. The inventory accounts remain unchanged during the period and a Purchases account is debited for purchases. Cost of goods sold is determined at the end of the period using a formula. Ending inventory is ascertained by physical count.

3. **Identify the effects of inventory errors on the financial statements.** *If the ending inventory is misstated:* (1) inventory and retained earnings will be misstated in the balance sheet, (2) cost of goods sold and net income will be misstated in the income statement, and (3) working capital and the current ratio will be misstated. *If purchases and the ending inventory are misstated by the same amount:* (1) inventory and accounts payable will be misstated in the balance sheet, (2) cost of goods sold and net income will **not** be misstated in the income statement (even though purchases and ending inventory are both misstated in the income statement), and (3) the current ratio will be misstated.

4. **Identify the items that should be included as inventory cost.** Product costs are the costs directly associated with the acquisition of goods and the conversion of such goods to a salable condition. Such charges would include purchases, freight charges on goods purchased, other direct costs of acquisition, labor, and other production costs incurred in processing the goods up to the time of sale. Manufacturing overhead costs (which include indirect material, indirect labor, and such items as depreciation, taxes, insurance, heat, and electricity incurred in the manufacturing process) are also allocated to inventory.

5. **Describe and compare the cost flow assumptions used in accounting for inventories.** (1) **Average cost** prices items in inventory on the basis of the average cost of all similar goods available during the period. (2) **First-in, first-out (FIFO)** assumes that costs are used in the order in which the related goods were purchased. The cost of inventory on hand at a balance sheet date must therefore represent the most recent purchase prices. (3) **Last-in, first-out (LIFO)** matches the cost of the last goods purchased against revenue.

6. **Explain the significance and use of a LIFO reserve.** The difference between the inventory method used for internal reporting purposes and LIFO is referred to as the Allowance to Reduce Inventory to LIFO. Either the LIFO reserve or the replacement cost of the inventory should be disclosed.

7. **Explain the effect of LIFO liquidations.** The effect of LIFO liquidations is that costs from preceding periods are matched against sales revenues reported in current dollars. This leads to a distortion in net income and a substantial tax bill in the current period. LIFO liquidations can occur frequently when a specific goods LIFO approach is employed.

8. **Explain the dollar-value LIFO method.** An important feature of the dollar-value LIFO method is that increases and decreases in a pool are determined and measured in terms of total dollar value, not the physical quantity of specific goods in the inventory pool.

9. **Identify the major advantages and disadvantages of LIFO.** The major advantages of LIFO are: (1) recent costs are matched against current revenues to provide a better measure of current earnings; (2) as long as the price level increases and inventory quantities do not decrease, a deferral of income tax occurs in LIFO; (3) because of the deferral of income tax, there is improvement of cash flow; and (4) a company's future reported earnings will not be affected substantially by future price declines (future earnings hedge). Major disadvantages are: (1) reduced earnings, (2) inventory is stated in terms of old costs rather than recent costs, and (3) the cost flow does **not** approximate the physical flow of the items except in unique situations.

10. **Identify the reasons why the LIFO cost method is selected.** Preferability for LIFO can ordinarily be established if: (1) selling prices and revenues have been increasing faster than costs; and (2) LIFO has been traditional, such as department stores and industries like refining, chemicals, and glass where a fairly constant "base stock" is present. Conversely, LIFO would probably not be appropriate: (1) where changes in sales prices tend to lag behind changes in costs; (2) in situations where specific identification is traditional, such as in the sales of automobiles, farm equipment, art, and antique jewelry; and (3) where unit costs tend to decrease as production increases, thereby nullifying the tax benefit that LIFO might provide.

TIPS ON CHAPTER TOPICS

TIP: The cost of an inventory item includes all costs necessary to acquire the item and bring it to the location and condition for its intended use. This cost would include the item's purchase price, transportation-in, and any special handling charges. However, transportation-out is **not** included in the cost of inventory; it is classified as a selling expense on the income statement for the period in which the expense was incurred.

TIP: The transportation terms designate the point at which title passes. F.o.b. shipping point (or seller) means the title passes to the buyer when it leaves the seller's dock. F.o.b. destination (or buyer) means the title passes to the buyer when it arrives at the buyer's dock. Assuming that Palmer Company in Bay Hill, Florida sells to Payne Stewart in Orlando, Florida, the following shows synonymous terms:

F.o.b. shipping point	**F.o.b. destination**
or f.o.b. seller	or f.o.b. buyer
or f.o.b. Bay Hill, Florida	or f.o.b. Orlando, Florida

TIP: FIFO (first-in, first-out) means the cost of the first items put into inventory are used to price the first items out to cost of goods sold. Thus, the earliest acquisition prices are used to price cost of goods sold for the period, and the latest (most current) acquisition prices are used to price items in the ending inventory. LIFO (last-in, first-out) uses the most recent costs to price the units sold during the period, and it uses the oldest prices to cost the items in the ending inventory. Thus, in a period of rising prices, the method that will yield the lowest net income on the income statement and the lowest ending inventory on the balance sheet is the LIFO method.

TIP: The cost of the ending inventory determined by using the weighted-average method is an amount between the cost of the ending inventory determined by using the LIFO method and the cost of the ending inventory determined by using the FIFO method.

TIP: When working a problem which requires the computation of either ending inventory or cost of goods sold, remember that the total of the ending inventory and the cost of goods sold should equal the total cost of goods available for sale during the period (beginning inventory plus the net cost of purchases).

TIP: Sales revenue represents the **selling prices** of goods sold, whereas cost of goods sold expense represents the **cost** of items sold.

TIP: The inventory pricing method selected by an entity does **not** have to correspond to the actual physical flow of goods. Thus, a company can use the LIFO method to determine the cost of ending inventory even though the first goods purchased are the first to be sold.

TIP: An understatement in ending inventory of year 1 will cause an understatement in net income for year 1 and an overstatement in net income for year 2. Thus, retained earnings and working capital at the end of year 1 are understated. However, assuming no more errors are committed at the end of year 2, retained earnings and working capital are not affected at the end of year 2.

TIP: When using the dollar-value LIFO method, you must determine the layers of inventory in terms of base prices. Then each of those layers must be priced in terms of the price level of the period in which each particular layer was added.

TIP: When performing the computations for the dollar-value LIFO method, watch that the results are what you would expect them to be. For instance, most companies experience a trend of increasing prices. Therefore, in converting the ending inventory at current cost to base prices, you would expect the ending inventory at base prices to be an amount that is less than the ending inventory at current cost.

TIP: When using the dollar-value LIFO method, a current price index may be given, or you may have to solve for it. For instance, if prices increased over the current year by 8%, the current price index would be 108. Using another example, if ending inventory is given as $128,800 at current cost and $115,000 at base prices, the current price index is 112 ($128,800 ÷ $115,000 = 1.12, which is 112 percent).

TIP: A company can use one inventory cost method for financial reporting purposes and a different method for income tax reporting purposes. However, the Internal Revenue Code generally requires that if an entity selects LIFO for income tax reporting, it must also use LIFO for its general purpose financial statements.

EXERCISE 8-1

Purpose: (L.O.3) This exercise will enable you to practice identifying the effects of inventory errors on the financial statements.

The net income per books of Wacky Wicks Company was determined without knowledge of the errors indicated.

Year	Net Income Per Books	Error in Ending Inventory	
1996	$ 150,000	Overstated	$ 9,000
1997	156,000	Overstated	21,000
1998	162,000	Understated	33,000
1999	168,000	No error	

Instructions
Compute the correct net income figure for each of the four years after taking into account the inventory errors.

Solution to Exercise 8-1

Year	Net Income Per Books	Add Over-statement Jan. 1	Deduct Under-statement Jan. 1	Deduct Over-statement Dec. 31	Add Under-statement Dec. 31	Corrected Net Income
1996	$ 150,000			$ 9,000		$ 141,000
1997	156,000	$ 9,000		21,000		144,000
1998	162,000	21,000			$ 33,000	216,000
1999	168,000		$ 33,000			135,000

Approach and Explanation: When more than one error affects a given year (such as in 1997), analyze each error separately then combine the effects of each analysis to get the net impact of the errors. The beginning inventory for 1997 (ending inventory for 1996) was overstated by $9,000. Therefore, cost of goods sold was overstated by $9,000, and net income for 1997 was understated by $9,000. The ending inventory for 1997 was overstated by $21,000. Therefore, cost of goods sold was understated, and net income for 1997 was overstated by $21,000. An understatement in net income of $9,000 and an overstatement of $21,000 in 1997 net to an overstatement of $12,000 for the net income figure reported for 1997. This overstatement of $12,000, combined with the $156,000 amount reported, yields a corrected net income figure of $144,000 for 1997.

Another way of analyzing the effects of an individual error is illustrated below for the $21,000 overstatement of inventory at the end of 1997.

		Effect on 1997		Effect on 1998	
	Beginning inventory			Overstated	$21,000
+	Cost of goods purchased				
=	Cost of goods available for sale			Overstated	21,000
-	Ending inventory	Overstated	$21,000		
=	Cost of goods sold	Understated	21,000	Overstated	21,000
	Sales				
-	Cost of goods sold	Understated	21,000	Overstated	21,000
=	Gross profit	Overstated	21,000	Understated	21,000
-	Operating expenses				
=	Net income	Overstated	21,000	Understated	21,000

Thus, the previously computed net income figure for 1997 must be reduced by $21,000 to correct for this error. Also, the net income figure for 1998 must be increased by $21,000 to correct for the same error.

> **TIP:** The ending inventory for year 1 is the beginning inventory for year 2. Thus, when the ending inventory for year 1 is overstated, it will cause an overstatement in the net income for year 1 and an understatement in net income for year 2 for the same amount. This error will cause retained earnings at the end of year 1 to be overstated because net income for year 1 (which is overstated) is closed into retained earnings. The balance of retained earnings at the end of year 2 will be unaffected by this error because the net income for year 2 (which is understated by the same amount as the overstatement in retained earnings at the end of year 1) is closed into retained earnings; the error at this point counterbalances. Working capital at the end of year 1 is overstated (because inventory is a current asset), but working capital at the end of year 2 is unaffected because the inventory figure at the end of year 2 is determined by a physical inventory counting and pricing procedure. No new error in this process is assumed unless otherwise indicated.

EXERCISE 8-2

Purpose: (L.O.5,9) This exercise reviews the characteristics and the effects of using various pricing methods to determine inventory costs.

Instructions

Answer each of the following questions by inserting one of these abbreviations in the space provided:

SI	(specific identification)
WA	(weighted-average)
FIFO	(first-in-first-out)
LIFO	(last-in-first-out)

_________ 1. Which inventory cost method **best** matches current costs with current revenues on the income statement?

_________ 2. Which inventory cost method yields the most realistic amount for inventory, compared to replacement cost, on the balance sheet?

_________ 3. Which method results in the most exact ending inventory valuation when inventory items of the same type are **not** homogenous?

_________ 4. Which method is based on the assumption that inventory flow is "mixed" and therefore "mixes" all acquisition prices?

During a period of **rising prices**, which method yields the:

_________ 5. lowest net income figure?

_________ 6. lowest amount for inventory on the balance sheet?

_________ 7. lowest cost of goods sold figure?

_________ 8. lowest owners' equity figure?

During a period of **declining prices**, which method yields the:

_________ 9. lowest net income figure?

_________ 10. lowest amount for inventory on the balance sheet?

_________ 11. lowest cost of goods sold figure?

_________ 12. lowest owners' equity figure.

Solution to Exercise 8-2

1.	LIFO	5.	LIFO	9.	FIFO
2.	FIFO	6.	LIFO	10.	FIFO
3.	SI	7.	FIFO	11.	LIFO
4.	WA	8.	LIFO	12.	FIFO

Approach: Write down a description of the weighted-average, FIFO, and LIFO cost flow assumptions. Note the relative effects of these methods on the income statement and the balance sheet in a period of rising prices.

TIP: **Inventory pricing method** is a synonymous term for **inventory costing method**.

TIP: **FIFO (first-in, first-out)** means the cost of the first items put into inventory are used to price the first items out to cost of goods sold. Thus, the earliest acquisition prices are used to price cost of goods sold for the period, and the latest (most current) acquisition prices are used to price items in the ending inventory. **LIFO (last-in, first-out)** uses the most recent costs to price the units sold during the period, and it uses the oldest prices to cost the items in ending inventory. Thus, in a period of rising prices, the method that will yield the lowest net income on the income statement **and** the lowest ending inventory on the balance sheet is the LIFO method.

TIP: Some corporations prefer to use the LIFO method for purposes of determining taxable income on the entity's tax return because, in periods of inflation, LIFO yields a lower taxable income figure than other inventory costing methods. LIFO is said to defer holding gains; therefore, the payment of related income taxes is deferred also. For example, assume two inventory items are purchased for $50. One is sold for $75 and the other is held for a while. In the meantime, the supplier raises his price to $60. One more item is purchased to keep the inventory quantity at two. Then the old item is sold at a new selling price of $90. There is a $10 gain experienced because an item was purchased at $50 and held while prices (both acquisition and selling) increased. Using the FIFO method, that holding gain will be recognized in the current period as a part of the gross profit figure [sales of $165 ($75 + $90) minus cost of goods sold of $100 ($50 + $50) = gross profit of $65 ($25 + $40)]. Whereas if the LIFO method is used, that holding gain is deferred to a future period when the LIFO base is liquidated. Thus, the gross profit would only amount to $55 under LIFO [sales of $165 ($75 + $90) minus cost of goods sold of $110 ($50 + $60) = gross profit of $55 ($25 + $30)]. The difference between $65 gross profit under FIFO and $55 gross profit under LIFO is the $10 deferral of holding gain under LIFO.

ILLUSTRATION 8-1
PERPETUAL VS. PERIODIC INVENTORY SYSTEMS (L.O.2)

Features of a Perpetual System

1. Purchases of merchandise for resale are debited to Inventory rather than to Purchases.
2. Freight-in, Purchase Returns and Allowances, and Purchase Discounts are recorded in Inventory rather than in separate accounts.
3. Cost of goods sold is recognized for each sale by debiting the account, Cost of Goods Sold, and crediting Inventory.
4. Inventory is a control account that is supported by a subsidiary ledger of individual inventory records. The subsidiary records show the quantity and cost of each type of inventory on hand. At any point during the accounting period (assuming all postings are up to date), the balance of the Inventory account reflects the cost of the items that should be on hand at that point in time.

Features of a Periodic System

1. Purchases of merchandise for resale are debited to Purchases.
2. The Freight-in, Purchase Returns and Allowances, and Purchase Discounts accounts are separate accounts which are used to record information about inventory acquisitions during the accounting period.
3. Cost of goods sold is recognized only at the end of the accounting period when the (1) ending inventory amount (determined by physical count, pricing, and extensions) is recorded in the Inventory account, (2) the Purchases, Freight-in, Purchase Returns and Allowances, and Purchase Discounts account balances are closed to the Income Summary account, and (3) the beginning inventory amount is transferred from the Inventory account to the Income Summary account.
4. There is no subsidiary ledger for inventory. All during the accounting period, the Inventory account reflects the cost of the inventory items on hand at the beginning of the period (beginning inventory). The Inventory account is **not** updated for acquisitions and withdrawals of inventory during the period; it is updated only at the end of the period to reflect the cost of the items on hand at the balance sheet date.

ILLUSTRATION 8-1 (Continued)

<table>
<tr><th colspan="2">EXAMPLE</th></tr>
<tr><th>PERPETUAL SYSTEM</th><th>PERIODIC SYSTEM</th></tr>
<tr><td colspan="2">1. There are 8 units in beginning inventory at a cost of $2,000 each.</td></tr>
<tr><td>The Inventory account shows the inventory on hand at $16,000.</td><td>The Inventory account shows the inventory on hand at $16,000.</td></tr>
<tr><td colspan="2">2. Purchase 12 items on account at $2,000 each.</td></tr>
<tr><td>Inventory 24,000
Accounts Payable 24,000</td><td>Purchases 24,000
Accounts Payable 24,000</td></tr>
<tr><td colspan="2">3. Return one defective item for $2,000 credit.</td></tr>
<tr><td>Accounts Payable 2,000
Inventory 2,000</td><td>Accounts Payable 2,000
Purchase Returns & Allowances 2,000</td></tr>
<tr><td colspan="2">4. Sell 15 items on account for $3,000 each.</td></tr>
<tr><td>Accounts Receivable 45,000
Sales 45,000
Cost of Goods Sold 30,000
Inventory 30,000</td><td>Accounts Receivable 45,000
Sales 45,000</td></tr>
<tr><td colspan="2">5. End of period entries for inventory-related accounts (4 units on hand at $2,000 each).</td></tr>
<tr><td>No entries are necessary:
The Inventory account shows the ending balance as $8,000 ($16,000 + $24,000 - $2,000 - $30,000)</td><td>Inventory (ending by physical count) 8,000
Purchase Returns & Allowances 2,000
Cost of Goods Sold 30,000
Purchases 24,000
Inventory (beginning) 16,000</td></tr>
</table>

EXERCISE 8-3

Purpose: (L.O.5) This exercise will allow you to practice performing calculations to determine inventory cost under each of three costing (pricing) methods, using both the periodic and the perpetual systems.

The Griggs Company is a multi-product firm. Presented below is information concerning one of their products, Infusion-39:

Date	Transaction	Quantity	Cost
1/1	Beginning inventory	1,000	$12
2/4	Purchase	2,000	18
2/20	Sale	2,500	
4/2	Purchase	3,000	22
11/4	Sale	2,000	

Instructions

Compute the cost of the ending inventory, assuming Griggs uses:

(a) Periodic system, FIFO cost method.
(b) Perpetual system, FIFO cost method.
(c) Periodic system, LIFO cost method.
(d) Perpetual system, LIFO cost method.
(e) Periodic system, average cost method.
(f) Perpetual system, moving-average cost method.

Solution to Exercise 8-3

(a) **Periodic-FIFO:**

	Units	
Beginning inventory	1,000	
Purchases (2,000 + 3,000)	5,000	
Units available for sale	6,000	
Sold (2,500 + 2,000)	4,500	
Goods on hand (assumed)	1,500	1,500 units x $22 = $33,000

(b) **Perpetual-FIFO:** Same as periodic: $33,000

> **TIP:** The use of FIFO with a perpetual system always yields the same results as the use of FIFO with a periodic system. The same does **not** hold true with the LIFO or average cost methods.

(c) **Periodic-LIFO:**

1,000 units x $12	=	$12,000
500 units x $18	=	9,000
1,500 units	=	$21,000

(d) **Perpetual-LIFO:**

Date	Purchased	Sold	Balance
1/1			1,000 x $12 = $12,000
2/4	2,000 x $18 = $36,000		(2,000 x $18) + (1,000 x $12) = $48,000
2/20		(2,000 x $18) + (500 x $12) = $42,000	500 x $12 = $ 6,000
4/2	3,000 x $22 = $66,000		(3,000 x $22) + (500 x $12) = $72,000
11/4		2,000 x $22 = $44,000	(1,000 x $22) + (500 x $12) = $28,000

(e) **Periodic-average:**

1,000 x $12 =	$ 12,000					
2,000 x $18 =	36,000					
3,000 x $22 =	66,000					1,500 Units
6,000	$114,000	÷	6,000	=	$19 each	x $19
						$28,500

(f) **Perpetual-average:**

Date	Purchased	Sold	Balance
1/1			1,000 x $12 = $12,000
2/4	2,000 x $18 = $36,000		3,000 x $16[a] = $48,000
2/20		2,500 x $16 = $40,000	500 x $16 = $ 8,000
4/2	3,000 x $22 = $66,000		3,500 x $21.14[b] = $73,990
11/4		2,000 x $21.14 = $42,280	1,500 x $21.14 = $31,710

[a]1,000 x $12 = $12,000
2,000 x $18 = 36,000
3,000 $48,000

$48,000 ÷ 3,000 = $16.00

[b] 500 x $16 = $ 8,000
3,000 x $22 = 66,000
3,500 $74,000

$74,000 ÷ 3,500 = $21.14

TIP: When using the average method and a perpetual system, a new average unit cost must be computed **only** after each new purchase; a sale will **not** affect the average unit cost. The average method applied to a perpetual system is often called the **moving-average** method.

TIP: Examine your solution to the exercise above and judge the reasonableness of your answers. What do you expect the relationship of the answers to be for the periodic system?

(1) Because the trend of the acquisition costs was upward, the ending inventory computed under LIFO should be lower than the ending inventory figure computed under FIFO.

(2) The cost of the ending inventory determined by using the average method should be between the amount of the ending inventory determined by using the LIFO method and the amount of the ending inventory determined by using the FIFO method.

EXERCISE 8-4

Purpose: (L.O.2) This exercise will enable you to practice determining how to handle goods in transit and other items necessary for proper inventory valuation.

Jennifer Laudermilch Company, a supplier of artworks, provided the following information from its account records for the year ended December 31, 1999.

Inventory at December 31, 1999 (at cost, based on a physical count of goods in Laudermilch's warehouse on 12/31/99)	$ 820,000
Accounts payable at December 31, 1999	460,000
Net sales (sales less sales returns)	7,000,000

Additional information is as follows:

1. Laudermilch received goods costing $32,000 on January 2, 2000. The goods had been shipped f.o.b. shipping point on December 27, 1999, by Geoffrey Harrill Company.

2. Laudermilch received goods costing $41,000 on January 4, 2000. The goods had been shipped f.o.b. destination on December 28, 1999 by Nanula Company.

3. Laudermilch sold goods costing $18,000 to O'Toole Company on December 29, 1999. The goods were picked up by the common carrier on that same date and shipped f.o.b. shipping point. They were expected to arrive at the buyer's business as early as January 3, 2000. An invoice for $29,000 was recorded and mailed on December 29.

4. Laudermilch sold goods costing $30,000 to Matheson Company on December 31, 1999. The goods were picked up by the common carrier on that same date and shipped f.o.b. destination. They were expected to arrive at the buyer's store as early as January 2, 2000. These goods were billed to the customer for $45,000 on December 31 and were not included in the physical count at December 31, 1999.

5. Laudermilch is the consignor for a collection of prints. The prints are hanging in the showroom of The Dizzy Decorator. They cost Laudermilch $62,000 and are priced to sell at $95,000. They were not included in the physical count.

6. Laudermilch is the consignee for some goods from Asian Collectibles. They cost the consignor $50,000 and are priced to sell for $76,000 with Laudermilch to get a commission of 10%. They were included in the ending inventory at the selling price.

7. Included in the physical count were goods billed to a customer f.o.b. shipping point on December 31, 1999. These items had a cost of $24,000 and were billed at $38,000. The shipment was on Laudermilch's loading dock waiting to be picked up by the common carrier and was included in the physical count at December 31, 1999.

8. Goods received from a vendor on December 26, 1999 were included in the physical count. However, the related $44,000 vendor invoice was not included in accounts payable at December 31, 1999 because the accounts payable copy of the receiving report was lost. These goods are marked to sell for $65,000.

Instructions

Using the format shown below, prepare a schedule of adjustments as of December 31, 1999 to the initial amounts per Laudermilch's accounting records. Show separately the effect, if any, of each of the eight transactions on the December 31, 1999 amounts. If the transactions would have no effect on the initial amount shown, state NONE.

Adjustments increase (or decrease)	Inventory	Accounts Payable	Net Sales
Initial Amounts	$ 820,000	$ 460,000	$ 7,000,000
1.			
2.			
3.			
4.			
5.			
6.			
7.			
8.			
Total Adjustments	$	$	$
Adjusted Amounts	$	$	$

Solution to Exercise 8-4

Adjustments increase (or decrease)	Inventory	Accounts Payable	Net Sales
Initial Amounts	$ 820,000	$ 460,000	$ 7,000,000
1.	32,000	32,000	None
2.	None	None	None
3.	None	None	None
4.	30,000	None	(45,000)
5.	62,000	None	None
6.	(76,000)	None	None
7.	None	None	(38,000)
8.	None	44,000	None
Total Adjustments	48,000	76,000	(83,000)
Adjusted Amounts	$ 868,000	$ 536,000	$6,917,000

Explanation:

1. When the terms of the purchase are f.o.b. shipping point, ownership of the goods passes to the buyer when the public carrier accepts the goods from the seller. Therefore, title passed to Laudermilch on December 27, 1999, but the goods were not physically present to be included in the physical count at December 31, 1999.

2. These goods would not have been included in the physical count at December 31, 1999, and are not to be included in the inventory at that date. Title did not pass to Laudermilch until the goods were received on January 4, 2000.

3. With shipping terms of f.o.b. shipping point, title passed to the customer (O'Toole) when the goods were picked up by the common carrier on December 29, 1999. Therefore, the goods are properly excluded from the ending inventory, and the sale has been properly recorded in 1999.

4. With shipping terms of f.o.b. destination, title did not pass to Matheson (the buyer) until the goods were received by the buyer, which had to be sometime in 2000. Therefore, the sale was improperly recorded in 1999. The goods were not on the premises late December 31, 1999, so were excluded from the physical count. However, their cost should be included in ending inventory to be reported on the balance sheet.

5. Under a consignment arrangement, the holder of the goods (called the **consignee**) does not own the goods. Ownership remains with the shipper of the goods (called the **consignor**) until the goods are sold to a customer. Laudermilch, the consignor, should include merchandise held by the consignee as part of its inventory. The goods were not in Laudermilch's warehouse when the physical count was taken; however, they should be included as part of the inventory balance at December 31, 1999.

6. Laudermilch does not own the goods which it holds on consignment. Therefore, these goods should be excluded from its inventory; they should be included in the inventory of Asian Collectibles.

7. The $24,000 of goods on the loading dock were properly included in the physical count because they had not been released to the common carrier by the end of the day, December 31, 1999. However, the sale was improperly recorded; therefore, an adjustment is needed to reduce sales by the billing price of $38,000.

8. The $44,000 of goods received on December 26, 1999 were properly included in the physical count of inventory; $44,000 must be added to accounts payable since the invoice was not included in the December 31, 1999 accounts payable balance.

EXERCISE 8-5

Purpose: (L.O.5) This exercise will illustrate the effect on net income when the LIFO cost method rather than the FIFO cost method is used in a period of rising prices. It also requires you to examine the effect of both the beginning inventory and the ending inventory on the net income computation.

Using the FIFO cost method, Worrell Company had a beginning inventory of $24,000, ending inventory of $30,000, and net income of $80,000. If Worrell had used the LIFO cost method, the beginning inventory would have been $20,000 and the ending inventory would have been $23,000.

Instructions

Compute what net income would have been if the LIFO cost method had been used.

Solution to Exercise 8-5

Using LIFO:

Beginning inventory would have been less by $4,000; therefore,
Cost of goods sold would have been less by $4,000 and
Net income would have been more by $4,000, and
Ending inventory would have been less by $7,000; therefore,
Cost of goods sold would have been more by $7,000 and
Net income would have been less by $7,000, therefore:

Net income using FIFO	$ 80,000
Decrease in beginning inventory using LIFO	4,000
Decrease in ending inventory using LIFO	(7,000)
Net income using LIFO	$ 77,000

CASE 8-1

Purpose: (L.O.6) This case will discuss the nature and use of a LIFO reserve. Many companies use LIFO for tax and external reporting purposes, but maintain a FIFO, average cost, or standard cost system for internal reporting purposes.

Instructions

(a) State a few reasons why a company may use LIFO for external reporting and FIFO for internal reporting purposes.

(b) Explain what a LIFO reserve is and how it works.

Solution to Case 8-1

(a) An entity may choose to use LIFO for tax purposes and for general purpose financial statements published for external users while using the FIFO inventory costing method for internal reports for several reasons such as:

1. Companies often base their pricing decisions on a FIFO, average, or standard cost assumption, rather than a LIFO basis.
2. Record keeping on some basis other than LIFO is easier because the LIFO assumption usually does not approximate the physical flow of the product.
3. Profit-sharing and other bonus arrangements are often not based on a LIFO inventory assumption.
4. The use of a pure LIFO system is troublesome for interim periods, for which estimates must be made of year-end quantities and prices.

(b) A **LIFO reserve** is the difference between the ending inventory amount derived by the inventory method used for internal reporting purposes (FIFO, for example) and the ending inventory amount derived by the use of the LIFO method employed for external reporting purposes. This difference is often recorded in an account called Allowance to Reduce Inventory to LIFO. The change in the balance of this account from one period to the next is called the **LIFO effect**. For example, assume the Sullivan Company uses FIFO for internal reports and LIFO for external reports. At January 1, 1999, the Allowance to Reduce Inventory to LIFO account balance was $45,000. At the end of 1999, the inventory balance is $460,000 under FIFO and $400,000 under LIFO. The LIFO effect for 1999 is $15,000 and is recorded as follows:

Cost of Goods Sold	15,000	
Allowance to Reduce Inventory to LIFO..................		15,000

The Allowance to Reduce Inventory to LIFO balance of $60,000 would be deducted from the $460,000 Inventory account balance on the balance sheet to ensure that the inventory is stated on a LIFO basis at year-end. Either the amount of the LIFO reserve or the replacement cost of the inventory should be disclosed in the financial statements or the accompanying notes.

EXERCISE 8-6

Purpose: (L.O.8) This exercise illustrates the use of the dollar-value LIFO method. It shows how a decrease in the ending inventory in terms of base prices from one year to the next affects the calculations and then what happens when an increase in the ending inventory at base prices occurs.

Presented below is information related to Tina Argentine Company.

Date	Ending Inventory (End of Year Prices)	Price Index (Percentage)
December 31, 1994	$ 160,000	100
December 31, 1995	231,000	105
December 31, 1996	216,000	120
December 31, 1997	247,000	130
December 31, 1998	308,000	140
December 31, 1999	348,000	145

Instructions

Compute the ending inventory for Tina Argentine Company for 1994 through 1999 using the dollar-value LIFO method.

Solution to Exercise 8-6

	Current $		Price Index (Percentage)		Base-Year $	Change
1994	$ 160,000	÷	100	=	$ 160,000	--
1995	231,000	÷	105	=	220,000	$+60,000
1996	216,000	÷	120	=	180,000	(40,000)
1997	247,000	÷	130	=	190,000	+10,000
1998	308,000	÷	140	=	220,000	+30,000
1999	348,000	÷	145	=	240,000	+20,000

Ending Inventory—Dollar Value LIFO:

1994		$ 160,000
1995	$160,000 @ 100 =	$160,000
	60,000 @ 105 =	63,000
		$223,000
1996	$160,000 @ 100 =	$160,000
	20,000 @ 105 =	21,000
		$181,000
1997	$160,000 @ 100 =	$160,000
	20,000 @ 105 =	21,000
	10,000 @ 130 =	13,000
		$194,000
1998	$160,000 @ 100 =	$160,000
	20,000 @ 105 =	21,000
	10,000 @ 130 =	13,000
	30,000 @ 140 =	42,000
		$236,000
1999	$160,000 @ 100 =	$160,000
	20,000 @ 105 =	21,000
	10,000 @ 130 =	13,000
	30,000 @ 140 =	42,000
	20,000 @ 145 =	29,000
		$265,000

Approach and Explanation: (1) The ending inventory must first be converted from current dollars to base-year dollars. This is done by dividing the ending inventory at current prices by the current price index. (2) Next, the ending inventory at base-year prices is apportioned into layers, according to individual years in which the inventory was acquired. (3) Each layer is then priced using the index of the year in which it was acquired in order to obtain the inventory at dollar-value LIFO cost.

> TIP: Whenever a layer, or a portion thereof, is eliminated (such as is the case in 1996), it is gone forever and cannot be restored. Notice how in 1997, when there is again an increase in inventory, the newly added layer for 1997 is priced at the index of the year in which that layer was added (1997) and **not** at the index of the portion of the 1995 layer that was eliminated in 1996. This process is consistent with the last costs into inventory being the first costs out (LIFO); thus, inventory is valued at the earliest purchase prices.

ANALYSIS OF MULTIPLE-CHOICE TYPE QUESTIONS

QUESTION

1. (L.O.2) At December 31, 1999, a physical count of merchandise inventory belonging to Rhoda Corp. showed $1,000,000 to be on hand. The $1,000,000 was calculated before any potential necessary adjustments related to the following:
   - Excluded from the $1,000,000 was $80,000 of goods shipped f.o.b. shipping point by a vendor to Rhoda on December 30, 1999 and received on January 3, 2000.
   - Excluded from the $1,000,000 was $72,000 of goods shipped f.o.b. destination to Rhoda on December 30, 1999 and received on January 3, 2000.

- Excluded from the $1,000,000 was $95,000 of goods shipped f.o.b. destination by Rhoda to a customer on December 28, 1999. The customer received the goods on January 4, 2000.

The correct amount to report for inventory on Rhoda's balance sheet at December 31, 1999 is:

a. $1,072,000.
b. $1,095,000.
c. $1,175,000.
d. $1,247,000.

Explanation:

(1) The $80,000 should be added to the $1,000,000 because f.o.b. shipping point means the title transferred to Rhoda when the goods left the seller's dock on December 30, 1999.

(2) The $72,000 is properly excluded from the ending inventory because title did not pass to Rhoda until Rhoda received the goods on January 3, 2000.

(3) The $95,000 should be added to the $1,000,000 because the goods belong to Rhoda until they are received by the customer (in 2000).

$1,000,000	
+ 80,000	
+ 95,000	
$1,175,000	Amount to report for ending inventory at December 31, 1999.

(Solution = c.)

QUESTION

2. (L.O.3) If beginning inventory is understated by $7,000, and ending inventory is overstated by $3,000, net income for the period will be:

a. overstated by $10,000.
b. overstated by $4,000.
c. understated by $4,000.
d. understated by $10,000.

Approach and Explanation: Each error's effect on net income should be determined separately. The effect on net income is dependent on the effect on the computation of cost of goods sold (which is an expense affecting net income). The effects are then combined to compute the **total** effect on net income for the period. (Solution = a.)

	First Error	Second Error	Total Effect
Beg. Inventory	Understated $7,000		Understated $7,000
+ Purchases			
= Goods Available	Understated $7,000		Understated $7,000
- Ending Inventory		Overstated $3,000	Overstated $3,000
= Cost of Goods Sold	Understated $7,000	Understated $3,000	Understated $10,000
Net Income	Overstated $7,000	Overstated $3,000	Overstated $10,000

QUESTION

3. (L.O.5,9) Which inventory costing method most closely approximates current cost for each of the following:

	Ending Inventory	Cost of Goods Sold
a.	FIFO	FIFO
b.	FIFO	LIFO
c.	LIFO	FIFO
d.	LIFO	LIFO

Approach and Explanation: Write down which inventory method (LIFO or FIFO) reports current cost for ending inventory and which uses current cost to price cost of goods sold and then look for your answer combination. FIFO uses the first cost in as the first cost out, so the last (most current) costs are used to price the ending inventory. Therefore, FIFO is the answer for the first column. In contrast, LIFO uses the last cost in (current cost) as the first cost out (to cost of goods sold), so LIFO reflects the most current costs experienced in cost of goods sold. Therefore, LIFO is the answer for the second column. Answer "b" is the determined combination. (Solution = b.)

QUESTION

4. (L.O.5) For 1999, Selma Co. had beginning inventory of $75,000, ending inventory of $90,000 and net income of $120,000, using the LIFO inventory method. If the FIFO method had been used, beginning inventory would have been $85,000, ending inventory would have been $105,000 and net income would have been:
   a. $125,000.
   b. $115,000.
   c. $145,000.
   d. $95,000.

Approach and Explanation: Develop the answer by analyzing the effects on the cost of goods sold computation and resulting effects on net income. (Solution = a.)

	LIFO	FIFO	Effect on Cost of Goods Sold		Effect on Net Income	
Beginning Inventory	$ 75,000	$ 85,000	Increase	$10,000	Decrease	$10,000
+ Purchases						
= Goods Available						
- Ending Inventory	90,000	105,000	Decrease	15,000	Increase	15,000
= Cost of Goods Sold						
Net Income	120,000	?	Decrease	5,000	Increase	5,000

Net income using LIFO	$ 120,000
Increase in net income	5,000
Net income using FIFO	$ 125,000

QUESTION

5. (L.O.4) Dong Company purchased goods with a list price of $50,000, subject to trade discounts of 20% and 10%, with a 2% cash discount allowed if payment is made within 10 days of receipt. Dong uses the gross method of recording purchases. Dong should record the cost of this merchandise as:
   a. $34,000.
   b. $35,000.
   c. $36,000.
   d. $50,000.
   e. None of the above.

Explanation: Trade discounts are not recorded in the accounts; they are means of computing a sales (purchase) price. Using the gross method of recording purchases, the cash discount allowed does not affect the amount recorded in the Purchases account; the cash discount allowed will be recorded if it is taken and will be recorded as a credit to Purchase Discounts. (Solution = c.)

Computations:

List price	$ 50,000
First trade discount ($50,000 x 20%)	(10,000)
Subtotal	40,000
Second trade discount ($40,000 x 10%)	(4,000)
Purchase price	$ 36,000

TIP: A chain discount occurs when a list price is subject to several trade discounts. When a chain discount is offered, the amount of each trade discount is determined by multiplying (1) the list price of the merchandise **less** the amount of prior trade discounts by (2) the trade discount percentage.

QUESTION

6. (L.O.4) Grennan Retail Company incurred the following costs in 1999:
   Freight-in on purchases
   Interest on loan to acquire inventory
   Selling costs

   Should the above items be included or excluded in determining Grennan's inventory valuation for its balance sheet?

	Freight-in	Interest	Selling Costs
a.	Include	Include	Include
b.	Include	Include	Exclude
c.	Include	Exclude	Exclude
d.	Exclude	Exclude	Exclude

Explanation: Freight-in is a product cost. The cost of inventory should include all costs necessary to get the inventory in the place and condition for its intended purpose (resale). Freight-in is necessary to get the merchandise to the location for resale. Interest costs should not be capitalized for inventories that are acquired by a merchandiser (because the goods do not require a period of time to ready them for sale) or inventories that are routinely manufactured or otherwise produced in large quantities on a repetitive basis. Therefore, the interest on this inventory is a period cost. Selling expenses are treated as a period cost. (Solution = c.)

QUESTION

7. (L.O.2,5) The following facts pertain to the cost of one product carried in the merchandise inventory of the Herara Store:

Inventory on hand, January 1	200 units @ \$20 =	\$ 4,000
Purchase, March 18	600 units @ \$24 =	14,400
Purchase, July 20	800 units @ \$26 =	20,800
Purchase, October 31	400 units @ \$30 =	12,000

A physical count of the inventory on December 31 reveals that 500 units are on hand. If the FIFO cost method is used with a periodic inventory system, the inventory should be reported on the balance sheet at:

a. \$40,000.
b. \$36,600.
c. \$14,600.
d. \$11,200.
e. None of the above.

Approach and Explanation: Think about what FIFO stands for: the first cost is in the first out to cost of goods sold. Therefore, ending inventory is comprised of the latest costs experienced. (Solution = c.)

400 units @ \$30 =	\$ 12,000
100 units @ \$26 =	2,600
Ending inventory at FIFO	\$ 14,600

QUESTION

8. (L.O.2,5) Refer to the data in question 7 above. If the average costing method is used, the cost of goods sold for the year amounts to:

a. \$38,400.
b. \$37,500.
c. \$12,800.
d. \$12,500.

Approach and Explanation: Read the question carefully. Notice it asks for the cost of goods sold and not for the ending inventory as you might expect.

Total cost of all units available for sale:

Beginning inventory	$ 4,000
Purchases ($14,400 + $20,800 + $12,000)	47,200
Cost of goods available for sale	$ 51,200

$51,200	Cost of goods available for sale
÷ 2,000[1]	Units available for sale
= $25.60	Average unit cost

$25.60 Average unit cost x 500 units =	$12,800 Ending inventory
$25.60 Average unit cost x 1,500[2] units =	$38,400 Cost of goods sold

[1]200 + 600 + 800 + 400 = 2,000 units available for sale.
[2]2,000 units available - 500 units in ending inventory = 1,500 units sold.
(Solution = a.)

QUESTION

9. (L.O.5) Refer to the data in question 7 above. If the LIFO costing method is used, the cost of goods sold for the year amounts to:
   a. $40,000.
   b. $36,600.
   c. $14,600.
   d. $11,200.

Approach and Explanation: Notice the question asks for the cost of goods sold rather than the cost of the ending inventory. You may approach the solution one of two ways: You may cost the items sold or compute the cost of the ending inventory and deduct that cost from the cost of goods available for sale. Using the first of these two approaches, think of what LIFO stands for: the last cost in is the first cost out to cost of goods sold. (Solution = a.)

Units available	2,000
Units on hand at end of period	(500)
Units sold	1,500

400 units @ $30 =	12,000	
800 units @ $26 =	20,800	
300 units @ $24 =	7,200	
1,500 units =	40,000	Cost of goods sold

TIP: The cost of the ending inventory using LIFO would be:

200 units @ $20	=	$ 4,000	
300 units @ $24	=	7,200	
500 units	=	$ 11,200	Ending inventory

QUESTION

10. (L.O.8) McGraty Corp. uses dollar-value LIFO. Its inventory was $500,000 in terms of base-year prices at December 31, 1999. At December 31, 2000, McGraty's inventory was $600,000 at base-year prices and $660,000 at current cost. McGraty's inventory at December 31, 2000, using dollar-value LIFO, is:
    a. $660,000.
    b. $610,000.
    c. $600,000.
    d. $550,000.

Approach and Explanation: Set up the problem as you normally would a dollar-value LIFO problem, even though the data given is not what you might expect.

Date	Ending Inventory @ Current Costs	÷	Price Index (Percentage)	=	Ending Inventory @ Base Prices	Dollar-Value LIFO Cost
12/31/99					$500,000	$500,000
12/31/00	$660,000		?		600,000	?

Normally you are told the index and are then able to divide the inventory at current cost by the index to get the inventory at base-year prices. Here, you need to solve for the index by dividing $660,000 by $600,000 which gives you 1.10; so the index, in percentage terms, is 110. The ending inventory at dollar-value LIFO therefore is: (Solution = b.)

Base-Year $	%		Dollar-Value LIFO Cost
$500,000 x	100	=	$ 500,000
$100,000 x	110	=	110,000
			$ 610,000

CHAPTER 9

INVENTORIES: ADDITIONAL VALUATION ISSUES

OVERVIEW

Sometimes a business is faced with the situation where impairments in the value of its inventory are so great relative to selling prices that items cannot be sold at a normal profit. In compliance with conservatism, any impairments in value should be recognized in the current period and the inventory should be reported at the lower-of-cost-or-market (LCM) on the balance sheet. By following the LCM rule, the impairment is recognized in the period in which it occurs, rather than in the later period of disposal of the inventory. Accounting for declines in inventory value is discussed in this chapter.

Sometimes a business may need to estimate the cost of inventory on hand at a certain date. Two estimation techniques—the gross profit and the retail method of inventory estimation—are discussed in this chapter. Although the conventional retail method yields results which are to approximate a lower-of-average-cost-or-market valuation for the inventory, the retail method also can be used to approximate FIFO cost, lower of FIFO cost or market, weighted-average cost, LIFO cost, etc. The conventional retail method and the LIFO retail method are discussed in this chapter.

SUMMARY OF LEARNING OBJECTIVES

1. **Explain and apply the lower of cost or market rule.** If inventory declines in value below its original cost for whatever reason, the inventory should be written down to reflect this loss. The general rule is that the historical cost principle is abandoned when the future utility (revenue-producing ability) of the asset is no longer as great as its original cost. The conservatism principle (or constraint) is the justification for this departure from the historical cost principle.

2. **Identify when inventories are valued at net realizable value.** Inventories are reported at net realizable value when (1) there is a controlled market with a quoted price applicable to all quantities, (2) no significant costs of disposal are involved, and (3) the cost figures are too difficult to obtain.

3. **Explain when the relative sales value method is used to value inventories.** When a group of varying units is purchased at a single lump-sum price, a so-called basket purchase, the total purchase price may be allocated to the individual items on the basis of relative sales value.

4. **Explain accounting issues related to purchase commitments.** Accounting for purchase commitments is controversial. Some argue that these contracts should be reported as assets and liabilities at the time the contract is signed; others believe that the present recognition at the delivery date is most appropriate. The FASB neither excludes nor recommends the recording of assets and liabilities for purchase commitments but notes that if they were recorded at the time of commitment, "the nature of the loss and the valuation account that records it when the price falls would be clearly seen."

5. **Determine ending inventory by applying the gross profit method.** The steps to determine ending inventory by applying the gross profit method are as follows: (1) compute the cost of goods available for sale, (2) compute the estimated cost of goods sold by multiplying the sales figure by the cost of goods sold percentage (the cost of goods sold percentage is 100% minus the gross profit expressed as a percentage of sales), and (3) compute the estimated ending inventory on hand by subtracting estimated cost of goods sold from the cost of goods available for sale.

6. **Determine ending inventory by applying the conventional retail method.** The steps to determine ending inventory by applying the conventional retail method are: (1) the sales for the period are deducted from the retail value of the goods available for sale to produce an estimated inventory at retail, (2) the ratio of cost to retail for all goods passing through a department or firm is then determined by dividing the total goods available for sale at cost by the total goods available for sale at retail, and (3) the inventory valued at retail is converted to an approximate lower of cost or market figure by applying the cost-to-retail ratio.

7. **Explain how inventory is reported and analyzed.** Accounting standards require financial statement disclosure of: (1) the composition of the inventory (in the balance sheet or in a separate schedule in the notes), (2) significant or unusual inventory financing arrangements, and (3) inventory costing methods employed (which may differ for different elements of inventory). Accounting standards also require the consistent application of costing methods from one period to another. Common ratios used in the management and evaluation of inventory levels are inventory turnover and a related measure, average days to sell the inventory.

8.* **Determine ending inventory by applying the LIFO retail method.** The application of LIFO retail is made under two assumptions: stable prices and fluctuating prices. **Procedures under stable prices:** (a) Because the LCM valuation method is not used with the LIFO cost method, both the markups and the markdowns are used to compute the purchases' cost-to-retail percentage. (b) Since the LIFO method is concerned primarily with the additional layer (or the amount that should be subtracted from the previous layer), the beginning inventory is excluded from the cost-to-retail percentage used to price a newly added layer. (c) The markups and markdowns apply only to the goods purchased during the current period and not to the beginning inventory. **Procedures under fluctuating prices:** The steps are the same as for stable prices except that in computing the LIFO inventory under a dollar-value LIFO approach, the dollar increase in inventory is found and deflated to beginning-of-the-year prices to determine whether actual increases or decreases in quantity have occurred. If quantities increase, this increase is priced at the new index to compute the new layer. If quantities decrease, the decrease is subtracted from the most recent layers to the extent necessary.

*This material is discussed in Appendix 9-A of the text.

TIPS ON CHAPTER TOPICS

TIP: As used in the phrase "lower of cost or market," the term **market** refers to the market in which the entity buys (not the market in which it sells). Thus, market means current replacement cost (by purchase or by reproduction) except that: (1) market should not exceed the net realizable value (ceiling) and (2) market should not be less than the net realizable value reduced by an allowance for an approximately normal profit margin (floor).

TIP: The **net realizable value of inventory** is the net amount of cash expected to ultimately be received from the sale of the inventory. Thus, the net realizable value of inventory is the estimated selling price in the ordinary course of business less reasonably predictable costs of completion and disposal.

TIP: There are two simple steps to follow in order to apply the **lower of cost or market rule** to an inventory item. Be sure to follow them in order:

Step 1: **Find market:** List the replacement cost, net realizable value (ceiling), and the net realizable value less a normal profit margin (floor) and choose the **middle** value of these three amounts. Thus:

(a) market is replacement cost **if** the replacement cost is in the range between the "ceiling" value and the "floor" value.

(b) market is the "ceiling" value if the replacement cost is equal to or above the ceiling.

(c) market is the "floor" value if the replacement cost is equal to or below the floor.

Step 2: **Compare market** (as determined in Step 1) **with cost and choose the lower** of the two. This choice is the amount at which the inventory is to be reported on the balance sheet.

TIP: If the utility of an inventory item declines prior to the period of sale (disposal), that loss of utility should be recognized in the period of decline rather than the period of disposal. Thus, if an inventory item has become obsolete, the amount of write down determined by the LCM rule should be recognized as a loss in the period of the decline in utility.

TIP: **Gross profit** is synonymous with **gross margin**.

TIP: The gross profit percentage (expressed as a percentage of selling price) and the cost of goods sold percentage (also expressed as a percentage of selling price) are complements; that is, they sum to 100%. When the gross profit method of inventory estimation is used and the gross margin is expressed in terms of cost, the gross margin must first be expressed in terms of selling price before you can proceed with the computations. One method of conversion is to memorize and use the following formula:

$$\text{Gross margin on selling price} = \frac{\text{Percentage markup on cost}}{100\% + \text{Percentage markup on cost}}$$

Another approach to deriving this formula is shown below. It uses the familiar formula: Sales (S) - Cost of Goods Sold (CGS) = GP.

Example: If GP = 25% of cost, then cost of goods sold is 100%.
Putting this much information into our formula above: S - 100% = 25%.
Therefore S = 125%.
Expressing GP as a percentage of S we get: 25% ÷ 125% = 20%.
Thus, gross profit = 20% of sales.

TIP: The conventional retail method is used to approximate a lower-of-average-cost-or-market figure for inventory valuation. There are other versions of the retail method. In each application, an amount of inventory expressed in terms of retail prices is converted to a cost or to a lower-of-cost-or-market amount by multiplying the retail figure by a ratio. The components of the ratio vary depending on which version of the retail method is desired.

TIP: The conventional retail method **includes** net markups (often called net additional markups) but **excludes** net markdowns from the **ratio computation**. The reason for this is that a lower-of-cost-or-market valuation is desired when the conventional retail method is used. (Net markdowns would also be included in the ratio if a straight average cost value rather than a lower-of-average-cost-or-market valuation were desired.) The omission of the net markdowns from the ratio computation results in a higher denominator and therefore a lower resulting ratio than what would be derived if the net markdowns were to be included in the ratio computation. When there have been markdowns, any related writedowns in inventory should be reflected in the current income statement (from a conservative point of view). This is accomplished by reporting the inventory at a lower value which means more of the cost of goods available for sale goes to the income statement as cost of goods sold expense.

TIP: In using the conventional retail method, the net markdowns are omitted from the ratio computation, but they must be **included** in determining the estimated ending inventory at retail.

TIP: The retail inventory method can be used only if sufficient information is accumulated and maintained. Purchases are recorded in the accounts at cost. Although not recorded in the accounts, the retail value of purchases and the changes in that value (markups, markup cancellations, markdowns, and markdown cancellations) must be recorded in supplemental records for use in inventory calculations utilizing the retail inventory method.

EXERCISE 9-1

Purpose: (L.O.1) This exercise reviews the steps involved in the determination of the lower-of-cost-or-market (LCM) valuation for inventory.

The Richard G. Long Company handles ten different inventory items. The normal profit on each item is 25% of the selling price.

Instructions

From the information below, complete the blanks to calculate the value to be used for the inventory figure for financial statements if the LCM rule is applied to individual items.

		Per Unit								
Item	No. of Units on Hand	Cost	Replace-ment Cost	Expected Selling Price	Expected Cost to Sell	Ceil-ing	Floor	Market	LCM	Item Total
1	100	$7.00	$ 7.50	$ 10.00	$ 1.00					
2	10	7.00	6.25	10.00	1.00					
3	50	7.00	9.25	10.00	1.00					
4	10	9.50	9.25	10.00	1.00					
5	20	5.00	6.25	10.00	1.00					
6	100	8.00	7.25	10.00	1.00					
7	30	12.00	11.50	16.00	1.00					
8	10	16.00	15.50	16.00	1.00					
9	20	14.00	11.00	20.00	2.00					
10	10	17.00	16.00	20.00	2.00					
					Grand Total					

Solution to Exercise 9-1

	Per Unit				# of Units	Item Total
Item	Ceiling	Floor	Market	LCM		
1	$ 9.00	$ 6.50	$ 7.50	$ 7.00	100	$ 700.00
2	9.00	6.50	6.50	6.50	10	65.00
3	9.00	6.50	9.00	7.00	50	350.00
4	9.00	6.50	9.00	9.00	10	90.00
5	9.00	6.50	6.50	5.00	20	100.00
6	9.00	6.50	7.25	7.25	100	725.00
7	15.00	11.00	11.50	11.50	30	345.00
8	15.00	11.00	15.00	15.00	10	150.00
9	18.00	13.00	13.00	13.00	20	260.00
10	18.00	13.00	16.00	16.00	10	160.00
				Grand	Total	$ 2,945.00

Approach and Explanation: Write down the two steps involved in determining the lower of cost or market and perform the steps in order for each of the items:

Step 1: Find market. Market is the middle value of replacement cost, ceiling, and floor. For example:

	Item 1	Item 2	Item 3	Item 4
Estimated selling price	$10.00	$10.00	$10.00	$10.00
- Cost to complete and dispose	1.00	1.00	1.00	1.00
= Net realizable value (ceiling)	9.00	9.00	9.00	9.00
- Normal profit margin	2.50*	2.50	2.50	2.50
= Floor	$ 6.50	$ 6.50	$ 6.50	$ 6.50

*$10.00 x 25% = $2.50.

Ceiling	$ 9.00	$ 9.00	$ 9.00	$ 9.00
Floor	6.50	6.50	6.50	6.50
Replacement cost	7.50	6.25	9.25	9.25
Middle of these three values	7.50	6.50	9.00	9.00

Step 2: Compare cost with market and choose the lower.

Cost	$ 7.00	$ 7.00	$ 7.00	$ 9.50
Market (from Step 1)	7.50	6.50	9.00	9.00
Lower of cost or market	7.00	6.50	7.00	9.00

EXERCISE 9-2

Purpose: (L.O.1) This exercise will illustrate the effects of the failure to properly apply the LCM rule.

Bava uses the lower-of-cost-or-market rule to value its inventory. At December 31, 1999, the following facts pertain to Product X-17.

Original cost	$420
Replacement cost	365
Expected selling price	400
Estimated selling expenses	50
Normal profit	25% of selling price
Quantity in ending inventory	100 units

The accountant for Bava used the replacement cost value ($365) to value Product X-17 at December 31, 1999.

Instructions

Answer the following questions:

1. Is $365 the correct unit value for Product X-17 for balance sheet reporting at December 31, 1999? Explain.
2. If $365 is not the correct value, explain the effect of the misstatement on the following: (a) income statement for the year ending December 31, 1999, (b) balance sheet at December 31, 1999, (c) income statement for the year ending December 31, 2000, and (d) balance sheet at December 31, 2000. Assume that all of Product X-17 on hand at December 31, 1999 was sold during 2000.

Solution to Exercise 9-2

1. $365 is **not** the correct value for Product X-17 at December 31, 1999.

Explanation: The ceiling value of $350 should have been used for the market figure (replacement cost of $365 exceeds the ceiling value of $350) and the ceiling is lower than original cost ($420); hence, $350 is the correct unit value for ending inventory at December 31, 1999.

Computations:

Expected selling price	$ 400
Estimated selling expenses	(50)
Ceiling	350
Normal profit ($400 x 25%)	(100)
Floor	$ 250

Ceiling	$ 350
Floor	250
Replacement cost	365
Middle of these three values	$ 350

Cost	$ 420
Market	350
Lower of cost or market	$ 350

2. (a) Net income for 1999 is overstated by $1,500.
(b) Assets are overstated by $1,500 and owners' equity is overstated by $1,500 at December 31, 1999.
(c) Net income for 2000 is understated by $1,500.
(d) No effect on the balance sheet at December 31, 2000.

Explanation:

(a) $365 - $350 = $15.
$15 x 100 = $1,500.
The error will cause an overstatement of ending inventory which results in an understatement of cost of goods sold expense which causes an overstatement in net income for 1999 in the amount of $1,500.

(b) Ending inventory is overstated by $1,500, so assets at December 31, 1999 are overstated by $1,500. Owners' equity at December 31, 1999 is also overstated by $1,500 because net income for 1999 (which is overstated by $1,500) is closed into owners' equity at the end of the accounting period.

TIP: Visualize the basic accounting equation. This error will maintain balance in the basic accounting equation. If assets are overstated, then something else in the equation must be effected to keep the equation in balance. In this case, it is an overstatement of owners' equity because the error affects income (and that effect flows into owners' equity).

(c) The inventory is all sold in 2000. Bava's accountant is using $365 as the carrying value for each of the 100 units when the correct unit value should be $350. This will cause net income for the year ending December 31, 2000 to be understated by $1,500 because cost of goods sold will be overstated by $1,500.

(d) The inventory in question is no longer on hand at December 31, 2000, so there is no effect on assets at that date. The $1,500 understatement in income for 2000 is closed into owners' equity which has a balance that is overstated by $1,500 at the beginning of 2000; thus, the owners' equity balance at December 31, 2000 is correct.

CASE 9-1

Purpose: (L.O.1,6) This case addresses three inventory topics: (1) inventoriable costs, (2) the LCM rule, and (3) the retail method.

Toastie Corporation, a retailer of small kitchen appliances, purchases its inventories from various suppliers.

Instructions

(a) 1. Explain what costs will be inventoriable for Toastie.
    2. Explain why Toastie's administrative costs would or would not be inventoriable.

(b) 1. Toastie uses the lower of cost or market rule for its inventory. What is the theoretical justification for this rule?
    2. The original cost of the inventory is above the replacement cost which is above the net realizable value of the inventory. Explain what amount should be used to value the inventory and why.

(c) Toastie currently uses the average cost method to determine the cost of its inventory. To simplify the procedures involved in counting and pricing its ending inventory, Toastie Corporation is considering the use of the conventional retail method. How should Toastie treat the beginning inventory and net markups in calculating the cost ratio to use to determine the ending inventory? Explain why.

Solution to Case 9-1

(a) 1. Toastie's inventoriable costs should include all costs incurred to get the appliances ready for sale to the customer. It includes not only the purchase price of the goods but also the other associated costs incurred for the appliances up to the time they are ready for sale to the customer, for example, transportation-in.

2. Administrative costs are assumed to expire with the passage of time and not to attach to the product. Furthermore, administrative costs do not relate directly to inventories, but are incurred for the benefit of all functions of the business. Thus, administrative costs should be treated as period costs, not as product costs; that is, they are not inventoriable.

(b) 1. The lower of cost or market rule is used for valuing inventories because of the conservatism principle (constraint) and because the decline in the utility of the inventories below their cost should be recognized as a loss in (and matched with) the period in which the decline took place.

2. The net realizable value should be used to value the inventory because market is less than cost. In this instance, "market" is the ceiling (net realizable value) because replacement cost > ceiling > floor and "market" is the middle value. This indicates that there has been a decline in the utility of the inventory. The inventory should be written down and a loss recorded. The inventory should never be valued at more than net realizable value. Apparently, not only will Toastie Corporation fail to realize a profit when it sells the inventory, it will not even recover its original cost.

(c) Toastie's beginning inventory at cost and at retail would be included in the calculation of the cost-to-retail ratio because the conventional retail method approximates a lower of **average** cost or market valuation. An average cost method reflects all costs experienced (both from the beginning inventory and from purchases) in the ending inventory calculation. Net markups would be included in the calculation of the cost ratio. This procedure reduces the cost ratio because there is a larger denominator for the cost ratio calculation. Thus, the concept of balance sheet conservatism is being followed and a lower of cost or market valuation is approximated.

EXERCISE 9-3

Purpose: (L.O.3) This exercise will demonstrate the use of the relative sales value method to value inventories.

Patrick Morley Corporation purchased a tract of unimproved land on Lake Sybelia for $1,000,000. Costs of subdividing and readying the land for residential lots amounted to $140,000. The lots are of two sizes and some are lakefront, so they vary in market prices as follows:

Type	No. of Lots	Sales Price per Lot
1	10	$ 60,000
2	15	80,000
3	6	100,000

Lots remaining unsold at December 31, 1999 were as follows:

Type	No. of Lots
1	4
2	9
3	2

Instructions

Compute the value to be reported for the inventory of lots on hand on the December 31, 1999 balance sheet.

Solution to Exercise 9-3

Type	# of Lots	Sales Price per Lot	Total Sales Price	Relative Sales Price	Total Cost	Cost Allocated to Lots	Cost per Lot
1	10	$ 60,000	$ 600,000	6/24	$1,140,000	$ 285,000	$ 28,500
2	15	80,000	1,200,000	12/24	1,140,000	570,000	38,000
3	6	100,000	600,000	6/24	1,140,000	285,000	47,500
			$2,400,000			$1,140,000	

Ending Inventory:

Type	Lots Left	Cost per Lot	Total
1	4	$ 28,500	$114,000
2	9	38,000	342,000
3	2	47,500	95,000
			$551,000

Explanation: When a group of varying units is purchased (acquired) at a single lump sum price (often called a basket purchase), the total cost is allocated to the various items based on their relative sales (market) values.

EXERCISE 9-4

Purpose: (L.O.5) This exercise will illustrate the use of the gross profit method of inventory estimation when: (1) gross profit is expressed as a percentage of cost, and (2) gross profit is expressed as a percentage of selling price.

Tim McInnes requires an estimate of the cost of goods lost by fire on April 2. Merchandise on hand on January 1 was $38,000. Purchases since January 1 were $72,000; freight-in, $3,400; and purchase returns and allowances, $2,400. Sales totaled $100,000 to April 2. Goods costing $7,700 were left undamaged by the fire; all other goods were destroyed.

Instructions

(a) Compute the cost of goods destroyed, assuming that the gross profit is 25% of cost.
(b) Compute the cost of goods destroyed, assuming that the gross profit is 25% of sales.

Solution to Exercise 9-4

(a)

Merchandise on hand, January 1		$ 38,000
Purchases	$ 72,000	
Purchase returns and allowances	(2,400)	
Net purchases	69,600	
Freight-in	3,400	73,000
Total merchandise available for sale		111,000
Estimated cost of goods sold*		(80,000)
Estimated ending inventory on April 2		31,000
Undamaged goods		(7,700)
Estimated fire loss		$ 23,300

*Gross profit = 25% ÷ (100% + 25%) = 20% of sales.
Therefore, cost of goods sold = 80% of sales of $100,000 = $80,000.

(b) Gross profit is 25% of sales.
Therefore, cost of goods sold = 75% of sales of $100,000 = $75,000.

Total merchandise available for sale (as computed above)	$ 111,000
Estimated cost of goods sold	(75,000)
Estimated ending inventory at April 2	36,000
Undamaged goods	(7,700)
Estimated fire loss	$ 28,300

TIP: It is important to understand that inventory is accounted for in terms of the **cost** of goods acquired, and the Sales account reflects the **selling prices** of goods that have been sold during the period. Therefore, the profit element must be removed from the sales amount to arrive at the cost of the goods sold.

Approach: Use these steps to perform the calculations:

(1) **Compute the cost of goods available for sale** for the period January 1 through April 2. This is done by combining the cost of inventory on hand at the beginning of the year (January 1) and the net cost of purchases during the period (net purchases plus freight-in).

(2) **Determine the estimated cost of goods sold** during the period. This is done by multiplying the sales figure for the period by the cost of goods sold percentage. The cost of goods sold percentage is 100% minus the gross margin percentage. **Caution:** *The gross margin percentage used here must be stated in terms of selling price.* In part (b) of this exercise, gross profit is given in terms of sales. In part (a), however, you must convert the "25% of cost" to "20% of sales" before the cost of goods sold percentage of 80% can be applied to the sales amount.

(3) **Compute the estimated inventory on hand at the end of the period** (April 2, date of fire) by subtracting the estimated cost of goods sold (Step 2) from the cost of goods available for sale (Step 1).

(4) **Determine the estimated loss** from fire by deducting the cost of the undamaged goods from the estimated cost of inventory on hand at April 2 (Step 3).

EXERCISE 9-5

Purpose: (L.O.6,8) This exercise illustrates two variations of the retail inventory method. It will provide an opportunity to compare and contrast these two approaches.

The records of Nancy Klintworth's Baubles report the following data for the month of May.

Sales	$ 79,000
Sales returns	1,000
Markups	10,000
Markup cancellations	1,500
Markdowns	9,300
Markdown cancellations	2,800
Freight on purchases	2,400
Purchases (at cost)	48,000
Purchases (at sales price)	88,000
Purchase returns (at cost)	2,000
Purchase returns (at sales price)	3,000
Beginning inventory (at cost)	30,000
Beginning inventory (at sales price)	46,500

Instructions

(a) Compute the ending inventory by the conventional retail inventory method.

(b) Compute the ending inventory using the retail method to approximate a LIFO cost figure (assuming stable prices).

Solution to Exercise 9-5

	Cost		Retail
Beginning inventory	$ 30,000		$ 46,500
Purchases	48,000		88,000
Purchase returns	(2,000)		(3,000)
Freight on purchase	2,400		
Goods available for sale	78,400		131,500
Net markups:			
Markups		$ 10,000	
Markup cancellations		(1,500)	8,500
	78,400		140,000
Net markdowns:			
Markdowns		9,300	
Markdown cancellations		(2,800)	(6,500)
	$ 78,400		133,500
Net sales ($79,000 - $1,000)			(78,000)
Ending inventory, at retail			$ 55,500

(a) Cost-to-retail ratio = $78,400 ÷ $140,000 = 56%
Ending inventory at lower of average cost or market = 56% x $55,500 = $31,080

(b) Cost-to-retail ratio = $48,400[a] ÷ 87,000[b] = 55.63%

	Retail	Ratio	LIFO Cost
Beginning inventory layer	$ 46,500		$ 30,000
Layer added in May	9,000[c]	55.63%	5,007
Ending inventory	$ 55,500		$ 35,007

[a]$78,400 - $30,000 = $48,400 — Net cost of purchases.
[b]$133,500 - $46,500 = $87,000 — Retail value of purchases plus net markups less net markdowns.
[c]$55,500 - $46,500 = $9,000 — Excess of ending inventory at retail over beginning inventory at retail.

Approach and Explanation:

(a) Step 1: **Compute the ending inventory at retail.** This is done by determining the retail value of goods available for sale, adjusting that figure for net markups and net markdowns, and deducting the retail value of goods no longer on hand (sales, estimated theft, etc.).

Step 2: **Compute the cost-to-retail ratio.** The conventional retail method approximates an average cost amount so both beginning inventory and net purchases information is used in the ratio. The conventional retail method is to approximate a lower-of-cost-or-market value so the net markups are included but the net markdowns are excluded from the ratio computation.

Step 3: **Determine the ending inventory at an approximate lower-of-average-cost-or-market value.** Apply the appropriate cost-to-retail ratio (Step 2) to the total ending inventory at retail (Step 1).

(b) Step 1: **Compute the ending inventory at retail.** This is done the same way as Step 1 in Part (a) above.

Step 2: **Compute the cost-to-retail ratio.** When the LIFO method is used, ending inventory is priced in layers. If the ending inventory at retail is higher than the beginning inventory at retail, a new inventory layer was added during the period [Part (b) assumes stable prices] and the beginning inventory is intact. Therefore, the ending inventory is composed of the beginning inventory layer(s) and a new layer. A cost-to-retail ratio is needed to cost the new layer. Because the layer added came from purchases of the current period, beginning inventory information is **not** included in this ratio. Because LIFO cost rather than a lower-of-cost-or-market valuation is desired, both the net markups and net markdowns are reflected in the ratio computation.

Step 3: **Determine the ending inventory at an approximate LIFO cost (assuming stable prices).** Determine the cost of each layer in the ending inventory. Because a new layer was added in May, the beginning inventory layer is still intact at the end of the period ($46,500 at retail and $30,000 at LIFO cost). The ratio for the added layer (55.63% as determined in Step 2) is used to convert the $9,000 increase in inventory during the period at retail prices to a LIFO cost amount.

TIP: If the ending inventory at retail had been equal to or less than the beginning inventory at retail figure ($46,500), then a different ratio would be needed. That ratio would be one which expresses the relationship of the cost of the beginning inventory ($30,000) to the retail value of the beginning inventory ($46,500). The ending inventory at retail would have been multiplied by that ratio (64.516%) to determine the LIFO cost of the ending inventory. Assuming an ending inventory at retail of $40,000, the ending inventory at LIFO cost would be $25,806.

TIP: If prices had not been stable, additional procedures would have been required to eliminate the effects of price-level changes in order to measure the real increases in inventory, not the dollar increase.

TIP: Compare the steps for each variation of the retail method utilized in this exercise. Notice that **Step 1** is the **same** for each of the two scenarios and, therefore, yields the same results ($55,500 ending inventory at retail). Notice that Step 3 always applies a ratio to this $55,500 (or a portion thereof). The differences between these two scenarios then stem from the appropriate ratio (Step 2) to be applied in each case and the layers that may exist in a LIFO situation. Look at each scenario and think through the logic of the ratio calculation as explained in this solution. This process should make it easier to recall how to handle similar situations as you encounter them. **Illustration 9-1** will help to summarize and compare these variations on the use of the retail method.

ILLUSTRATION 9-1
HOW TO COMPUTE AND APPLY THE COST/RETAIL RATIO FOR THE RETAIL METHOD (L.O.6,8)

Method (Basis)	Cost/Retail Ratio	How to Compute Ending Inventory
1. Conventional (Lower of Average Cost or Market).	(Beginning inventory at cost + net cost of purchases) ÷ (beginning inventory at retail + net purchases at retail + net markups).	Ending inventory at retail x ratio.
2. LIFO Cost (ignoring change in price level).		
a. If ending inventory at retail is higher than beginning inventory at retail (added layer).	(Net cost of purchases) ÷ (net purchases at retail + net markups - net markdowns).	(Beginning inventory at cost) + (added layer at retail x ratio).
b. If ending inventory at retail is less than beginning inventory at retail.	Beginning inventory at cost ÷ beginning inventory at retail.	Ending inventory at retail x ratio.

EXERCISE 9-6

Purpose: (L.O.8) This exercise will illustrate the use of the dollar-value LIFO retail method when there is: (a) a decrease in inventory and (b) an increase in inventory.

You assemble the following information for Henrietta's Department Store, which computes its inventory under the dollar-value LIFO retail method.

	Cost	Retail
Inventory on January 1, 1999	$ 227,200	$ 320,000
Purchases	340,400	460,000
Increase in price level for year		8%

Instructions

(a) Compute the cost of the inventory on December 31, 1999, assuming that the ending inventory at retail is $286,200.

(b) Compute the cost of the inventory on December 31, 1999, assuming that the ending inventory at retail is $351,000.

Solution to Exercise 9-6

(a)

Ending inventory at current retail prices	$ 286,200
Ending inventory at base retail prices ($286,200 ÷ 1.08)	265,000

This calculation reveals that the inventory quantity has declined below the beginning level (compare $265,000 with $320,000); the ending inventory is merely a portion of the beginning inventory. Therefore, the cost-to-retail ratio reflected in the beginning inventory layer is used to price the ending inventory.

$227,200 ÷ $320,000 = 71% Cost-to-retail ratio for beginning inventory

$265,000 x 71% = $ 188,150

Approach and Explanation:

Step 1: **Deflate the $286,200 ending inventory at current retail prices to base retail prices of $265,000.** The ending inventory at current retail prices is reduced to base retail prices by dividing the $286,200 by the ending price level index (108%). The price level increased 8% during the year so assigning an index of 100 (base) to the beginning of the year would mean the index at the end of the year would be 108% (8% higher than 100).

Step 2: **Determine whether a real increase or a decrease has occurred in inventory.** This is done by comparing the ending inventory at base retail prices ($265,000) with the beginning inventory at base retail prices ($320,000).

Step 3: **Determine the ending inventory at dollar-value LIFO.** The ending inventory is merely a portion of the beginning inventory layer. The ending inventory at base retail prices is then converted to a cost figure by using the appropriate cost-to-retail ratio which is the ratio reflected in the beginning inventory.

(b)

Ending inventory at current retail prices	$ 351,000
Ending inventory at base retail prices ($351,000 ÷ 1.08)	325,000
Beginning inventory at base retail prices	320,000
Layer added—at base prices	5,000

Ending Inventory:	**Retail at Base Price**	**Dollar-Value LIFO**
Beginning inventory	$ 320,000	$ 227,200
Additional layer	5,000	3,996*
Ending inventory	$ 325,000	$ 231,196

*The $5,000 layer at base prices must be restored to the price level of the period in which it was added: $5,000 x 1.08 = $5,400 and then the cost-to-retail ratio for items purchased during the current year must be applied to that $5,400: $5,400 x 74%** = $3,996.

**The cost-to-retail ratio for items purchased during 1999 is computed as follows: $340,400 ÷ $460,000 = 74%.

Approach and Explanation:

Step 1: **Deflate the $351,000 ending inventory at current retail prices to base retail prices of $325,000.** This is done by dividing the $351,000 by 108%.

Step 2: **Determine whether a real increase or a decrease has occurred in inventory.** This is done by comparing the ending inventory at base retail prices ($325,000) with the beginning inventory at base retail prices ($320,000). A real increase of $5,000 in terms of base retail prices has occurred.

Step 3: **Determine the ending inventory at dollar-value LIFO.** The ending inventory is composed of two layers—the beginning inventory layer and a layer added during 1999. The cost of the beginning inventory layer is carried over from last period. The added layer must first be priced in terms of current retail prices (multiply $5,000 x 1.08) because the layer was added in 1999 and then that result ($5,400) is converted to a cost figure by multiplying it by the appropriate cost-to-retail ratio (74%). The appropriate cost-to-retail ratio is the relationship of cost to retail of the purchases made in 1999.

ANALYSIS OF MULTIPLE-CHOICE TYPE QUESTIONS

QUESTION

1. (L.O.1) Crosby Co. is just beginning its first year of operations. Crosby intends to use either the perpetual moving average method or the periodic weighted average method, and to apply the lower of cost or market rule either to individual items or to the total inventory. Prices of most inventory items are expected to increase throughout 1999, although the prices of a few items are expected to decrease. What inventory system should Crosby Co. select if it wants to minimize the inventory carrying amount at the end of the first year?

	Inventory Method	Cost or Market Application
a.	Perpetual	Individual items
b.	Perpetual	Total inventory
c.	Periodic	Individual items
d.	Periodic	Total inventory

Approach and Explanation: Think about the results of using the perpetual moving average method versus the results of using the periodic weighted average method. In a period of rising prices, the periodic weighted average method will yield the lower ending inventory figure (the ending weighted average unit cost for the perpetual system will be higher than the weighted average unit cost for the period for the periodic system). Then think about the results of applying the lower-of-cost-or-market rule to individual items versus the results of applying it to the total inventory. The individual item approach gives the most conservative valuation for balance sheet purposes. When categories or total inventory is used, situations caused by products whose replacement cost is higher than original cost are allowed to offset situations where replacement cost is lower than original cost. When an item-by-item approach is used, all possible declines in utility are recognized and not offset by inventory items whose replacement cost exceeds original cost. Combine the results of these analyses to get the final answer. (Solution = c.)

QUESTION

2. (L.O.1) Peachy Products has an item in inventory with a cost of $85. Current replacement cost is $75. The expected selling price is $100, estimated selling costs are $18, and the normal profit is $5. Using the lower-of-cost-or-market rule, the item should be included in the inventory at:
   a. $75.
   b. $77.
   c. $82.
   d. $85.

Approach and Explanation: Write down the two steps in determining LCM and follow them:

(1) Find market: Three possibilities:
Ceiling ($100 - $18) = $82
Floor ($82 - $5) = $77
Replacement cost = $75
Choose the middle value of these three: $77 = market

(2) Compare market with cost and choose the lower.
Market of $77 versus cost of $85. Lower = $77 (Solution = b.)

QUESTION

3. (L.O.1) In applying the lower-of-cost-or-market rule to inventories at December 31, 1999, Xavier Corporation wrote the inventory down from $500,000 to $420,000. This writedown should be reported:
   a. as a prior period adjustment of $80,000.
   b. as an operating expense in 1999.
   c. as an extraordinary item on the 1999 income statement.
   d. as a part of cost of goods sold expense.
   e. immediately after cost of goods sold or immediately after gross profit on the 1999 income statement.

Explanation: The $80,000 loss should be shown separately from cost of goods sold in the income statement; it is not an extraordinary item. (Solution = e.)

QUESTION

4. (L.O.4) In 1999, Lucas Manufacturing signed a contract with a supplier to purchase raw materials in 2000 for $700,000. Before the December 31, 1999 balance sheet date, the market price for these materials dropped to $510,000. The journal entry to record this situation at December 31, 1999 will result in a credit that should be reported:
   a. as a valuation account to Inventory on the balance sheet.
   b. as a current liability.
   c. as an appropriation of retained earnings.
   d. on the income statement.

Approach and Explanation: Draft the entry referred to in the question. Think about the classification of each account in the entry. Focus on the credit part addressed in the stem of the question. The journal entry is:

Estimated Loss on Purchase Commitments	190,000	
Estimated Liability on Purchase Commitments		190,000

The loss would be reported on the income statement under Other Expenses and Losses. The liability is reported as a current liability because the contract is to be executed within the year that immediately follows the balance sheet date. (Solution = b.)

QUESTION

5. (L.O.5) The following information pertains to the Godfrey Company for the six months ended June 30 of the current year:

Merchandise inventory, January 1	$ 700,000
Purchases	5,000,000
Freight-in	400,000
Sales	6,000,000

Gross profit is normally 25% of sales. What is the estimated amount of inventory on hand at June 30?

a. $100,000
b. $1,600,000
c. $2,100,000
d. $4,600,000

Approach and Explanation: Use the following steps to solve a gross profit inventory method question:

(1) Compute the cost of goods available for sale during the period:

Beginning inventory	$ 700,000
Purchases	5,000,000
Freight-in	400,000
Cost of goods available for sale	$ 6,100,000

(2) Determine the estimated cost of goods sold during the period:

Sales	$ 6,000,000
Cost of goods sold percentage (100% - 25%)	x 75%
Estimated cost of goods sold	$ 4,500,000

TIP: This problem was simple because the gross profit percentage given in the problem is stated in terms of sales. When the gross margin percentage is expressed in terms of cost, that percentage must first be converted to the equivalent percentage of selling price before the other computations can be performed.

(3) Compute the estimated inventory on hand at the end of the period:

Cost of goods available for sale	$ 6,100,000
Estimated cost of goods sold	4,500,000
Estimated ending inventory	$ 1,600,000

(Solution = b.)

QUESTION

6. (L.O.6) A company uses the retail method to estimate ending inventory for interim reporting purposes. If the retail method is used to approximate a lower-of-average-cost-or-market valuation, which of the following describes the proper treatment of net markups and net markdowns in the cost-to-retail ratio calculation?

	Net Markups	Net Markdowns
a.	Include	Include
b.	Include	Exclude
c.	Exclude	Include
d.	Exclude	Exclude

Approach and Explanation: First notice that the lower-of-average-cost-or-market approach to the retail method is often referred to as the conventional retail method. Recall that using a lower-of-cost-or-market figure is an application of the principle of conservatism. Also recall that the retail method involves multiplying the ending inventory at retail by a ratio. The lower the ratio, the lower the computed inventory value. Including the net markups (increases in retail prices) but excluding the net markdowns (decreases in retail prices) gives the highest denominator possible for the ratio calculation which yields the lowest ratio possible. (Note: Net markups are often called net additional markups.) (Solution = b.)

QUESTION

7. (L.O.6) The following data relate to the merchandise inventory of the Hofma Company:

Beginning inventory at cost	$ 13,800
Beginning inventory at selling price	20,000
Purchases at cost	31,000
Purchases at selling price	50,000

The cost to retail percentage (ratio) to be used in calculating an estimate of ending inventory by use of the conventional retail method is:

a. 156%.
b. 145%.
c. 69%.
d. 64%.

Explanation:

Ratio = Cost ÷ Retail
Ratio = ($13,800 + $31,000) ÷ ($20,000 + $50,000)
Ratio = $44,800 ÷ $70,000
Ratio = 64% (Solution = d.)

QUESTION

8. (L.O.6) The Ruffier Department Store uses the conventional retail inventory method. The following information is available at December 31, 1999:

	Cost	Retail
Beginning inventory	$ 37,800	$ 60,000
Purchases	200,000	290,000
Freight-in	7,200	
Sales		275,000

What is the estimated cost of the ending inventory?

a. $47,250.
b. $52,500.
c. $53,586.
d. $192,500.

Computations:

	Cost	Retail
Beginning inventory	$ 37,800	$ 60,000
Purchases	200,000	290,000
Freight-in	7,200	
Cost of goods available for sale	$ 245,000	350,000
Sales		(275,000)
Step 1: Ending inventory at retail		$ 75,000

Step 2: Cost to retail ratio = $245,000 ÷ $350,000 = 70%
Step 3: Estimated cost of ending inventory = $75,000 x 70% = $ 52,500

Approach and Explanation: Think about how the conventional retail method of inventory estimation works. An estimate of the ending inventory at retail is made by deducting sales from the retail value of goods available for sale, and the ending inventory at retail is converted to a cost value by applying an appropriate ratio which is an expression of the relationship between inventory cost and its retail value. Apply the following steps to compute the amount required:

Step 1: **Compute the ending inventory at retail.** Deduct net sales from the retail price of all of the goods available for sale during the period. Arrive at $75,000.

Step 2: **Compute the cost to retail ratio.** Divide the cost of the goods available for sale ($245,000) by the retail value of those same goods ($350,000). Arrive at 70%.

Step 3: **Determine the estimated cost of the ending inventory.** Apply the cost to retail ratio (70%) to the ending inventory at retail ($75,000). Arrive at $52,500. (Solution = b.)

QUESTION

9. (L.O.7) Which of the following statements is **false** regarding an assumption of inventory cost flow?

a. The cost flow assumption need not correspond to the actual physical flow of goods.
b. The assumption selected may be changed each accounting period.
c. The FIFO assumption uses the earliest acquired prices to cost the items sold during a period.
d. The LIFO assumption uses the earliest acquired prices to cost the items on hand at the end of an accounting period.

Explanation: Once a method is selected from acceptable alternative methods, the entity must consistently apply that method for successive periods. The reason for this **consistency concept** is that **comparability** of financial statements is reduced or lost if methods are changed from period to period. However, an entity may change a method if it becomes evident that another method is more appropriate. (Solution = b.)

QUESTION

10. (L.O.8) The Billy Dial Department Store uses a calendar year and the LIFO retail inventory method (assuming stable prices). The following information is available at December 31, 1999:

	Cost	Retail
Beginning inventory	$ 37,200	$ 60,000
Purchases	200,000	290,000
Freight-in	4,000	
Net markups		30,000
Net markdowns		20,000
Sales		285,000

What is the ending inventory at LIFO cost?

a. $46,763.
b. $47,400.
c. $47,603.
d. $50,250.

Computations:

	Cost	Retail
Beginning inventory	$ 37,200	$ 60,000
Purchases	200,000	290,000
Freight-in	4,000	
Goods available for sale	241,200	350,000
Net markups		30,000
Subtotals	$ 241,200	380,000
Net markdowns		(20,000)
Sales		(285,000)
Ending inventory at retail		$ 75,000

Ending inventory:

	Retail	Ratio	Cost
Beginning layer	$ 60,000		$ 37,200
Added layer	15,000	68%*	10,200
Ending inventory	$ 75,000		$ 47,400

*$204,000[a] ÷ $300,000[b] = 68%

[a]$200,000 + $4,000 = $204,000
[b]$290,000 Purchases + $30,000 Markups - $20,000 Markdowns = $300,000

Approach and Explanation: Think about how LIFO works. If the ending inventory is greater than the beginning inventory, the ending inventory is comprised of the beginning inventory plus a new layer; if the ending inventory is less than the beginning inventory, the ending inventory is comprised of a remaining portion of the beginning inventory layer. Think about how the retail method of inventory estimation works. An estimate of the ending inventory at retail is made by deducting sales from the retail value of goods available for sale and the ending inventory at retail is converted to a cost or to a lower-of-cost-or-market value by applying an appropriate ratio which is an expression of the relationship between inventory cost and its retail value. Apply the following steps to compute the amount required:

Step 1: **Compute the ending inventory at retail.** Arrive at $75,000.

Step 2: **Compute the cost-to-retail ratio.** Comparing ending inventory at retail ($75,000) with beginning inventory at retail ($60,000) indicates a layer was added during 1999. Therefore, a ratio is needed to cost the layer which was added during 1999. The ratio for the new layer should exclude the beginning inventory. The ratio should include both net markups and net markdowns to approximate a cost (rather than a LCM valuation).

Step 3: **Determine the ending inventory at an approximate LIFO cost.** Use the beginning layer ($37,200 at LIFO cost) and apply the purchases' cost-to-retail ratio (68%) to the added layer at retail ($15,000). (Solution = b.)

QUESTION

11. (L.O.7) The inventory turnover ratio is a measure of the liquidity of the inventory. This ratio is computed by dividing:
    a. the cost of goods sold by 365 days.
    b. the cost of goods sold by the average amount of inventory on hand.
    c. net credit sales by the average amount of inventory on hand.
    d. 365 days by the cost of goods sold.

Approach and Explanation: Write down the formula to compute the inventory turnover ratio. Think about the logic of each of the computation's components. The formula is as follows:

$$\text{Inventory Turnover ratio} = \frac{\text{Cost of Goods Sold}}{\text{Average Inventory}}$$

The cost of goods sold figure is a cost figure whereas net credit sales is a figure reflecting the selling prices of items sold. The cost of an inventory item is reflected in the Inventory account until such time when the item is sold; then, the cost is transferred to the Cost of Goods Sold account. If an item is sold on credit, the selling price of the item is recorded in the Accounts Receivable account. Hence, the accounts receivable turnover ratio uses net credit sales and average accounts receivable balance; whereas, the inventory turnover ratio uses cost of goods sold and the average inventory balance for its computation. A variant of the inventory turnover ratio is the **average days to sell inventory** which is computed by dividing 365 days by the inventory turnover ratio. (Solution = b.)

CHAPTER 10

ACQUISITION AND DISPOSITION OF PROPERTY, PLANT, AND EQUIPMENT

OVERVIEW

Assets that have physical existence and that are expected to be used in revenue-generating operations for more than one year or operating cycle, whichever is longer, are classified as long-term tangible assets. Some problems may arise in determining the acquisition cost of a fixed asset, such as: the initial acquisition may be the result of several expenditures, one fixed asset may be exchanged for another fixed asset, a plant asset may be obtained on a deferred payment plan, or additional expenditures may be involved subsequent to acquisition. These and other issues and their related accounting procedures are examined in this chapter.

SUMMARY OF LEARNING OBJECTIVES

1. **Describe the major characteristics of property, plant, and equipment.** The major characteristics of property, plant, and equipment are: (1) They are acquired for use in operations and not for resale, (2) they are long-term in nature and usually subject to depreciation, and (3) they possess physical substance.

2. **Identify the costs included in the initial valuation of land, buildings, and equipment.**
   Cost of land: Includes all expenditures made to acquire land and to ready it for use. Land costs typically include (1) the purchase price; (2) closing costs, such as title to the land, attorney's fees, and recording fees; (3) costs incurred in getting the land in condition for its intended use, such as grading, filling, draining, and clearing; (4) assumption of any liens, mortgages or encumbrances on the property; (5) any additional land improvements that have an indefinite life; and (6) cost to remove unwanted building (less scrap proceeds) on newly acquired land.
   Cost of buildings: Includes all expenditures related directly to their acquisition or construction. Costs related to constructed assets include (1) materials, labor, overhead costs, and avoidable interest cost incurred during construction and (2) professional fees and building permits.
   Cost of equipment: Includes (1) the purchase price, (2) freight and handling charges incurred, (3) insurance on the equipment while in transit, (4) cost of special foundations if required, (5) assembling and installation costs, and (6) costs of conducting trial runs.

3. **Describe the accounting problems associated with self-constructed assets.** The assignment of indirect costs of manufacturing creates special problems because these costs cannot be traced directly to work and material orders related to the fixed assets constructed. These costs might be handled in one of three ways: (1) Assign no fixed overhead to the cost of the constructed asset, (2) assign a portion of all overhead to the construction process, or (3) allocate on the basis of lost production. The second method is used extensively in practice.

4. **Describe the accounting problems associated with interest capitalization.** Only avoidable actual interest (with modifications) incurred during the acquisition period should be capitalized. The rationale for this approach is that during construction, the asset is not generating revenue

and therefore interest cost should be deferred (capitalized); once construction is completed, the asset is ready for its intended use and revenues can be earned. Any interest cost incurred in purchasing an asset that is ready for its intended use should be expensed.

5. **Understand accounting issues related to acquiring and valuing plant assets.** The following issues relate to acquiring and valuing plant assets: (1) *Cash discounts:* Whether taken or not, they are generally considered a reduction in the cost of the asset; the real cost of the asset is the cash or cash equivalent price of the asset. (2) *Assets purchased on long-term credit contracts:* Are accounted for at the present value of the consideration exchanged between the contracting parties. (3) *Lump sum purchase:* Allocate the total cost among the various assets on the basis of their relative fair market values. (4) *Issuance of stock:* If the stock is being actively traded, the market value of the stock issued is a fair indication of the cost of the property acquired; if the market value of the capital stock exchanged is not determinable, the value of the property should be established and used as the basis for recording the asset and issuance of the capital stock. (5) *Exchanges of property, plant, and equipment:* See **Illustration 10-1** for a summary of how to account for exchanges of nonmonetary assets. (6) *Contributions:* A contribution is a nonreciprocal transfer. A nonreciprocal transfer is to be recorded at the fair value of the asset received or given. In general, contributions received are to be recorded by a credit to revenue; however, the receipt of land, buildings, or other assets from a government to entice a business to its community is usually recorded by a credit to Donated Capital. Contributions given are recorded by a debit to Contribution Expense.

6. **Describe the accounting treatment for costs incurred subsequent to acquisition.** See **Illustration 10-2** for a summary of how to account for costs subsequent to acquisition.

7. **Describe the accounting treatment for the disposal of property, plant, and equipment.** Regardless of the time of disposal, depreciation must be taken up to the date of disposition, and then all accounts related to the retired asset should be removed. Gains or losses on the retirement of plant assets should be shown in the income statement along with other items that arise from customary business activities. Gains or losses on involuntary conversions should be reported as extraordinary items. If an asset is scrapped or abandoned without any cash recovery, a loss should be recognized equal to the asset's book value. If scrap value or insurance proceeds exist, the gain or loss that occurs is the difference between the proceeds and the asset's book value.

8.* **Understand interest capitalization involving noninterest-bearing liabilities, interim period computations, and interest compounding.** In defining expenditures to which interest capitalization rates should be applied, only expenditures that involve the payment of cash, the transfer of other assets, or the incurrence of a liability with which interest is recognized should be considered.

Noninterest-bearing liabilities, such as trade payables and short-term accruals, should be excluded from the computation of average accumulated expenditures. When computing weighted-average accumulated expenditures on an interim basis, the capitalized interest for the prior period must be included.

*This material is covered in Appendix 10-A in the text.

TIPS ON CHAPTER TOPICS

TIP: **Property, plant, and equipment** is a classification that is often referred to as **fixed assets** or **plant assets**. Included in this section should be long-lived tangible assets that are currently being used in operations to generate goods and services for customers. Two exceptions to this guideline are: (1) Construction of Plant in Process, and (2) Deposits on Machinery. In each of these cases, the asset is not yet being used in operations but an expenditure has been made which is to be classified in the property, plant, and equipment section of the balance sheet. Idle fixed assets are to be classified as other assets and plant assets no longer used and held for sale are to be classified either as current assets or other assets, depending on whether they are expected to be sold within the next year or not.

TIP: In determining the cost of a plant asset, keep in mind the same guideline we had for inventory. The cost includes all costs necessary to get the item to the location and condition for its intended use.

TIP: In determining the cost of a plant asset, keep in mind the historical cost principle. **Cost** is measured by the cash or the fair market value of the noncash consideration given or the fair market value of the consideration received, whichever is the more objectively determinable. Fair market value refers to cash equivalent value. When cash is given to acquire an asset, it is a relatively simple matter to determine the asset's cost. However, when a noncash asset is given in exchange or when a deferred payment plan is involved, more thought is required to determine the asset's cost. Pay close attention to these areas as they are often the subjects from which discriminating exam questions are derived.

TIP: When one noncash asset is exchanged for another noncash asset, it is important to determine if it is a dissimilar or similar asset exchange. If it is a **similar** asset exchange **and** if a gain is experienced on the disposal of the old asset, then we are to depart from the historical cost principle in determining the cost of the new asset; the entire gain or a portion of the gain (depending on whether boot is received) is to be deferred because the earning process did not culminate with the exchange.

TIP: When a deferred payment plan is involved in the acquisition of a noncash asset, pay careful attention to whether a fair rate of interest is stated in the agreement. When an unreasonably low stated interest rate is present, interest must be imputed so that the effective amount of interest reported reflects the market rate of interest.

TIP: In the context of accounting for property, plant, and equipment, the term "capitalize" means to record and carry forward into one or more periods expenditures from which benefits or proceeds will be realized; thus, a balance sheet account is debited.

TIP: In accounting for the many expenditures related to the operation and maintenance of property, plant, and equipment, the accountant must determine whether to record these individual expenditures by a debit to the income statement or by a debit to the balance sheet. In making this determination, keep in mind that expenditures benefiting the company for more than the current accounting period should be capitalized in order to properly match expenses with revenues over successive accounting periods; expenditures for items that do not yield benefits beyond the current accounting period should be expensed.

TIP: In the context of the topic of property, plant, and equipment, the term **carrying value** refers to the amount derived by deducting the balance in the Accumulated Depreciation account from the balance in the related asset account. Synonymous terms are: **book value**, net asset value, undepreciated value, and **carrying amount**. Book value may be very different from fair value. Fair value is often referred to as fair market value or market value. The computation of book value is **not** affected by the estimated residual value or salvage value.

TIP: The net cost (cost less scrap proceeds) of tearing down an old building should be charged (debited) to the Land account if the building was someone else's old building and recently acquired along with the land as a site to be used for another structure. (The cost is charged to Land because it was necessary to get the land in the condition for its intended purpose—to provide space upon which to erect a new building.) The cost of tearing down an old building should be charged to Loss on Disposal of Building if the building has been used in the entity's operations and is now demolished to make way for another building or an alternative use of the land. Therefore, the cost of tearing down an old building is **never** charged to the Building account.

TIP: There are several areas in accounting which utilize the formula to allocate a single sum between two or more items based on the relative fair market values of the items involved. That formula is as follow:

$$\frac{\text{Market Value of One Item in Group}}{\text{Market Value of All Items in Group}} \times \text{Amount to be Allocated} = \text{Amount to be Assigned to Item Designated in the Numerator}$$

This formula is used in Chapter 10 to allocate one lump-sum amount of cost to the individual assets acquired in a **lump sum purchase** (often called a **basket purchase**). The formula will also be used in volume two of this book in Chapter 15 to allocate the proceeds from the issuance of several classes of securities, in Chapter 17 to allocate the proceeds from the issuance of bonds with detachable warrants, and in Chapter 18 to allocate the cost of an investment. The formula is also useful in the managerial accounting arena such as in the case where there are joint costs to be allocated to joint products. The same formula was used in Chapter 8 to allocate the cost of certain inventory items to units based on their relative sales values.

TIP: A nonreciprocal transfer of a nonmonetary asset is to be recorded at the fair market value of the asset at the date of transfer. Property donated to a for-profit entity is an example of this type of transaction and results in a credit to Revenue or to Donated Capital (Additional Paid-in Capital), depending on whether the donor is a for-profit entity or a governmental entity.

CASE 10-1

Purpose: (L.O.2,6) This case will review the costs to be capitalized for property, plant, and equipment.

Property, plant, and equipment generally represents a large portion of the total assets of a company. Accounting for the acquisition and usage of such assets is, therefore, an important part of the financial reporting process.

Instructions

(a) Distinguish between a revenue expenditure and a capital expenditure. Explain why its distinction is important.

(b) Identify at least six costs that should be capitalized as the cost of land. Assume that land with an existing building is acquired for cash and that the existing building is to be removed immediately in order to provide space for a new building on that site.

(c) Identify at least five costs that should be capitalized as the cost of a building.

(d) Identify at least six costs that should be capitalized when equipment is acquired for cash.

(e) Describe the factors that determine whether expenditures relating to property, plant, and equipment already in use should be capitalized.

(AICPA Adapted)

Solution to Case 10-1

(a) A **capital expenditure** is expected to yield benefits either in all future accounting periods (acquisition of land) or in a limited number of accounting periods (acquisition of buildings and equipment). Capital expenditures are capitalized, that is, recorded as assets, and, if related to assets of limited life, amortized over the periods which will be benefited. A **revenue expenditure** is an expenditure for which the benefits are **not** expected to extend beyond the current period. Hence, they benefit only the current period (recorded as an expense) or they benefit no period at all (recorded as a loss).

The distinction between capital and revenue expenditures is of significance because it involves the timing of the recognition of expense and, consequently, the determination of periodic earnings. This distinction also affects the costs reflected in the asset accounts which will be recovered from future periods' revenues.

If a revenue expenditure is improperly capitalized, net income of the current period is overstated, assets are overstated, and future earnings are understated for all the periods to which the improperly capitalized cost is amortized. If the cost is not amortized, future earnings will not be affected, but assets and retained earnings will continue to be overstated for as long as the cost remains on the books. If a nonamortizable capital expenditure is improperly expensed, current earnings are understated and assets and retained earnings are understated for all foreseeable periods in the future. If an amortizable capital expenditure is improperly expensed, net income of the current period is understated, assets and retained earnings are understated, and net income is overstated for all future periods to which the cost should have been amortized.

(b) The cost of land may include:
(1) purchase price.
(2) survey fees.
(3) title search fees.
(4) escrow fees.
(5) delinquent property taxes assumed by buyer.
(6) broker's commission.
(7) legal fees.
(8) recording fee.
(9) unpaid interest assumed by buyer.
(10) cost of clearing, grading, landscaping, and subdividing (less salvage).
(11) cost of removing old building (less salvage).
(12) special assessments such as lighting or sewers if they are permanent in nature.
(13) landscaping of permanent nature.
(14) any other cost necessary to acquire the land and get it in the condition necessary for its intended purpose.

> **TIP:** Typically, the cost of land includes the cost of elements that occur prior to excavation for a new building. Costs related to the foundation of the building are elements of building cost.

(c) The cost of a building may include:
(1) purchase price or construction costs (including an allocation of overhead if self-constructed).
(2) excavation fees.
(3) architectural fees.
(4) building permit fee.
(5) cost of insurance during construction (if paid by property owner).
(6) property taxes during construction.
(7) interest during construction (only interest actually incurred).
(8) cost of temporary buildings.
(9) any other cost necessary to acquire the building and get it in the location and condition for its intended purpose.

(d) The cost of equipment may include:
(1) purchase price (less discounts allowed).
(2) sales tax.
(3) installation charges.
(4) freight charges during transit.
(5) insurance during transit.
(6) cost of labor and materials for test runs.
(7) cost of special platforms.
(8) ownership search.
(9) ownership registration.
(10) breaking-in costs.
(11) other costs necessary to acquire the equipment and get it to the location and condition for its intended use.

(e) The factors that determine whether expenditures relating to property, plant, and equipment already in use should be capitalized are as follows:
(1) Expenditures are material.
(2) They are nonrecurring in nature.

(3) They benefit future periods in some way such as by doing one of the following:
   a. They extend the useful life of a plant asset.
   b. They enhance the quality of existing services.
   c. They add new asset services.
   d. They reduce future operating costs of existing assets.
   e. They are required to meet environmental concerns and regulations.

Approach:

1. Scan all requirements before you begin on the first question. Sometimes the latter requirements will help you to see more clearly what is really being requested in the earlier requirements. Sometimes the solution to one requirement appears to overlap with the solution to another part of the question.
2. Prepare a key word outline before you begin writing detailed answers. This outline should very briefly list the concepts you want to cover in your paragraph(s). This outline will help you to organize your thoughts before you begin writing sentences.

EXERCISE 10-1

Purpose: (L.O.2,6) This exercise will help you identify which expenditures related to property, plant, and equipment should be capitalized and which should be expensed.

> **TIP:** Remember that expenditures which benefit the company for more than the current accounting period should be capitalized in order to properly match expenses with revenues over successive accounting periods. Expenditures for items that do not yield benefits beyond the current accounting period should be expensed.

Instructions

Assume all amounts are material. For each of the following independent items, indicate by use of the appropriate letter if it should be:

C = Capitalized or E = Expensed

______ 1. Invoice price of drill press.

______ 2. Sales tax on computer.

______ 3. Costs of permanent partitions constructed in an existing office building.

______ 4. Installation charges for new conveyer system.

______ 5. Costs of trees and shrubs planted in front of office building.

______ 6. Costs of surveying new land site.

_____ 7. Costs of major overhaul of delivery truck.

_____ 8. Costs of building new counters for show room.

_____ 9. Costs of powders, soaps, and wax for office floors.

_____ 10. Cost of janitorial services for office and show room.

_____ 11. Costs of carpets in a new office building.

_____ 12. Costs of annual termite inspection of warehouse.

_____ 13. Insurance charged for new equipment while in transit.

_____ 14. Property taxes on land used for parking lot.

_____ 15. Cost of a fan installed to help cool old factory machine.

_____ 16. Cost of exterminator's services.

_____ 17. Costs of major redecorating of executives' offices.

_____ 18. Cost of fertilizers for shrubs and trees.

_____ 19. Cost of labor services for self-constructed machine.

_____ 20. Costs of materials used and labor services expended during trial runs of new machine.

Solution to Exercise 10-1

1.	C	6.	C	11.	C	16.	E
2.	C	7.	C	12.	E	17.	C
3.	C	8.	C	13.	C	18.	E*
4.	C	9.	E*	14.	E	19.	C
5.	C	10.	E	15.	C	20.	C

*This answer assumes the products were consumed during the current period. Material amounts of unused supplies on hand at the balance sheet date should be reported as a prepaid expense.

TIP: As used in this chapter, the term **capital expenditure** refers to one which is expected to benefit more than one period; hence, it is initially recorded as an asset and should be expensed over the periods benefited. A **revenue expenditure** is one which is expected **not** to be of benefit to any period beyond the current period; hence, it is recorded by a debit to either an expense account or to a loss account in the period incurred.

EXERCISE 10-2

Purpose: (L.O.2) This exercise will give you practice in identifying capital versus revenue expenditures.

Hughes Supply Company, a newly formed corporation, incurred the following expenditures related to Land, to Buildings, and to Machinery and Equipment.

Cash paid for land and dilapidated building thereon		$ 300,000
Removal of old building	$ 60,000	
Less salvage	16,500	43,500
Surveying before construction to determine best position for building		1,110
Interest on short-term loans during construction		22,200
Excavation before construction for basement		57,000
Fee for title search charged by abstract company		1,560
Architect's fees		8,400
Machinery purchased (subject to 2% cash discount, which was not taken)		165,000
Freight on machinery purchased		4,020
Storage charges on machinery, necessitated by noncompletion of building when machinery was delivered on schedule		6,540
New building constructed (building construction took 8 months from date of purchase of land and old building)		1,500,000
Assessment by city for sewers (a one-time assessment)		4,800
Transportation charges for delivery of machinery from storage to new building		1,860
Installation of machinery		6,000
Trees, shrubs, and other landscaping after completion of building (permanent in nature)		16,200

Instructions

(a) Identify the amounts that should be debited to Land.
(b) Identify the amounts that should be debited to Buildings.
(c) Identify the amounts that should be debited to Machinery and Equipment.
(d) Indicate how the costs above **not** debited to Land, Buildings, or Machinery and Equipment should be recorded.

Solution to Exercise 10-2

	(a) Land	(b) Bldgs.	(c) M&E	(d) Other
Cash paid for land & old bldg.	$300,000			
Removal of old building ($60,000 - $16,500)	43,500			
Surveying before construction		$ 1,110		
Interest on loans during construction		22,200		
Excavation before construction		57,000		
Abstract fees for title search	1,560			
Architect's fees		8,400		
Machinery purchased			$161,700	$ 3,300 Misc. Exp. (Int. Exp.)
Freight on machinery			4,020	
Storage charges caused by noncompletion of building				6,540 Misc. Exp. (Loss)
New building construction		1,500,000		
Assessment by city	4,800			
Transportation charges—machinery				1,860 Misc. Exp. (Loss)
Installation—machinery			6,000	
Landscaping	16,200			
Totals	$366,060	$1,588,710	$171,720	$11,700

TIP: The purchase price of the machine is the **cash equivalent price** at the date of acquisition which is the $165,000 reduced by the 2% cash discount allowed ($3,300), whether or not the discount is taken. The additional outlay of $3,300 is due to extending the time for payment which is equivalent to interest (time value of money). The cost of the machine does **not** include the $6,540 storage charges and $1,860 transportation charges out of storage because these costs were not planned costs necessary to get the equipment to the location intended for use; rather they were caused by the lack of completing the building on schedule (hence, a loss or miscellaneous expense).

CASE 10-2

Purpose: (L.O.5) This case will review the rules for determining a plant asset's cost when the asset is acquired on a deferred payment plan or in a nonmonetary exchange.

A company often acquires property, plant, and equipment by means other than immediate cash payment.

Instructions

(a) Explain how to determine a plant asset's cost if it is acquired on a deferred payment plan.

(b) Explain how to determine a plant asset's cost if it is acquired in exchange for a dissimilar nonmonetary asset.

(c) Explain how to determine a machine's cost if it is acquired in exchange for a similar machine and a small cash payment is also made.

(d) Explain how to determine a machine's cost if it is acquired in exchange for a similar machine and a small amount of cash is received.

Solution to Case 10-2

(a) A plant asset acquired on a deferred-payment plan should be recorded at an equivalent cash price excluding interest. If a fair rate of interest is not stated in the sales contract, an imputed interest rate should be determined. The asset should then be recorded at the contract's present value, which is computed by discounting the payments at the stated or imputed interest rate. The interest portion (stated or imputed) of the contract price should be charged to interest expense over the life of the contract.

(b) A plant asset acquired in exchange for a dissimilar nonmonetary asset should be recorded at the fair value (cash equivalent value) of the consideration given or the fair value of the consideration received, whichever is more clearly determinable. This is an application of the historical cost principle. Any gain or loss on the exchange should be recognized because the earning process is considered complete.

(c) When exchanging an old machine and paying cash for a new machine, the new machine should be recorded at the amount of monetary consideration (cash) paid plus the undepreciated cost of the nonmonetary asset (old machine) surrendered if there is no indicated loss. If a loss is indicated, it should be recognized. This would reduce the recorded amount of the new machine. An experienced loss is indicated when the old asset's market value is less than its carrying value at the date of exchange; a gain is indicated if the asset's market value exceeds its carrying value. No experienced gain, however, should be recognized by the party paying monetary consideration.

> **TIP:** When cash is paid in an exchange of similar assets and the market value of the asset to be exchanged is less than its book value (an experienced loss), the historical cost principle is followed in determining the cost of the new asset. Additionally, the loss on the old asset is recognized in total. When cash is paid in an exchange of similar assets and the market value of the asset to be exchanged is greater than its book value (a gain), there is a departure from the historical cost principle in determining the cost of the new asset and the gain is **not** recognized. The gain is deferred because the earning process has not been culminated.

(d) If a loss is experienced on the old asset, the cost of a machine acquired along with a small amount of boot in exchange for a similar machine is equal to the carrying value of the old asset minus the boot received minus the loss recognized on the old asset. If a gain is experienced on the old asset, the cost of a machine acquired along with a small amount of boot in exchange for a similar machine is equal to the carrying value of the old machine minus the boot received plus the portion of the gain that is recognized. The portion of the gain to be recognized is determined by the ratio of monetary assets to the total fair market value of the consideration received.

EXERCISE 10-3

Purpose: (L.O.4) This exercise will provide an example of the capitalization of interest cost incurred during construction.

Marvel Company engaged Invention Company to construct a special purpose machine to be used in its factory. The following data pertain:

1. The contract was signed by Marvel on August 30, 1999. Construction was begun immediately and was completed on December 1, 1999.
2. To aid in the financing of this construction, Marvel borrowed $600,000 from Bank of Okahumpa on August 30, 1999 by signing a $600,000 note due in 3 years. The note bears an interest rate of 12% and interest is payable each August 30.
3. Marvel paid Invention $200,000 on August 30, 1999, and invested the remainder of the note's proceeds ($400,000) in 5% government securities until December 1.
4. On December 1, Marvel made the final $400,000 payment to Invention.
5. Aside from the note payable to the Bank of Okahumpa, Marvel's only outstanding liability at December 31, 1999 is a $60,000, 9%, 5-year note payable dated January 1, 1996, on which interest is payable each December 31.

Instructions

(a) Calculate the weighted-average accumulated expenditures, interest revenue, avoidable interest, total interest incurred, and interest cost to be capitalized during 1999. Round all computations to the nearest dollar.

(b) Prepare the journal entries needed on the books of Marvel Company at each of the following dates: August 30, 1999; December 1, 1999; and December 31, 1999.

Solution to Exercise 10-3

(a) **Computation of Weighted-Average Accumulated Expenditures:**

Expenditures			Capitalization		Weighted-Average
Date	Amount	x	Period	=	Accumulated Expenditures
August 30	$200,000		3/12		$50,000
December 1	400,000		0		0
					$50,000

Interest Revenue: $400,000 x 5% x 3/12 = $5,000

Avoidable Interest:

Weighted-Average Accumulated Expenditures	x	Interest Rate	=	Avoidable Interest
$50,000		12%		$6,000

Total Interest Incurred:

$600,000 x 12% x 4/12	=	$ 24,000
$60,000 x 9%	=	5,400
		$ 29,400

Interest to be capitalized: $6,000

(b)	8/30	Cash	600,000	
		Notes Payable		600,000
		Machine	200,000	
		Short-term Investments	400,000	
		Cash		600,000
	12/1	Cash	405,000	
		Interest Revenue ($400,000 x 5% x 3/12)		5,000
		Short-term Investments		400,000
		Machine	400,000	
		Cash		400,000
	12/31	Machine [computed in part (a)]	6,000	
		Interest Expense ($29,400 - $6,000)	23,400	
		Cash ($60,000 x 9%)		5,400
		Interest Payable ($600,000 x 12% x 4/12)		24,000

Explanation: Paragraphs 6 and 7 of *SFAS No. 34* state:

> "The historical cost of acquiring an asset includes the costs necessarily incurred to bring it to the condition and location for its intended use. If an asset requires a period of time in which to carry out the activities necessary to bring it to that condition and location, the interest cost incurred during that period as a result of expenditures for the asset is a part of the historical cost of acquiring the asset. The objectives of capitalizing interest are (a) to obtain a measure of acquisition cost that more closely reflects the enterprise's total investment in the asset and (b) to charge a cost that relates to the acquisition of a resource that will benefit future periods against the revenues of the periods benefited."

Examples of assets that qualify for interest capitalization are: (1) assets that an enterprise constructs for its own use (such as facilities), and (2) assets intended for sale or lease that are constructed as discrete projects (such as ships or real estate projects). Interest cannot be capitalized for inventories that are routinely manufactured or otherwise produced in large quantities on a repetitive basis. Marvel's machine is a qualifying asset.

The amount to be capitalized is that portion of the interest cost incurred during the asset's acquisition period that theoretically could have been avoided (for example, by avoiding additional borrowings or by using the funds expended for the asset to repay existing borrowings) if expenditures for the asset had not been made.

Avoidable interest is determined by applying an appropriate interest rate(s) to the weighted-average amount of accumulated expenditures for the asset during the period. The appropriate rate is that rate associated with a specific new borrowing, if any. If average accumulated expenditures for the asset exceed the amount of a specific new borrowing associated with the asset, the capitalization rate to be applied to such excess shall be a weighted average of the rates applicable to other borrowings of the enterprise.

The weighted-average amount of accumulated expenditures for the asset represents the average investment tied up in the qualifying asset during the period. For Marvel, a $200,000 balance in Machine for the three-month capitalization period (date of expenditures to the date the asset is ready for use) means an equivalent (average) investment of $50,000 on an annual basis. Marvel uses only the 12% rate applicable to the specific new borrowing to compute the avoidable interest because the specific borrowing ($600,000) exceeds the weighted-average accumulated expenditures.

The amount of interest to be capitalized is not to exceed the actual interest costs incurred. Thus, Marvel compares its avoidable interest of $6,000 and its actual interest incurred of $29,400 and chooses the lower amount to capitalize. Any interest amounts earned on funds borrowed which are temporarily in excess of the company's needs are to be reported as interest revenue rather than be used to offset the amount of interest to be capitalized. Thus, Marvel will report $5,000 as interest revenue and that $5,000 will not affect the amount of interest to be capitalized.

EXERCISE 10-4

Purpose: (L.O.5) This exercise will give you practice in accounting for the acquisition of a plant asset on a deferred payment plan.

Starstruck, Inc. purchased a computer network on December 31, 1999 for $200,000, paying $50,000 down and agreeing to pay the balance in five equal installments of $30,000 payable each December 31 beginning in 2000. An assumed interest rate of 10% is implicit in the purchase price.

Instructions (Round to the nearest cent)

(a) Prepare the journal entry(ies) at the date of purchase.
(b) Prepare an amortization schedule for the installment agreement.
(c) Prepare the journal entry(ies) at December 31, 2000, to record the cash payment and the applicable interest expense (assume the effective interest method is employed).
(d) Prepare the journal entry(ies) at December 31, 2001, to record the cash payment and the applicable interest expense (assume the effective interest method is employed).

Solution to Exercise 10-4

(a) Time diagram:

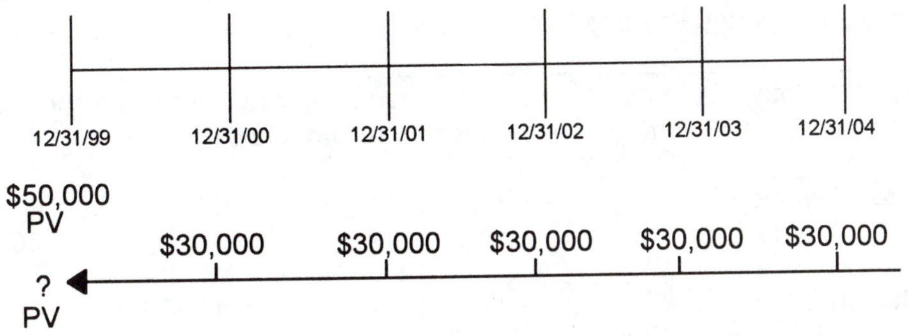

Entry:

Equipment	163,723.70*	
Discount on Notes Payable	36,276.30	
Cash		50,000.00
Notes Payable ($30,000 x 5)		150,000.00

*PV of a $30,000 ordinary annuity @ 10% for 5 years ($30,000 x 3.79079)	$ 113,723.70
Down payment	50,000.00
Capitalized value of equipment	$ 163,723.70

(b)

Date	Cash Payment	10% Interest Expense	Reduction of Principal	Liability Balance
12/31/99				$113,723.70
12/31/00	$ 30,000.00	$ 11,372.37	$ 18,627.63	95,096.07
12/31/01	30,000.00	9,509.61	20,490.39	74,605.68
12/31/02	30,000.00	7,460.57	22,539.43	52,066.25
12/31/03	30,000.00	5,206.63	24,793.37	27,272.88
12/31/04	30,000.00	2,727.12*	27,272.88	-0-
Totals	$ 150,000.00	$ 36,276.30	$113,723.70	

*This is a plug figure, which includes a rounding error of $0.17.

(c)

December 31, 2000

Notes Payable	30,000.00	
Interest Expense (see schedule)	11,372.37	
Cash		30,000.00
Discount on Notes Payable		11,372.37

(d) **December 31, 2001**

Notes Payable	30,000.00	
Interest Expense (see schedule)	9,509.61	
Cash		30,000.00
Discount on Notes Payable		9,509.61

TIP: For each entry in (c) and (d), two entries could replace the one compound entry. For example, the two equivalent entries for (c) would be:

Notes Payable	30,000.00	
Cash		30,000.00
Interest Expense	11,372.37	
Discount on Notes Payable		11,372.37

EXERCISE 10-5

Purpose: (L.O.5) This exercise reviews the computations involved in a lump-sum purchase of plant assets.

The Eliason Company paid $750,000 cash for a package of plant assets. The package consisted of the following:

	Seller's Book Value	Market Value
Land	$ 60,000	$ 300,000
Building	120,000	400,000
Equipment	220,000	250,000
Tools	100,000	50,000
Total	$ 500,000	$ 1,000,000

Instructions

(a) Prepare the journal entry for Eliason to record the acquisition of these assets on the company's books.

(b) Why must you allocate the total cost to separate accounts for the individual assets? Why can't you simply use "Plant Assets" as an account and record the total cost to that account? Explain.

Solution to Exercise 10-5

(a)

Land	225,000	
Building	300,000	
Equipment	187,500	
Tools	37,500	
Cash		750,000

Approach and Explanation: The total cost ($750,000) is to be allocated to the individual assets based on the relative market values of these assets. The formula that can be used to accomplish this objective is as follows:

$$\frac{\text{Market Value of One Item in Group}}{\text{Market Value of All items in Group}} \times \text{Amount to be Allocated} = \text{Amount to be Assigned to Item Designated in the Numerator}$$

Land:	($300,000 ÷ $1,000,000) x $750,000 =	$225,000
Building:	($400,000 ÷ $1,000,000) x $750,000 =	$300,000
Equipment:	($250,000 ÷ $1,000,000) x $750,000 =	$187,500
Tools:	($50,000 ÷ $1,000,000) x $750,000 =	$37,500

TIP: Sum the four answers obtained by using the formula. They should total to the amount you set out to allocate ($750,000, in this case).

(b) The total cost must be allocated to the individual assets because land is not subject to the process of depreciation, and the depreciable assets normally are subject to different service lives and maybe even different depreciation methods.

ILLUSTRATION 10-1
SUMMARY OF REQUIREMENTS FOR RECOGNIZING GAINS AND LOSSES ON EXCHANGES OF NONMONETARY ASSETS (L.O.5)

1. Compute the total gain or loss experienced on the transaction, which is equal to the difference between the fair value of the asset given up and the book value of the asset given up. An excess of fair value over book value indicates an experienced gain; an excess of book value over fair value indicates an experienced loss.

2. If a loss is computed in 1, always recognize the entire loss.

3. If a gain is computed in 1,
   (a) and the earning process is considered completed, the entire gain is recognized (dissimilar assets).
   (b) and the earning process is not considered completed (similar assets),
      (1) and no boot is received, no gain is recognized.
      (2) and boot is received, the following portion of the gain is recognized:

$$\frac{\text{Cash Received (Boot)}}{\text{Cash Received (Boot)} + \text{Fair Value of Other Assets Received}} \times \text{Total Gain Experienced}$$

TIP: "Boot" is a term used to describe monetary consideration (such as cash or a receivable which is a claim for cash) given or received in an exchange of nonmonetary assets. When boot is received in the exchange of similar assets, part of the exchanged asset is considered to be sold; therefore, part of the earning process is considered complete and a **proportionate** amount of the gain is recognized by the party receiving the boot if a gain has been experienced.

TIP: Recall that it is the conservatism constraint that requires **all losses to be recognized** rather than deferred to future periods.

TIP: The rules stated here for recognition of gain or loss pertain to reporting on general purpose financial statements. These rules differ from the treatment called for on an income tax return.

EXERCISE 10-6

Purpose: (L.O.5) This exercise will allow you to practice recording the exchange of similar productive assets.

Soon Yoon Company exchanged equipment used in its manufacturing operations plus $15,000 in cash for similar equipment used in the operations of Peggy Gunshanan Company. The following information pertains to the exchange:

	Soon Yoon Co.	Peggy Gunshanan Co.
Equipment (cost)	$ 84,000	$ 84,000
Accumulated depreciation	66,000	30,000
Fair value of equipment	31,500	46,500
Cash given up	15,000	

Instructions

(a) Prepare the journal entries to record the exchange on the books of both companies.

(b) Prepare the journal entries to record the exchange on the books of both companies assuming the fair value of Soon Yoon Co.'s old asset is $16,500 (rather than $31,500) and the fair value of Peggy Gunshanan's old equipment is $31,500 (rather than $46,500).

(c) Prepare the journal entries to record the exchange on the books of both companies, assuming the fair value of Soon Yoon Co.'s old asset is $46,500 (rather than $31,500) and the fair value of Peggy Gunshanan's old equipment is $61,500 (rather than $46,500).

Solution to Exercise 10-6

(a) **Soon Yoon Company:**

Equipment (New)	33,000	
Accumulated Depreciation	66,000	
Equipment (Old)		84,000
Cash		15,000

Computation of book value:

Cost of old asset	$ 84,000
Accumulated depreciation	(66,000)
Book value of old asset	$ 18,000

Computation of gain:

Fair value of equipment given	$ 31,500
Book value of equipment given	(18,000)
Gain experienced on old asset	$ 13,500

Valuation of new equipment:

Book value of equipment given	$18,000
Boot given	15,000
Cost of new equipment	$33,000

OR

Fair value of equipment received	$46,500
Gain deferred	(13,500)
Cost of new equipment	$33,000

Peggy Gunshanan Company:

Cash	15,000	
Equipment (New)	31,500	
Accumulated Depreciation	30,000	
Loss on Disposal of Plant Asset	7,500	
Equipment (Old)		84,000

Computation of book value:

Cost of old asset	$84,000
Accumulated depreciation	(30,000)
Book value of old asset	$54,000

Computation of loss:

Fair value of equipment given	$ 46,500
Book value of equipment given	(54,000)
Loss experienced on old asset	$ (7,500)

Valuation of new equipment:

Book value of equipment given	$54,000
Loss recognized on disposal	(7,500)
Fair value of equipment given	46,500
Boot received	(15,000)
Cost of new equipment	$31,500

Approach and Explanation: Refer to **Illustration 10-1** which summarizes the rules for recognizing gains and losses experienced on exchanges of nonmonetary assets.

Soon Yoon has experienced a gain of $13,500 on the old asset. It is an exchange of similar productive assets; hence, the earning process is not considered complete. Boot is given; therefore, the gain is not recognized. Rather than crediting a gain, the gain is reflected in the cost of the new asset by reducing what otherwise would have been recorded as the new asset's cost. Thus, the gain is deferred and there is a departure from the historical cost principle in determining the cost of the new asset.

Peggy Gunshanan has experienced a loss. A loss is always recognized, regardless of whether the exchange is of dissimilar or similar assets and regardless of whether boot is given or received. (Think about the principle of conservatism here to help you to remember this.) The historical cost principle is followed in determining the amount to record for the equipment received.

> **TIP:** The parties will bargain so that the total fair value given equals the total fair value received. Therefore, since Peggy Gunshanan is giving up equipment worth $46,500, but Soon Yoon's equipment is only worth $31,500, Soon Yoon is also giving $15,000 cash to Peggy Gunshanan.

(b) **Soon Yoon Company:**

Equipment (New)	31,500	
Accumulated Depreciation	66,000	
Loss on Disposal of Plant Asset	1,500	
Equipment (Old)		84,000
Cash		15,000

Computation of loss:

Fair value of equipment given	$16,500
Book value of equipment given	18,000
Loss experienced on old asset	$ (1,500)

Valuation of new equipment:

Book value of equipment given	$18,000
Loss recognized on disposal	(1,500)
Boot given	15,000
Cost of new equipment	$31,500

OR

Fair value of equipment given	$16,500
Boot given	15,000
Cost of new equipment	$31,500

Peggy Gunshanan Company:

Cash	15,000	
Equipment (New)	16,500	
Accumulated Depreciation	30,000	
Loss on Disposal of Plant Asset	22,500	
Equipment (Old)		84,000

Computation of loss:

Fair value of equipment given	$ 31,500
Book value of equipment given	(54,000)
Loss experienced on old asset	$ (22,500)

Valuation of new equipment:

Book value of equipment given	$ 54,000
Loss recognized on disposal	(22,500)
Fair value of equipment given	31,500
Boot received	(15,000)
Cost of new equipment	$16,500

Explanation: Both Soon Yoon and Peggy Gunshanan experienced losses on the disposal of their old plant assets. A loss is always to be recognized (because of conservatism). The historical cost principle is followed in determining the cost of the new plant asset.

(c) **Soon Yoon Company:**

Equipment (New)	33,000	
Accumulated Depreciation	66,000	
Equipment (Old)		84,000
Cash		15,000

Computation of gain:

Fair value of equipment given	$46,500
Book value of equipment given	(18,000)
Gain experienced on old asset	$ 28,500

Valuation of new equipment:

Book value of equipment given	$18,000
Boot given	15,000
Cost of new equipment	$33,000

OR

Fair value of equipment given	$46,500
Gain deferred	(28,500)
Boot given	15,000
Cost of new equipment	$33,000

Peggy Gunshanan Company:

Cash	15,000	
Equipment (New)	40,830	
Accumulated Depreciation	30,000	
Equipment (Old)		84,000
Gain on Disposal of Plant Asset		1,830

Computation of gain experienced:

Fair value of equipment given	$61,500
Book value of equipment given	(54,000)
Gain experienced on old asset	$ 7,500

Computation of gain recognized:

[$15,000 ÷ ($15,000 + $46,500)] x $7,500 = $1,830

Valuation of new equipment:

Book value of equipment given	$54,000
Fair value of boot received	(15,000)
Gain recognized	1,830
Cost of new equipment	$40,830

OR

Fair value of equipment given	$61,500
Boot received	(15,000)
Gain deferred ($7,500 - $1,830)	(5,670)
Cost of new equipment	$40,830

Explanation: Soon's entire gain is deferred (**not** recognized currently) because Soon is giving boot in an exchange of similar productive assets. The reasoning for the restriction on recognition of gain is that no portion of the earning process has been completed (since no boot was received). The "gain" serves to reduce the recorded value of the new asset. Peggy Gunshanan's gain is partially recognized because boot is being received in an exchange of similar productive assets. The portion of the gain recognized is determined by a ratio of the boot received to the total fair value of the consideration received. The portion of the gain experienced but not recognized reduces what otherwise would have been recorded as the cost of the new equipment.

ILLUSTRATION 10-2
EXPENDITURES SUBSEQUENT TO ACQUISITION (L.O.6)

A plant asset often requires expenditures subsequent to acquisition. Generally, four major types of expenditures may be incurred relative to existing plant assets; they are as follows:

- **Additions.** Increase or extension of existing assets.
- **Improvements and Replacements.** Substitution of an improved asset for an existing one.
- **Rearrangement and Reinstallation.** Movement of assets from one location to another.
- **Repairs.** Expenditures that maintain assets in condition for operation.

Costs that are incurred subsequent to acquisition are to be capitalized (by a debit to an asset account or to an accumulated depreciation account, depending on the circumstances) if they are material, nonrecurring in nature, and benefit future periods in some manner such as by doing one or more of the following:

a. They extend the useful life of a plant asset.
b. They enhance the quality of existing services.
c. They add new asset services.
d. They reduce future operating costs of existing assets.
e. They are required to meet governmental regulations (such as for environmental reasons).

The accounting treatment appropriate for various costs incurred subsequent to the acquisition of capitalized assets is summarized as follows:

ILLUSTRATION 10-2 (Continued)

Type of Expenditure	Normal Accounting Treatment
Additions	Capitalize cost of addition to asset account.
Improvements and Replacements	(a) **Carrying value of old asset known:** Remove cost of and accumulated depreciation on old asset, recognizing any gain or loss. Capitalize cost of improvement/replacement. (b) **Carrying value of old asset unknown:** 1. If the asset's useful life is extended, debit accumulated depreciation for cost of improvement/replacement. 2. If the quantity or quality of the asset's productivity is increased, capitalize cost of improvement/replacement to asset account.
Rearrangement and Reinstallation	(a) If original installation cost is **known**, account for cost of rearrangement/reinstallation as a replacement (carrying value known). (b) If original installation cost is **unknown** and rearrangement/reinstallation cost is **material** in amount and benefits future periods, capitalize as an asset. (c) If original installation cost is **unknown** and rearrangement/reinstallation cost is **not material or future benefit is questionable**, expense the cost when incurred.
Repairs	(a) **Ordinary:** Expense cost of repairs when incurred. (b) **Major:** As appropriate, treat as an addition, improvement, or replacement.

CASE 10-3

Purpose: (L.O.6) This case will provide a few examples of the accounting for costs subsequent to the acquisition of fixed assets.

Hardent Resources Group has been in its plant facility for twenty years. Although the plant is quite functional, numerous repair costs are incurred to maintain it in sound working order. The company's plant asset book value is currently $750,000, as indicated below:

Original cost	$ 1,350,000
Accumulated depreciation	600,000
Book value	$ 750,000

During the current year, the following expenditures were made involving the plant facility:

(a) The entire plant was repainted at a cost of $26,000.

(b) The roof was an asbestos cement slate; for safety purposes, it was removed and replaced with a new and better quality roof at a cost of $62,000. Book value of the old roof was $31,000.

(c) Because of increased demands for its product, the company increased its plant capacity by building a new addition at a cost of $315,000.

(d) The plumbing system was completely updated at a cost of $53,000. The cost of the old plumbing system was not known. It is estimated that the useful life of the building will not change as a result of this updating.

(e) A series of major repairs were made at a cost of $50,000, because parts of the wood structure were rotting. The cost of the old wood structure was not known. These extensive repairs are estimated to increase the useful life of the building.

Instructions

Indicate how each of these transactions would be recorded in the accounting records.

Solution to Case 10-3

(a) Expenditures that do not increase the service benefits of the asset are expensed. Painting costs are considered ordinary repairs because they maintain the existing condition of the asset or restore it to normal operating efficiency.

(b) The approach to follow is to remove the old book value of the roof and substitute the cost of the new roof. It is assumed that the expenditure increases the future service potential of the asset. Recognize a loss equal to the book value of the old roof removed.

(c) Any addition to plant assets is capitalized because a new asset has been created. This addition increases the service potential of the plant.

(d) Conceptually the book value of the old plumbing system should be removed. However, in practice, it is often difficult if not impossible to determine this amount. In this case, one of two approaches is followed. One approach is to capitalize the cost of the replacement on the theory that sufficient depreciation was taken on the item to reduce the carrying amount to almost zero. A second approach is to debit accumulated depreciation on the theory that the replacement extends the useful life of the asset and thereby recaptures some or all of the past depreciation. In our present situation, the problem specifically states that the useful life is not extended and therefore debiting accumulated depreciation is inappropriate. Thus, this expenditure should be added to the cost of the plant facility.

(e) See discussion in (d) above. In this case, because the useful life of the asset has increased, a debit to accumulated depreciation would appear to be the most appropriate treatment.

EXERCISE 10-7

Purpose: (L.O.7) This exercise will (1) illustrate several different ways in which you may dispose of property, and (2) discuss the appropriate accounting procedures for each.

Presented below is a schedule of property dispositions for Friedlander Co.

Schedule of Property Dispositions

	Cost	Accumulated Depreciation	Cash Proceeds	Fair Market Value	Nature of Disposition
Land	$ 80,000	---	$ 64,000	$ 64,000	Condemnation
Building	30,000	---	7,200	---	Demolition
Warehouse	130,000	$22,000	148,000	148,000	Destruction by fire
Machine	16,000	6,400	3,600	14,400	Trade-in
Furniture	20,000	15,700	---	5,600	Contribution
Automobile	16,000	6,920	5,920	5,920	Sale

The following additional information is available:

- **Land.** On January 7, a condemnation award was received as consideration for unimproved land held primarily as an investment, and on April 7, another parcel of unimproved land to be held as an investment was purchased at a cost of $70,000.

- **Building.** On May 4, land and building were purchased at a total cost of $150,000, of which 20% was allocated to the building on the corporate books. The real estate was acquired with the intention of demolishing the building, and this was accomplished during the month of August. Cash proceeds received in August represent the net proceeds from demolition of the building.

- **Warehouse.** On January 2, the warehouse was destroyed by fire. The warehouse was purchased January 2, 1995, and had been depreciated $22,000. On June 15, part of the insurance proceeds was used to purchase a replacement warehouse at a cost of $130,000.

- **Machine.** On October 31, the machine was exchanged for another similar machine having a fair market value of $10,800 and cash of $3,600 was received.

- **Furniture.** On July 2, furniture was contributed to a qualified charitable organization. No other contributions were made or pledged during the year.

- **Automobile.** On December 31, the automobile was sold to Dee Dee Burgess, a stockholder.

Instructions

Indicate how these items would be reported on the income statement of Friedlander Co.

(AICPA adapted)

Solution to Exercise 10-7

The following accounting treatment appears appropriate for these items:

- **Land.** The loss on the condemnation of the land of $16,000 ($80,000 - $64,000) should be reported as an extraordinary item on the income statement. A condemnation comes about from a government unit exercising its right of eminent domain. *Eminent domain* is defined as "expropriation of assets by a government." Expropriation of assets is given as an example of an extraordinary item in *APB Opinion 30*. The $70,000 land purchase has no income statement effect.

- **Building.** There is no recognized gain or loss on the demolition of the building. The entire purchase cost ($30,000), decreased by the demolition proceeds ($7,200), is allocated to land.

- **Warehouse.** The gain on the destruction of the warehouse should be reported in the "other revenues and gains" section of the income statement. A fire can happen in any environment; therefore, it is not an extraordinary item. The gain is computed as follows:

Insurance proceeds		$148,000
Cost	$130,000	
Accumulated depreciation	(22,000)	(108,000)
Realized gain		$ 40,000

Some contend that a portion of this gain should be deferred because the proceeds are reinvested in similar assets. Deferral of the gain in this situation is not permitted under GAAP.

- **Machine.** The recognized gain on the exchange would be computed as follows:

Fair market value of old machine		$14,400
Cost	$16,000	
Accumulated depreciation	(6,400)	(9,600)
Total gain experienced		$ 4,800

Total gain recognized = $4,800 x [$3,600 ÷ ($3,600 + $10,800)] = $1,200

This gain would probably be reported in the "other revenues and gains" section. It might be considered an unusual item, but it would usually not be infrequent. The cost of the new machine would be capitalized at $7,200:

Carrying value of old asset ($16,000 - $6,400)	$9,600
Boot received	(3,600)
Gain recognized	1,200
Cost of new machine	$7,200

OR

Fair market value of new machine		$10,800
Gain experienced	$4,800	
Gain recognized	(1,200)	
Gain deferred		3,600
Cost of new machine		$ 7,200

- **Furniture.** The contribution of the furniture to a charitable organization would be reported as a contribution expense of $5,600 with a related gain on disposition of furniture of $1,300 [$5,600 - ($20,000 - $15,700)]. The contribution expense and the related gain may be netted, if desired, for reporting purposes.

- **Automobile.** The loss on sale of the automobile of $3,160 [$5,920 - ($16,000 - $6,920)] should probably be reported in the "other expenses and losses" section. This is a related party transaction; such transactions require special disclosure.

TIP: The receipt of the condemnation award (January 7) represents an **involuntary conversion of nonmonetary assets to monetary assets**. Any gain or loss related to the transaction shall be recognized even though the enterprise reinvests or is obligated to reinvest the monetary assets in replacement nonmonetary assets. The receipt of insurance proceeds due to the destruction of the warehouse is also an involuntary conversion of nonmonetary assets to monetary assets.

TIP: The sale of property, plant, and equipment for cash should be accounted for as follows:
(1) The carrying value at the date of the sale (cost of the property, plant, and equipment less the accumulated depreciation) should be removed from the accounts.
(2) The excess of cash from the sale over the carrying value removed is accounted for as a gain on the sale, while the excess of carrying value removed over cash from the sale is accounted for as a loss on the sale.

TIP: When a plant asset is disposed of, the accumulated depreciation must be updated before the gain or loss can be computed. The discussions above assume that updating has taken place.

EXERCISE 10-8

Purpose: (L.O.2,6) This exercise is designed to give you additional practice in analyzing changes in property, plant, and equipment accounts during a period. Problems of this type frequently appear on professional exams.

At December 31, 1998, certain accounts included in the property, plant, and equipment section of the Busch Company's balance sheet had the following balances:

Land	$ 100,000
Buildings	800,000
Leasehold improvements	500,000
Machinery and equipment	700,000

During 1999 the following transactions occurred:

- Land site number 52 was acquired for $1,000,000. Additionally, to acquire the land Busch paid a $60,000 commission to a real estate agent. Costs of $15,000 were incurred to clear the land. During the course of clearing the land, timber and gravel were recovered and sold for $5,000.

- A second tract of land (site number 53) with a building was acquired for $300,000. The closing statement indicated that the land value was $200,000 and the building value was $100,000. Shortly after acquisition, the building was demolished at a cost of $30,000. A new building was constructed for $150,000 plus the following costs:

Excavation fees	$ 11,000
Architectural design fees	8,000
Building permit fee	1,000
Imputed interest on equity funds used during construction (The company had no debt outstanding and no actual interest cost incurred.)	6,000

  The building was completed and occupied on September 30, 1999.

- A third tract of land (site number 54) was acquired for $600,000 and was put on the market for resale.

- Extensive work was done to a building occupied by Busch under a lease agreement that expires on December 31, 2008. The total cost of the work was $125,000, which consisted of the following:

Painting of ceilings	$ 10,000	estimated useful life is 1 year
Electrical work	35,000	estimated useful life is 10 years
Construction of extension to current working area	80,000	estimated useful life is 30 years
	$ 125,000	

  The lessor paid one-half of the costs incurred in connection with the extension to the current working area.

- During December 1999, costs of $65,000 were incurred to improve leased office space. The related lease will terminate on December 31, 2001, and is not expected to be renewed.

- A group of new machines were purchased under a royalty agreement which provides for payment of royalties based on units of production for the machines. The invoice price of the machines was $75,000, freight costs were $2,000, unloading charges were $1,500, and royalty payments for 1999 were $13,000.

Instructions

(a) Prepare a detailed analysis of the changes in each of the following balance sheet accounts for 1999:

Land	Leasehold improvements
Buildings	Machinery and equipment

Disregard the related accumulated depreciation accounts.

(b) List the items in the fact situation which were not used to determine the answer to (a) above, and indicate **where, or if,** these items should be included in Busch's financial statements.

(AICPA Adapted)

Solution to Exercise 10-8

(a)

Busch Company
ANALYSIS OF LAND ACCOUNT
for 1999

Balance at January 1, 1999			$ 100,000
Land site number 52			
Acquisition cost		$ 1,000,000	
Commission to real estate agent		60,000	
Clearing costs	$ 15,000		
Less amounts recovered	5,000	10,000	
Total land site number 52			1,070,000
Land site number 53			
Land value		200,000	
Building value		100,000	
Demolition cost		30,000	
Total land site number 53			330,000
Balance at December 31, 1999			$ 1,500,000

Busch Company
ANALYSIS OF BUILDING ACCOUNT
for 1999

Balance at January 1, 1999		$ 800,000
Cost of new building constructed on land site number 53		
Construction costs	$ 150,000	
Excavation fees	11,000	
Architectural design fees	8,000	
Building permit fee	1,000	170,000
Balance at December 31, 1999		$ 970,000

Busch Company
ANALYSIS OF LEASEHOLD IMPROVEMENTS ACCOUNT
for 1999

Balance at January 1, 1999	$500,000
Electrical work	35,000
Construction of extension to current work area ($80,000 x 1/2)	40,000
Office space improvements	65,000
Balance at December 31, 1999	$640,000

Busch Company
ANALYSIS OF MACHINERY AND EQUIPMENT ACCOUNT
for 1999

Balance at January 1, 1999		$ 700,000
Cost of new machines acquired		
Invoice price	$ 75,000	
Freight costs	2,000	
Unloading charges	1,500	78,500
Balance at December 31, 1999		$ 778,500

(b) Items in the fact situation which were not used to determine the answer to (a) above are:

- Imputed interest of $6,000 on equity funds used during construction should not be included anywhere in Busch's financial statements. Only interest actually incurred should be capitalized during construction.
- Land site number 54, which was acquired for $600,000 and held for resale, should be included in Busch's balance sheet in the investment classification.
- Painting of ceilings for $10,000 should be included as a normal operating expense in Busch's income statement.
- Royalty payments of $13,000 should be included as a normal operating expense in Busch's income statement.

ANALYSIS OF MULTIPLE-CHOICE TYPE QUESTIONS

QUESTION

1. (L.O.2) Jacobson Manufacturing Company purchased a machine for $65,000 on January 2, 1999. At the date of purchase, Jacobson incurred the following additional costs:

Loss on sale of old machine	$ 2,000
Freight-in	900
Installation cost	1,500
Breaking-in costs	650

The amount to record for the acquisition cost of the new machine is:

a. $65,000.
b. $67,400.
c. $68,050.
d. $69,400.

Approach and Explanation: Apply the guideline: The cost of a plant asset includes all costs required to get the item to the location and condition for its intended purpose.

Purchase price	$ 65,000
Freight-in	900
Installation cost	1,500
Breaking-in costs	650
Total acquisition cost	$ 68,050

The loss on sale of the old machine should be charged to an income statement account so it will not impact the new asset's value. (Solution = c.)

QUESTION

2. (L.O.2) Buena Vista Hotel purchases Embassy Hotel with the intention of demolishing the Embassy Hotel and building a new high-rise hotel on the site. The cost of the Embassy Hotel should be:
   a. capitalized as part of the cost of the land.
   b. capitalized as part of the cost of the new hotel.
   c. written off as a loss when it is torn down.
   d. depreciated over the life of the new hotel structure.

Explanation: The cost of the land should include all costs necessary to acquire it and prepare it for its intended use by the buyer—which is to provide a site for a new building. (Solution = a.)

QUESTION

3. (L.O.3) A manufacturing company decides to build its own factory equipment. The cost of self-constructed plant assets may include which of the following:

	Materials	Labor	Mfg. Overhead
a.	Yes	Yes	Yes
b.	Yes	Yes	No
c.	Yes	No	No
d.	No	Yes	No

Explanation: In addition to the materials and labor used to build a plant asset, the manufacturer should assign a pro rata portion of the manufacturing overhead to obtain the asset's cost. However, the asset should not be recorded for more than its fair value (the total amount that would be charged by an outside independent producer). (Solution = a.)

QUESTION

4. (L.O.4) Herndon Inc. has a fiscal year ending October 31. On November 1, 1998, Herndon borrowed $20,000,000 at 15% to finance construction of a new plant. Repayments of the loan are to commence the month following completion of the plant. During the year ending October 31, 1999, expenditures for the partially completed structure totaled $12,000,000. These expenditures were incurred evenly through the year. Interest earned on the unexpended portion of the loan amounted to $800,000 for the year. What amount of interest should be capitalized as of October 31, 1999?
   a. $0.
   b. $100,000.
   c. $900,000.
   d. $2,200,000.

Explanation: The situation is one which qualifies for the capitalization of interest. The following steps should help to compute the amount:

(1) **Find the weighted-average accumulated expenditures** for the period:

Total expenditures at beginning of the period	$ 0
Total expenditures at end of the period	12,000,000
Sum	$ 12,000,000

$12,000,000 ÷ 2 = average of $6,000,000

(2) **Determine the interest rate to use.** Because the amount of a specific borrowing ($20,000,000) exceeds the weighted-average accumulated expenditures ($6,000,000), use the interest rate for that specific borrowing (15%).

(3) **Compute the avoidable interest** by multiplying the appropriate interest rate (15% from Step 2) by the weighted-average accumulated expenditures ($6,000,000 from Step 1).

$6,000,000 x 15% = $900,000 Avoidable interest

(4) **Determine the amount of interest to capitalize** by selecting the lower of the actual interest incurred (15% x $20,000,000 = $3,000,000) or the amount of avoidable interest ($900,000 from Step 3). The lower in this case is the $900,000 avoidable interest. (Solution = c.)

> **TIP:** The interest earned ($800,000) is to be reported as revenue on the income statement and should not be used to offset the interest to be capitalized.

QUESTION

5. (L.O.5) A large plot of land was donated by the City of Moberly to the Dupont Corporation to entice the company to build a plant and provide new jobs in the community. The land should be recorded on Dupont's books at:
   a. the cost of the attorney's fees involved in handling the transaction.
   b. the value assigned by Dupont's board of directors.
   c. the land's market value.
   d. no more than one dollar because the land was obtained for no cost.

Explanation: A donation (contribution) is a nonreciprocal transfer (value goes in only one direction rather than in both directions as happens in an exchange transaction). A nonreciprocal transfer is to be recorded at the fair value of the property, goods, or services involved. Although contributions received are normally credited to revenue, a donation from a governmental entity to a for-profit entity to entice the business to its community is better credited to Donated Capital (an element of additional paid-in capital on the balance sheet). (Solution = c.)

QUESTION

6. (L.O.5) The Holstrum Corporation intends to acquire some plant assets from Bailey Corporation by issuing common stock in exchange. The cost of the assets should be measured by:
   a. the par value of the stock.
   b. the market value of the stock.
   c. the book value of the stock.
   d. Bailey's carrying value of the assets.

Explanation: Cost is measured by the fair market value (cash equivalent) of the consideration given (the stock in this case), or the fair market value of the consideration received (the plant assets in this case), whichever is the more objectively determinable. If the market value of the common stock is not determinable, the fair market value of the plant assets should be used. (Solution = b.)

QUESTION

7. (L.O.5) In January 1999, Barbie Company entered into a contract to acquire a new machine for its factory. The machine, which had a cash price of $300,000, was acquired in exchange for the following:

Down payment	$ 30,000
Note payable in 24 equal monthly installments	240,000
500 shares of Barbie common stock, with an agreed value of $100 per share	50,000
Total	$ 320,000

   Prior to the machine's use, installation costs of $8,000 were incurred. The amount to record for the acquisition cost of the machine is:
   a. $300,000.
   b. $308,000.
   c. $320,000.
   d. $328,000.

Approach and Explanation: Any time you have a question regarding the acquisition cost of a plant asset, write down (or mentally review) the two rules regarding asset cost: (1) Cost is measured by the fair market value (cash equivalent) of the consideration given or the fair market value of the consideration received, whichever is the more objectively determinable; and (2) An asset's cost includes all costs necessary to get it to the location and condition for its intended purpose. Then apply the rules to the situation given.

The cash equivalent of the machine acquired is $300,000 (cash price). The cash equivalent of the consideration given is the cash down payment of $30,000 plus the fair value of the stock ($50,000) plus the present value of the note payable (something less than $240,000). Because no information is given about the market value of the note or the appropriate interest rate for the note, but the cash equivalent price is given for the asset received, the more objectively determinable figure is the $300,000. The $8,000 installation cost must be added to get the total acquisition cost. (Solution = b.)

QUESTION

8. (L.O.5) Two home builders agree to exchange tracts of land that each holds for purposes of development. An appraiser was hired and the following information is available:

	Batson	Beamer
Book value of land	$ 50,000	$ 72,000
Fair value of land	80,000	100,000
Cash paid	20,000	

In recording this exchange should a gain be recognized by Batson, Beamer, or both parties?

	Batson	Beamer
a.	Yes	Yes
b.	Yes	No
c.	No	Yes
d.	No	No

Approach and Explanation:

(1) **Determine if it is an exchange of similar or dissimilar assets.** One tract of land for another to use for the same purpose is an exchange of similar assets.

(2) **Determine if a gain or loss is experienced.** Fair value exceeds book value for both parties so both have experienced a gain.

(3) **Determine if boot is given or received.** Batson is giving boot; Beamer is receiving boot.

(4) **Write down the rules for recognition of gain in a similar asset exchange.** The party giving boot (Batson) is not to recognize any gain. The party receiving boot is to recognize a portion of the gain experienced. In this case, the receipt of cash by Beamer represents a partial sale of the land, thus completing a portion of the earning process. (Solution = c.)

QUESTION

9. (L.O.5) Refer to the facts of question 8. The amount to be recorded by Batson for the acquisition cost of the new tract of land is:
   a. $50,000.
   b. $70,000.
   c. $72,000.
   d. $80,000.
   e. $100,000.

Approach and Explanation: When boot is given in a similar asset exchange, no gain is to be recognized. The cost of the new asset is equal to the recorded value (book value) of the old asset, reduced for any impairment (minus any loss recognized), plus the boot given. There was no loss in this case; therefore, $50,000 book value + $20,000 boot = $70,000 cost. A journal entry approach can also be used (the debit to the new asset account is a plug figure): (Solution = b.)

Land (New)	70,000		**Plug last.**
Land (Old)		50,000	**Do second.**
Cash		20,000	**Do first.**

QUESTION

10. (L.O.6) In accounting for plant assets, which of the following outlays made subsequent to acquisition should be fully expensed in the period the expenditure is made?

a. Expenditure made to increase the efficiency or effectiveness of an existing asset.
b. Expenditure made to extend the useful life of an existing asset beyond the time frame originally anticipated.
c. Expenditure made to maintain an existing asset so that it can function in the manner intended.
d. Expenditure made to add new asset services.

Explanation: If an expenditure benefits future periods, it should be capitalized (debited to a balance sheet account); if the expenditure does not yield benefits to a future period, it should be recorded by a debit to an income statement account. An expenditure made to maintain an existing asset in good working condition does not provide any benefits other than those that were in potential when the original asset was acquired; hence, it should be expensed. Answer selections "a," "b," and "d" all represent future economic benefits; hence, they should be debited to an asset account or to an accumulated depreciation account, depending on whether or not an asset's life is increased by the expenditure subsequent to acquisition. (Solution = c.)

CHAPTER 11

DEPRECIATION, IMPAIRMENTS, AND DEPLETION

OVERVIEW

Expenses arise from the cost of goods or services that are consumed in the process of generating revenue. When a long-term tangible asset is acquired, it actually represents a bundle of future asset services. The total cost of these services equals the acquisition cost of the asset **minus the asset's expected (estimated) market value at the end of its useful life.** As a productive asset is used, services (benefits) are consumed; therefore, a portion of the original asset cost should be charged to expense in order to comply with the matching principle. The process of allocating (expensing) the cost of long-term tangible assets over the accounting periods during which the asset is used is called **depreciation**. The process of allocating the costs of natural resources to inventory (and later to cost of goods sold) is called **depletion**. Depreciation and depletion are discussed in this chapter.

SUMMARY OF LEARNING OBJECTIVES

1. **Explain the concept of depreciation.** Depreciation is the accounting process of allocating the cost of long-lived tangible assets to expense in a systematic and rational manner to those periods expected to benefit from the use of the asset.

2. **Identify the factors involved in the depreciation process.** Three factors involved in the depreciation process are: (1) determining the depreciation base for the asset, (2) estimating service life, and (3) selecting a method of cost apportionment (depreciation).

3. **Compare activity, straight-line, and decreasing-charge methods of depreciation.** (1) *Activity method:* Assumes that depreciation is a function of use or productivity instead of the passage of time. The life of the asset is considered in terms of either the output it provides, or an input measure such as the number of hours it works. (2) *Straight-line method:* Considers depreciation a function of time instead of a function of usage. This method is widely employed in practice because of its simplicity. The straight-line procedure is often the most conceptually appropriate when a decline in usefulness is constant from period to period. (3) *Decreasing-charge method:* Provides for a higher depreciation charge in the earlier years and lower charges in later periods. The main justification for this approach is that the asset suffers the greatest loss of services in the earlier years.

4. **Explain special depreciation methods.** There are five special depreciation methods: (1) *Inventory method:* Used to value small tangible assets such as hand tools or utensils. (2) *Retirement and replacement methods:* Used principally by public utilities and railroads that own many similar units of small value such as poles, ties, conductors, and telephones. The purpose of these approaches is to avoid elaborate depreciation schedules for individual assets. (3) *Group and composite methods:* The term "group" refers to a collection of assets that are similar in nature; "composite" refers to a collection of assets that are dissimilar in nature. The group method is frequently used where the assets are fairly homogeneous and have approximately the same useful lives. The composite approach is used when the assets are heterogeneous and have different lives. (4) *Compound interest methods:* Unlike most depreciation methods, the compound interest methods are increasing-charge methods that result in lower depreciation charges in the early years and higher depreciation charges in the later years. (5) *Hybrid or combination methods:* A hybrid depreciation method widely used in the steel

industry is a combination straight line/activity approach referred to as the production variable method.

5. **Identify reasons why depreciation methods are selected.** The selection of a depreciation method involves factors such as the nature and uncertainty of revenue flows, matching costs and revenues, effect on income and asset book values, tax considerations, and record-keeping costs.

6. **Explain the accounting issues related to asset impairment.** The process to determine an impairment loss is as follows: (1) Review events and changes in circumstances for possible impairment. (2) If events or changes suggest impairment, determine if the sum of the expected future net cash flows from the long-lived asset is less than the carrying amount of the asset. If less, measure the impairment loss. (3) The impairment loss is the amount by which the carrying amount of the asset is greater than the fair value of the asset. After an impairment loss is recorded, the reduced carrying amount of the long-lived asset is now considered its new cost basis. An impairment loss may not be restored for an asset held for use. If the asset is expected to be disposed of, the impaired asset should be reported at the lower of cost or net realizable value. It is not depreciated. An impaired asset held for disposal can be continuously written up or down in future periods as long as the write-up is never greater than the carrying amount before impairment.

7. **Explain the accounting procedures for depletion of natural resources.** The accounting procedures for depletion of natural resources are: (1) establishment of depletion base, and (2) allocation of resource cost. Four factors are involved in establishing the depletion base: (a) *Acquisition costs*, (b) *Exploration costs*, (c) *Development costs*, and (d) *Restoration costs*. To allocate resource cost, normally, depletion is computed on the units of production method, which means that depletion is a function of the number of units withdrawn during the period. In adopting this approach, the total cost of the natural resource less salvage value is divided by the number of units estimated to be in the resource deposit to obtain a cost per unit of product. This cost per unit is multiplied by the number of units extracted to compute depletion.

8. **Explain how property, plant, and equipment and natural resources are reported and analyzed.** The basis of valuation for property, plant, and equipment and natural resources should be disclosed along with pledges, liens, and other commitments related to these assets. Any liability secured by property, plant, and equipment and natural resources should **not** be offset against these assets, but should be reported in the liability section. Property, plant, and equipment not currently employed as producing assets in the business should be segregated from assets used in operations. When assets are depreciated, a valuation account normally called Accumulated Depreciation is credited. When assets are depleted, an accumulated depletion account may be used or the depletion may be credited directly to the natural resource account. Companies engaged in significant oil and gas producing activities must provide significant additional disclosures about these activities. Analysis may be performed to evaluate the asset turnover rate and the rate of return on assets.

9. **Describe financial statement disclosures for natural resources.** The FASB requires both publicly traded and privately held companies engaged in significant oil and gas producing activities to disclosure in their financial statements (1) the basic method of accounting for those costs incurred in oil and gas productivity activities, and (2) the manner of disposing of costs relating to oil and gas producing activities. Public companies, in addition to these two required disclosures, must include as supplementary information numerous schedules reporting reserve quantities; capitalized costs; acquisition, exploration, and development activities; and a standardized measure of discounted future net cash flows related to proved oil and gas reserve quantities.

*10. **Describe income tax methods of depreciation.** A Modified Accelerated Cost Recovery System (MACRS) was enacted by Congress in the Tax Reform Act of 1986. It applies to depreciable assets placed in service in 1987 and later. The computation of depreciation under MACRS differs from the computation under GAAP in three respects: (1) a mandated tax life, which is generally shorter than the economic life; (2) cost recovery on an accelerated basis; and (3) an assigned salvage value of zero.

*This material is covered in Appendix 11-A in the text.

TIPS ON CHAPTER TOPICS

TIP: **Residual value** is often referred to as **salvage value**, and sometimes it is called estimated **scrap value**.

TIP: Residual value is used in the computation of depreciation for the early years of life of an asset whenever the straight-line method or the sum-of-the-years'-digits method or an activity method is used. Salvage value is **not** a factor in determining depreciation for the early years of life if a declining-balance method is used; however, salvage value can effect the amount computed for depreciation in the last year(s) of an asset's life. An asset should **not** be depreciated below its salvage value.

TIP: The **activity method** is often called the **variable charge** approach or the **units of output** or the **units of production method**.

TIP: The **declining-balance depreciation method** applies a constant rate to a declining book value to calculate depreciation. The rate used is often twice the straight-line rate, in which case the method is then referred to as the **200% declining-balance method** or the **double declining-balance method**. Sometimes the rate is one and one-half times the straight-line rate, in which case the method is called the **150% declining-balance method**.

TIP: The **book value** of a plant asset is determined by deducting the balance of accumulated depreciation from the balance of the related asset account. The balance in the related asset account is generally the asset's original cost. Thus, the estimated residual value does not directly affect the book value computation. Book value is often called **carrying value**, **carrying amount**, **net asset value**, or **undepreciated value**. An asset's book value at a given date may be far different than its market (fair) value at the same date.

TIP: **Depreciable cost** or **depreciation base** is a term that refers to the total amount to be depreciated over the life of the asset. It is determined by deducting the estimated residual value from the cost of the asset.

TIP: When an asset being depreciated by a group or composite depreciation method is disposed of, no gain or loss is recorded; the difference between the original cost of the asset and the proceeds from disposal is charged to Accumulated Depreciation.

CASE 11-1

Purpose: (L.O.1,2) This case examines the process of matching the cost of fixed assets with the revenues which the assets help to generate.

Plant assets provide services for two or more periods. There is a cost to the services consumed; this cost should be matched with the periods benefited.

Instructions

(a) Briefly define depreciation as used in accounting.

(b) Identify the factors that are relevant in determining the annual depreciation and explain whether these factors are determined objectively or whether they are based on judgment.

(AICPA Adapted)

Solution to Case 11-1

(a) Depreciation is the accounting process of allocating an asset's historical cost (recorded amount) to the accounting periods benefited by the use of the asset. It is a process of cost allocation, not valuation. Depreciation is not intended to provide funds for an asset's replacement; it is merely an application of the matching principle.

(b) The factors relevant in determining the annual depreciation for a depreciable asset are the initial recorded amount (acquisition cost and any subsequent capitalized costs), estimated salvage value, estimated useful life, and deprecation method.

Assets are typically recorded at their acquisition cost, which is in most cases objectively determinable. But cost assignments in other cases—"basket purchases" and selection of an implicit interest rate in asset acquisition under deferred-payment plans—may be quite subjective and involve considerable judgment.

The salvage value is an estimate of an amount potentially realizable when the asset is retired from service. It is initially a judgment factor and is affected by the length of the asset's useful life to the enterprise.

The useful life is also a judgment factor. It involves selecting the "unit" of measure of service life and estimating the number of such units embodied in the asset. Such units may be measured in terms of time periods or in terms of activity (for example, years or machine hours). When selecting the life, one should select the lower (shorter) of the physical life or the economic life to the user. Physical life involves wear and tear and casualties; economic life involves such things as technological obsolescence and inadequacy.

Selecting the depreciation method is generally a judgment decision; but, a method may be inherent in the definition adopted for the units of service life, as discussed earlier. For example, if such units are machine hours, the method is a function of the number of machine hours used during each period. A method should be selected that will best measure the portion of services expiring each period. Once a method is selected, it may be applied by using a predetermined, objectively derived formula.

EXERCISE 11-1

Purpose: (L.O.3) This exercise will give you practice in computing depreciation for three successive periods for three commonly used methods.

Hudspeth Company purchases equipment on January 1, Year 1, at a cost of $645,000. The asset is expected to have a service life of 12 years and a salvage value of $60,000.

Instructions

(a) Compute the amount of depreciation for each of Years 1 through 3 using the straight-line depreciation method.

(b) Compute the amount of depreciation for each of Years 1 through 3 using the sum-of-the-years'-digits method.

(c) Compute the amount of depreciation for each of Years 1 through 3 using the double-declining balance method. (In performing your calculations, round the constant percentage to the nearest one-hundredth of a percentage point and round final answers to the nearest dollar.)

Solution to Exercise 11-1

(a) $$\frac{\$645,000 - \$60,000}{12} = \underline{\underline{\$48,750}}$$ Depreciation for each of Years 1 through 3 using the straight-line method.

(b) $$\frac{12 \times 13}{2} = 78$$

12/78 x ($645,000 - $60,000) =	$90,000	depreciation Year 1
11/78 x ($645,000 - $60,000) =	$82,500	depreciation Year 2
10/78 x ($645,000 - $60,000) =	$75,000	depreciation Year 3

(c) $$\frac{100\%}{12} \times 2 = 16.67\%$$

$645,000 x 16.67% =	$107,522	depreciation Year 1
($645,000 - $107,522) x 16.67% =	$ 89,598	depreciation Year 2
($645,000 - $107,522 - $89,598) x 16.67% =	$ 74,662	depreciation Year 3

EXERCISE 11-2

Purpose: (L.O.3) This exercise will provide an illustration of the computations for depreciation of partial periods using three common methods.

Scanlan Company purchased a new plant asset on April 1, 1999, at a cost of $345,000. It was estimated to have a service life of 20 years and a salvage value of $30,000. Scanlan's accounting period is the calendar year.

Instructions (Round all final answers to the nearest dollar.)

(a) Compute the amount of depreciation for this asset for 1999 and 2000 using the straight-line method.

(b) Compute the amount of depreciation for this asset for 1999 and 2000 using the sum-of-the-years'-digits method.

(c) Compute the amount of depreciation for this asset for 1999 and 2000 using the double-declining balance method.

Solution to Exercise 11-2

(a) $\frac{\$345,000 - \$30,000}{20 \text{ years}} \times 9/12 = \underline{\underline{\$11,813}}$ depreciation for 1999

$\frac{\$345,000 - \$30,000}{20 \text{ years}} = \underline{\underline{\$15,750}}$ depreciation for 2000

Approach and Explanation: Write down and apply the formula for straight-line depreciation. Multiply the annual depreciation amount by the portion of the asset's first year of service that falls in the given accounting period.

$$\frac{\text{Cost - Salvage Value}}{\text{Estimated Service LIfe}} = \text{Depreciation Charge}$$

(b) $\frac{20\ (20 + 1)}{2} = 210$

	9/12 x 20/210 x ($345,000 - $30,000)	=	$\underline{\underline{\$22,500}}$ depreciation for 1999
	3/12 x 20/210 x ($345,000 - $30,000)	=	$ 7,500
+	9/12 x 19/210 x ($345,000 - $30,000)	=	$\underline{21,375}$
			$\underline{\underline{\$28,875}}$ depreciation for 2000

Approach and Explanation: Write down and apply the formula for sum-of-the-years'-digits depreciation. Apportion the depreciation for the given asset year between the two accounting periods involved. The first nine months of the asset's first year of life fall in the 1999 calendar year. The last three months of the asset's first year of life and the first nine months of the asset's second year of life fall in the 2000 calendar year. There is no shortcut to the two-part computation of depreciation for 2000, as illustrated above.

Formula: $\frac{n\ (n + 1)}{2}$ = Sum of the Years

$$\frac{\text{No. of Years Remaining at Beginning of Asset Year}}{\text{Sum of the Years}} \times (\text{Cost - Salvage}) = \text{Depreciation for Full Asset Year}$$

(c) Straight-line rate $\frac{100\%}{20}$ = 5%; 5% x 2 = 10%

10% x \$345,000 = \$34,500 depreciation for asset's first year
10% x (\$345,000 - \$34,500) = \$31,050 depreciation for asset's second year

9/12 x \$34,500 = \$25,875 depreciation for 1999

3/12 x \$34,500 =	\$ 8,625	
+ 9/12 x \$31,050 =	23,288	
	\$ 31,913	depreciation for 2000

Approach and Explanation: Write down and apply the formula for the declining balance method. Apportion the depreciation for a given **asset year** between the two accounting periods involved.

Constant Percentage x Book Value at Beginning of Asset Year = Depreciation for Asset Year

An alternative approach is as follows:

After the first partial year, calculate depreciation for a full **accounting year** by multiplying the constant percentage by the book value of the asset at the beginning of the accounting period.

Thus, the computation for 2000 would be as follows:
10% x (\$345,000 - \$25,875) = \$31,913.

EXERCISE 11-3

Purpose: (L.O.3) This exercise is designed to test your ability to solve for missing data by applying your knowledge regarding depreciation computations.

Landenberger Company acquired a plant asset at the beginning of Year 1. The asset has an estimated service life of 5 years. An employee has prepared depreciation schedules for this asset using three different methods to compare the results of using one method with the results of using other methods. You are to assume that the following schedules have been correctly prepared for this asset using (1) the straight-line (St.-line) method, (2) the sum-of-the-years'-digits (SYD) method, and (3) the double-declining balance (DDB) method (switching to the straight-line method after the mid-life of the asset).

Year	Straight-line	Sum-of-the-Years'-Digits	Double-declining Balance
1	\$ 6,000	\$ 10,000	\$ 14,400
2	6,000	8,000	8,640
3	6,000	6,000	5,184
4	6,000	4,000	888
5	6,000	2,000	888
Total	\$ 30,000	\$ 30,000	\$ 30,000

Instructions

Answer the following questions:

(a) What is the cost of the asset being depreciated?

(b) What amount, if any, was used in the depreciation calculations for the salvage value of this asset?

(c) Which method will produce the highest charge to income in Year 1?

(d) Which method will produce the highest charge to income in Year 4?

(e) Which method will produce the highest book value for the asset at the end of Year 3?

(f) If the asset is sold at the end of Year 3, which method would yield the highest gain (or lowest loss) on disposal of the asset?

Solution to Exercise 11-3

(a) If there is any salvage value and the amount is unknown (as is the case here), the cost would have to be determined by looking at the data for the double-declining balance method.

100% ÷ 5 = 20%; 20% x 2 = 40%
Cost x 40% = $14,400; $14,400 ÷ .40 = $36,000 cost of asset

Approach: Write down the formula for each of the depreciation methods mentioned. Fill in the data given for Year 1. Examine what remains to be solved.

(Cost - Salvage Value) ÷ Estimated Service Life = St.-line Depreciation
(Cost - Salvage Value) ÷ 5 = $6,000

(# of Years Remaining at Beginning of Asset Year ÷ Sum of the Years)
x (Cost - Salvage Value) = SYD Depreciation
5 ÷ 15 x (Cost - Salvage Value) = $10,000

Constant Percentage x Cost = DDB Depreciation
40% x Cost = $14,400

There are two variables (cost and salvage value) unknown for each of the first two methods, and there is no way to solve for either of them. However, cost can easily be determined for the third method (DDB). Once you solve for cost, it is a simple matter to solve for salvage value.

(b) $36,000 cost (answer a) - $30,000 total depreciation = $6,000 salvage value

Approach: The difference between the answer to part (a) and the total depreciation per the schedule ($30,000) is the salvage value used.

(c) The highest charge to income for Year 1 will be yielded by the double-declining balance method.

Approach: Examine the depreciation schedules. Notice the method that results in the highest depreciation amount for Year 1.

(d) The highest charge to income for Year 4 will be yielded by the straight-line method.

Approach: Examine the depreciation schedules given. Notice the method that results in the highest depreciation amount for Year 4.

(e) The method to yield the highest book value at the end of Year 3 would be the method that yields the lowest accumulated depreciation at the end of Year 3 which is the straight-line method. Computations:

St.-line = $36,000 - ($6,000 + $6,000 + $6,000)
= $18,000 book value at the end of Year 3.

SYD = $36,000 - ($10,000 + $8,000 + $6,000)
= $12,000 book value at the end of Year 3.

DDB = $36,000 - ($14,400 + $8,640 + $5,184)
= $7,776 book value at the end of Year 3.

Approach: Write down the formula to compute book value: Cost - Accumulated Depreciation = Book Value. To obtain a high book value, you need a low accumulated depreciation. Examine the depreciation schedules to determine the method that would yield the lowest total depreciation for the first three years.

(f) The method that will yield the highest gain (or lowest loss) if the asset is sold at the end of Year 3 is the method which will yield the lowest book value at the end of Year 3. In this case, it is the double-declining balance method.

Approach: Write down the formula to compute gain or loss on disposal: Selling Price - Book Value = Gain (Loss). To obtain a high gain, you need a low book value. Examine the formula for book value. To get a low book value, you need high depreciation charges. Use the depreciation schedules to determine the method that would yield the highest accumulated depreciation balance at the end of three years.

EXERCISE 11-4

Purpose: (L.O.4) This exercise will enable you to practice working with the composite method for computing depreciation.

Presented below is information related to the Bosshardt Corporation (all assets are acquired at the beginning of Year 1):

Asset	Cost	Estimated Scrap	Estimated LIfe (in years)
A	$60,750	$8,250	10
B	50,400	7,200	9
C	54,000	4,800	8
D	28,500	2,250	7
E	35,250	3,750	6

Instructions

(a) Compute the rate of depreciation per year to be applied to the plant assets under the composite method.

(b) Compute the composite life.

(c) Prepare the adjusting entry necessary at the end of the year to record depreciation for Year 1.

(d) Prepare the entry at the end of Year 6 to record the sale of fixed asset D for cash of $7,500. It was used for 6 years, and depreciation was recorded under the composite method.

Solution to Exercise 11-4

(a)

Asset	Cost	Estimated Scrap	Depreciable Cost	Estimated Life	Depreciation Per Year
A	$ 60,750	$ 8,250	$ 52,500	10	$ 5,250
B	50,400	7,200	43,200	9	4,800
C	54,000	4,800	49,200	8	6,150
D	28,500	2,250	26,250	7	3,750
E	35,250	3,750	31,500	6	5,250
	$228,900	$26,250	$202,650		$25,200

Composite rate = $25,200 ÷ $228,900; or 11.009%

Approach and Explanation: Steps to compute the composite rate:

1. Compute what would be the amount of annual straight-line depreciation for each asset by dividing each asset's **depreciable cost** by its estimated service life. Sum these amounts ($25,200).

2. Compute the composite rate by dividing the total depreciation per year (results of Step 1—$25,200) by the amount of **original cost** ($228,900).

(b) Composite life = $202,650 ÷ $25,200; or 8.04 years

Approach and Explanation: Compute the composite life by dividing the total depreciable cost ($202,650) by the total annual depreciation charge ($25,200).

(c) **End of Year 1**

Depreciation Expense on Plant Assets	25,200	
Accumulated Deprecation on Plant Assets		25,200
($228,900 x 11.009% = $25,200)		

Approach and Explanation: Compute the depreciation for any given year by multiplying the balance in the asset account by the composite rate (results of Step 2). The balance in the asset account will change over time due to the acquisition of new assets and the disposal of old assets.

(d) **End of Year 6**

Cash	7,500	
Accumulated Depreciation on Plant Assets	21,000	
Plant Assets		28,500

Approach and Explanation: When using the group or composite method, no gain or loss on disposition is recorded. The difference between the proceeds (if any) on disposal and the original cost of the asset is debited (or credited) to the Accumulated Depreciation account. Thus, if an asset is retired before, or after, the average service of the group is reached, the resulting gain or loss is buried in the Accumulated Depreciation account.

EXERCISE 11-5

Purpose: (L.O.5) This exercise will provide you with an illustration of how to account for a change in the estimated service life and salvage value of a plant asset due to an expenditure subsequent to acquisition.

The Russell Company purchased a machine on January 1, 1989 for $105,000. The machine was being depreciated using the straight-line method over an estimated life span of 20 years, with a $15,000 salvage value. At the beginning of 1999, when the machine had been in use for 10 years, the company paid $25,000 to overhaul the machine. As a result of this improvement, the company estimated that the useful life of the machine would be extended an additional 5 years and the salvage value would be reduced to $10,000.

Instructions

Compute the depreciation charge for 1999.

Solution to Exercise 11-5

Cost	$ 105,000
Accumulated depreciation at 1/1/99	45,000[a]
Book value at 1/1/99	60,000
Additional expenditure capitalized	25,000
Revised book value	85,000
Current estimate of salvage value	10,000
Remaining depreciable cost at 1/1/99	75,000
Remaining years of useful life at 1/1/99	÷ 15[b]
Depreciation expense for 1999	$ 5,000

[a]Cost	$105,000
Original estimate of salvage value	15,000
Original depreciable cost	90,000
Original service life in years	÷ 20
Original depreciation per year	4,500
Number of years used	x 10
Accumulated depreciation at 1/1/99	$ 45,000

[b]Original estimate of life in years	20
Number of years used	(10)
Additional years	5
Remaining years of useful life at 1/1/99	15

TIP: A change in the estimated useful life and/or salvage value of an existing depreciable asset is to be accounted for prospectively (in current and/or future periods). Therefore, the book value at the beginning of the period of change, less the current estimate of salvage value, is to be allocated over the remaining periods of life, using the appropriate depreciation method. The book value at the beginning of the period of change is calculated using the original estimates of service life and salvage value.

TIP: The $25,000 cost of overhaul is capitalized in this case because the cost benefits future periods by extending the useful life of the machine.

Approach: Whenever you have a situation that involves a change in the estimated service life and/or salvage value of a depreciable asset, use the format shown above to compute the remaining depreciable cost and allocate that amount over the remaining useful life using the given depreciation method.

EXERCISE 11-6

Purpose: (L.O.3) This exercise will allow you to practice using various depreciation methods and it will also give you the opportunity to compare the results of using one method to the results of using another method.

On January 1, 1999, Irish Company, a machine-tool manufacturer, acquires a piece of new industrial equipment for $1,000,000. The new equipment has a useful life of five years and the salvage value is estimated to be $100,000. Irish estimates that the new equipment can produce a total of 40,000 units and expects it to produce 10,000 units in its first year. Production is then estimated to decline by 1,000 units per year over the remaining useful life of the equipment.

The following depreciation methods may be used:

- Double declining-balance
- Straight-line
- Sum-of-the-years'-digits
- Units-of-output

Instructions

(a) Identify which depreciation method would result in the maximization of profits for financial statement reporting for the **three**-year period ending December 31, 2001. Prepare a schedule showing the amount of accumulated depreciation at December 31, 2001, under the method selected. Show supporting computations in good form. Ignore present value and income tax considerations in your answer.

(b) Identify which depreciation method would result in the minimization of profits for the **three**-year period ending December 31, 2001. Prepare a schedule showing the amount of accumulated depreciation at December 31, 2001, under the method selected. Show supporting computations in good form. Ignore present value and income tax considerations in your answer.

(AICPA Adapted)

Solution to Exercise 11-6

(a) The straight-line method of depreciation would result in the maximization of profits for financial statement reporting for the three-year period ending December 31, 2001.

Irish Company
ACCUMULATED DEPRECIATION USING STRAIGHT-LINE METHOD
December 31, 2001

(Cost - Salvage Value) ÷ Estimated Service LIfe

($1,000,000 - $100,000) ÷ 5 years = $180,000

Year	Depreciation Expense	Accumulated Depreciation
1999	$ 180,000	$ 180,000
2000	180,000	360,000
2001	180,000	540,000
	$ 540,000	

(b) The double declining balance method of depreciation would result in the minimization of profits for the three-year period ending December 31, 2001.

Irish Company
ACCUMULATED DEPRECIATION USING
DOUBLE DECLINING-BALANCE METHOD
December 31, 2001

Straight-line rate is 5 years, or 20%. Double declining-balance rate is 40% (20% x 2). Ignore salvage value.

Year	Book Value at Beginning of Year	Depreciation Expense	Accumulated Depreciation
1999	$1,000,000	$400,000	$400,000
2000	600,000	240,000	640,000
2001	360,000	144,000	784,000
		$784,000	

Other supporting computations:

Irish Company
ACCUMULATED DEPRECIATION USING
SUM-OF-THE-YEARS'-DIGITS METHOD
December 31, 2001

[n x (n + 1)] ÷ 2 = [5 x (5 + 1)] ÷ 2 = 15

5/15 X ($1,000,000 - $100,000) = $300,000
4/15 x ($1,000,000 - $100,000) = $240,000
3/15 X ($1,000,000 - $100,000) = $180,000

Year	Depreciation Expense	Accumulated Depreciation
1999	$ 300,000	$ 300,000
2000	240,000	540,000
2001	180,000	720,000
	$ 720,000	

Irish Company
ACCUMULATED DEPRECIATION USING
UNITS-OF-OUTPUT METHOD
December 31, 2001

(Cost - Salvage Value) ÷ Total Units of Output =
($1,000,000 - $100,000) ÷ 40,000 =
$22.50 Depreciation per Unit

10,000 x $22.50 = $225,000
9,000 x $22.50 = $202,500
8,000 x $22.50 = $180,000

Year	Depreciation Expense	Accumulated Depreciation
1999	$ 225,000	$ 225,000
2000	202,500	427,500
2001	180,000	607,500
	$ 607,500	

EXERCISE 11-7

Purpose: (L.O.7) This exercise will give you practice in computing depletion.

During 1999, Alston Corporation acquired a mineral mine for $2,700,000, of which $450,000 is attributable to the land value after the mineral has been removed. Engineers estimate that 15 million units of mineral can be recovered from this mine. During 1999, 1,200,000 units were extracted and 800,000 units were sold.

Instructions

Compute the depletion for 1999.

Solution to Exercise 11-7

($2,700,000 - $450,000) ÷ 15,000,000 = $.15

$.15 x 1,200,000 = $180,000 Depletion for 1999

Approach and Explanation: Write down the formula to compute depletion, enter the data given, and solve.

$$\frac{\text{Acquisition Cost} + \text{Costs to Explore and Develop} - \text{Residual Value of Land} + \text{Costs to Restore Land to Alternative Use}}{\text{Number of Units to be Extracted}} = \text{Depletion Cost Per Recoverable Unit}$$

Depletion Cost Per Recoverable Unit	x	Units Extracted During Period	=	Depletion for the Period

TIP: The depletion charge for the period is the amount to be removed from the property, plant, and equipment classification ($180,000 in this case). It is based on the units **extracted** from the earth during the period. The portion of this $180,000 which gets to the income statement is dependent upon the number of units **sold**. When the number of units extracted exceed the number sold, as in this exercise, a portion of the depletion costs goes into the Inventory account on the balance sheet.

ILLUSTRATION 11-1
ACCOUNTING FOR IMPAIRMENTS (L.O.6)

A summary of the key concepts in accounting for impairments is presented below:

A **recoverability test** is used to determine whether an impairment has occurred: If the sum of the expected future net undiscounted cash flows (from the use of the asset and its eventual disposition) is less than the carrying amount of the asset, the asset has been impaired.

If the recoverability test indicates that an impairment has occurred, a loss is computed. The impairment loss is the amount by which the carrying amount of the asset exceeds its fair value. The fair value of an asset is measured by its market value (if an active market exists) or by the present value of expected future net cash flows (if an active market does not exist). If an asset is to be disposed of instead of held for use, the asset's net realizable value (fair value less cost to sell) is used as a measure of the net cash flows that will be received from this asset.

Subsequent to recognizing the loss from impairment, the following guidelines are to be followed:

1. If the asset is to be held for use, it will be depreciated based on the new cost basis.
2. If the asset is to be sold, no more depreciation is taken once the asset is no longer used.
3. Restoration of the impairment loss is not permitted for an asset which is held for use.
4. Restoration of the impairment loss is allowed for an asset held for sale. Because assets held for disposal will be recovered through sale rather than through use in operations, they are continually revalued. Each period they are reported at the lower of cost or net realizable value. Thus, an asset held for disposal can be written up or down in future periods, as long as the write-up does not produce a new carrying value greater than the carrying amount of the asset before an adjustment was made to reflect a decision to dispose of the asset.

TIP: Losses or gains related to impaired assets should be reported as part of income from continuing operations. Thus, they are **not** classified as extraordinary items.

ANALYSIS OF MULTIPLE-CHOICE TYPE QUESTIONS

QUESTION

1. (L.O.3,8) A machine was purchased for $8,000,000 on January 1, 1999. It has an estimated useful life of 8 years and a residual value of $800,000. Depreciation is being computed using the sum-of-the-years'-digits method. What amount should be shown for this machine, net of accumulated depreciation, in the company's December 31, 2000 balance sheet?
   a. $4,200,000
   b. $5,000,000
   c. $6,300,000
   d. $6,600,000

Approach and Explanation: Write down the formula to compute book value and the formula to compute depreciation using the sum-of-the-years'-digits method. Fill in the data from the scenario at hand and solve. Be careful that you don't get so involved with the computation for depreciation that you lose sight of the question—and that is, to compute the book value of the equipment. It would be helpful to underline the middle of the last sentence of the stem of the question in order to keep your focus on what is being asked.

Cost - Accumulated Depreciation = Book Value

$$\frac{\text{No. of Years Remaining Life}}{\text{Sum of the Years}} \times (\text{Cost - Salvage}) = \text{Depreciation Charge}$$

$$\frac{n\,(n + 1)}{2} = \text{Sum of the Years} \qquad \frac{8\,(8 + 1)}{2} = 36$$

8/36 x ($8,000,000 - $800,000) = $1,600,000 depreciation for 1999.
7/36 x ($8,000,000 - $800,000) = $1,400,000 depreciation for 2000.

Depreciation for 1999	$ 1,600,000
Depreciation for 2000	1,400,000
Accumulated depreciation at 12/31/00	$ 3,000,000

Cost	$ 8,000,000	
Accumulated depreciation	3,000,000	
Book value at 12/31/00	$ 5,000,000	(Solution = b.)

QUESTION

2. (L.O.3,5) Tammy Corporation purchased a machine on July 1, 1999 for $900,000. The machine has an estimated life of five years and a salvage value of $120,000. The machine is being depreciated by the 150% declining-balance method. What amount of depreciation should be recorded for the year ended December 31, 2000?
   a. $229,500
   b. $198,900
   c. $189,000
   d. $163,800

Approach and Explanation: Write down the formula to use for the declining-balance approach. (Notice the facts indicate there is a partial period for the first year (1999) and the question asks for the depreciation for the 2000 reporting period.) Compute the rate that is 150% of the straight-line rate. Apply the formula to the facts given. Remember that salvage value is not used with this method in computing depreciation in the early years of the asset's life.

Constant Percentage x Book Value at Beginning of the Year = Depreciation

$$\frac{100\%}{\text{Life}} = \frac{100\%}{5 \text{ years}} = 20\% \qquad 20\% \times 150\% = 30\% \text{ constant percentage}$$

30% x $900,000 = $270,000 First year of life
30% x (900,000 - $270,000) = $189,000 Second year of life
1/2 x $270,000 = $135,000 for 1996
(1/2 x $270,000) + (1/2 x $189,000) = $229,500 for 2000

OR

30% x ($900,000 - $135,000) = $229,500 for 2000 (Solution = a.)

QUESTION

3. (L.O.3,5) A plant asset with a five-year estimated useful life and no salvage value is sold during the second year of the asset's life. How would the use of the straight-line method of depreciation instead of an accelerated depreciation method affect the amount of gain or loss on the sale of the plant asset?

	Gain	Loss
a.	Increase	Decrease
b.	Decrease	Increase
c.	No Effect	Increase
d.	No Effect	No Effect

Approach and Explanation: An accelerated method would result in more accumulated depreciation and, therefore, a lower book value. In contrast, the straight-line method results in less accumulated depreciation and a higher book value. This means a lower gain or a higher loss is computed if the asset is sold and the straight-line method is in use. One way you can prove this to yourself is to make up a set of facts (cost, service life, accelerated method to use) and assume the asset is sold for a given amount at the end of the second year. Compare that gain or loss with the gain or loss that would result if the straight-line method is used. (Solution = b.)

QUESTION

4. (L.O.4) Roberts Truck Rental uses the group depreciation method for its fleet of trucks. When it retires one of its trucks and receives cash from a salvage company, the carrying value of property, plant, and equipment will be decreased by the:
   a. original cost of the truck.
   b. original cost of the truck less the cash proceeds.
   c. cash proceeds received.
   d. cash proceeds received and original cost of the truck.

Approach and Explanation: Write down the journal entry to record the disposal of the truck and analyze its effect. Remember that no gain or loss is recorded on the disposal when the group or composite method is used.

Cash	Proceeds	
Accumulated Depreciation	**Plug**	
Truck		Original Cost

In analyzing the entry's net effect on the book value (carrying amount) of property, plant, and equipment we find the following: (1) The decrease in Truck will reduce PP&E by the truck's original cost. (2) The debit to Accumulated Depreciation will increase PP&E by the excess of the truck's original cost over the proceeds from disposal. (3) Therefore, the net effect is to decrease PP&E by the amount of the cash proceeds from the sale. (Solution = c.)

QUESTION

5. (L.O.2) The term "depreciable cost," or "depreciable base," as it is used in accounting, refers to:
   a. the total amount to be charged (debited) to expense over an asset's useful life.
   b. cost of the asset less the related depreciation recorded to date.
   c. the estimated market value of the asset at the end of its useful life.
   d. the acquisition cost of the asset.

Approach and Explanation: Write down a definition of depreciable cost **before** you read any of the answer selections. **Depreciable cost** or **depreciable base** is the total amount of asset cost that can be expensed over the life of the asset; thus, it is original cost less estimated residual (salvage) value. Answer selection "b" describes the term book value. Answer selection "c" describes salvage value or residual value. Selection "d" represents the total cost of the asset. (Solution = a.)

QUESTION

6. (L.O.2) A machine is purchased by the Dunnagin Company for $18,000. Dunnagin pays $6,000 in cash and gives a note payable for $12,000 that is payable in installments over a four-year period. Dunnagin estimates that the machine could physically last for 12 years, even though Dunnagin expects to use it in its business for only 9 years. The period of time to be used by Dunnagin for depreciation purposes is:
   a. 4 years.
   b. 5 years.
   c. 9 years.
   d. 12 years.

Approach and Explanation: Think about the objective of the depreciation process—to allocate an asset's cost to the periods benefited. The asset should be depreciated over its useful life, which is the length of time the asset will be of service to the entity using it. (Solution = c.)

QUESTION

7. (L.O.8) The book value of a plant asset is:
   a. the fair market value of the asset at a balance sheet date.
   b. the asset's acquisition cost less the total related depreciation recorded to date.
   c. equal to the balance of the related accumulated depreciation account.
   d. the assessed value of the asset for property tax purposes.

Approach and Explanation: Write down the definition for the term book value: **book value** is the asset's original cost (acquisition cost) less accumulated depreciation. Look for the answer selection that agrees with your definition. (Solution = b.)

QUESTION

8. (L.O.3) A machine with an estimated service life of five years and an expected salvage value of $5,000 was purchased on January 1, 1999 for $50,000. The amount to be recorded for depreciation for 1999, 2000, and 2001, respectively, using the sum-of-the-years'-digits method will be:
   a. $20,000; $12,000; $7,200.
   b. $16,667; $13,333; $10,000.
   c. $15,000; $12,000; $9,000.
   d. $15,000; $8,000; $4,400.

Approach and Explanation: Write down the formula to compute SYD depreciation. Enter the data given and solve.

$$\frac{n\,(n+1)}{2} = \text{Sum of the Years} \qquad \frac{5\,(6)}{2} = 15$$

$$\frac{\text{\# of Years Life Remaining at Beginning of Asset Year}}{\text{Sum of the Years}} \times (\text{Cost - Salvage}) = \text{Depreciation for Full Asset Year}$$

1999: ($50,000 - $5,000) x 5/15 =	$ 15,000	
2000: ($50,000 - $5,000) x 4/15 =	$ 12,000	
2001: ($50,000 - $5,000) x 3/15 =	$ 9,000	(Solution = c.)

QUESTION

9. (L.O.3) A machine with an estimated service life of five years and an expected salvage value of $5,000 was purchased on January 1, 1999, for $50,000. The amount to be recorded for depreciation for years 1999, 2000, and 2001, respectively, using the 200% declining-balance method will be:
   a. $20,000; $12,000; $7,200.
   b. $18,000; $10,800; $6,480.
   c. $16,667; $13,333; $10,000.
   d. $10,000; $8,000; $6,400.

Approach and Explanation: Write down the formula for the declining-balance method. Enter the data given and solve.

Book Value at Beginning of Year x Constant Percentage = Depreciation

Constant Percentage = 2 x (100% ÷ Life) = 2 x (100% ÷ 5) = 40%

1999:	$50,000 x 40% =	$20,000
2000:	($50,000 - $20,000) x 40% =	$12,000
2001:	($50,000 - $20,000 - $12,000) x 40% =	$ 7,200

(Solution = a.)

QUESTION

10. (L.O.3) Salvage (residual) value may or may not be used in computing depreciation expense in the early years of an asset's life. Net income is understated if, in the first year, estimated salvage value is excluded from the depreciation computation when using the:

	Units of Output Method	Sum-of-the-Years'-Digits Method
a.	Yes	Yes
b.	No	No
c.	No	Yes
d.	Yes	No

Approach and Explanation: Before looking at the methods addressed directly in the question, think about how salvage value affects the depreciation computation under various methods. In considering the common depreciation methods such as straight-line, activity methods, sum-of-the-years'-digits, and declining-balance methods, the declining-balance methods are the only methods that do not use the residual value in computing depreciation in the early years of the asset's life. However, the residual value may affect the computations with the declining-balance method in the latter years of the asset's life because the asset should not be depreciated below its residual value. The units-of-output method is an activity method. (Solution = a.)

QUESTION

11. (L.O.5) The Schoen Company purchased a piece of equipment at the beginning of 1989 for $60,000. The equipment was being depreciated using the straight-line method over an estimated life of 20 years, with no salvage value. At the beginning of 1999, when the equipment had been in use for 10 years, the company paid $10,000 to overhaul the equipment. As a result of this improvement, the company estimates that the useful life of the equipment will be extended an additional five years. What should be the depreciation expense for this equipment in 1999?
    a. $2,000
    b. $2,667
    c. $3,000
    d. $1,867

Approach and Explanation: Write down the model or format to compute depreciation whenever there has been a change in the estimated service life and/or salvage value. Fill in the data of the case at hand and solve.

Cost	$ 60,000
Accumulated depreciation at 1/1/99	30,000[a]
Book value (before overhaul) at 1/1/99	30,000
Additional expenditure capitalized (if any)	10,000
Revised book value (after overhaul)	40,000
Current estimate of salvage value	0
Remaining depreciable cost at 1/1/99	40,000
Remaining years of useful life at 1/1/99	÷ 15[b]
Depreciation expense for 1999	$ 2,667
	(Solution = b.)

[a]Cost	$ 60,000
Original estimate of salvage	0
Original depreciable cost	60,000
Original service life in years	÷ 20
Original depreciation per year	3,000
Number of years used	x 10
Accumulated depreciation at 1/1/99	$ 30,000

[b]Original estimate of life in years	20
Number of years used	(10)
Additional years	5
Remaining years of useful life at 1/1/99	15

TIP: Be careful when computing the length of time between two dates. The length of time between the beginning of 1989 and the beginning of 1999 is 10 years; whereas, the length of time between the end of 1989 and the beginning of 1999 is nine years. It is a common mistake to deduct one year from the other (1999 - 1989 = 10 years). As you can see from the foregoing, that will not always work. It is wise to write down the years that fall between the two dates and then count those years on your list. For example, the length of time between the end of 1996 and the beginning of 1999 is two years and is determined as follows:

1997	1
1998	2

QUESTION

12. (L.O.8) The rate of return on total assets can be computed by which of the following computations?

1. $\dfrac{\text{Net income}}{\text{Net sales}}$

2. $\dfrac{\text{Net sales}}{\text{Average total assets}}$

3. Profit margin on sales x Asset turnover

4. $\dfrac{\text{Net income}}{\text{Average total assets}}$

a. Formula 1.
b. Formula 2.
c. Formula 3.
d. Formula 4.
e. Formula 3 or 4.

Explanation: Formula 1 above measures the rate of return on sales (profit margin on sales ratio). Formula 2 computes the asset turnover ratio. Formula 3 is one of two ways to compute the rate of return on total assets; Formula 4 is the second of two ways to compute the rate of return on total assets. (Solution = e.)

CHAPTER 12

INTANGIBLE ASSETS

OVERVIEW

The balance sheet classification for intangible assets is used to report assets which lack physical existence and are not properly classifiable elsewhere. For instance (1) bank deposits and accounts receivable both are intangible by a legal definition but are properly classified as current assets for accounting purposes, and (2) investment in stock is intangible in nature but should be classified as either a current asset or a long-term investment for accounting purposes. Assets such as patents, trademarks, copyrights, and franchises are intangible in nature and are classified in the intangible asset section of a balance sheet. Intangible assets are discussed in this chapter.

SUMMARY OF LEARNING OBJECTIVES

1. **Describe the characteristics of intangible assets.** A major characteristic of an intangible asset is the high degree of uncertainty concerning the *future benefits* that are to be received from its employment. Intangibles may be subdivided on the basis of the following characteristics: (1) *Identifiability:* separately identifiable or lacking specific identification. (2) *Manner of acquisition:* acquired singly, in groups, or in business combinations, or developed internally. (3) *Expected period of benefit:* limited by law or contract, related to human or economic factors, or indefinite or indeterminate duration. (4) *Separability from the enterprise:* rights transferable without title, salable, or inseparable from the enterprise or a substantial part of it.

2. **Explain the procedure for valuing and amortizing intangible assets.** Intangibles are recorded at cost. **Cost** includes all costs of acquisition and expenditures necessary to make the intangible asset ready for its intended use. If intangibles are acquired for stock or in exchange for other assets, the cost of the intangible is the fair market value of the consideration given or the fair market value of the intangible received, whichever is more clearly evident. When several intangibles, or a combination of intangibles and tangibles, are bought in a "basket purchase," the cost should be allocated on the basis of fair market values or on the basis of relative sales values. Intangible assets should be amortized by systematic charges to expense over their useful lives; however, the amortization period should not exceed 40 years.

3. **Identify the types of specifically identifiable intangible assets.** The major identifiable intangible assets are: (1) **Patent:** gives the holder exclusive right to use, manufacture, and sell a product or process for a period of 17 years without interference or infringement by others. (2) **Copyright:** a federally granted right that all authors, painters, musicians, sculptors, and other artists have in their creations and expressions. (3) **Trademark and trade name:** a word, phrase, or symbol that distinguishes or identifies a particular enterprise or product. (4) **Leasehold:** a contractual understanding between a lessor (owner of property) and a lessee (renter or property) that grants the lessee the right to use specific property, owned by the lessor, for a specific period of time in return for stipulated, and generally periodic, cash payments. (5) **Organization costs:** costs incurred in the formation of a corporation such as legal fees, state fees of various sorts, and certain promotional expenditures. (6) **Franchise or license:** a contractual arrangement under which the franchisor grants the franchisee the right to sell certain products or services, to use certain trademarks or trade names, or to perform certain functions, usually within a designated geographical area.

4. **Explain the conceptual issues related to goodwill.** Goodwill is unique because unlike receivables, inventories, and patents that can be sold or exchanged individually in the marketplace, goodwill can be identified only with the business as a whole. Goodwill is a "going-concern" valuation and is recorded only when an entire business is purchased. Goodwill generated internally should not be capitalized in the accounts, because measuring the components of goodwill is simply too complex and associating any costs with future benefits too difficult. The future benefits of goodwill may have no relationship to the costs incurred in the development of that goodwill. Goodwill may exist even in the absence of specific costs to develop it. Costs to maintain and restore goodwill are not capitalized.

5. **Describe the accounting procedures for recording goodwill.** To record goodwill, the fair market value of the net tangible and identifiable intangible assets is compared with the purchase price of the acquired business. The difference is considered goodwill. Goodwill is the residual—the excess of cost over fair value of the identifiable net assets acquired. Goodwill is often identified on the balance sheet as the excess of cost over the fair value of the net assets acquired.

6. **Identify the conceptual issues related to research and development costs.** R & D costs are not in themselves intangible assets, but research and development activities frequently result in the development of something that is patented or copyrighted. The difficulties in accounting for R & D expenditures are (1) identifying the costs associated with particular activities, projects, or achievements; and (2) determining the magnitude of the future benefits and length of time over which such benefits may be realized. Because of these latter uncertainties, the FASB has standardized and simplified accounting practice by requiring that all research and development costs be charged to expense when incurred.

7. **Describe the accounting procedures for research and development costs.** The costs associated with R & D activities and the accounting treatment accorded them are as follows: (1) **Materials, equipment, and facilities:** Expense the entire costs, unless the items have alternative future uses (in R & D activities or otherwise), then carry materials as inventory (and allocate to R & D expense as consumed) and capitalize equipment and facilities (and depreciate as used). (2) **Personnel:** Salaries, wages, and other related costs of personnel engaged in R & D should be expensed as incurred. (3) **Purchased intangibles:** Expense the entire cost, unless the items have alternative future uses, then capitalize and amortize. (4) **Contract services:** The costs of services performed by others in connection with the reporting company's R & D should be expensed as incurred. (5) **Indirect costs:** A reasonable allocation of indirect costs shall be included in R & D costs, except for general and administrative costs, which must be related to be included.

8.* **Identify the accounting treatment for computer software costs.** Costs incurred in creating a computer software product should be charged to R & D expense when incurred until technological feasibility has been established for the product. Subsequent costs should be capitalized and amortized to current and future periods. Computer software that is purchased for sale or lease to third parties and has alternative future uses may be capitalized and amortized using the greater of the percent of revenue approach or the straight-line approach.

*This material appears in Appendix 12-A in the text.

9.** **Explain various approaches to valuing goodwill.** One method of valuing goodwill is the excess earnings approach. Using this approach, the total earning power that the company commands is computed. The next step is to calculate "normal earnings" by determining the normal rate of return on assets in that industry. The difference between what the firm earns and what is normal in the industry is referred to as the excess earning power. This excess earning power indicates that there are unidentifiable values that provide the increased earning power. Finding the value of goodwill then is a matter of discounting these excess future earnings to the present. The number of years method of valuing goodwill, which simply multiplies the excess earnings by the number of years of expected excess earnings, is used to provide a rough measure for the goodwill factor. A third method of valuing goodwill is the discounted free cash flow method, which projects the amount of cash that will accumulate over a specified number of

years and then finds the present value of that amount as today's value of the firm.
**This material appears in Appendix 12-B in the text.

TIPS ON CHAPTER TOPICS

TIP: An intangible asset is to be amortized over its useful life; however, the amortization period should not exceed 40 years. This rule applies even to assets which may appear to have an unlimited or indefinite life (such as organization costs and goodwill).

TIP: Research and development (R & D) costs are to be expensed in the period incurred. The FASB established this guideline after a study revealed that very few R & D projects ever culminate in a successfully marketed product. When great uncertainty exists, the conservatism constraint (or principle) dictates that we choose the alternative with the **least** favorable effect on net income and on assets.

TIP: To capitalize earnings means to discount or calculate the present worth of the projected future earnings of an asset or business. If the earnings are assumed to continue indefinitely, the present value is determined by dividing the appropriate earnings figure by the appropriate rate. This procedure is often used in determining the value of existing goodwill when a going business is to be bought or sold.

TIP: In 1996, the AICPA proposed a new rule that requires companies to capitalize and amortize the cost of software they use internally. Companies would also be permitted to capitalize and amortize the cost of upgrading or enhancing computer programs. However, the rule would force companies to immediately write off any money spent on training related to the internal use of software, as well as expenses related to internally developed software that is not used. The FASB is reviewing this proposal.

EXERCISE 12-1

Purpose: (L.O.2,7) This exercise will give you practice in identifying items that are to be classified as costs associated with various intangible assets.

The Redskins Corporation incurred the following costs during January 1999:

1. Attorneys' fees in connection with organization of the corporation
2. Meetings of incorporators, state filing fees, and other organization costs
3. Improvements to leased offices prior to occupancy
4. Costs to design and construct a prototype
5. Testing of prototype
6. Troubleshooting breakdowns during commercial production
7. Fees paid to engineers and lawyers to prepare patent application; patent granted January 22
8. Payment of six months rent on leased facilities
9. Stock issue costs
10. Payment for a copyright

11. Materials purchased for future research and development projects; materials have alternative future use
12. Costs to advertise new business

Instructions

(a) For each item above, identify what account should be debited to record the expenditure.

(b) Indicate in which classification the related account will be reported in the financial statements.

Solution to Exercise 12-1

(a) Account Debited	**(b) Classification**
1. Organization Costs	Intangible Asset
2. Organization Costs	Intangible Asset
3. Leasehold Improvements	Property, Plant, and Equipment (or Intangible Asset)
4. Research and Development Expense	Operating Expense
5. Research and Development Expense	Operating Expense
6. Factory Overhead	Allocated to Inventory and Cost of Goods Sold
7. Patent	Intangible Asset
8. Prepaid Rent	Current Asset
9. Organization Costs (or reduction of Additional Paid-in Capital)	Intangible Asset (or reduction of Additional Paid-in Capital)
10. Copyright	Intangible Asset
11. Raw Materials Inventory	Current Asset
12. Advertising Expense	Operating Expense

EXERCISE 12-2

Purpose: (L.O.2,3) This exercise will review the accounting guidelines related to three types of intangible assets—patent, franchise, and trademark.

Information concerning Linda Heckenmueller Corporation's intangible assets follows:

1. Heckenmueller incurred $85,000 of experimental and development costs in its laboratory to develop a patent which was granted on January 2, 1999. Legal fees and other costs associated with registration of the patent totaled $16,000. Heckenmueller estimates that the useful life of the patent will be 8 years.

2. On January 1, 1999, Heckenmueller signed an agreement to operate as a franchisee of Cluck-Cluck Fried Chicken, Inc. for an initial franchise fee of $150,000. Of this amount, $30,000 was paid when the agreement was signed and the balance is payable in 4 annual payments of $30,000 each, beginning January 1, 2000. The agreement provides that the downpayment is not refundable and no future services are required of the franchisor. The present value at January 1, 1999, of the 4 annual payments discounted at 14% (the implicit rate for a loan of this type) is $87,400. The agreement also provides that 5% of the revenue from the franchise must be paid to the franchisor annually. Heckenmueller's revenue from the franchise for 1999 was $1,800,000. Heckenmueller estimates the useful life of the franchise to be 10 years.

3. A trademark was purchased from Wolfe Company for $64,000 on July 1, 1996. Expenditures for successful litigation in defense of the trademark totalling $16,000 were paid on July 1, 1999. Heckenmueller estimates that the useful life of the trademark will be 20 years from the date of acquisition.

Instructions

(a) Prepare a schedule showing the intangible asset section of Heckenmueller's balance sheet at December 31, 1999. Show supporting computations in good form.

(b) Prepare a schedule showing all expenses resulting from the transactions that would appear on Heckenmueller's income statement for the year ended December 31, 1999. Show supporting computations in good form.

(AICPA adapted)

Solution to Exercise 12-2

(a)

Linda Heckenmueller Corporation
INTANGIBLE ASSETS
December 31, 1999

Patent, net of accumulated amortization of $2,000 (Schedule 1)	$ 14,000
Franchise, net of accumulated amortization of $11,740 (Schedule 2)	105,660
Trademark, net of accumulated amortization of $11,671 (Schedule 3)	68,329
Total intangible assets	$ 187,989

Schedule 1: Patent

Cost of securing patent on 1/2/99	$ 16,000
1999 amortization ($16,000 x 1/8)	(2,000)
Cost of patent, net of amortization	$ 14,000

Schedule 2: Franchise

Cost of franchise on 1/1/99 ($30,000 + $87,400)	$ 117,400
1999 amortization ($117,400 x 1/10)	(11,740)
Cost of franchise, net of amortization	$ 105,660

Schedule 3: Trademark

Cost of trademark on 7/1/96	$ 64,000
Amortization, 7/1/96 to 1/1/99 ($64,000 x 1/20 x 2.5)	(8,000)
Book value on 1/1/99	56,000
Cost of successful legal defense on 7/1/99	16,000
Book value after legal defense	72,000
Amortization, 1/1/99 to 12/31/99 (Schedule 4)	(3,671)
Cost of trademark, net of amortization	$ 68,329

(b)

Linda Heckenmueller Corporation
EXPENSES RESULTING FROM SELECTED INTANGIBLES TRANSACTIONS
For the Year Ended December 31, 1999

Interest expense ($87,400 x 14%)	$ 12,236
Patent amortization (Schedule 1)	2,000
Franchise amortization (Schedule 2)	11,740
Franchise fee ($1,800,000 x 5%)	90,000
Trademark amortization (Schedule 4)	3,671
Total expenses	$119,647

TIP: The $85,000 of research and development costs incurred in developing the patent would have been expensed prior to 1999 (per *SFAS No. 2*).

Schedule 4: Trademark Amortization

Amortization of original cost ($64,000 x 1/20)	$ 3,200
Amortization of legal fees ($16,000 x 1/17 x 6/12)	471
Total trademark amortization	$ 3,671

Approach: The ideal approach would be to prepare the journal entries associated with the facts given and post them to T-accounts to determine the balances to be reported on the income statement for the year ending December 31, 1999 and on the balance sheet at December 31, 1999. Under some circumstances (such as exam conditions), time may not permit these additional steps. You should at least think about and visualize the flow of the information through the accounts. This will greatly aid the successful completion of the schedules required.

Explanation:

1. Research and development costs are to be expensed in the period incurred. Thus, the $85,000 of experimental and development costs incurred in developing the patent would have been expensed prior to 1999. Legal fees and other costs associated with obtaining the patent should be matched with each of the eight years estimated to be benefited; therefore, the $16,000 of legal fees and registration costs should be capitalized and amortized.

2. The franchise rights will benefit future periods. Therefore, the costs associated with obtaining those rights should be capitalized and amortized over future periods. The acquisition cost is determined by the cash given (down payment of $30,000) and the cash equivalent of the related payable (present value of the four annual payments at 14%—$87,400). The fact that "the down payment is not refundable and no future services are required of the franchisor" has no impact on how the franchisee accounts for the franchise. The provision in the agreement which calls for the franchisee to pay 5% of the annual revenue from the franchise to the franchisor does not initially require

any accounting treatment; an expense accrues as revenues are earned from use of the franchise. The capitalized franchise costs are to be amortized over the useful period of 10 years. The interest expense resulting from deferred payment is to be recognized annually by applying the implicit interest rate of 14% to the outstanding payable balance.

3. The purchase price of the trademark ($64,000) was capitalized in mid-1996 when the trademark was acquired. That cost is being amortized over the 20-year useful life. (Note that only one-half year of amortization was recorded in 1996.) Expenditures of $16,000 for successful litigation in defense of the trademark rights are to be charged to the Trademark account because such a suit establishes the legal rights of the holder of the trademark (which benefits future periods). Because the litigation was settled in the middle of 1999, only one-half year of amortization of these legal costs is recorded for 1999. The $16,000 is to be amortized over the remaining useful life of the trademark (17 years in this case).

EXERCISE 12-3

Purpose: (L.O.3) This exercise reviews the subject of leasehold improvements.

On January 1, 1999, Mr. Howard Anderson's Prize Paints entered into a lease contract with the Regency Mall Corp. The agreement provides for a 10-year lease on store space in a suburban mall. Mr. Anderson is leasing the space for his wholesale paint business. In order to prepare the facilities for his purpose, Mr. Anderson constructed several partitions at a cost of $3,200 and lowered the ceiling at a cost of $1,400. The partitions and ceiling revert to the owner of the property at the end of the lease term. Mr. Anderson assumes they will last as long as the building, which he estimates to have a 20-year life. The company uses a calendar year reporting period.

Instructions

(a) Prepare the journal entry to record the payment to the builder who put in the partitions and ceiling.

(b) Identify the period of time over which the improvements should be amortized. Explain why.

(c) Prepare the related adjusting entry (if any) at December 31, 1999.

(d) Explain how the improvements would appear on the balance sheet at the end of the third year of the lease.

Solution to Exercise 12-3

(a) Leasehold improvements ($3,200 + $1,400) 4,600
Cash.. 4,600

(b) Leasehold improvements are to be amortized over their useful life or the remaining term of the lease, whichever is less. In this scenario, the remaining term of the lease is 10 years, which is less than the 20-year useful life of the improvements. The 10-year period should be used.

(c) The adjusting entry to amortize the improvements at December 31, 1999, would be:
Amortization of Leasehold Improvements Expense...................... 460
Leasehold Improvements ($4,600 ÷ 10 years = $460)............ 460

(d) Leasehold Improvements would most likely appear in the property, plant, and equipment section of Prize Paints' balance sheet at an amount of $3,220 [$4,600 - (3 x $460) = $3,220] at the end of the third year of the lease, although some accountants would prefer to report this item in the intangible asset classification.

EXERCISE 12-4

Purpose: (L.O.6,7) This exercise will give you practice in identifying activities that constitute R & D activities.

Listed below are four independent situations involving research and development costs:

1. During 1999 Bebe Co. incurred the following costs:

Research and development services performed by Way Co. for Bebe	$ 325,000
Testing for evaluation of new products	300,000
Laboratory research aimed at discovery of new knowledge	375,000
Research and development services performed by Bebe for Elway Co.	220,000

How much should Bebe report as research and development expense for the year ended December 31, 1999?

2. Holly Corp. incurred the following costs during the year ended December 31, 1999:

Design, construction, & testing of preproduction prototypes & models	$ 220,000
Routine, on-going efforts to refine, enrich, or otherwise improve upon the qualities of an existing product	250,000
Quality control during commercial production including routine testing of products	300,000
Laboratory research aimed at discovery of new knowledge	360,000
Conceptual formulation and design of possible product alternatives	100,000

What is the total amount to be classified and expensed as research and development for 1999?

3. Polanski Company incurred costs in 1999 as follows:

Equipment acquired for use in various R & D projects (current and future)	$ 890,000
Depreciation on the equipment above	135,000
Materials used in R & D	300,000
Compensation costs of personnel in R & D	400,000
Outside consulting fees for R & D work	150,000
Indirect costs appropriately allocated to R & D	260,000

What is the total amount of research and development expense that should be reported in Polanski's 1999 income statement?

4. Liverpool Inc. incurred the following costs during the year ended December 31, 1999:

Laboratory research aimed at discovery of new knowledge	$ 175,000
Routine design of tools, jigs, molds, and dies	60,000
Radical modification to the formulation of a chemical product	125,000
Research and development costs reimbursable under a contract to perform R & D for Johnathon King, Inc.	350,000
Testing for evaluation of new products	275,000

What is the total amount to be classified and expensed as research and development for 1999?

Instructions

Provide the correct answer to each of the four situations.

Solution to Exercise 12-4

1.

Research and development services performed by Way Co. for Bebe	$ 325,000
Testing for evaluation of new products	300,000
Laboratory research aimed at discovery of new knowledge	375,000
Total R & D expense	$ 1,000,000

> **TIP:** R & D costs related to R & D activities conducted for other entities are classified as a receivable (because of the impending reimbursement).

2.

Design, construction & testing of preproduction prototypes & models	$ 220,000
Laboratory research aimed at discovery of new knowledge	360,000
Conceptual formulation & design of possible product alternatives	100,000
Total R & D expense	$ 680,000

3.

Depreciation on the equipment acquired for use in various R & D projects	$ 135,000
Materials used in R & D	300,000
Compensation costs of personnel in R & D	400,000
Outside consulting fees for R & D work	150,000
Indirect costs appropriately allocated to R & D	260,000
Total R & D expense	$ 1,245,000

> **TIP:** Equipment, facilities, and purchased intangibles that have **alternative future uses** (in other R & D projects or otherwise) are to be **capitalized**; the **related depreciation and amortization are to be classified as R & D.**

4.

Laboratory research aimed at discovery of new knowledge	$ 175,000
Radical modification to the formulation of a chemical product	125,000
Testing for evaluation of new products	275,000
Total R & D expense	$ 575,000

Approach: Read the requirement of each situation before you begin detailed work on the first one. Notice that all four items deal with research and development costs. Therefore, review in your mind the definitions of the words "research" and "development." Recall what you can from the list of activities considered to be R & D and the list of activities which are **not** considered to be R & D. Think of why the items logically appear on a particular list. It is important to think about these items **before** you dig into the questions because details in the situations may mislead you. To minimize confusion, organize your thoughts and recall what you know about the subject before you begin to process the data at hand.

Explanation: To differentiate research and development costs from other similar costs, the FASB issued the following definitions in *SFAS No. 2*:

> **Research** is planned search or critical investigation aimed at discovery of new knowledge with the hope that such knowledge will be useful in developing a new product or service ... or a new process or technique ... or in bringing about a significant improvement to an existing product or process.
>
> **Development** is the translation of research findings or other knowledge into a plan or design for a new product or process or for a significant improvement to an existing product or process whether intended for sale or use. It includes the conceptual formulation, design, and testing of product alternatives, construction of prototypes, and operation of pilot plants. It does not include routine or periodic alterations to existing products, production lines, manufacturing processes, and other on-going operations even though those alterations may represent improvements; it does not include market research or market testing activities.

Many costs have characteristics similar to those of research and development costs, for instance, costs of relocation and rearrangement of facilities, start-up costs for a new plant or new retail outlet, marketing research costs, promotion costs of a new product or service, and costs of training new personnel. To distinguish between R & D and those other similar costs, the following schedule (from *SFAS No. 2*) provides (1) examples of activities that typically would be **included** in research and development, and (2) examples that typically would be **excluded** from research and development.

1. R & D Activities

(a) Laboratory research aimed at discovery of new knowledge.
(b) Searching for applications of new research findings.
(c) Conceptual formulation and design of possible product or process alternatives.
(d) Testing in search for or evaluation of product or process alternatives.
(e) Modification of the design of a product or process.
(f) Design, construction, and testing of preproduction prototypes and models.
(g) Design of tools, jigs, molds, and dies involving new technology.
(h) Design, construction, and operation of a pilot plant not useful for commercial production.
(i) Engineering activity required to advance the design of a product to the manufacturing stage.

2. Activities Not Considered R & D

(a) Engineering follow-through in an early phase of commercial production.
(b) Quality control during commercial production including routine testing.
(c) Trouble-shooting breakdowns during commercial production.
(d) Routine, on-going efforts to refine, enrich, or improve the qualities of an existing product.
(e) Adaptation of an existing capability to a particular requirement or customer's need.
(f) Periodic design changes to existing products.
(g) Routine design of tools, jigs, molds, and dies.
(h) Activity, including design and construction engineering related to the construction, relocation, rearrangement, or startup of facilities or equipment.
(i) Legal work on patent applications, sale, licensing, or litigation.

ILLUSTRATION 12-1
DETERMINATION OF GOODWILL AND PURCHASE PRICE (L.O.9)

Step 1: **Determine an estimate of future average annual earnings.** This is usually done by computing the adjusted average net earnings of the company in the past. Adjust for accounting changes, extraordinary items, and other such special items.

Step 2: **Determine normal earnings.** Multiply *the industry average rate of return* times *the fair market value of the identifiable net assets* of the company.

Step 3: **Determine excess earnings.** This is the average earnings from Step 1 less the normal earnings from Step 2.

Step 4: **Determine the value of goodwill.** This can be done by using an appropriate discount rate and choosing the number of periods for which the excess earnings will be maintained. It could be treated as a perpetuity by capitalizing the excess earnings (dividing excess earnings by an appropriate capitalization rate). Alternatively, the number of years method could be used.

Step 5: **Determine purchase price.** This will be the sum of the value of goodwill and the fair value of identifiable net assets of the firm.

EXERCISE 12-5

Purpose: (L.O.9) This exercise illustrates the steps in estimating the value of goodwill.

Mr. Judski is contemplating the sale of his business, Classic Vettes. The following data are available:

Book value of tangible & identifiable intangible assets less liabilities	$ 185,000
Market value of tangible & identifiable intangible assets less liabilities	$ 200,000
Estimated average future annual income for Classic Vettes	$ 28,000
Normal rate of return for the industry	10%

Instructions

(a) Compute the estimated value of goodwill if excess income is capitalized at a 10% rate.
(b) Compute the estimated value of goodwill if excess income is capitalized at a 25% rate.

Solution to Exercise 12-5

(a) $200,000 x 10% = $20,000 normal earnings
$28,000 - $20,000 = $8,000 excess earnings
$8,000 ÷ 10% = $80,000 goodwill

Approach and Explanation: Perform the applicable steps described in **Illustration 12-1**:

Step 1: Determine an estimate of future average annual earnings. This is given data in the exercise at hand—$28,000.

Step 2: Determine normal earnings. Multiply the industry average rate of return times the fair market value of the identifiable net assets of the firm.
10% x $200,000 = $20,000 Normal earnings

Step 3: Determine excess earnings. Deduct normal earnings from future average annual earnings.
$28,000 - $20,000 = $8,000 Excess earnings

Step 4: Determine the value of goodwill. Capitalize excess earnings by dividing excess earnings by the chosen capitalization rate.
$8,000 ÷ 10% = $80,000 goodwill

(b) $200,000 x 10% = $20,000 normal earnings
$28,000 - $20,000 = $8,000 excess earnings
$8,000 ÷ 25% = $32,000 goodwill

TIP: The higher the capitalization rate, the lower the resulting value for goodwill.

TIP: Excess earnings are often referred to as superior earnings.

TIP: Net identifiable assets are determined by deducting total liabilities from total identifiable (tangible and intangible) assets.

TIP: Fair value, market value, and fair market value are terms which are often used interchangeably.

EXERCISE 12-6

Purpose: (L.O.9) This exercise will provide an example of how to use the present value method to estimate the value of goodwill.

As president of Winnie Audio Corp., you are considering purchasing Winkle Video Corp., whose balance sheet is summarized as follows:

Current assets	$ 400,000	Current liabilities	$ 400,000
Fixed assets (net of depreciation)	800,000	Long-term liabilities	500,000
		Common stock	300,000
Other assets	200,000	Retained earnings	200,000
Total	$1,400,000	Total	$ 1,400,000

The fair market value of current assets is $700,000. The normal rate of return on net assets for the industry is 15%. The average expected annual earnings projected for Winkle Video Corp. is $160,000.

Instructions

Assuming that the excess earnings continue for 5 years, determine the value for goodwill by use of the present-value method.

Solution to Exercise 12-6

Step 1: Average expected annual earnings are $160,000 (data given).

Step 2:	Fair market value of net assets	$ 800,000*
	Normal rate of return	15%
	Normal earnings	$ 120,000
Step 3:	Expected earnings	$ 160,000
	Normal earnings	(120,000)
	Excess earnings	$ 40,000
Step 4:	Excess earnings	$ 40,000
	Present value of an annuity of 1 factor, 5 years @ 15%	3.35216
	Estimated goodwill	$ 134,086.40

*Book value of total assets	$ 1,400,000
Excess fair market value over book value of current assets	300,000**
Fair value of total assets	1,700,000
Total liabilities ($400,000 + $500,000)	900,000
Fair market value of net identifiable assets of Winkle	$ 800,000

**Fair market value of current assets	$ 700,000
Book value of current assets	400,000
Excess fair market value over book value of current assets	$ 300,000

Approach: Apply the steps listed in **Illustration 12-1**.

TIP: You should also be able to compute the purchase price that would result if both parties agree with the estimated goodwill figure computed above. The fair value of the net identifiable assets ($800,000) plus the value of the unidentifiable asset (goodwill of $134,086) equals a total fair value of $934,086 for Winkle Video Corp.

TIP: You should also be able to record the purchase of Winkle Video Corp. if Audio Corp. pays $934,086 to purchase it. The identifiable assets would be recorded at their fair values ($1,700,000), Goodwill would be debited for $134,086, the liabilities would be recorded at their fair values ($900,000) and Cash would be credited for $934,086.

ANALYSIS OF MULTIPLE-CHOICE TYPE QUESTIONS

QUESTION

1. (L.O.3) The adjusted trial balance of the Laventhal Corporation as of December 31, 1999 includes the following accounts:

Trademark	$ 30,000
Discount on bonds payable	37,500
Organization costs	12,500
Excess of cost over fair value of identifiable net assets of acquired business	175,000
Advertising costs (to promote goodwill)	20,000

What should be reported as total intangible assets on Laventhal's December 31, 1999 balance sheet?

a. $217,500
b. $230,000
c. $237,500
d. $275,000

Approach and Explanation: Identify the classification of each item listed. Sum the ones you identify as being intangible assets.

Trademark	$ 30,000
Organization costs	12,500
Excess of cost over fair value of identifiable net assets of acquired business	175,000
Total intangible assets	$ 217,500

Discount on bonds payable is to be classified as a contra liability. Advertising costs incurred are to be reported as an expense on the income statement. The costs to develop, maintain, or restore goodwill are not to be capitalized. Only the costs to acquire goodwill with a going business can be recorded as goodwill. The "excess of cost over fair value of net identifiable net assets of acquired business" is a technical term referring to goodwill. (Solution = a.)

QUESTION

2. (L.O.3) A patent with a remaining legal life of 12 years and an estimated useful life of 8 years was acquired for $288,000 by Bradley Corporation on January 2, 1995. In January 1999, Bradley paid $18,000 in legal fees in a successful defense of the patent. What should Bradley record as patent amortization for 1999?

a. $24,000
b. $36,000
c. $38,250
d. $40,500

Approach and Explanation: Analyze the Patent account. Use the data given to compute the amounts reflected therein and the resulting amortization for 1999.

Cost at beginning of 1995	$ 288,000	
Amortization for 1995-1998	(144,000)*	
Book value at beginning of 1999	144,000	
Legal fees capitalized	18,000	
Revised book value, beginning of 1999	162,000	
Remaining years of life	÷ 4	
Amortization for 1999	$ 40,500	(Solution = d.)

*Beginning of 1995, patent cost	$ 288,000
Estimated years of service life	÷ 8
Annual amortization for 1995-1998	36,000
Number of years used	4
Total amortization 1995-1998	$ 144,000

QUESTION

3. (L.O.3) On January 1, 1999, Teeple Corporation incurred organization costs of $30,000. For financial reporting purposes, Teeple is amortizing these costs on the same basis as the maximum allowable for federal income tax purposes. What portion of the organization costs will Temple defer to years subsequent to 1999?

a. $0
b. $6,000
c. $24,000
d. $30,000

Explanation: The **maximum amount of amortization** will result from using the **minimum amortization period** which, for tax purposes, is 60 months (5 years).

$30,000 ÷ 5 yrs. = $6,000 amortization per year.

If $6,000 is amortized, then the amount to defer is computed as follows:

Total organization costs	$ 30,000	
Amount amortized in 1999	(6,000)	
Amount to defer to subsequent periods	$ 24,000	(Solution = c.)

TIP: Note the importance of reading the question carefully. An intermediate step—the computation of the $6,000 amortization amount for 1999—is one of the distractors. You should read the last sentence of the question stem first to understand the essence of the problem. It is wise to write down the essential computation to keep your focus:

Total Organization Costs
- Amount to Amortize in 1999
= Amount to Defer

QUESTION

4. (L.O.2) Innoventions Inc. acquired a patent from Whizkid Inc. on January 1, 1999, in exchange for $7,000 cash and an investment security that had been acquired in 1995. The following facts pertain:

Original cost of investment	$ 14,000
Carrying value of patent on books of Whizkid Inc.	4,500
Fair market value of the investment security on January 1, 1999	23,000

The cost of the patent to be recorded by Innoventions Inc. is:

a. $7,000.
b. $11,500.
c. $21,000.
d. $30,000.
e. None of the above.

Approach and Explanation: Recall the guideline for determining the cost of any intangible asset. The cost of an intangible asset includes all costs incurred to acquire the asset. The historical cost principle dictates that cost be measured by the fair market value (i.e., cash equivalent value) of the consideration given or by the fair market value of the consideration received, whichever is the more objectively determinable. Innoventions Inc. gave $7,000 cash plus the investment security with a fair market value of $23,000 at the date of the exchange. The cost of the patent is, therefore, $30,000. (Solution = d.)

QUESTION

5. (L.O.3) A development stage enterprise should use the same generally accepted accounting principles that apply to established operating enterprises for:

	Recognition of Revenue	Recognition of Expenses
a.	Yes	Yes
b.	No	No
c.	No	Yes
d.	Yes	No

Explanation: In *SFAS No.* 7 the FASB indicates that the accounting practices and reporting standards should be no different for an enterprise trying to establish a new business than they are for other enterprises. Thus, the "same generally accepted accounting principles that apply to established operating enterprises shall govern the recognition of revenue by a development stage enterprise (DSE) and shall determine whether a cost incurred by a DSE is to be charged to expense when incurred or is to be capitalized or deferred." This means that items constituting preoperating costs should be expensed unless the same costs would be deferred by an established business; the fact that the costs are incurred before the entity has any significant revenue earned is not by itself justification for deferral of such costs. (Solution = a.)

QUESTION

6. (L.O.3) Windsor Corporation was organized in 1998 and began operations at the beginning of 1999. Prior to the start of operations, the following costs were incurred in 1998:

Attorneys' fees for assistance in obtaining corporate charter and drafting related documents	$ 33,000
Meetings of incorporators	14,000
Improvements to leased office space prior to occupancy	48,000
Fees to promoters to help locate buyers for Windsor's common stock	21,000
	$116,000

What should be the balance of the Organization Costs account before any amortization is recorded?

a. $21,000.
b. $33,000.
c. $68,000.
d. $116,000.
e. None of the above.

Approach and Explanation: Before reading through the list of costs incurred, define "organization costs" and think of the most common examples. **Organization costs** are costs incurred in the formation of a corporation such as fees to promoters and underwriters for handling stock issues, legal fees, state fees of various sorts, and certain promotional expenditures. They benefit all periods of a corporation's life so they should be capitalized and amortized over a period not to exceed 40 years. Because they are required to be amortized over a minimum of five years for tax purposes, companies often choose five years for the amortization period for financial reporting purposes. Windsor should charge the following to Organization Costs:

Attorneys' fees for incorporation	$ 33,000	
Meetings of incorporators	14,000	
Fees to promoters	21,000	
Total organization costs	$ 68,000	(Solution = c.)

TIP: The $48,000 of improvements to leased office space prior to occupancy should be recorded in the Leasehold Improvements account.

QUESTION

7. (L.O.7) Motts Corporation purchased the following items at the beginning of 1999:

Materials to be used in R & D activities; these materials have alternative future uses and they remain unused at the end of 1999.	$ 50,000
Materials to be used in R & D activities; these materials do not have alternative future uses and $12,000 of them remain unused at the end of 1999.	33,000
Equipment to be used in R & D activities; this equipment was used in one R & D project during 1999 and is expected to be used in other R & D projects to be undertaken over the next 5 years. It has no residual value. Motts normally uses the straight-line depreciation method for equipment.	100,000
Total	$ 183,000

Based on the above information, Motts should report R & D expenses for 1999 of:

a. $183,000.
b. $103,000.
c. $53,000.
d. $21,000.
e. None of the above.

Approach and Explanation: Mentally review the proper accounting treatment for materials and equipment acquired for use in R & D activities. The cost of materials acquired for use in R & D activities should be expensed in the period acquired unless the items have alternative future uses (in R & D projects or otherwise); then they should be carried as inventory and allocated to R & D expense as used. The cost of equipment and facilities acquired for use in R & D activities should be expensed in the period acquired unless the items have alternative future uses (in R & D projects or otherwise); then they should be capitalized and depreciated as used (the resulting depreciation should be classified as R & D expense). Thus, Motts would have the following R & D expense for 1999: (Solution = c.)

Materials acquired, no future alternative use	$ 33,000
Depreciation on equipment used in R & D activities ($100,000 ÷ 5 years)	20,000
Total R & D expense for 1999	$ 53,000

QUESTION

8. (L.O.7) In 1999, Barry Sanders Corporation incurred research and development costs as follows:

Equipment	$ 200,000
Personnel	300,000
Indirect costs	100,000
Total	$ 600,000

These costs relate to a product that will be marketed in 2000. It is estimated that these costs will be recouped by December 31, 2002. The equipment has no alternative future use. What is the amount of research and development costs that should be charged to income in 1999?

a. $0
b. $100,000
c. $400,000
d. $600,000

Explanation: All R & D costs are to be expensed in the period incurred. Equipment used in R & D activities that has alternative future use would be capitalized and depreciated. This equipment has no alternative use, so it is expensed immediately. A reasonable allocation of indirect costs should be included in R & D. Costs of personnel engaged in R & D activities are to be expensed in the period incurred. (Solution = d.)

QUESTION

9. (L.O.8) Gates Inc. develops computer software to be sold to the general public. The costs incurred in creating a new piece of software should be:

a. charged to R & D expenses.
b. capitalized and amortized.
c. charged to R & D expense when incurred until technological feasibility has been established for the product; the costs incurred after this point are to be capitalized.
d. charged to cost of goods sold expense.

Explanation: Costs incurred in creating computer software to be sold to external parties should be charged to research and development expense when incurred until technological feasibility has been established for the product (which occurs upon completion of a detailed program design or working model). Costs incurred subsequent to this point are to be capitalized and amortized to current and future periods. Companies are required to use the greater of (1) the ratio of current revenues to current and anticipated revenues (percent of revenue approach) or (2) the straight-line method over the remaining useful life of the asset (straight-line approach) as a basis of amortization. (Solution = c.)

QUESTION

10. (L.O.9) The owners of Tellmart Shoe Store are contemplating selling the business to new interests. The cumulative earnings for the past 5 years amounted to $750,000, including extraordinary gains of $25,000. The annual earnings based on an average rate of return on investment for this industry would have been $115,000. If excess earnings are to be capitalized at 15%, then implied goodwill should be:
    a. $175,000.
    b. $233,334.
    c. $200,000.
    d. $725,000.

Approach and Explanation: Follow the steps in **Illustration 12-1**.

Step 1:	Cumulative earnings over the past 5 years	$ 750,000
	Extraordinary gains included in above	(25,000)
	Total earnings excluding extraordinary items	725,000
	Number of years included above	÷ 5
	Average earnings in past 5 years assumed to be average annual earnings	$ 145,000
Step 2:	Normal earnings = $115.000.	
Step 3:	Expected average earnings	$ 145,000
	Normal earnings	(115,000)
	Excess earnings	$ 30,000
Step 4:	Excess earnings	$ 30,000
	Capitalization rate	÷ 15%
	Estimated value of goodwill	$ 200,000
		(Solution = c.)

CHAPTER 13

CURRENT LIABILITIES AND CONTINGENCIES

OVERVIEW

Initially, the resources (assets) of a business have to come from entities outside of the particular organization. Two main sources of resources are creditor sources (liabilities) and owners' sources (owners' equity). In this chapter, we begin our in-depth discussion of liabilities.

Due to the nature of some business activities, it is common to find some goods and services being received while payment for these items is made days or weeks later. Therefore, at a specific point in time, such as a balance sheet date, we may find that a business has obligations for merchandise received from suppliers (accounts payable), for money it has borrowed (notes payable), for interest incurred (interest payable), for property taxes (property taxes payable), for sales tax charged to customers which has not yet been remitted to the government (sales taxes payable), for salaries and wages (salaries and wages payable), and for other amounts due to government agencies in connection with employee compensation. Such payables are reported as current (short-term) liabilities, because they will fall due within the next 12 months and will require the use of current assets (cash, in these cases) to liquidate them. Accounting for current liabilities is discussed in this chapter.

SUMMARY OF LEARNING OBJECTIVES

1. **Define current liabilities and describe how they are valued.** Current liabilities are obligations whose liquidation is reasonably expected to require the use of current assets or the creation of other current liabilities. Theoretically, liabilities should be measured by the present value of the future outlay of cash required to liquidate them. In practice, current liabilities are usually recorded in accounting records and reported in financial statements at their full maturity value.

2. **Identify the nature and types of current liabilities.** There are several types of current liabilities. The following list details the most common types: (1) accounts payable, (2) notes payable, (3) current maturities of long-term debts, (4) dividends payable, (5) returnable deposits, (6) unearned revenue, (7) taxes payable, and (8) employee-related liabilities.

3. **Explain the classification issues of short-term debt expected to be refinanced.** An enterprise should exclude a short-term obligation from current liabilities if both of the following conditions are met: (1) It must intend to refinance the obligation on a long-term basis, *and* (2) it must demonstrate an ability to consummate the refinancing.

4. **Identify types of employee-related liabilities.** The employee-related liabilities are: (1) payroll deductions; (2) compensated absences; (3) postretirement benefits, which consist of pensions and postretirement health care and life insurance benefits, and (4) bonus agreements,

5. **Indicate how current liabilities are disclosed.** The current liability accounts are commonly presented as the first classification in the liabilities and stockholders' equity section of the balance sheet. Within the current liability section, the accounts may be listed in order of maturity, in descending order of amount, or in order of liquidation preference. Detail and supplemental information concerning current liabilities should be sufficient to meet the requirement of full disclosure.

6. **Identify the criteria used to account for and disclose loss contingencies.** An estimated loss from a loss contingency should be accrued by a charge to expense and a liability recorded only if both of the following conditions are met: (1) Information available prior to the issuance of the financial statements indicates that it is probable that a liability has been incurred at the date of the financial statements, and (2) the amount of the loss can be reasonably estimated. If the loss is either probable or estimable but not both, or if there is only a reasonable possibility that a liability may have been incurred, disclosure should be made in the notes of the nature of the contingency and an estimate of the possible loss.

7. **Explain the accounting for different types of loss contingencies.** (1) **Litigation:** The following factors must be considered in determining whether a liability should be recorded with respect to pending or threatened litigation and actual or possible claims and assessments: (a) the time period in which the underlying cause for action occurred; (b) the probability of an unfavorable outcome; and, (c) the ability to make a reasonable estimate of the amount of loss. (2) **Warranties:** If it is probable that customers will make claims under warranties relating to goods or services that have been sold and a reasonable estimate of the costs involved can be made, the accrual method must be used. Warranty costs under the accrual basis are charged to operating expense in the year of sale. (3) **Sales promotions:** Premiums, coupon offers, and rebates are made to stimulate sales, and their costs should be charged to expense in the period of the sale that benefits from the promotion plan.

8.* **Compute employee bonuses under differing arrangements.** Because a bonus is often based on net income and is deductible in determining net income, the bonus may have to be determined algebraically. Its computation is made more difficult by the bonus being deductible for tax purposes and the taxes being deductible from the income on which the bonus is based.

*This material is covered in Appendix 13-A in the text.

TIPS ON CHAPTER TOPICS

TIP: **Current liabilities** are often called **short-term liabilities** or **short-term debt**. **Noncurrent liabilities** are often called **long-term liabilities** or **long-term debt**.

TIP: **Current liabilities** are obligations whose liquidation is reasonably expected to require the use of existing resources properly classifiable as current assets, or the creation of other current liabilities. **Noncurrent liabilities** are obligations which do not meet the criteria to be classified as current.

TIP: An estimated loss from a loss contingency should be accrued by a charge to expense and a credit to a liability if both of the following conditions are met: (1) it is **probable** (likely) that a liability has been incurred at the date of the balance sheet, and (2) the amount of the loss can be **reasonably estimated**. If the loss is either probable or estimable but not both, or if there is at least a **reasonable possibility** that a liability has been incurred, the contingency must be disclosed in the notes (but not accrued). If it is only **remotely possible** (unlikely) that a liability has been incurred, no accrual or note disclosure is required (there are some exceptions to this guideline).

TIP: Self-insurance is not insurance; rather, it is risk assumption. Any company that assumes its own risks puts itself in the position of incurring expenses or losses as they occur. It is **not** generally acceptable to charge expense and report a liability prior to the occurrence of the event even if the amount of loss is reasonably estimable.

EXERCISE 13-1

Purpose: (L.O.2) This exercise tests your ability to distinguish between current and noncurrent (long-term) liabilities.

Instructions

Indicate how each of the following items would be reported on a balance sheet being prepared at December 31, 1999.

1. Obligation to supplier for merchandise purchased on credit. (Terms 2/10, n/30)
2. Note payable to bank maturing 90 days after balance sheet date.
3. Bonds payable due January 1, 2002.
4. Property taxes payable.
5. Interest payable on long-term bonds payable.
6. Income taxes payable.
7. Portion of lessee's lease obligations due in years 2001 through 2005.
8. Revenue received in advance, to be earned over the next six months.
9. Salaries payable.
10. Rent payable.
11. Short-term notes payable.
12. Pension obligations maturing in ten years.
13. Installment loan payment due three months after balance sheet date.
14. Installment loan payments due after one year.
15. Portion of lessee's lease obligations due within a year after the December 31, 1999 balance sheet date.
16. Bank overdraft.
17. Accrued officer bonus.
18. Premium offers outstanding.
19. Cash dividends declared but not paid.
20. Deferred rent revenue.
21. Stock dividends payable.
22. Bonds payable due June 1, 2000.
23. Bonds payable due July 1, 2000 for which a sinking fund will be used to pay off the debt. The sinking fund is classified as a long-term investment.
24. Discount to the bonds payable in item 3 above.
25. Current maturities of long-term debt.
26. Accrued interest on notes payable.
27. Customer deposits.
28. Sales taxes payable.
29. FICA withholdings.
30. Contingent liability (reasonable possibility of loss).
31. Contingent liability (probable and estimable).
32. Obligation for warranties.
33. Unearned warranty revenue.
34. Gift certificates outstanding.
35. Loan from stockholder.

Solution to Exercise 13-1

TIP: Apply the definition of a current liability. Analyze each situation and determine if the liability will fall due within a year (or operating cycle) of the balance sheet date and whether it will require the use of current assets or the incurrence of another current liability to be liquidated. If so, it is current; if not, it is long-term. Recall that current assets include cash and assets expected to be converted to cash or sold or consumed within the next year or operating cycle, whichever is longer.

1. Current liability (called Accounts Payable).
2. Current liability.
3. Noncurrent liability.
4. Current liability.
5. Current liability; interest on bonds is usually due semi-annually or annually.
6. Current liability.
7. Noncurrent liability.
8. Current liability.
9. Current liability.
10. Current liability.
11. Current liability.
12. Noncurrent liability.
13. Current liability.
14. Noncurrent liability.
15. Current liability.
16. Current liability (assuming no other bank accounts with positive balances in the same bank).
17. Current liability.
18. Current liability; may also classify a portion as a noncurrent liability.
19. Current liability
20. Current liability or noncurrent liability, depending on when the revenue is expected to be earned.
21. Paid-in capital; it does not meet the definition of a liability. ("Stock dividends payable" is a poor caption for "stock dividend distributable.")
22. Current liability.
23. Noncurrent liability; even though it is coming due within a year, it will not require the use of current assets to be liquidated.
24. Contra noncurrent liability (deducted from the related bonds payable).
25. Current liability.
26. Current liability, generally; in rare cases may be noncurrent.
27. Current liability or noncurrent liability, depending on the time left before they are to be returned or earned.
28. Current liability.
29. Current liability.
30. Note disclosure only.
31. Current liability or noncurrent liability, depending on the date settlement is expected.
32. Current liability and/or noncurrent liability, depending on term of warranty (this account title is used with the expense warranty method).
33. Current liability and/or noncurrent liability, depending on term of warranty (this account title is used with the sales warranty method).

34. Current liability, most likely; could have a portion as a noncurrent liability.
35. Current liability or noncurrent liability, depending on the due date of the loan; loans with related parties are required to be separately disclosed; if this loan is due on demand, the payable must be classified as a current liability.

EXERCISE 13-2

Purpose: (L.O.2) This exercise will provide an example of the proper accounting for an obligation to an agency of the state government—unremitted sales taxes.

During the month of September, Chelsea's Boutique had cash sales of $702,000 and credit sales of $411,000, both of which include the 6% sales tax that must be remitted to the state by October 15. Sales taxes on September sales were lumped with the sales price and recorded as a credit to the Sales Revenue account.

Instructions

(a) Prepare the adjusting entry that should be recorded to fairly present the financial statements at September 30.

(b) Prepare the entry to record the remittance of the sales taxes on October 5 if a 2% discount is allowed for payments received by the State Revenue Department by October 10.

Solution to Exercise 13-2

(a)	9/30	Sales Revenue		63,000	
		Sales Taxes Payable			63,000
		Computation:			
		Sales plus sales tax ($702,000 + $411,000)	$1,113,000		
		Sales exclusive of tax ($1,113,000 ÷ 1.06)	1,050,000		
		Sales tax	$ 63,000		
(b)	10/5	Sales Taxes Payable		63,000	
		Cash (98% x $63,000)			61,740
		Gain on Sales Tax Collections (2% x $63,000)			1,260

Explanation: Sales taxes on transfers of tangible personal property and on certain services must be collected from customers and remitted to the proper government authority. A liability is set up to provide for taxes collected from customers but as yet unremitted to the tax authority. The Sales Taxes Payable account should reflect the liability for sales taxes due to the government.

When the sales tax collections credited to the liability account are not equal to the liability as computed by the governmental formula, an adjustment of the liability account may be made by recognizing a gain or a loss on sales tax collections.

EXERCISE 13-3

Purpose: (L.O.3) This exercise will provide you with two examples of the proper treatment of short-term debt expected to be refinanced.

Situation 1

On December 31, 1998, Mayor Frederick Specialty Foods Company had $1,000,000 of short-term debt in the form of notes payable due February 4, 1999. On January 22, 1999, the company issued 20,000 shares of its common stock for $40 per share, receiving $800,000 proceeds after brokerage fees and other costs of issuance. On February 4, 1999, the proceeds from the stock sale, supplemented by an additional $200,000 cash, are used to liquidate the $1,000,000 debt. The December 31, 1998 balance sheet is issued on February 20, 1999.

Situation 2

Included in Hubbard Corporation's liability account balances on December 31, 1998 were the following:

14% note payable issued October 1, 1998, maturing September 30, 1999	$500,000
16% note payable issued April 1, 1995, payable in six annual installments of $200,000 beginning April 1, 1996	600,000

Hubbard's December 31, 1998 financial statements were issued on March 31, 1999. On January 13, 1999, the entire $600,000 balance of the 16% note was refinanced by issuance of a long-term obligation payable in a lump-sum. In addition, on March 8, 1999, Hubbard consummated a noncancelable agreement with the lender to refinance the 14%, $500,000 note on a long-term basis, with readily determinable terms that have not yet been implemented. Both parties are financially capable of honoring the agreement, and there have been no violations of the agreement's provisions.

Instructions

Situation 1: Show how the $1,000,000 of short-term debt should be presented on the December 31, 1998 balance sheet, including note disclosure.

Situation 2: Explain how the liabilities should be classified on the December 31, 1998 balance sheet. How much should be classified as a current liability?

Solution to Exercise 13-3

Situation 1

Mayor Frederick Specialty Foods Co.
PARTIAL BALANCE SHEET
December 31, 1998

Current liabilities:	
Notes payable (Note 1)	$ 200,000
Long-term debt:	
Notes payable refinanced in February 1999 (Note 1)	800,000

Note 1—Short-term debt refinanced

As of December 31, 1998, the Company had notes payable totaling $1,000,000 due on February 4, 1999. These notes were refinanced on their due date to the extent of $800,000 received from the issuance of common stock on January 22, 1999. The balance of $200,000 was liquidated using current assets.

OR

Current liabilities:	
Notes payable (Note 1)	$ 200,000
Short-term debt expected to be refinanced (Note 1)	800,000
Long-term debt	XXX,XXX
(Same Note as above)	

Situation 2

The entire $600,000 balance of the 16% note is properly excluded from short-term obligations since before the balance sheet was issued, Hubbard refinanced the note by issuance of a long-term obligation. The $500,000, 14% note is properly excluded from short-term obligations due to the fact that, before the balance sheet was issued, Hubbard entered into a financing agreement that clearly permits Hubbard to refinance the short-term obligation on a long-term basis with terms that are readily determinable.

Approach and Explanation: Review the criteria which will require an enterprise to exclude a short-term obligation from current liabilities and apply the criteria to the situation at hand.

In accordance with *SFAS No. 6*, an enterprise is allowed to exclude a short-term obligation from current liabilities only if both of the following conditions are met:

1. It must **intend to refinance** the obligation on a long-term basis, and
2. It must **demonstrate an ability** to consummate the refinancing.

Intention to refinance on a long-term basis means the enterprise intends to refinance the short-term obligation so that the use of working capital will not be required during the ensuing fiscal year or operating cycle, if longer. The **ability** to consummate the refinancing must be demonstrated by:

(a) **Actually refinancing** the short-term obligation by issuance of a long-term obligation or equity securities after the date of the balance sheet but before it is issued; or

(b) Entering into a **financing agreement** that clearly permits the enterprise to refinance the debt on a long-term basis with terms that are readily determinable.

If an actual refinancing occurs, the portion of the short-term obligation to be excluded from current liabilities may not exceed the proceeds from the new obligation or equity securities issued that are to be used to retire the short-term obligation. When a financing agreement is relied upon to demonstrate ability to refinance a short-term obligation on a long-term basis, the amount of short-term debt that can be excluded from current liabilities cannot exceed the amount available for refinancing under the agreement.

> TIP: By excluding short-term debt expected to be refinanced from the current liability classification, the company's working capital position and its current ratio are improved.

EXERCISE 13-4

Purpose: (L.O.4) This exercise will review accounting for compensated absences.

Marsha Diebler Company began operations on January 2, 1998. It employs 9 individuals who work 8-hour days and are paid hourly. Each employee earns 10 paid vacation days and 6 paid sick days annually. Vacation days may be taken after January 15 of the year following the year in which they are earned. Sick days may be taken as soon as they are earned; unused sick days accumulate but do not vest. Additional information is as follows:

Actual Hourly Wage Rate		Vacation Days Used by Each Employee		Sick Days Used By Each Employee	
1998	1999	1998	1999	1998	1999
$7.00	$8.00	0	9	4	5

Marsha Diebler has chosen not to accrue paid sick leave until used, and has chosen to accrue paid vacation time at expected future rates of pay without discounting. The company used the following projected rates to accrue vacation time:

Year in Which Vacation Time Was Earned	Projected Future Pay Rates Used to Accrue Vacation Pay
1998	$7.90
1999	8.60

Instructions

(a) Prepare journal entries to record transactions related to compensated absences during 1998 and 1999.

(b) Compute the amounts of any liability for compensated absences that should be reported on the balance sheet at December 31, 1998 and 1999.

Solution to Exercise 13-4

(a) **1998**

To accrue the expense and liability for vacations:	Wages Expense	5,688 (1)	
	Vacation Wages Payable		5,688
To record sick time paid:	Wages Expense	2,016 (2)	
	Cash		2,016
To record vacation time paid:	No entry.		

1999

To accrue the expense and liability for vacations:	Wages Expense	6,192 (3)	
	Vacation Wages Payable		6,192
To record sick time paid:	Wages Expense	2,880 (4)	
	Cash		2,880
To record vacation time paid:	Wages Expense	65	
	Vacation Wages Payable	5,119 (5)	
	Cash		5,184 (6)

(1) 9 employees x $7.90/hr. x 8 hrs./day x 10 days = $5,688.
(2) 9 employees x $7.00/hr. x 8 hrs./day x 4 days = $2,016.
(3) 9 employees x $8.60/hr. x 8 hrs./day x 10 days = $6,192.
(4) 9 employees x $8.00/hr. x 8 hrs./day x 5 days = $2,880.
(5) 9 employees x $7.90/hr. x 8 hrs./day x 9 days = $5,119.
(6) 9 employees x $8.00/hr. x 8 hrs./day x 9 days = $5,184.

(b) Accrued liability at year-end:

	1998 Vacation Wages Payable	1999 Vacation Wages Payable
Jan. 1 balance	$ 0	$ 5,688.00
+ accrued	5,688.00	6,192.00
- paid	(0)	(5,119.20)
Dec. 31 balance	$ 5,688.00 (1)	$ 6,760.80 (2)

(1) 9 employees x $7.90/hr. x 8 hrs./day x 10 days = $ 5,688.00

(2) 9 employees x $7.90/hr. x 8 hrs./ day x 1 day = $ 568.80
9 employees x $8.60/hr. x 8 hrs./day x 10 days = 6,192.00
$ 6,760.80

TIP: The expense and related liability for compensated absences should be recognized in the year in which the employees earn the rights to those absences. Vacation and holiday pay must be accrued if it vests or accumulates. Sick pay must be accrued only if it vests.

ILLUSTRATION 13-1
ACCOUNTING TREATMENT OF LOSS CONTINGENCIES (L.O.6,7)

Loss Related to	Usually Accrued	Not Accrued	May Be Accrued*
1. Collectibility of receivables	X		
2. Obligations related to product warranties and product defects	X		
3. Premiums offered to customers	X		
4. Risk of loss or damage of enterprise property by fire, explosion, or other hazards		X	
5. General or unspecified business risks		X	
6. Risk of loss from catastrophes assumed by property and casualty insurance companies including reinsurance companies		X	
7. Threat of expropriation of assets			X
8. Pending or threatened litigation			X
9. Actual or possible claims and assessments**			X
10. Guarantees of indebtedness of others***			X
11. Obligations of commercial banks under "standby letters of credit"***			X
12. Agreements to repurchase receivables (or the related property) that have been sold***			X

*Should be accrued when both criteria are met (probable and reasonably estimable).
**Estimated amounts of losses incurred prior to the balance sheet date but settled subsequently should be accrued as of the balance sheet date.
***Should be disclosed even though possibility of loss may be remote.

EXERCISE 13-5

Purpose: (L.O.2,6,7) This exercise will enable you to practice analyzing situations to determine whether a liability should be reported, and if so, at what amount.

John Cleese Inc., a publishing company, is preparing its December 31, 1999 financial statements and must determine the proper accounting treatment for each of the following situations:

1. Cleese sells subscriptions to several magazines for a two- or three-year period. Cash receipts from subscribers are credited to Unearned Magazine Subscriptions Revenue. This account had a balance of $5,300,000 at December 31, 1999, before adjustment. An analysis of outstanding subscriptions at December 31, 1999 shows that they expire as follows:

During 2000:	$ 800,000
During 2001:	900,000
During 2002:	1,200,000

2. A suit for breach of contract seeking damages of $1,000,000 was filed by an author against Cleese on June 1, 1999. The company's legal counsel believes that an unfavorable outcome is probable. A reasonable estimate of the court's award to the plaintiff is in the range between $200,000 and $800,000. The company's legal counsel believes the best estimate of potential damages is $350,000.

3. On January 2, 1999, Cleese discontinued collision, fire, and theft coverage on its delivery vehicles and became self-insured for these risks. Actual losses of $40,000 during 1999 were charged to Delivery Expense. The 1998 premium for the discontinued coverage amounted to $75,000, and the controller wants to set up a reserve for self-insurance by a debit to Delivery Expense of $35,000 and a credit to Liability for Self-insurance of $35,000.

4. During December 1999, a competitor company filed suit against Cleese for copyright infringement claiming $600,000 in damages. In the opinion of management and company counsel, it is reasonably possible that damages will be awarded to the plaintiff. The best estimate of potential damages is $175,000.

Instructions

For each of the situations above, prepare the journal entry that should be recorded as of December 31, 1999, or explain why an entry should not be recorded. Show supporting computations in good form.

Solution to Exercise 13-5

1.	Unearned Magazine Subscription Revenue........................	2,400,000*	
	Magazine Subscriptions Revenue...........................		2,400,000
	(To adjust the unearned revenue account)		

***Liability account:**

Book balance at December 31, 1999	$ 5,300,000
Adjusted balance ($800,000 + $900,000 + $1,200,000)	2,900,000
Adjustment required	$ 2,400,000

2.	Estimated Loss from Pending Lawsuit..............................	350,000	
	Estimated Liability from Pending Lawsuit...............		350,000
	(To record estimated minimum damages on breach-of-contract litigation)		

This situation involves a contingent liability. Because it is **probable** that a liability has been incurred and the loss is reasonably estimable, the loss should be accrued. When the expected loss amount is in a range, the best estimate within the range is used for the accrual. When no amount within the range is a better estimate than any other amount, the dollar value at the low end is accrued and the dollar amount at the high end of the range is disclosed in the notes.

3. No entry should be made to accrue for an expense because the absence of insurance coverage does not mean that an asset has been impaired or a liability has been incurred as of the balance sheet date. Cleese may, however, appropriate retained earnings for self-insurance as long as actual costs or losses are not charged against the appropriation of retained earnings and no part of the appropriation is transferred to income. Appropriation of retained earnings and/or disclosure in the notes to the financial statements are not required, but are recommended.

4. No entry should be made for this loss contingency, because it is not probable that an asset has been impaired or a liability has been incurred as of the balance sheet date. The loss contingency (along with the best estimate of amount) should be disclosed in the notes to financial statements because the likelihood of loss is judged to be reasonably possible.

EXERCISE 13-6

Purpose: (L.O.7) This exercise will provide an example of accounting for premium claims outstanding.

Jo-Ann Beiler Company includes 1 coupon in each box of cereal that it packs and 10 coupons are redeemable for a premium (a toy). In 1999, Jo-Ann Beiler company purchased 9,000 premiums at 90 cents each and sold 100,000 boxes of cereal at $2.00 per box; 40,000 coupons were presented for redemption in 1999. It is estimated that 60% of the coupons will eventually be presented for redemption. This is the first year for this premium offering.

Instructions

Prepare all the entries that would be made relative to sales of cereal and to the premium plan in 1999.

Solution to Exercise 13-6

Inventory of Premiums (9,000 x $.90)	8,100	
Cash		8,100
Cash (100,000 x $2.00)	200,000	
Sales		200,000
Premium Expense	3,600	
Inventory of Premiums [(40,000 ÷ 10) x $.90]		3,600
Premium Expense	1,800*	
Estimated Liability for Premiums		1,800

*[(100,000 x 60%) - 40,000] ÷ 10 x $.90 = $1,800

Explanation: The first entry records the purchase of 9,000 toys which will be used as premiums. The second entry records the sales of cereal (100,000 boxes). The third entry records the redemption of 40,000 coupons with customers receiving one premium for every 10 coupons. The cost of the 4,000 toys distributed to these customers is recorded by a debit to expense. The fourth entry is an adjusting entry at the end of the accounting period to accrue the cost of additional premiums included in boxes of cereal sold this period that are likely to be redeemed in future periods. This is an application of the matching principle. The expense of a premium should be recognized in the same period as the related revenue which, in this case, is from the sale of cereal boxes containing the coupons that customers will redeem for a premium.

EXERCISE 13-7

Purpose: (L.O.7) This exercise will provide an example of the journal entries involved in accounting for a warranty that is included with the sale of a product (warranty is not sold separately). Two methods are examined—the cash basis and the expense warranty method (an accrual method).

Colleen Mahla Corporation sells laptop computers under a two-year warranty contract that requires the corporation to replace defective parts and to provide the necessary repair labor. During 1998 the corporation sells for cash 400 computers at a unit price of $2,000. On the basis of past experience, the two-year warranty costs are estimated to be $90 for parts and $100 for labor per unit. (For simplicity, assume that all sales occurred on December 31, 1998, rather than evenly throughout the year.)

Instructions

(a) Record any necessary journal entries in 1998, applying the cash basis method.

(b) Record any necessary journal entries in 1998, applying the expense warranty accrual method.

(c) What liability relative to these transactions would appear on the December 31, 1998 balance sheet and how would it be classified if the cash basis method is applied?

(d) What liability relative to these transactions would appear on the December 31, 1998 balance sheet and how would it be classified if the expense warranty accrual method is applied?

In 1999 the actual warranty costs to Colleen Mahla Corporation were $14,800 for parts and $18,200 for labor.

(e) Record any necessary journal entries in 1999, applying the cash basis method.

(f) Record any necessary journal entries in 1999, applying the expense warranty accrual method.

(g) Under what conditions is it acceptable to use the cash basis method? Explain.

Solution to Exercise 13-7

(a)	Cash (400 x $2,000)	800,000	
	Sales of Computers		800,000
(b)	Cash (400 x $2,000)	800,000	
	Sales of Computers		800,000
	Warranty Expense [400 x ($90 + $100)]	76,000	
	Estimated Liability Under Warranties		76,000

(c) No liability would be disclosed under the cash basis method relative to future costs due to warranties on past sales.

(d) Current Liabilities:

Estimated Liability Under Warranties	$38,000

Long-term Liabilities:

Estimated Liability Under Warranties	$38,000

(e)	Warranty Expense	33,000	
	Parts Inventory		14,800
	Wages Payable		18,200
(f)	Estimated Liability Under Warranties	33,000	
	Parts Inventory		14,800
	Wages Payable		18,200

(g) The cash basis is used for income tax purposes. Theoretically, the accrual basis (expense warranty method in this case) should be used for financial reporting purposes. However, the cash basis is often justifiably used for accounting purposes when warranty costs are immaterial or when the warranty period is relatively short.

EXERCISE 13-8

Purpose: (L.O.7) This exercise will exemplify the journal entries involved in accounting for a warranty that is sold separately from the related product. The sales warranty accrual method is used for such situations.

Terence Trent Company sells scanners for $800 each and offers to each customer a three-year warranty contract for $90 that requires the company to perform periodic services and to replace defective parts. During 1998, the company sold 500 scanners and 400 warranty contracts for cash. It estimates the three-year warranty costs as $30 for parts and $50 for labor and accounts for warranties on the sales warranty accrual method. Assume all sales occurred on December 31, 1998, and revenue from the sale of the warranties is to be recognized on a straight-line basis over the life of the contract.

Instructions

(a) Record any necessary journal entries in 1998.
(b) What liability relative to these transactions would appear on the December 31, 1998 balance sheet and how would it be classified?

In 1999, Terence Trent Company incurred actual costs relative to 1998 scanner warranty sales of $3,800 for parts and $6,000 for labor.
(c) Record any necessary journal entries in 1999 relative to 1998 scanner warranties.
(d) What amounts relative to the 1998 scanner warranties would appear on the December 31, 1999 balance sheet and how would they be classified?

Solution to Exercise 13-8

(a)	Cash ($400,000 + $36,000)	436,000	
	Sales of Scanners (500 x $800)		400,000
	Unearned Warranty Revenue (400 x $90)		36,000

(b) Current Liabilities:
Unearned Warranty Revenue $12,000
(Note: Warranty costs are assumed to be incurred equally over the three-year period)

Long-term Liabilities:
Unearned Warranty Revenue $24,000

(c)	Warranty Expense	9,800	
	Parts Inventory		3,800
	Wages Payable		6,000
	Unearned Warranty Revenue	12,000	
	Revenue from Warranties		12,000

(d) Current Liabilities:
Unearned Warranty Revenue $12,000

Long-term Liabilities:
Unearned Warranty Revenue $12,000

EXERCISE 13-9

Purpose: (L.O.8) This exercise will show you how to compute a bonus under two different agreements.

Merry Rawls, president of the Merry Music Company, has a bonus arrangement with the company under which she receives 15% of the net income (after deducting taxes and bonus) each year. For the current year, the net income before deducting either the provision for income taxes or the bonus is $719,400. The bonus is deductible for tax purposes, and the effective income tax rate is 40%.

Instructions

(a) Compute the amount of Merry's bonus.
(b) Compute the appropriate provision for federal income taxes for the year.
(c) Recompute the amount of Merry's bonus if the bonus is to be 15% of income after bonus but before tax. (Round to the nearest dollar.)

Solution to Exercise 13-9

(B = bonus; T = taxes)

(a)	B	=	.15 ($719,400 - B - T)
	T	=	.40 ($719,400 - B)
	B	=	.15 [$719,400 - B - .4 ($719,400 - B)]
	B	=	.15 ($719,400 - B - $287,760 + .4B)
	B	=	.15 ($431,640 - .6B)
	B	=	$64,746 - .09B
	1.09B	=	$64,746
	Bonus	=	$59,400
(b)	T	=	.40 ($719,400 - B)
	T	=	.40 ($719,400 - $59,400)
	T	=	.40 ($660,000)
	Taxes	=	$264,000
(c)	B	=	.15 ($719,400 - B)
	B	=	$107,910 - .15B
	1.15B	=	$107,910
	Bonus	=	$93,835

TIP: Examine the equation to compute the bonus. Make sure it is consistent with the wording of the agreement. For instance, if the bonus is based on income **after** bonus and **after** taxes, then income must be reduced by both bonus and taxes in your formula (Income - B - T) [see part (a)]. But if the bonus is to be based on income after bonus and before taxes, then taxes are **not** part of your equation [see part (c)].

TIP: Always "prove" the bonus figure computed.

Proof—parts (a) and (b)

Income before bonus and before taxes	$ 719,400
Bonus	(59,400)
Income before taxes	660,000
Income taxes (40% x $660,000) [agrees with (b)]	(264,000)
Income after bonus and after taxes	396,000
Bonus rate	15%
Bonus [agrees with (a)]	$ 59,400

Proof—part (c)

Income before bonus and before taxes	$ 719,400
Bonus	(93,835)
Income before taxes	625,565
Bonus rate	15%
Bonus [agrees with (c)]	$ 93,835

ANALYSIS OF MULTIPLE-CHOICE TYPE QUESTIONS

QUESTION

1. (L.O.1) A current liability is an obligation that:
   a. was paid during the current period.
   b. will be reported as an expense within the year or operating cycle that follows the balance sheet date, whichever is longer.
   c. will be converted to a long-term liability within the next year.
   d. is expected to require the use of current assets or the creation of another current liability to liquidate it.

Approach and Explanation: Before you read the answer selections, write down the definition for "current liability." Compare each answer selection with your definition. A **current liability** is an obligation which will come due within one year and whose liquidation is reasonably expected to require the use of existing resources properly classifiable as current assets or the creation of other current liabilities. (Solution = d.)

QUESTION

2. (L.O.2) Burt Reynolds Company borrowed money from Loni Anderson Company for nine months by issuing a zero-interest-bearing note payable with a face value of $106,000. The proceeds amounted to $100,000. In recording the issuance of this note, what account should Burt debit for $6,000?
   a. Interest Payable
   b. Interest Expense
   c. Prepaid Interest
   d. Discount on Note Payable

Approach and Explanation: The excess of the face value of a zero-interest-bearing note payable and the proceeds collected upon its issuance is the cost of borrowing. This cost of borrowing (interest expense) should be recognized over the months the loan is outstanding. Therefore, the total interest ($6,000) is initially debited to a Discount on Note Payable Account. The balance of that account is then amortized (allocated) to interest expense over the life of the note. (Solution = d.)

TIP:	A **zero-interest-bearing note** is often called a **non-interest-bearing-note**.

QUESTION

3. (L.O.2) Martha's Boutique sells gift certificates. These gift certificates have no expiration date. Data for the current year are as follows:

Gift certificates outstanding, January 1	$ 225,000
Gift certificates sold	750,000
Gift certificates redeemed	660,000
Gross profit expressed as percentage of sales	40%

   At December 31, Martha should report unearned revenue of:
   a. $90,000.
   b. $126,000.
   c. $261,000.
   d. $315,000.

Approach and Explanation: Draw a T-account for the liability and enter the data given.

Gift Certificates Outstanding

		Beginning Balance	225,000
Redeemed	660,000	Sold	750,000
		Ending Balance	315,000

(Solution = d.)

> **TIP:** The gross profit percentage is not used in the solution for the balance of unearned revenue. Revenue and unearned revenue are gross amounts, not net amounts.

QUESTION

4. (L.O.3) Included in Arnold Company's liability accounts at December 31, 1999 was the following:

12% Note payable issued in 1997 for cash and due in May 2000	$2,000,000

On February 1, 2000 Arnold issued $5,000,000 of five-year bonds with the intention of using part of the bond proceeds to liquidate the $2,000,000 note payable maturing in May. On March 2, 2000, Arnold used $2,000,000 of the bond proceeds to liquidate the note payable. Arnold's December 31, 1999 balance sheet is being issued on March 15, 2000. How much of the $2,000,000 note payable should be classified as a current liability on the balance sheet?

a. $0
b. $800,000
c. $1,000,000
d. $2,000,000

Approach and Explanation: Mentally review the definition of a current liability and the guidelines for reporting short-term debt expected to be refinanced. At the date the balance sheet is issued, we have evidence of the intent and ability to refinance the debt on a long-term basis. That evidence is the post balance sheet issuance of long-term debt securities. The proceeds from the bond issuance exceed the reported amount of the note. Therefore, the entire $2,000,000 note payable should be classified as a long-term liability. (Solution = a.)

QUESTION

5. (L.O.4) An employee's net (or take-home) pay is determined by gross earnings minus amounts for income tax withholdings and the employee's:

a. portion of FICA taxes, and unemployment taxes.
b. and employer's portion of FICA taxes, and unemployment taxes.
c. portion of FICA taxes, unemployment taxes, and any voluntary deductions.
d. portion of FICA taxes, and any voluntary deductions.

Approach and Explanation: Before you read the answer selections, write down the model for the net (take-home) pay computation. Then find the answer selection that agrees with your model.

Employee's gross earnings for the current period
- Federal income tax withholdings
- FICA tax withholdings
- Withholdings for voluntary deductions; such as for charitable contributions, group health and life insurance premiums, savings, retirement fund contributions, and loan repayments

= Net (or take-home) pay (Solution = d.)

> **TIP:** The employer bears the burden of all unemployment taxes and its share of FICA taxes.

QUESTION

6. (L.O.6) An example of a contingent liability is:
   a. sales taxes payable.
   b. accrued salaries.
   c. property taxes payable.
   d. a pending lawsuit.

Approach and Explanation: Mentally define contingent liability and think of examples before you read the alternative answer selections. A contingent liability is a situation involving uncertainty as to possible loss or expense that will ultimately be resolved when one or more future events occur or fail to occur. Examples are pending or threatened lawsuits, pending IRS audits, and product warranties. Accrued salaries result in an actual liability. Sales taxes payable and property taxes payable are both actual liabilities if they exist at a balance sheet date. (Solution = d.)

QUESTION

7. (L.O.6,7) A contingent loss which is judged to be reasonably possible and estimable should be:

	Accrued	Disclosed
a.	Yes	Yes
b.	Yes	No
c.	No	Yes
d.	No	No

Explanation: A contingent loss that is probable and estimable is to be accrued. A contingent loss that is reasonably possible should be disclosed, but it should not be accrued. A contingent loss that is remotely possible can be ignored (unless it is one of the items on a list of contingencies that must always be disclosed, regardless of the likelihood of loss occurrence, such as guarantees of indebtedness of others). (Solution = c.)

QUESTION

8. (L.O.7) Scott Corporation began operations at the beginning of 1998. It provides a two-year warranty with the sale of its product. Scott estimates that warranty costs will equal 4% of the selling price the first year after sale and 6% of the selling price the second year after the sale. The following data are available:

	1998	1999
Sales	$400,000	$500,000
Actual warranty expenditures	10,000	38,000

The balance of the warranty liability at December 31, 1999 should be:

a. $12,000.
b. $42,000.
c. $44,000.
d. $50,000.

Approach and Explanation: Draw a T-account and enter the amounts that would be reflected in the account and determine its balance.

Estimated Liability Under Warranties

(2) Expenditures in 1998	10,000	(1) Expense for 1998	40,000
(4) Expenditures in 1999	38,000	(3) Expense for 1999	50,000
		12/31/99 Balance	42,000

(Solution = b.)

(1) $400,000 x (4% + 6%) = $40,000 expense for 1998.
The total warranty cost related to the products sold during 1998 should be recognized in the period of sale (matching principle).
(2) Given data. Actual expenditures during 1998.
(3) $500,000 x (4% + 6%) = $50,000 expense for 1999.
(4) Given data. Actual expenditures during 1999.

TIP: Because some items are sold near the end of the year and the warranty is for two years, a portion of the warranty liability should be classified as a current liability (the amount pertaining to the actual expenditures estimated to occur in 2000) and the remainder as a long-term liability.

QUESTION

9. (L.O.7) Crazy Pete Theme Park is self-insured. Premiums for insurance used to cost $100,000 per year before Crazy Pete discontinued coverage. During 1999, Crazy Pete suffered losses of $39,000 that used to be (but are no longer) covered by insurance. Crazy Pete thinks this was a "light" year and greater losses in future years will offset the lower amount sustained in 1999. In order to avoid volatility in earnings due to being self-insured, Crazy Pete wants to set up a Liability for Self-insurance. A reasonable estimate of losses to be incurred in 2000 is $120,000. The liability to be reported by Crazy Pete at December 31, 1999 due to this situation is:

a. $0.
b. $61,000.
c. $100,000.
d. $120,000.

Approach and Explanation: Even if the amount is estimable, the future losses from self-insurance do not result in liabilities at the December 31, 1999 balance sheet date because the losses in the future will result from future events, not from a past event. It is not generally acceptable to accrue future losses from self-insurance. (Solution = a.)

TIP: Crazy Pete should report $39,000 of losses on its 1999 income statement.

QUESTION

10. (L.O.8) Garth Brooks, a manager of a local business, is to receive an annual bonus equal to 10% of the company's income in excess of $100,000 before income taxes but after deduction of the bonus. If income before income taxes and bonus is $820,000 and the tax rate is 40%, the amount of the bonus would be:
    a. $22,800.
    b. $36,981.
    c. $65,455.
    d. $72,000.

Approach and Explanation: Carefully write an equation that expresses the agreement. Notice what should be deducted from income before the bonus percentage is applied—$100,000 and the bonus (but **not** taxes). Solve for bonus. Prove your answer.

B	=	10% ($820,000 - $100,000 - B)	
B	=	$82,000 - $10,000 - .1B	
1.1B	=	$72,000	
B	=	$72,000 ÷ 1.1	
B	=	$65,455	(Solution = c.)

Proof:		
	Income before taxes and bonus	$ 820,000
	Exclusion	(100,000)
	Bonus expense	(65,455)
	Income after bonus and before taxes	654,545
	Bonus rate	10%
	Bonus	$ 65,455

QUESTION

11. (L.O.7) The ratio of current assets to current liabilities is called the:
    a. current ratio.
    b. acid-test ratio.
    c. current asset turnover ratio.
    d. current liability turnover ratio.

Explanation: Two major ratios used to measure liquidity of an entity are the (1) current ratio and the (2) acid-test ratio. The current ratio is computed by dividing current assets by current liabilities. The acid-test ratio is computed by dividing quick assets (cash + marketable securities + net receivables) by current liabilities. Marketable securities in this context refer to short-term (temporary) investments. The current ratio is sometimes called the working capital ratio; the acid-test ratio is often called the quick ratio. (Solution = a).

CHAPTER 14

LONG-TERM LIABILITIES

OVERVIEW

Sources of assets include current liabilities, long-term liabilities, and owners' equity. Liabilities are considered a "temporary" source of assets, whereas owners' equity is a more "permanent" source of assets. When a company borrows money, it does so with the expectation of using the borrowed funds to acquire assets that can be used to generate more income. The objective is to generate an amount of additional income which exceeds the cost of borrowing the funds (interest).

Long-term debt consists of probable future sacrifices of economic benefits arising from present obligations that are not payable within a year or the operating cycle of the business, whichever is longer. Bonds payable, long-term notes payable, mortgages payable, pension liabilities, and lease obligations are examples of long-term liabilities. This chapter will focus on the first two of these.

Although the subject of accounting for bonds is included in the principles of accounting course, many intermediate students don't remember the details of the procedures and look upon this topic as one of the most difficult they have encountered. Perhaps they have problems with the material because they try to memorize their way through the topic. As a result, it is imperative that you think about the time value of money concepts introduced in Chapter 6 and grasp how they are applied in the computations involved in accounting for long-term debt. When you see the logic and rationale of the accounting procedures, you will find it easier to recall these guidelines years from now.

SUMMARY OF LEARNING OBJECTIVES

1. **Describe the formal procedures associated with issuing long-term debt.** Incurring long-term debt is often a formal procedure. The bylaws of corporations usually require approval by the board of directors and the stockholders before bonds can be issued or other long-term debt arrangements can be contracted. Generally, long-term debt has various covenants or restrictions. The covenants and other terms of the agreement between the borrower and the lender are stated in the bond indenture or note agreement.

2. **Identify various types of bond issues.** (1) *Secured and unsecured bonds*. (2) *Term, serial bonds, and callable bonds*. (3) *Convertible, commodity-backed, and deep discount bonds*. (4) *Registered and bearer (coupon) bonds*. (5) *Income and revenue bonds*. The variety in the types of bonds are a result of attempts to attract capital from different investors and risk takers and to satisfy the cash flow needs of the issuers.

3. **Describe the accounting valuation for bonds at the date of issuance.** The investment community values a bond at the present value of its future cash flows, which consist of interest and principal. The rate used to compute the present value of these cash flows is the interest rate that provides an acceptable return on an investment commensurate with the issuer's risk

characteristics. The interest rate written in the terms of the bond indenture and ordinarily appearing on the bond certificate is the stated, coupon, or nominal rate. This rate, which is set by the issuer of the bonds, is expressed as a percentage of the face value, also called the par value, principal amount, or maturity value, of the bonds. If the rate employed by the buyers differs from the stated rate, the present value of the bonds computed by the buyers will differ from the face value of the bonds. The difference between the face value and the present value of the bonds is either a discount or premium.

4. **Apply the methods of bond discount and premium amortization.** The discount (premium) is amortized and charged (credited) to interest expense over the period of time that the bonds are outstanding. Bond interest expense is increased by amortization of a discount and decreased by amortization of a premium. The profession's preferred procedure for amortization of a discount or premium is the effective interest method. Under the effective interest method, (1) interest expense is computed by multiplying the carrying value of the bonds at the beginning of the period by the effective interest rate, and (2) the bond discount or premium amortization is then determined by comparing the bond interest expense with the interest to be paid for the same interest period.

5. **Describe the accounting procedures for the extinguishment of debt.** At the time of reacquisition, the unamortized premium or discount and any costs of issue applicable to the debt must be amortized up to the reacquisition date. The amount paid on extinguishment or redemption before maturity, including any call premium and expense of reacquisition, is the reacquisition price. On any specified date, the net carrying amount of the debt is the amount payable at maturity, adjusted for unamortized premium or discount, and cost of issuance. Any excess of the net carrying amount over the reacquisition price is a gain from extinguishment, whereas the excess of the reacquisition price over the net carrying amount is a loss from extinguishment.

6. **Explain the accounting procedures for long-term notes payable.** Accounting procedures for notes and bonds are quite similar. Like a bond, a note is valued at the present value of its future interest and principal cash flows, with any discount or premium being similarly amortized over the life of the note. Whenever the face amount of the note does not reasonably represent the present value of the consideration given or received in the exchange, the entire arrangement must be evaluated to properly record the exchange and the subsequent interest.

7. **Describe off-balance-sheet financing arrangements.** Off-balance-sheet financing is an attempt to borrow funds in such a way that the obligations are not recorded. Two examples of off-balance sheet financing transactions are take-or-pay contracts and through-put agreements. Two additional off-balance-sheet approaches are interest rate swaps and project financing arrangements.

8. **Indicate how long-term debt is presented and analyzed.** Companies that have large amounts and numerous issues of long-term debt frequently report only one amount in the balance sheet and support this with comments and schedules in the accompanying notes. Any assets pledged as security for the debt should be shown in the asset section of the balance sheet. Long-term debt that matures within one year should be reported as a current liability, unless retirement is to be accomplished with other than current assets or the creation of a new liability other than a current liability. If the debt is to be refinanced, converted into stock, or is to be retired from a bond retirement fund, it should continue to be reported as noncurrent and accompanied with a footnote explaining the method to be used in its liquidation. Disclosure is required of future payments for sinking fund requirements and maturity amounts of long-term debt during each of the next 5 years. Debt to total assets and times interest earned are two ratios that provide information about debt-paying ability and long-run solvency.

9.* **Distinguish between and account for (1) a loss on loan impairment, (2) a troubled debt restructuring that results in the settlement of a debt, and (3) a troubled debt restructuring that results in a continuation of debt with modification of terms.** An impairment loan loss is based on the difference between the present value of the future cash flows and the carrying amount of the note. There are two types of settlement of debt restructurings: (1) transfer of noncash assets and (2) granting of equity interest. For accounting purposes, there are also two types of restructurings with continuation of debt with modified terms: (1) the carrying amount of debt is less than the total future cash flows, and (2) the carrying amount of debt is greater than the total future cash flows. (See **Illustration 14-4** for a summary of the related accounting procedures.)

*This material is covered in Appendix 14-A in the text.

TIPS ON CHAPTER TOPICS

TIP: The denomination of a bond is called the **face value**. Synonymous terms are **par value**, **principal amount**, **maturity value**, and **face amount**.

TIP: Bond prices are quoted in terms of percentage of par. Thus, a bond with a par value of $4,000 and a price quote of 102 is currently selling for a price of $4,080 (102% of $4,000). A bond with a quote of 100 is selling for its par value.

TIP: The bond contract is called an **indenture**. This term is often confused with the term "debenture." A **debenture** bond is an unsecured bond.

TIP: The interest rate written in the bond indenture and ordinarily appearing on the bond certificate is known as the **stated rate**. Synonymous terms are **coupon rate**, **nominal rate**, and **contract rate**.

TIP: The rate of interest actually earned by bondholders is called the **effective**, **yield**, or **market rate**.

TIP: A bond's **issuance price** is determined by the present value of all of the future cash flows promised by the bond indenture. The future cash flows include the face value and interest payments. The bond's present value is determined by using the market rate of interest at the date of issuance. An excess of the issuance price over par is called a **premium**; an excess of par value over the issuance price is called a **discount**.

TIP: In computing the present value of a bond's (1) maturity value and (2) interest payments, the **same** interest rate is used. That rate is the effective interest rate on a per interest period basis. As an example, if a ten-year bond has a stated rate of 10%, pays interest semiannually, and is issued to yield 12%, a 6% rate is used to perform **all** of the present value calculations.

TIP: Bond prices vary inversely with changes in the market rate of interest. This means that as the market rate of interest goes down, bond prices go up; and as the market rate of interest goes up, bond prices go down. It also means that at the date of issuance, if the market rate of interest is below the stated rate, the price will be above par; likewise, if the market rate is above the stated rate, the issuance price will be below par. Hence, **a premium or a discount is an adjustment to interest via an adjustment to price**. The adjustment to interest is recorded by the process of amortizing the premium or discount over the periods the bond is outstanding.

TIP: Interest payments on notes payable are generally made on a monthly or quarterly basis. Interest payments on bonds payable are usually made semiannually. Despite these common practices, interest rates generally are expressed on an annual basis. Therefore, care must be taken that the annual rate be converted to a "rate per period" before other computations are performed.

TIP: The **Discount on Bonds Payable account** is a contra liability account so its balance should be deducted from Bonds Payable on the balance sheet. The **Premium on Bonds Payable account** is an adjunct type valuation account so its balance should be added to the balance of Bonds Payable on the balance sheet. Unamortized Bond Issuance Costs are to be classified as a deferred charge in the "Other Assets" classification on the balance sheet; they should be amortized over the bond's life using the straight-line method.

TIP: The **effective interest method** of amortization is sometimes called the **interest method** or the **present value method** or the **effective method**. When the effective interest method is used, the bond's carrying value will equal its present value (assuming the amortization is up to date).

TIP: When the accounting period ends on a date other than an interest date, the amortization schedule for a bond or a note payable is unaffected by this fact. That is, the schedule is prepared and computations are made according to the bond periods, ignoring the details of the accounting period. The interest expense amounts shown in the amortization schedule are then apportioned to the appropriate accounting period(s). As an example, if the interest expense for the six months ending April 30, 1999 is $120,000, then $40,000 (2/6) of that amount would go on the income statement for the 1998 calendar year and $80,000 (4/6) of it should be reflected on the income statement for the 1999 calendar year.

ILLUSTRATION 14-1
COMPUTATION AND PROOF OF BOND ISSUANCE PRICE (L.O.3,4)

Guemple Company issues a 5-year bond on January 1, 1999 (maturity date is January 1, 2004), with a stated interest rate of 6%. The market rate of interest at the date of issuance is 5%, the par value is $1,000, and interest is due annually on January 1.

The bond is a promise to pay $1,000 on January 1, 2004 and $60 (6% x $1,000) every January 1 beginning January 1, 2000 and ending January 1, 2004. The price of the bond is determined by the present value of all future cash flows related to the bond. The present value of the bond is found by discounting all of the promised payments at the market rate of interest (5%). This process is illustrated by the following timeline and present value calculations:

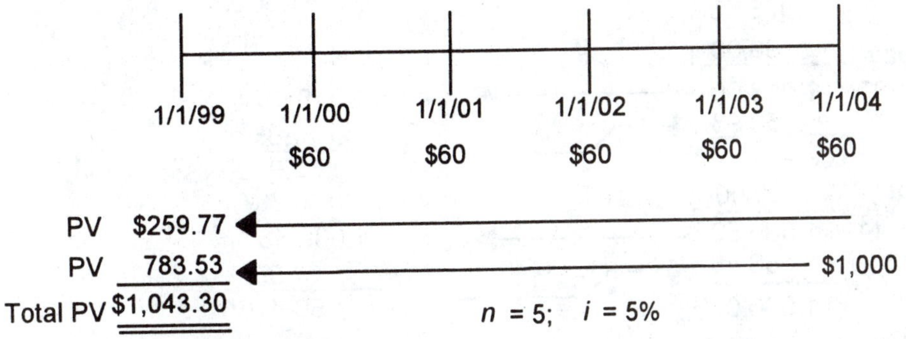

Present value of an ordinary annuity of $60 per period for 5 years at 5% interest ($60 x 4.32948)	$ 259.77
Present value of $1,000 due in 5 periods at 5% interest ($1,000 x .78353).	783.53
Total present value	$ 1,043.30

TIP: The factor of .78353 was derived from the Present Value of 1 table and the factor of 4.32948 was derived from the Present Value of an Ordinary Annuity of 1 table.

Thus, the bond price would be $1,043.30. Theoretically, this is the sum that would be required to be invested now at 5% compounded annually (market rate) to allow for the periodic (annual in this case) withdrawal of $60 (stated amount of interest) at the end of each of 5 years and the withdrawal of $1,000 at the end of 5 years. The following is proof that $1,043.30 is the amount required in this case.

ILLUSTRATION 14-1 (Continued)

Jan. 1, 1999	$1,043.30	→	$1,043.30	
	+ 52.17	interest at 5% ←	x .05	market rate effective interest
	1,095.47		52.1650	
1st interest payment on 1/1/00	- 60.00			
	1,035.47	→	1,035.47	
	+ 51.77	←	x .05	
	1,087.24		51.7735	
2nd interest payment on 1/1/01	- 60.00			
	1,027.24	→	1,027.24	
	+ 51.36	←	x .05	
	1,078.60		51.3620	
3rd interest payment on 1/1/02	- 60.00			
	1,018.60	→	1,018.60	
	+ 50.93	←	x .05	
	1,069.53		50.9300	
4th interest payment on 1/1/03	- 60.00			
	1,009.53	→	1,009.53	
	+ 50.48	←	x .05	
	1,060.01		50.4765	
5th interest payment on 1/1/04	- 60.00			
	1,000.01			
Principal payment	- 1,000.00			
	$ .01	Rounding error		

An amortization schedule can be constructed using the computations above. It would appear as follows:

Date	Stated Interest	Effective Interest	Premium Amortization	Carrying Value
1/1/99				$ 1,043.30
1/1/00	$ 60.00	$ 52.17	$ 7.83	1,035.47
1/1/01	60.00	51.77	8.23	1,027.24
1/1/02	60.00	51.36	8.64	1,018.60
1/1/03	60.00	50.93	9.07	1,009.53
1/1/04	60.00	50.47*	9.53	1,000.00
	$300.00	$256.70	$ 43.30	

*The rounding error of $.01 is plugged to interest expense in the last interest period.

ILLUSTRATION 14-2
FORMATS FOR COMMON COMPUTATIONS INVOLVING BONDS PAYABLE (L.O.4)

1. Cash Interest Per Period.

		Par value	Cash interest is always a constant amount each period.
	x	Stated rate of interest per period	
	=	Cash interest per period	

2. Interest Expense Using Straight-line Amortization Method.

		Cash interest for the period	Interest expense is a constant amount each period using this method.
	+	Discount amortization for the period	
OR	-	Premium amortization for the period	
	=	Interest expense for the period	

3. Amortization Amount Using Straight-line Method.
   Issuance premium or discount ÷ Periods in bonds life = Amortization per period

4. Interest Expense Using Effective Interest Method.

		Carrying value at the beginning of the period	The carrying value changes each interest period so the interest expense changes each period.
	x	Effective rate of interest per interest period	
	=	Interest expense for the interest period	

5. Amortization Amount Using Effective Interest Method.

		Interest expense for the interest period	Interest expense is greater than cash interest for bonds issued at a discount.
	-	Cash interest for the interest period	
	=	Amortization of discount for the interest period	
		OR	
		Cash interest for the interest period	Cash interest is greater than interest expense for bonds issued at a premium.
	-	Interest expense for the interest period	
	=	Amortization of premium for the interest period	

6. Carrying Value and Net Carrying Value.

		Par value	The process of amortization decreases the unamortized amount of discount or premium; hence the carrying value moves toward the par value.
	-	Unamortized discount	
OR	+	Unamortized premium	
	=	Carrying value	
	-	Unamortized debt issue costs	
	=	Net carrying amount	

7. Gain or Loss on Redemption.

		Net carrying amount
	-	Redemption price
	=	Gain if positive, that is, if net carrying value is the greater.
OR	=	Loss if negative, that is, if redemption price is the greater.

ILLUSTRATION 14-2 (Continued)

TIP: An **interest payment** promised by a bond is computed by multiplying the bond's par value by its stated interest rate. This amount is often referred to as the **cash interest** or **stated interest**.

TIP: Using the **straight-line method of amortization**, interest expense is determined by either adding the amount of discount amortization to the cash interest or deducting the amount of premium amortization from the cash interest. The periodic amount of amortization is determined by dividing the issuance premium or discount by the number of periods in the bond's life.

TIP: The **life** of a bond is measured by the time between the date of issuance and the date of maturity. The bond's life is shorter than the term of the bond if the bond is issued on a date later than it is dated.

TIP: The **effective interest expense** (interest expense using the effective interest method of amortization) is determined by multiplying the bond's carrying value at the beginning of the period by the effective interest rate. The difference between the interest payment (cash interest) and the effective interest expense for a period is the amount of premium or discount amortization for the period. The amount of amortization for a period causes a reduction in the balance of the unamortized premium or unamortized discount which in turn causes the carrying value to change.

TIP: A bond's **carrying value** (**book value**, **carrying amount**) is equal to the (1) par value plus any unamortized premium, or (2) par value minus any unamortized discount. When the effective interest method of amortization is used and the amortization is up to date, the bond's carrying value will equal its present value (determined by using the bond's effective interest rate to discount all remaining interest payments and par value). A bond's **net carrying value** is equal to its carrying value minus any related unamortized bond issuance costs.

TIP: The pattern of interest expense using the effective interest method may be compared to the pattern of interest expense using the straight-line method for both a bond issued at a discount and a bond issued at a premium by reference to the graph in **Illustration 14-3**. The relationship between interest expense and cash interest should also be noted. The difference between the cash interest and interest expense for a period is the amount of amortization for the period. The pattern of the periodic amount of amortization is also depicted by the graph.

TIP: If you use the effective interest rate (market rate at the date of a bond's issuance) to compute the (1) present value of the bond at the beginning of a given period, and (2) the present value of the same bond at the end of the given period, the difference between the two present value figures equals the amortization of the bond's premium or discount during that same period. This is true because the effective interest method results in reporting the present value of the liability (using the bond's effective interest rate for the discounting process) at a balance sheet date. That's why the effective interest method is the only method that is GAAP.

EXERCISE 14-1

Purpose: (L.O.3,4,5) This exercise will illustrate (1) the computations and journal entries throughout a bond's life for a bond issued at a discount and (2) the accounting required when bonds are called prior to their maturity date.

Arnold Howell Company issued bonds with the following details:

Face value	$100,000
Stated interest rate	7%
Market interest rate	10%
Maturity date	January 1, 2002
Date of issuance	January 1, 1999
Bond issue costs	$8,000
Call price	102
Interest payments due	Annually on January 1
Method of amortization	Effective interest

Instructions

(a) Compute the amount of issuance premium or discount.

(b) Prepare the journal entry for the issuance of bonds.

(c) Prepare the amortization schedule for these bonds.

(d) Prepare all of the journal entries (subsequent to the issuance date) for 1999 and 2000 that relate to these bonds. Assume the accounting period coincides with the calendar year. Assume reversing entries are not used.

(e) Prepare the journal entry to record the retirement of bonds assuming they are called on January 1, 2001.

Solution to Exercise 14-1

(a) $100,000 par x 7% stated rate = $7,000 annual cash interest

Factor for present value of a single sum, i = 10%, n = 3	.75132
Factor for present value of an ordinary annuity, i = 10%, n = 3	2.48685

$100,000 x .75132 =	$ 75,132.00
$7,000 x 2.48685 =	17,407.95
Issuance price	$ 92,539.95

Face value	$ 100,000.00
Issuance price	92,539.95
Discount on bonds payable	$ 7,460.05

(b)

Cash ($92,539.95 - $8,000.00)	84,539.95	
Discount on Bonds Payable	7,460.05	
Unamortized Bond Issue Costs	8,000.00	
Bonds Payable		100,000.00

Approach and Explanation: Always start with the easiest part of a journal entry. The issuance of a bond is **always** recorded by a credit to the Bonds Payable account for the par value of the bonds ($100,000 in this case). Because the issuance price is less than par, a contra type valuation account must be established; it is titled Discount on Bonds Payable and is debited for the issuance discount of $7,460.05. The $8,000 issuance costs are to be amortized over the periods benefited by the loan in order to comply with the matching principle; hence they are initially charged to an asset account. Cash was received for the issuance price less the issuance costs (fees to attorneys, accountants, printers, and underwriters) so debit Cash for the net proceeds of $84,539.95.

TIP: The Unamortized Bond Issue Costs account can be titled Bond Issue Costs. The Discount on Bonds Payable account is sometimes called Unamortized Bond Discount. Regardless of whether the word unamortized appears in the account titles or not, the balances of these accounts at a balance sheet date (after adjustments) represent the unamortized amounts.

(c)

Date	7% Stated Interest	10% Interest Expense	Discount Amortization	Carrying Value
1/1/99				$ 92,539.95
1/1/00	$ 7,000.00	$ 9,254.00	$ 2,254.00	94,793.95
1/1/01	7,000.00	9,479.40	2,479.40	97,273.35
1/1/02	7,000.00	9,726.65[a]	2,726.65	100,000.00
	$ 21,000.00	$ 28,460.05	$ 7,460.05	

[a]Includes rounding error of $.69.

Explanation: Stated interest is determined by multiplying the par value ($100,000) by the contract rate of interest (7%). Interest expense is computed by multiplying the carrying value at the beginning of the interest period by the effective interest rate (10%). The amount of discount amortization for the period is the excess of the interest expense over the stated interest (cash interest) amount. The carrying value at an interest payment date is the carrying value at the beginning of the interest period plus the discount amortization for the period.

TIP: The amount of interest expense of $9,479.40 appearing on the "1/1/01" payment line is the amount of interest expense for the interest period ending on that date. Thus, in this case, $9,479.40 is the interest expense for the twelve months preceding the date 1/1/01, which would be the calendar year of 2000.

TIP: Any rounding error should be plugged to (included in) the interest expense amount for the last interest period. Otherwise, there would forever be a small balance left in the Discount on Bonds Payable account long after the bonds were extinguished.

TIP: Notice that the total interest expense ($28,460.05) over the three-year period equals the total cash interest ($21,000.00) plus the total issuance discount ($7,460.05). Thus, you can see that the issuance discount represents an additional amount of interest to be recognized over the life of the bonds.

(d) **December 31, 1999**

Bond Interest Expense	9,254.00	
Interest Payable		7,000.00
Discount on Bonds Payable		2,254.00
Bond Issue Expense	2,666.67	
Unamortized Bond Issue Costs		2,666.67
($8,000.00 ÷ 3 = $2,666.67)		

January 1, 2000

Interest Payable	7,000.00	
Cash		7,000.00

December 31, 2000

Bond Interest Expense	9,479.40	
Interest Payable		7,000.00
Discount on Bonds Payable		2,479.40
Bond Issue Expense	2,666.67	
Unamortized Bond Issue Costs		2,666.67

(e) **January 1, 2001**

Interest Payable	7,000.00	
Bonds Payable	100,000.00	
Loss on Redemption of Bonds	7,393.31	
Discount on Bonds Payable		2,726.65
Unamortized Bond Issue Costs		2,666.66
Cash ($102,000 + $7,000)		109,000.00

($7,460.05 - $2,254.00 - $2,479.40 = $2,726.65 unamortized discount)
($8,000.00 - $2,666.67 - $2,666.67 = $2,666.66 unamortized issue costs)
($100,000.00 x 102% = $102,000.00 price to retire)
($100,000.00 - $2,726.65 = $97,273.35 carrying value)
($97,273.35 - $2,666.66 = $94,606.69 net carrying value)
($102,000.00 - $94,606.69 = $7,393.31 loss)

TIP: There was a **call premium** (amount in excess of par required) of $2,000.00 in this situation which is included in the loss computation.

TIP: Gains or losses on extinguishment of debt are to be classified as **extraordinary items** on the income statement (even though they may not meet the criteria of being unusual in nature and infrequent in occurrence) because of the guidelines contained in *SFAS No. 4*.

ILLUSTRATION 14-3
GRAPH TO DEPICT INTEREST PATTERNS FOR BONDS (L.O.4)

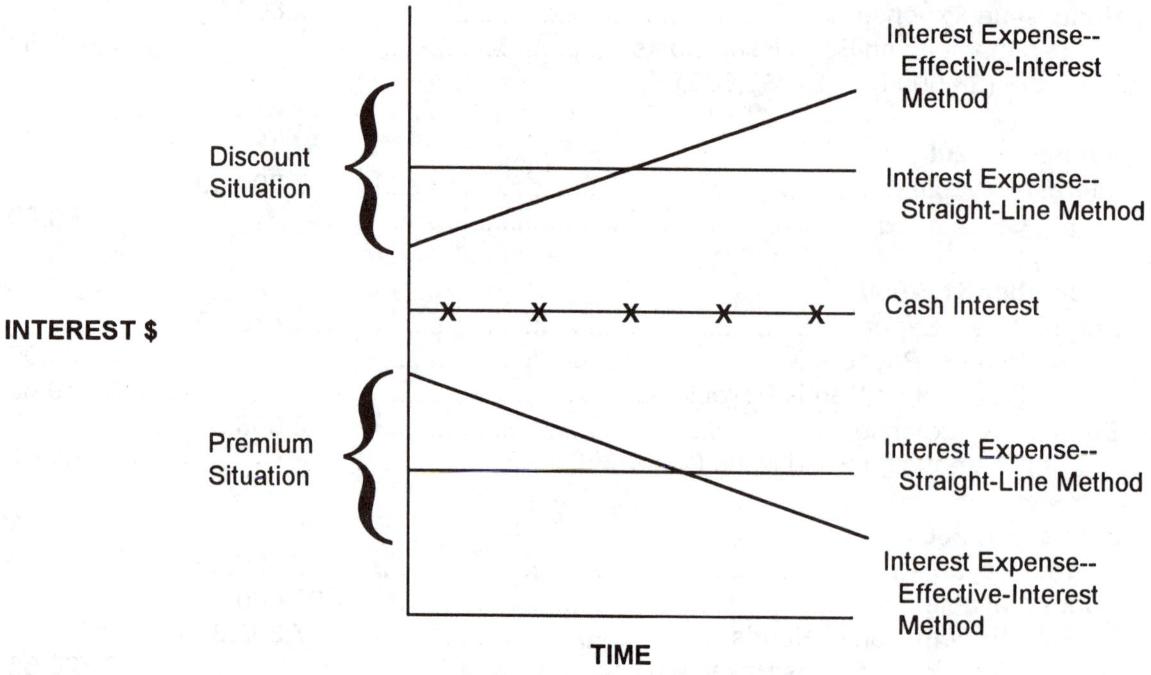

TIP: Regardless of whether the straight-line method of amortization or the effective interest method of amortization is used, the following will occur:

1. The amount of cash interest (stated interest) is a constant amount each period.
2. The bond's carrying amount increases over the bond's life if it is issued at a discount, due to the amortization of the discount.
3. The bond's carrying amount decreases over the bond's life if it is issued at a premium, due to the amortization of the premium.

TIP: If the straight-line method of amortization is used, the following relationships will exist:

1. The amount of amortization is a constant amount each period.
2. The amount of interest expense is a constant amount each period.

TIP: If the effective interest method of amortization is used, the following relationships will exist:

1. The effective interest rate is constant each period.
2. The interest expense is an increasing amount each period if the bond is issued at a discount (because a constant rate is applied to an increasing carrying amount each period).
3. The interest expense is a decreasing amount each period if the bond is issued at a premium (because a constant rate is applied to a decreasing carrying amount each period).
4. The amount of amortization **increases** each period because the difference between the effective interest expense and the cash interest widens each period.

EXERCISE 14-2

Purpose: (L.O.4) This exercise will serve as an example for both the issuance of bonds between interest payment dates and the use of the straight-line method of amortization.

On May 1, 1999, Peter Pan Tools Corporation issued bonds payable with a face value of $1,400,000 at 104 plus accrued interest. They are registered bonds dated January 1, 1999, bear interest at 9% payable semiannually on January 1 and July 1, and mature January 1, 2009. The company uses the straight-line method of amortization.

Instructions

(a) Compute the amount of bond interest expense to be reported on Peter Pan's income statement for the year ended December 31, 1999. (Round computations to the nearest dollar.)

(b) Compute the amount of bond interest payable to be reported on Peter Pan's balance sheet at December 31, 1999.

(c) Compute the amount of bond interest expense to be reported on Peter Pan's income statement for the year ended December 31, 2000.

Solution to Exercise 14-2

(a)	Interest paid on July 1, 1999 ($1,400,000 x 9% x 6/12)	$ 63,000
	Premium amortized on July 1, 1999 ($56,000 x 2/116)	(966)
	Accrued interest collected on May 1, 1999 ($1,400,000 x 9% x 4/12)	(42,000)
	Interest accrued on December 31, 1999 ($1,400,000 x 9% x 6/12)	63,000
	Premium amortized on December 31, 1999 ($56,000 x 6/116)	(2,897)
	Total bond interest expense for the year ending December 31, 1999	$ 80,137

Approach and Explanation: Prepare the journal entries to record the issuance of the bonds, the payment of interest and amortization of premium on July 1, 1999, and the year-end adjusting entry. Post the entries to the Interest Expense account and determine its balance at December 31, 1999.

May 1, 1999

Cash	1,498,000[c]	
Bonds Payable		1,400,000
Premium on Bonds Payable		56,000[a]
Bond Interest Expense		42,000[b]
(To record sale of bonds at a premium plus accrued interest)		

[a](104% x $1,400,000) - $1,400,000 = $56,000 issuance premium.
[b]9% x $1,400,000 x 4 months/12 months = $42,000 accrued interest (for January through April 1999).
[c]$1,400,000 face value x 104% = $1,456,000 issuance price.
$1,456,000 issuance price + $42,000 accrued interest = $1,498,000 cash proceeds.

July 1, 1999

Bond Interest Expense ($63,000 - $966)	62,034	
Premium on Bonds Payable ($56,000 x 2/116)	966	
Cash ($1,400,000 x 9% x 6/12)		63,000
(To record semiannual payment of interest and amortization of premium for two months)		

TIP: A premium or discount is to be amortized over the period the bonds are outstanding (from the date of issuance to the date of maturity). In this case, May 1, 1999 to January 1, 2009 is 4 months shy of 10 years (which is 116 months).

December 31, 1999

Bond Interest Expense ($63,000 - $2,897)	60,103	
Premium on Bond Payable ($56,000 x 6/116)	2,897	
Bond Interest Payable ($1,400,000 x 9% x 6/12)		63,000
(To record accrual of interest since last payment date and amortization of premium for 6 months)		

Bond Interest Expense

7/1/99	62,034	5/1/99	42,000
12/31/99	60,103		
Balance 12/31/99	80,137		

Bond Interest Payable

		12/31/99	63,000
		Balance 12/31/99	63,000

TIP: Bonds are often issued between interest payment dates. When this occurs, the issuer requires the investor to pay the market price for the bonds plus accrued interest since the last interest date. At the next interest payment date, the corporation will return the accrued interest to the investor by paying the full amount of interest due on outstanding bonds. In the situation at hand, the issuer collects from the investor interest from the date the bonds are dated to the date of issuance (from January 1, 1999 to May 1, 1999 is 4 months). When the next interest date rolls around (July 1, 1999), a full interest payment is made to the investor. Thus, the investor receives the two months' interest earned from May 1, 1999 to June 30, 1999, plus the accrued interest for four months that the investor paid in at the purchase date. Accrued interest at the date bonds are sold by an issuer is handled in this manner to expedite the issuer's payment procedures. At any interest payment date, interest for a full interest period is paid to each bondholder, there is no need to compute the actual time the bond investment was held by a particular bondholder and to prorate the interest because the investor has already paid in any portion of the full interest payment not earned by them during that interest period.

TIP: The journal entry to record the second interest payment on January 1, 2000 would be as follows (assuming reversing entries are not used):

Bond Interest Payable	63,000	
Cash		63,000
(To record a full interest payment)		

TIP: Refer to the journal entry made at the date of issuance (May 1, 1999). Rather than credit Bond Interest Expense for $42,000, you may credit Bond Interest Payable for the accrued interest of $42,000. This procedure will then require a modification to the entry on July 1, 1999. That entry would then include a debit to Bond Interest Payable for $42,000 and a debit to Bond Interest Expense for $20,034 rather than a debit to Bond Interest Expense for $62,034.

TIP: Refer to the journal entry made at December 31, 1999. You may wish to make two separate entries rather than the one compound entry. The equivalent single entries would be as follows:

December 31, 1999

Bond Interest Expense	63,000	
Bond Interest Payable		63,000
(To record accrued interest for the 6 months) ($1,400,000 x 9% x 6/12 = $63,000)		
Premium on Bonds Payable	2,897	
Bond Interest Expense		2,897
(To record premium amortization for 6 months) ($56,000 x 6/116 = $2,897)		

(b) Accrued interest payable at December 31, 1999:
$1,400,000 x 9% x 6/12 = $63,000

TIP: Refer to explanation of part (a) above and balance of T-account for Bond Interest Payable.

(c)

Interest paid on July 1, 2000 ($1,400,000 x 9% x 6/12)	$ 63,000
Premium amortized on July 1, 2000 ($56,000 x 6/116)	(2,897)
Interest accrued on December 31, 2000 ($1,400,000 x 9% x 6/12)	63,000
Premium amortized on December 31, 2000 ($56,000 x 6/116)	(2,897)
Total bond interest expense for the year ending December 31, 2000	$ 120,206

EXERCISE 14-3

Purpose: (L.O.4) This exercise will illustrate the computation of the bond price when interest is due semiannually. Additionally, it will present the accounting for bonds where the effective interest method of amortization is used and the end of the accounting period does not coincide with the end of an interest period.

P&J Chase Company sells $500,000 of 10% bonds on November 1, 1999. The bonds pay interest on May 1 and November 1 and are to yield 12%. The due date of the bonds is May 1, 2003. The accounting period is the calendar year. No reversing entries are made. Bond premium or discount is to be amortized at interest dates and at year-end.

Instructions

(a) Compute the price of the bonds at the issuance date.
(b) Prepare the amortization schedule for this issue.
(c) Prepare all of the relevant journal entries for this bond issue from the date of issuance through May 2001

Solution to Exercise 14-3

(a) Time diagram:

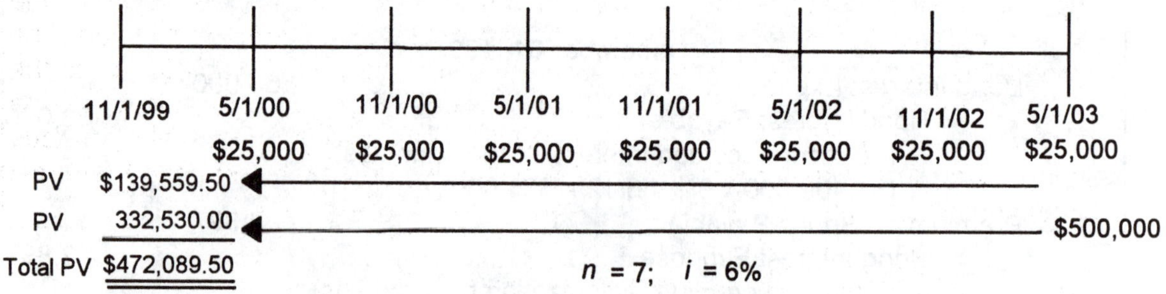

Factor for present value of a single sum, $i = 6\%$, $n = 7$ .66506
Factor for present value of an ordinary annuity, $i = 6\%$, $n = 7$ 5.58238
$500,000 x 5% = $25,000 interest per period

$500,000 x .66506 =	$ 332,530.00
$25,000 x 5.58238 =	139,559.50
Issuance price	$ 472,089.50

(b)

Date	5% Stated Interest	6% Interest Expense	Discount Amortization	Carrying Value
11/1/99				$ 472,089.50
5/1/00	$ 25,000.00	$ 28,325.37	$ 3,325.37	475,414.87
11/1/00	25,000.00	28,524.89	3,524.89	478,939.76
5/1/01	25,000.00	28,736.39	3,736.39	482,676.15
11/1/01	25,000.00	28,960.57	3,960.57	486,636.72
5/1/02	25,000.00	29,198.20	4,198.20	490,834.92
11/1/02	25,000.00	29,450.10	4,450.10	495,285.02
5/1/03	25,000.00	29,714.98*	4,714.98	500,000.00
	$ 175,000.00	$202,910.50	$ 27,910.50	

*Includes a rounding error of $2.12.

TIP: There are two interest periods per year; therefore, the stated interest rate per interest period is the annual rate (10%) divided by 2, which is 5%.

TIP: If you round all of your computations to the nearest cent, your rounding error will be small. A small (less than $5.00) rounding error provides some comfort that the amortization schedule is largely correct. A large rounding error (more than $10.00) indicates that one or more mistakes are likely included in the computation within the schedule or in the determination of the starting point (issuance price of the debt).

TIP: The amortization schedule displays amounts according to bond periods. If one interest period overlaps two different accounting periods, the amount of expense and amortization for that interest period must be appropriately allocated to the respective accounting periods.

TIP: Instead of just memorizing what goes on an amortization schedule, think about the reason the amounts have been included. That will help you to construct a schedule without much effort. In the date column, start with the issuance date, followed by each interest date. The stated interest amount is computed by multiplying the face value of the instrument by the stated rate of interest per interest period. Interest expense is computed by multiplying the carrying value at the beginning of the period (end of the prior line on the amortization schedule) by the market rate of interest per period. The difference between the stated interest and the interest expense for the period is the amount of the amortization for the period. Discount amortization is added to the previous carrying value (or premium amortization is deducted from the previous carrying value) to arrive at the carrying value at the end of the interest period (interest payment date).

(c)

November 1, 1999		
Cash	472,089.50	
Discount on Bonds Payable	27,910.50	
Bonds Payable		500,000.00
December 31, 1999		
Bond Interest Expense	9,441.79	
Discount on Bonds Payable		1,108.46
Interest Payable		8,333.33
($28,325.37 x 2/6 = $9,441.79)		
($3,325.37 x 2/6 = $1,108.46)		
($25,000.00 x 2/6 = $8,333.33)		
May 1, 2000		
Interest Payable	8,333.33	
Bond Interest Expense	18,883.58	
Discount on Bonds Payable		2,216.91
Cash		25,000.00
($28,325.37 - $9,441.79 = $18,883.58)		
($3,325.37 - $1,108.46 = $2,216.91)		
November 1, 2000		
Bond Interest Expense	28,524.89	
Discount on Bonds Payable		3,524.89
Cash		25,000.00
December 31, 2000		
Bond Interest Expense	9,578.80	
Discount on Bond Payable		1,245.47
Interest Payable		8,333.33
($28,736.39 x 2/6 = $9,578.80)		
($3,736.39 x 2/6 = $1,245.46 + $.01 to balance)		
($25,000.00 x 2/6 = $8,333.33)		

May 1, 2001

Bond Interest Expense	19,157.59	
Interest Payable	8,333.33	
Discount on Bonds Payable		2,490.92
Cash		25,000.00

($28,736.39 - $9,578.80 = $19,157.59)
($3,736.39 - $1,245.47 = $2,490.92)

EXERCISE 14-4

Purpose: (L.O.3,4) This exercise will enable you to practice identifying data required to perform computations involving bonds payable and applying the terminology associated with bonds.

On January 1, 1999, Tuna Fishery sold $100,000 (face value) worth of bonds. The bonds are dated January 1, 1999 and will mature on January 1, 2004. Interest is to be paid annually on January 1. Issue costs related to these bonds amounted to $2,000, and these costs are being amortized by the straight-line method. The following amortization schedule was prepared by the accountant for the first 2 years of the life of the bonds:

Date	Stated Interest	Effective Interest	Amortization	Carrying Value of Bonds
1/1/99				$ 104,212.37
1/1/00	$ 7,000.00	$ 6,252.74	$ 747.26	103,465.11
1/1/01	7,000.00	6,207.91	792.09	102,673.02

Instructions

On the basis of the information above, answer the following questions (round your answers to the nearest cent or percent) and explain the reasoning or computations, as appropriate.

(a) What is the nominal or stated rate of interest for this bond issue?
(b) What is the effective or market rate of interest for this bond issue?
(c) Prepare the journal entry to record the sale of the bond issue on January 1, 1999, including the issue costs.
(d) Prepare the appropriate entry(ies) at December 31, 2001, the end of the accounting year.
(e) Show how the account balances related to the bond issue will be presented on the December 31, 2001 balance sheet. Indicate the major classification(s) involved.
(f) What is the book value of the bonds at December 31, 2001?
(g) What is the net book value of the bonds at December 31, 2001?
(h) If the bonds are retired for $100,500 (excluding interest) at January 1, 2002, will the bonds be retired at a gain or a loss? What is the amount of that gain or loss? Where will it be reported on the income statement for the year ending December 31, 2002?

Solution to Exercise 14-4

(a) Stated interest = Stated rate of interest x Par
$7,000 = Stated rate of interest x $100,000
$7,000 ÷ $100,000 = Stated rate of interest
7% = Stated rate of interest

(b) Effective interest = Market rate x Carrying value at beginning of period
$6,252.74 = Market rate x $104,212.37
$6,252.74 ÷ $104,212.37 = Market rate
6% = Market rate

(c)

Cash	102,212.37	
Unamortized Bond Issue Costs	2,000.00	
Bonds Payable		100,000.00
Premium on Bonds Payable		4,212.37

(d)

Bond Interest Expense	6,160.38	
Premium on Bonds Payable	839.62	
Interest Payable		7,000.00
($102,673.02 x 6% = $6,160.38)		
Bond Issue Expense	400	
Unamortized Bond Issue Costs		400

(e)

Other Assets	
Unamortized bond issue costs	$ 800
Long-term liabilities	
Bonds payable, 7%, due 1/1/04	$ 100,000.00
Unamortized premium*	1,833.40
	$ 101,833.40

*$4,212.37 - $747.26 - $792.09 - $839.62 = $1,833.40

(f) $101,833.40 [See solution for part (e).]
Book value is another name for carrying value.

The amount, $101,833.40, can also be computed by:

Carrying value at 1/1/01 per schedule	$ 102,673.02
Amortization for 2001 [part (d)]	(839.62)
Carrying value at 12/31/01	$ 101,833.40

(g)

Bonds payable balance	$ 100,000.00
Premium on bonds payable balance	1,833.40
Book value	101,833.40
Unamortized bond issue costs	(800.00)*
Net book value at 12/31/01	$ 101,033.40

*[$2,000 - 3($400) = $800]

(h) Gain. A gain will result because the retirement price is less than the net carrying value at the date of retirement.

Net carrying value at 1/1/02 [part (g)]	$ 101,033.40
Retirement price	100,500.00
Gain on retirement of debt	$ 533.40

This gain from retirement of debt should be classified as an extraordinary item on the income statement; therefore, it is to be reported net of any related income tax effect.

EXERCISE 14-5

Purpose: (L.O.3) This exercise will illustrate how to account for the redemption of bonds by cash payment prior to maturity.

The balance sheet for Sea Willy Corporation reports the following information on December 31, 1998:

Long-term liabilities		
9% Bonds payable, due December 31, 2002	$ 1,000,000	
Less: Discount on bonds payable	60,000	
		$ 940,000

Interest is payable annually on December 31. The straight-line method of amortization is used. Interest rates have declined in the market place since the above mentioned bonds were issued. Sea Willy decides to borrow money from another source at a lower interest rate to lower its annual interest charges. Therefore, on July 1, 1999, Sea Willy redeems all of the old outstanding bonds at 102 (recall that bond prices vary inversely with changes in the market rate of interest).

Instructions

Prepare the journal entry(ies) to record the redemption of these bonds on July 1, 1999.

Solution to Exercise 14-5

Bond Interest Expense	45,000	
Cash		45,000
(To record the payment of accrued interest at July 1, 1999) ($1,000,000 x 9% x 6/12 = $45,000)		

Bond Interest Expense	7,500	
Discount on Bonds Payable		7,500
(To record the amortization of discount for six months) [($60,000 ÷ 4) x 6/12]		

Bonds Payable	1,000,000	
Loss on Bond Redemption	72,500[3]	
Discount on Bonds Payable		52,500[2]
Cash		1,020,000[1]
(To record the redemption of the bonds payable at 102)		

[1]$1,000,000 face value x 1.02 = $1,020,000 redemption price.
[2]$60,000 - $7,500 = $52,500 balance at July 1, 1999.
[3]$1,020,000 redemption price - $947,500 carrying value = $72,500 loss on redemption.

Approach and Explanation: Break the required entries into three simple parts— payment of accrued interest, update of discount amortization, and extinguishment of the liability. The bond holder is entitled to interest for the months between the last interest payment date and the redemption date, which is six months in this case. The amortization of the discount must be updated to arrive at the carrying value of the debt at the redemption date. In this case, six months of amortization must be recorded. The straight-line amortization method is being used so the $60,000 balance in the discount account at December 31, 1999 applies evenly to the remaining four years of the bond's term. The amortization for six months would, therefore, be one-half of the $15,000 annual amount.

For the entry to record the redemption, do the following: (1) Begin with the easiest part of the journal entry. Credit Cash to record the payment of the redemption price which is 102% of the face value of the bonds. (2) Remove the carrying value of the bonds from the accounts by debiting Bonds Payable for the face value of the bonds and crediting Discount on Bonds Payable for the balance of the related unamortized discount ($60,000 balance at December 31, 1998 less the $7,500 amortization for the first six months of 1999 = $52,500). (3) Record the difference between the redemption (retirement) price and the carrying value of the bonds as a gain or loss on redemption. An excess of carrying value over redemption price results in a gain. In the case at hand, the redemption price ($1,020,000) exceeds the carrying value of the bonds ($1,020,000 - $52,500 = $947,500). Since it cost $1,020,000 to eliminate a debt that appears on the books at only $947,500, a loss results.

TIP: Gains or losses on extinguishment of debt are classified as extraordinary items on the income statement (even though they may not meet the criteria of being unusual in nature and infrequent in occurrence) because of the guidelines contained in *SFAS No. 4*. Therefore, a gain or loss is reported net of any related income tax effect.

ILLUSTRATION 14-4
SUMMARY OF ACCOUNTING FOR IMPAIRMENT AND TROUBLED DEBT RESTRUCTURINGS (L.O.9)

Event	Accounting Procedure
1. Impairment	**Creditor:** Loss based upon difference between present value of future cash flows discounted at historical effective interest rate and carrying amount of note. Recognize interest revenue (or bad debt expense reduction) based upon new carrying amount and original effective rate. **Debtor:** No recognition.
2. Restructuring—Settlement of Debt	
a. Transfer of noncash assets.	**Creditor:** Recognize ordinary loss on restructure. **Debtor:** Recognize extraordinary gain on restructure and recognize ordinary gain or loss on asset transfer.
b. Granting of equity interest.	**Creditor:** Recognize ordinary loss on restructure. **Debtor:** Recognize extraordinary gain on restructure.
3. Restructurings—Continuation of Debt with Modified Terms	
a. Carrying amount of debt is less than future cash flows (no gain for debtor).	**Creditor:** Recognize ordinary loss based upon present value of restructured cash flows. Use the historical effective rate of the loan to compute this present value amount. Recognize interest revenue based upon new recorded value and original effective rate. **Debtor:** Recognize no gain on restructure. Determine new effective interest rate to be used in recording interest expense.
b. Carrying amount of debt is greater than total future cash flows (gain for debtor)	**Creditor:** Recognize ordinary loss based upon present value of restructured cash flows. Recognize interest revenue based upon new recorded value and original effective rate. **Debtor:** Recognize extraordinary gain on restructure and reduce carrying amount to the sum of the undiscounted cash flows. Recognize no interest expense over the remaining life of the debt.

TIP: When there is a restructuring that involves the continuation of debt with modification of terms, the computations made by the creditor to assess impairment are based on discounted future cash flows (at the original effective interest rate). However, the debtor's gain is calculated based upon undiscounted amounts. As a consequence, the gain recorded by the debtor will not equal the loss recorded by the creditor under many circumstances.

TIP: When there is a restructuring that involves a settlement of debt by transfer of noncash assets, the debtor has the following gain-loss computations:

(1) The excess of the carrying amount of the debt over the fair market value of the assets is recorded as a gain on restructuring; this gain is classified as an **extraordinary item** on the income statement.

(2) The difference between the fair market value of the assets and their recorded value (book value) is recorded as a gain or loss on disposition of assets; this gain or loss is **not** classified as an extraordinary item on the income statement (rather, it goes in the other gains or other losses section of a multiple-step income statement).

(a) If the fair market value of the assets exceeds their book value, a gain results.

(b) If the book value of the assets exceeds their fair market value, a loss results.

EXERCISE 14-6

Purpose: (L.O.9) This exercise will illustrate the accounting for a transfer of noncash assets to settle a debt obligation in a troubled debt situation.

Navajo Co. owes $194,400 to Mohawk Trust Co. The debt is a 10-year, 8% note. Because Navajo Co. is in financial trouble, Mohawk agrees to accept some property and cancel the entire debt. The property has a cost of $150,000, accumulated depreciation of $80,000, and a fair market value of $110,000.

Instructions

(a) Prepare the journal entry on Navajo's books for the debt restructure.

(b) Prepare the journal entry on Mohawk's books for the debt restructure.

Solution to Exercise 14-6

(a) **NAVAJO'S ENTRY:**

Notes Payable	194,400	
Accumulated Depreciation	80,000	
Property		150,000
Gain on Property Disposition (Not extraordinary)		40,000*
Gain on Restructuring of Debt (Extraordinary)		84,400**

*$110,000 - ($150,000 - $80,000) = $40,000
**$194,400 - $110,000 = $84,400

Approach and Explanation: (1) Begin with the easiest part of the journal entry. Remove the debt amount by a debit to Notes Payable for $194,400. (2) Remove the carrying value of the property by a debit to Accumulated Depreciation for $80,000 and a credit to Property for the $150,000 cost. (3) Compute and record the gain from settlement ($84,400 credit) and, (4) compute and record the gain from disposition of assets ($40,000). (5) Double check the entry to make sure it balances.

The debtor is required to determine the excess of the carrying amount of the payable ($194,400) over the fair value of the assets transferred ($110,000) and report that difference as an extraordinary gain ($84,400). The difference between the fair value of those assets and their carrying amounts is to be recognized as a gain or loss on disposition of assets. In this case, the fair value of $110,000 exceeds the carrying amount of $70,000; therefore, an ordinary gain of $40,000 is to be recognized. Although the gain on troubled debt restructuring is to be classified as an extraordinary item, the gain (or loss) from disposition of assets is to be classified as other revenues and gains (or other expenses and losses) on the debtor's income statement.

(b) **MOHAWK'S ENTRY:**

Property	110,000	
Allowance for Doubtful Accounts	84,400	
(or Loss on Restructuring)		
Notes Receivable		194,400

Approach and Explanation: (1) Remove the carrying amount of the receivable from the accounts by a credit to Notes Receivable for $194,400. (2) Record the acquisition of the property by a debit to Property for its fair value of $110,000. (3) Record the loss on settlement of $84,400 by a debit to Allowance for Doubtful Accounts or to a loss account. (4) Double check the entry to make sure it balances.

The creditor is required to determine the excess of the carrying amount of the receivable over the fair value of the assets being transferred to the creditor and record it as a charge against the Allowance for Doubtful Accounts account or to a loss account (such a loss is not to be classified as an extraordinary item).

EXERCISE 14-7

Purpose: (L.O.9) This exercise will illustrate the accounting for a troubled debt restructuring involving a modification of terms of an existing debt arrangement.

Pawnee Corp. owes $165,000 to Mohawk Trust Co. The debt is a 10-year, 10% note due December 31, 1998. Because Pawnee Corp. is in financial trouble, Mohawk agrees to extend the maturity date to December 31, 2000, reduce the principal to $150,000, and reduce the interest rate to 4%, payable annually on December 31. This restructuring takes place on December 31, 1998.

Instructions

(a) Prepare the journal entries on Pawnee's books on December 31, 1998, 1999, and 2000.

(b) Prepare the journal entries on Mohawk's books on December 31, 1998, 1999, and 2000.

Round all computations to the nearest dollar.

Solution to Exercise 14-7

(a) **PAWNEE'S ENTRIES:**

December 31, 1998		
Notes Payable	3,000	
Gain on Restructuring (Extraordinary)		3,000
December 31, 1999		
Notes Payable	6,000	
Cash (4% x $150,000)		6,000
December 31, 2000		
Notes Payable	156,000	
Cash [$150,000 + (4% x $150,000)]		156,000

Explanation: The situation described is a troubled debt restructuring involving continuation of debt with modified terms. Because in this situation the carrying amount of the debt ($165,000) at the time of restructure exceeds the undiscounted total future cash flows [$150,000 + ($150,000 x 4% x 2) = $162,000], the debtor will adjust the debt's carrying amount for the difference and recognize a gain ($3,000). Also, from the debtor's viewpoint, all future cash payments will go to reduce the principal; no interest expense will be recognized in the future in connection with this loan.

(b) **MOHAWK'S ENTRIES:**

December 31, 1998		
Allowance for Doubtful Accounts (or Bad Debt Expense)	30,619	
Notes Receivable		30,619

Explanation: The creditor in this case is required to calculate the loss based upon the expected future cash flows **discounted** at the historical effective rate on the loan. This write-down of the receivable will allow interest revenue to be reported in future years based on the historical effective rate (10%).

Pre-restructure carrying amount		$165,000
Present value of restructured cash flows:		
Present value of $150,000 due in 2 years at 10% ($150,000 x .82645)	$123,968	
Present value of $6,000 interest payable annually for 2 years at 10% ($6,000 x 1.73554)	10,413	134,381
Creditor's ordinary loss on restructure		$ 30,619

December 31, 1999		
Cash	6,000	
Notes Receivable	7,438	
Interest Revenue		13,438*

*A new amortization schedule would appear as follows:

Date	Cash Interest	10% Effective Interest	Increase in Carrying Value	Carrying Value of Note
12/31/98				$ 134,381
12/31/99	$ 6,000[a]	$ 13,438[b]	$ 7,438[c]	141,819
12/31/00	6,000	14,181	8,181	150,000

[a]$150,000 x 4% = $6,000.
[b]$134,381 x 10% = $13,438.
[c]$13,438 - $6,000 = $7,438.

December 31, 2000

Cash	6,000	
Notes Receivable..	8,181	
Interest Revenue..		14,181**

**Refer to the amortization schedule above.

Cash.	150,000	
Notes Receivable		150,000

ANALYSIS OF MULTIPLE-CHOICE TYPE QUESTIONS

QUESTION

1. (L.O.2) Bonds for which the owners' names are **not** registered with the issuing corporation are called:
   a. bearer bonds.
   b. term bonds.
   c. debenture bonds.
   d. secured bonds.

Approach and Explanation: Briefly define each answer selection. Choose the one that is described in the question's stem. **Bearer** (or **coupon**) **bonds** are bonds for which the name of the owner is not registered with the issuer; bondholders are required to send in coupons to receive interest payments and the bonds may be transferred directly to another party. **Registered bonds** are bonds registered in the name of the owner. **Term bonds** are bonds that mature (become due for payment) at a single specified future date. **Debenture bonds** are unsecured bonds. **Secured bonds** are bonds having specific assets pledged as collateral by the issuer. (Solution = a.)

QUESTION

2. (L.O.3) The periodic amortization of a premium on bonds payable will:
   a. cause the carrying value of the bonds to increase each period.
   b. cause the carrying value of the bonds to decrease each period.
   c. have no effect on the carrying value of the bonds.
   d. cause the carrying value always to be less than the par value of the bonds.

Approach and Explanation: Think about the process of amortizing a premium on bonds payable and how it affects the carrying value of the bonds. The Premium on Bonds Payable account has a normal credit balance. A premium is an adjustment to interest via an adjustment to price. Therefore, the entry to amortize the premium involves a debit to Premium on Bonds Payable and a credit to Bond Interest Expense. The amortization process reduces the balance of the unamortized premium. The carrying value of a bond issued at a premium is calculated by adding the premium balance to the face value of the bond. Thus, the carrying value of bonds payable issued at a premium will decrease each period until the maturity date (at which time the carrying value will equal the face value). (Solution = b.)

QUESTION

3. (L.O.3) A large department store issues bonds with a maturity date that is 20 years after the issuance date. If the bonds are issued at a discount, this indicates that at the date of issuance, the:
   a. nominal rate of interest and the stated rate of interest coincide.
   b. nominal rate of interest exceeds the yield rate.
   c. yield rate of interest exceeds the coupon rate.
   d. stated rate of interest exceeds the effective rate.

Approach and Explanation: Before reading the answer selections, write down the relationship that causes a bond to be issued at a discount: market rate of interest exceeds the stated rate of interest. Then list the synonymous terms for market rate and for stated rate: (1) market rate, effective rate, and yield rate; (2) stated rate, coupon rate, nominal rate, and contract rate. Selection "a" is incorrect because the nominal rate and the stated rate are just different names for the same thing. Selections "b" and "d" are incorrect because an excess of nominal rate (stated rate) over the yield rate (effective rate) will result in a premium, not a discount. Selection "c" is correct because when the yield rate (market rate) exceeds the coupon rate (stated rate), an issuance discount will result. (Solution = c.)

QUESTION

4. (L.O.4) If bonds are initially sold at a discount and the straight-line method of amortization is used, interest expense in the earlier years of the bond's life will:
   a. be less than the amount of interest actually paid.
   b. be less than it will be in the latter years of the bond's life.
   c. be the same as what it would have been had the effective interest method of amortization been used.
   d. exceed what it would have been had the effective interest method of amortization been used.

Approach and Explanation: Quickly sketch the graph that shows the patterns of and relationships between interest paid, interest expense using the straight-line method, and interest expense using the effective interest method. The graph appears in **Illustration 14-3**. Treat each of the possible answer selections as a True-False question. Look at the graph after reading each of the answer selections to determine if it is a correct answer.

Selection "a" is False because interest expense for a bond issued at a discount will be greater than interest actually paid throughout the bond's entire life, regardless of the amortization method used. Selection "b" is False because interest expense is a constant amount each period when the straight-line method is used; hence interest expense will be the same amount in the latter years as it is in the earlier years. Selection "c" is False because in the earlier years of life for a bond issued at a discount, interest expense computed using the straight-line method is greater than interest expense computed using the effective interest method. Selection "d" is True. The interest expense will increase over a bond's life when the bond is issued at a discount and the effective interest method of amortization is used. In the earlier years of life, that expense amount is less than interest expense using the straight-line method; and, in the latter years of life, that expense amount is more than interest expense computed using the straight-line method. (Solution = d.)

QUESTION

5. (L.O.4) At the beginning of 1999, the Alston Corporation issued 10% bonds with a face value of $400,000. These bonds mature in five years, and interest is paid semiannually on June 30 and December 31. The bonds were sold for $370,560 to yield 12%. Alston uses a calendar-year reporting period. Using the preferable method of amortization, what amount of interest expense should be reported for 1999? (Round all computations to the nearest dollar.)
   a. $44,333
   b. $44,467
   c. $44,601
   d. $45,888

Approach and Explanation: Write down the formula for computing interest using the effective method of amortization. Use the data in the question to work through the formula.

	Carrying value at the beginning of the period	$ 370,560.00
x	Effective rate of interest per interest period	6%
=	Interest expense for the first interest period	22,233.60
-	Cash interest for the interest period	20,000.00*
=	Amortization of discount for the first interest period	2,233.60
+	Carrying value at the beginning of the first period	370,560.00
=	Carrying value at the beginning of the second period	372,793.60
x	Effective rate of interest per interest period	6%
=	Interest expense for the second interest period	22,367.62
+	Interest expense for the first interest period	22,233.60
=	Interest expense for the calendar year of 1999	$ 44,601.22

*$400,000 x (10% ÷ 2) = $20,000

(Solution = c.)

TIP: The interest must be computed on a per interest period basis. In this question, the interest period is six months. The interest for 1999 is comprised of the interest for the bond's first two interest periods.

QUESTION

6. (L.O.5) At December 31, 1999 the following balances existed on the books of the Malloy Corporation:

Bonds Payable	$ 500,000
Discount on Bonds Payable	40,000
Interest Payable	12,500
Unamortized Bonds Issue Costs	30,000

If the bonds are retired on January 1, 2000, at 102, what will Malloy report as a loss on redemption?

a. $92,500
b. $80,000
c. $67,500
d. $50,000

Approach and Explanation: Write down the format for the computation of the gain or loss on redemption and plug in the amounts from this question.

	Par value	$ 500,000
-	Unamortized discount	40,000
=	Carrying amount	460,000
-	Unamortized debt issue costs	30,000
=	Net carrying amount	430,000
-	Redemption price	510,000*
=	Gain (Loss) on redemption	$ (80,000)

*$500,000 x 102% = $510,000.

(Solution = b.)

QUESTION

7. (L.O.5) "In-substance defeasance" is a term used to refer to an arrangement whereby:

a. a company gets another company to cover its payments due on long-term debt.
b. a governmental unit issues debt instruments to corporations.
c. a company provides for the future repayment of a long-term debt by placing purchased securities in an irrevocable trust.
d. a company legally extinguishes debt before its due date.

Explanation: In-substance defeasance is an arrangement whereby a company provides for the future repayment of one or more of its long-term debt issues by placing purchased securities in an irrevocable trust, the principal and interest of which are pledged to pay off the principal and interest of its own debt securities as they mature. The company, however, is not legally released from being the primary obligor under the debt that is still outstanding. (Solution = c.)

QUESTION

8. (L.O.6) On December 31, 1999 Sugar Products Company borrows $100,000 from Candy Factory Company and gives Candy Factory a 5-year, noninterest-bearing note with a face value of $100,000. The conditions of the note provide that Candy Factory can purchase $400,000 of products from the issuer of the note at something less than the regular market price over the next 5 years. Sugar Products normally has to pay an interest rate of 10% when it borrows money from a bank to finance purchases of raw materials. Which of the following is **true**?
   a. Sugar Products should report the note payable at a carrying value of $100,000 on its balance sheet at December 31, 1999.
   b. Sugar Products should record no interest expense over the next five years in connection with this loan.
   c. At the inception of the note, Sugar Products should record a debit to Cash for the present value of the note using a 10% interest rate for discounting purposes.
   d. At the inception of the note, Sugar Products should record unearned revenue for the excess of the note's face value over its present value.

Approach and Explanation: Record the journal entry for Sugar Products for the inception of the note. The difference between the present value of the note and the amount of cash received should be recorded as both a discount on the note and unearned revenue by the issuer of the note. The journal entry would be as follows:

Cash	100,000	
Discount on Notes Payable	37,908	
Notes Payable		100,000
Unearned Revenue		37,908*

*Present value of $100,000 due 5 years at 10% =
$100,000 x .62092 = $62,092;
$100,000 face value - $62,092 present value =
$37,908 discount.

The Discount on Notes Payable will be amortized to interest expense over the five-year term using the effective interest method. The Unearned Revenue will be recognized as revenue from the sale of products and is prorated on the same basis that each period's sales to the lender-customer bear to the total sales to that customer for the term of the note. Thus, in this situation, the amortization of the discount and the recognition of the unearned revenue are at different rates. (Solution = d.)

QUESTION

9. (L.O.6) Bandy Rentals borrowed money from a local savings and loan to build new mini-warehouses. Bandy gave a 20-year mortgage note in the amount of $100,000 with a stated rate of 10.75%. The lender charged 4 points to close the financing. Based on this information:
   a. Bandy should debit Interest Expense in recording the points at the date the money is borrowed.
   b. Bandy's effective interest rate is now less than the 10.75% stated rate.
   c. Bandy should record the Mortgage Note Payable for only $96,000 since only $96,000 cash was received.
   d. Bandy should amortize the points to interest expense over the life of the loan.

Explanation: Bandy will receive $96,000 cash but will have to repay $100,000 plus interest at 10.75% on the $100,000. Thus, the points raise the effective interest rate above the stated rate and should be accounted for as interest expense over the life of the loan. (Solution = d.)

QUESTION

10. (L.O.9) A debtor in a troubled debt restructuring has debt that is settled by a transfer of land with a fair value that is less than the carrying amount of the debt but is more than the book value of the land. Should a gain or loss on restructuring of debt be recognized? Should a gain or loss on the disposition of assets be recognized?

	Gain or Loss on Restructuring of Debt	Gain or Loss on Disposition of Assets
a.	Gain	Gain
b.	Gain	Loss
c.	Loss	Loss
d.	Loss	Gain

Approach and Explanation: Assign amounts to the (1) carrying amount of the debt, (2) carrying amount of the loan, and (3) fair value of the land. Be sure your assigned amounts maintain the relationships stated in the question. Then use a journal entry approach to solve. For instance: Fair value of land, $100,000; carrying amount of debt, $127,000; and book value of land, $65,000. For the journal entry, debit the debt account(s) for $127,000; credit Land for $65,000; credit Gain on Disposition of Assets for $35,000 (an excess of the fair value over the book value indicates that a gain has been experienced on the old asset). The rest of the entry is due to a gain or loss on restructuring of debt. A credit for $27,000 is needed for the entry to balance; hence, there is a gain on settlement. If you are able to settle a debt by giving an asset with a value that is less than the carrying amount of the debt, you have an advantageous settlement of debt; hence a gain on restructuring of debt should be recognized.

Debt	127,000	
Land		65,000
Gain on Disposition of Assets		35,000
Gain on Restructuring of Debt		27,000

(Solution = a.)

Notes

Notes

Notes

Notes

Notes

Notes

Notes

Notes

Notes

Notes

Notes

Notes

Notes

Notes